RELIGIOUS EPISTEMOLOGY THROUGH
SCHILLEBEECKX AND TIBETAN BUDDHISM

T&T Clark Studies in Edward Schillebeeckx

Series editors
Kathleen McManus
Frederiek Depoortere
Stephan van Erp

RELIGIOUS EPISTEMOLOGY THROUGH SCHILLEBEECKX AND TIBETAN BUDDHISM

Reimagining Authority Amidst Modern Uncertainty

Jason M. VonWachenfeldt

LONDON • NEW YORK • OXFORD • NEW DELHI • SYDNEY

T&T CLARK

Bloomsbury Publishing Plc

50 Bedford Square, London, WC1B 3DP, UK
1385 Broadway, New York, NY 10018, USA
29 Earlsfort Terrace, Dublin 2, Ireland

BLOOMSBURY, T&T CLARK and the T&T Clark logo are trademarks
of Bloomsbury Publishing Plc

First published in Great Britain 2021
Paperback edition published 2022

Copyright © Jason M. VonWachenfeldt, 2021

Jason M. VonWachenfeldt has asserted his right under the Copyright, Designs
and Patents Act, 1988, to be identified as Author of this work.

For legal purposes the Acknowledgments on p. vi constitute an extension
of this copyright page

All rights reserved. No part of this publication may be reproduced or
transmitted in any form or by any means, electronic or mechanical,
including photocopying, recording, or any information storage or retrieval
system, without prior permission in writing from the publishers.

Bloomsbury Publishing Plc does not have any control over, or responsibility for, any
third-party websites referred to or in this book. All internet addresses given in this
book were correct at the time of going to press. The author and publisher regret any
inconvenience caused if addresses have changed or sites have ceased to exist, but can
accept no responsibility for any such changes.

A catalogue record for this book is available from the British Library.

Library of Congress Cataloging-in-Publication Data
Names: VonWachenfeldt, Jason, author.
Title: Religious epistemology through Schillebeeckx and Tibetan Buddhism :
reimagining authority amidst modern uncertainty / Jason VonWachenfeldt.
Description: London ; New York : T&T Clark, [2021] | Series: T&T Clark
studies in Edward Schillebeeckx | Includes bibliographical references and index. |
Identifiers: LCCN 2020045360 (print) | LCCN 2020045361 (ebook) |
ISBN 9780567698636 (hardback) | ISBN 9780567699350 (paperback) |
ISBN 9780567698643 (pdf) | ISBN 9780567698667 (epub)
Subjects: LCSH: Knowledge, Theory of (Religion) | Religions. |
Schillebeeckx, Edward, 1914–2009. | Dge-'dun-chos-'phel, A-mdo,
1903-1951. | Catholic Church–Relations–Buddhism. |
Buddhism–Relations–Catholic Church.
Classification: LCC BL51 .V59 2021 (print) | LCC BL51 (ebook) |
DDC 210–dc23
LC record available at https://lccn.loc.gov/2020045360
LC ebook record available at https://lccn.loc.gov/2020045361

ISBN: HB: 978-0-5676-9863-6
PB: 978-0-5676-9935-0
ePDF: 978-0-5676-9864-3
eBook: 978-0-5676-9866-7

Series: T&T Clark Studies in Edward Schillebeeckx

Typeset by Newgen KnowledgeWorks Pvt. Ltd., Chennai, India

To find out more about our authors and books visit www.bloomsbury.com
and sign up for our newsletters.

CONTENTS

Acknowledgments	vi
Introduction THE PROBLEM OF OBJECTIVE "TRUTH" AND THE THREAT OF RELATIVISM FOR RELIGIOUS PRACTITIONERS IN THE MODERN WORLD	1
Chapter 1 COMPARATIVE THEOLOGY, RELIGIOUS DIVERSITY, AND THE QUESTION OF ULTIMATE TRUTH	5
Chapter 2 THE "BRIDGE CONCEPT" AND ITS MATERIALS	23
Chapter 3 THE ROLES OF INDIVIDUAL INTELLECT AND THE COLLECTIVE INTELLIGENCE OF THE COMMUNITY IN KNOWLEDGE FORMATION	67
Chapter 4 THE ROLE OF THE HISTORICAL FOUNDERS OF RELIGIOUS TRADITIONS IN SHAPING AND CONVEYING RELIGIOUS KNOWLEDGE, MEANING, AND TRUTH FOR CONTEMPORARY BELIEVERS	111
Chapter 5 THE ROLE AND AUTHORITY OF PERSONAL EXPERIENCE IN THE APOPHATIC KNOWLEDGE OF ULTIMATE REALITY	163
Conclusion POSSIBLE MADHYAMAKA IMPLICATIONS FOR CATHOLIC THEOLOGY	215
Bibliography	241
Index	247

ACKNOWLEDGMENTS

One cannot embark on a voyage of comparative dialogue without becoming acutely aware of just how much one's insights are shaped by the countless influences of so many others.

I am deeply indebted to the director of this original project, my dissertation advisor, Leo Lefebure, who helped me focus my arguments and cultivate my own distinct voice within the field. There is no doubt that the quality of this work was dramatically improved because of his participation and guidance in its production. I am also equally indebted to Georgetown University as well as the other three members of my dissertation committee. Francisca Cho not only introduced me to the academic study of Buddhism and awakened my interest in Madhyamaka philosophy but also served as a close confidant, mentor, and friend. Her willingness to persistently garner wisdom from numerous voices, regardless of the academic or religious field, in order to strengthen one's own understanding truly embodies the spirit of pluralism that the Georgetown program seeks to emulate. Similarly, this project would not have been possible without the guidance of Benjamin Bogin, who added a necessary historical depth to my study and passion for the Buddhist tradition and, in so doing, paired my broader personal interests with Tibetan Buddhist philosophy generally and with the Tibetan Madhyamaka traditions more specifically through introducing me to the thought of Gendun Chopel. Finally, Roger Haight has been one of the most influential individuals of my entire life. Not only did he introduce me to both the theology of Edward Schillebeeckx and the contemporary Catholic theological questions concerning Christology and pluralism during my graduate studies at Union Theological Seminary in New York, but he also immeasurably shaped my own academic interests and spiritual seeking, which are in large part the result of his own commitments to his faith and pastoral ministry amidst his various trials and controversies. It was because of him that I took interest in comparative studies, and through him I personally witnessed how such exercises truly can, and should, affect individuals' thought and practice in contemporary society. It has been an honor to be personally and professionally enriched by four individuals of such intellectual and professional acumen— a privilege for which I will be forever grateful and cherish as a highlight of my life.

Besides those who directly aided in the development of this project, there are many others who deserve recognition and gratitude for their involvement in its formation. In particular, Demian Wheeler, my closest intellectual companion and by far the most formative influence of my own thought, and Paul Knitter, who has been a close advocate, mentor, and friend since my graduate studies at Union Seminary. I would also like to thank the faculty members of the Lawrenceville

School's Religion and Philosophy Department—in particular Phil Jordan who has provided guidance and invaluable advice. Similarly, my intellectual and professional development continue to be sharpened by many other Lawrenceville colleagues and students—including Hunter Cuniff, Chris Cunningham, Blake Eldridge, Dana Kooistra, Pier Kooistra, Dave Laws, Kate Liu, Julie Mellor, Noelle Niu, Bernadette Teeley, Richard Wang, and Annie Wilcox. Their collaborative and congenial spirit has fostered my continued love for theological and philosophical inquiry.

Finally, the completion of this entire enterprise would certainly not have been possible without the enduring love, support, and encouragement of my family. I would especially like to thank my immediate and extended siblings: Jeff VonWachenfeldt, Laurie Lutsch, Tiffany and Jesse Sloane, and Philip and Hannah Varvaris. More specifically my brother, Jeff VonWachenfeldt, will forever be an integral part of my own spiritual biography and continues to inspire me with his determined progress and unfailing joy amidst unspeakable hardships. I would also be remiss not to mention my lifelong best friend, Jared Hubbard, who has selflessly supported me and been with me on my highest mountaintops and lowest valleys. In this sense, he truly exemplifies the sage's ideal of the "friend who sticks closer than a brother" (Prov. 18:24). I am grateful as well for my warmhearted father- and mother-in-law, Peter and Cathy Varvaris, whose enduring spirit of service has led them to repeatedly travel to take care of my family whenever any need arose. Lastly, I would not be the person I am today were it not for my own mother and father, Jean and Mike VonWachenfeldt, both of whom have come to symbolize the walking definition of perseverance, strength, compassion, and faith for my own life. What is more, my father's gift of a passion for theological inquiry was the greatest inheritance I could have ever received.

Above all, I wish to acknowledge Kristen VonWachenfeldt, the love of my life, my closest companion of more than fifteen years, and the mother of our beautiful children—Ava and Jack. All of my accomplishments are as much hers as they are my own, and none of them would mean anything without her. I dedicate this work to them.

Introduction

THE PROBLEM OF OBJECTIVE "TRUTH" AND THE THREAT OF RELATIVISM FOR RELIGIOUS PRACTITIONERS IN THE MODERN WORLD

How many winds of doctrine have we known in recent decades, how many ideological currents, how many ways of thinking. The small boat of the thought of many Christians has often been tossed about by these waves—flung from one extreme to another: from Marxism to liberalism, even to libertinism; from collectivism to radical individualism; from atheism to a vague religious mysticism; from agnosticism to syncretism and so forth. Every day new sects spring up, and what St. Paul says about human deception and the trickery that strives to entice people into error (cf. Eph 4:14) comes true.

Today, having a clear faith based on the Creed of the Church is often labeled as fundamentalism. Whereas relativism, that is, letting oneself be "tossed here and there, carried about by every wind of doctrine," seems the only attitude that can cope with modern times. We are building a dictatorship of relativism that does not recognize anything as definitive and whose ultimate goal consists solely of one's own ego and desires.
—Cardinal Joseph Ratzinger, 2005[1]

What can one ever know for certain? On what basis or "authority" can one ever assert any knowledge of objective "truth"? Such questions are not only quite common within much of contemporary society but are indeed becoming more and more common within religious communities and among the individual practitioners that comprise them as well. In fact, when Cardinal Joseph Ratzinger made the now almost infamous declaration above in his homily directly preceding the conclave that would elect him as Pope Benedict XVI, many speculated that its harsh tone and its seemingly hardline stance toward a position seen as antithetical to much of mainstream society might prevent him from being elected pontiff. Needless to say, these predictions proved untrue. Yet the apparently polemical response to this statement, especially in the subsequent wake of the speaker's emergence as the new

---

1. Joseph Ratzinger, "Pro Eligendo Romano Pontifice," http://www.vatican.va/gpII/documents/homily-pro-eligendo-pontifice_20050418_en.html (2014).

vicar of Christ and face of the Catholic Church toward the world, highlights the commonly felt tension within many of the members of the contemporary Catholic Church between a belief and participation in a tradition that proclaims to have the one universal truth of all reality that is essential for humanity's well-being and survival, and a citizenship within a (post)modern society that has become ever-increasingly suspicious of any claims to knowledge of "universal truth."[2] The (not always acknowledged) worldview that undergirds contemporary society is one that accepts the notion that, as Sheila Davaney summarizes it, "There is, for humans, no cosmic point of view, unfettered by historical particularity."[3]

In the introduction to his seminal work *The Postmodern Condition: A Report on Knowledge*, Jean-François Lyotard famously summarized the pervasive contemporary attitude toward knowledge and truth within much of society, by "simplifying [it] to the extreme," as a "postmodern" worldview that has an "incredulity toward metanarratives"[4]—or, as Paul Knitter helpfully interprets this statement, a worldview "that does not allow any universal stories or truths."[5] What this effectively means then is that individuals are not only becoming more

---

2. It should be noted here that what Cardinal Ratzinger is rejecting is not the recognition of a "conceptual plurality" in humans' perception of the nature of knowledge and truth about reality (in the sense of what Lonergan called the merely subjective "mental composition" element of knowledge) across obvious contextual diversities. Rather, what he means by "relativism" is the judgment of truth that this recognition of conceptual plurality directly corresponds with the "real composition," or "real synthesis" (to borrow two more expressions from Lonergan), of reality as it is in itself (see Bernard J. F. Lonergan, *Verbum: Word and Idea in Aquinas*, 22 vols., Collected Works of Bernard Lonergan, vol. 2 (Toronto: University of Toronto Press for Lonergan Research Institute of Regis College, 1980; reprint, 2005), 62-3)). By making such a jump from conceptual recognition to ultimate judgment, Cardinal Ratzinger is clearly voicing the fear that Christians will adopt a stance of "relativism" toward their understanding of ultimate reality and ultimate truth. The Jesuit theologian Roger Haight helpfully defines this notion of "relativism" as "the position that, whether or not transcultural or ultimate truths exist, they cannot be known as such or agreed upon. All knowledge is particular and culturally determined *without remainder*" (see Roger Haight S. J., *Ecclesial Existence*, 3 vols., Christian Community in History, vol. 3 (New York: Continuum, 2008), x n. 2.). And as such, a primary focus of this particular project is to show how a comparison between the two thinkers examined might assist in displaying multiple ways for doing theological reflection that can acknowledge the relativizing effect of conceptual diversity while not necessarily requiring a judgment of relativism to the nature of ultimate reality in itself.

3. Sheila Greeve Davaney, *Pragmatic Historicism: A Theology for the Twenty-First Century* (Albany: State University of New York Press, 2000), 84.

4. Jean François Lyotard, *The Postmodern Condition: A Report on Knowledge* (Minneapolis: University of Minnesota Press, 1984), xxiv.

5. Paul F. Knitter, *One Earth, Many Religions: Multifaith Dialogue and Global Responsibility* (Maryknoll, NY: Orbis Books, 1995), 41.

comfortable with but are in fact seeing it as *necessary* to agree with and make sense of the proclamations of philosophers, such as Walter Truett Anderson and Richard Rorty, who insist that one can and must justifiably make a distinction between the affirmation that there is a reality "out there" and that "truth" is "out there." Or as Anderson pointedly phrases it,

> Seeing truth as made, not found—seeing reality as socially constructed—doesn't mean deciding there is nothing "out there." It means understanding that all our stories about what's out there—all our scientific facts, our religious teachings, our society's beliefs, even our personal perceptions—are the products of a highly creative interaction between human minds and the cosmos.[6]

In light of such declarations by contemporary philosophers, Ratzinger's comments above about the fear of there being a new "dictatorship of relativism" within contemporary culture seem much more understandable in expressing the apparent threat that such thinking might have on the credibility and subsequent efficaciousness of religious belief for individuals within contemporary society. At the same time, as Knitter aptly situates the dilemma, no matter what one thinks of the "anything goes" relativism seemingly lurking in such "'anti-foundational' proclamations" of Anderson, Rorty, and the like, these types of statements signal a growing assumption within many individuals—not just within secular society at large but also within particular faith communities—that "there is no one foundation for, or expression of, or criterion for truth which is, as it were, given to us from outside the diversity of historical filters. There is no universal perspective hovering over these filters to which we can appeal for our grasp of truth."[7] Thus, it would seem that if religious institutions and traditions insist on maintaining age-old depictions of religious knowledge, truth, and especially *authority*, which were cultivated within premodern worldviews and present them as the exclusively valid understanding and interpretation of reality, these institutions will run the

---

6. Walt Truett Anderson, "Introduction: What's Going on Here?," in *The Truth about the Truth: De-Confusing and Re-Constructing the Postmodern World*, ed. Walt Truett Anderson (New York: Putnam, 1995), 8. Or, in the words of the neopragmatist Richard Rorty,

> We need to make a distinction between the claim that the world is out there and the claim that truth is out there. To say that the world is out there, that it is not our creation, is to say, with common sense, that most things in space and time are the effects of causes which do not include human mental states. To say that truth is not out there is simply to say that where there are no sentences there is no truth, that sentences are elements of human languages, and that human languages are human creations ... The world is out there, but descriptions of the world are not.

See Richard Rorty, *Contingency, Irony, and Solidarity* (New York: Cambridge University Press, 1989), 5.

7. Knitter, *One Earth*, 41.

risk of speaking in a language that is incomprehensible to vast portions of their constituents. Consequently, therefore, in the end they risk losing much of the same legitimacy and authority in the minds of those followers that these traditions and institutions are so desperately seeking to protect through their opposition to this perceived "relativism." Nevertheless, on the other hand, one could also ask, if religious traditions completely succumb to the pressures of these worldviews and relinquish any definitive assertion of possessing an authoritative knowledge of truth, they do not lose this credibility and viability among their practitioners anyways. And so the dilemma persists.

The intention of this project, therefore, is to approach this ostensibly impenetrable quandary by asking the question of whether the relationship between religious traditions and the current modern epistemological challenges of philosophy and society must be deemed a "zero-sum game" that truly demands an "either/or" decision by contemporary religious believers. This examination will construct and critically assess an imaginary dialogue between the lives and thought of two religious thinkers of the twentieth century from quite disparate theological and philosophical traditions—the Dutch Catholic theologian Edward Schillebeeckx (1914–2009) and the Tibetan Buddhist historian and philosopher Gendun Chopel (1903–1951)—particularly in regard to their theories of religious epistemology and the nature of ultimate truth in light of the challenging interruption of modern thought and development. This project will attempt to present at least two theories of how religious belief might be able to adapt to the contemporary epistemological mentality while at the same time not sacrificing the potency and efficacy of religious faith and participation among a given tradition's followers. Moreover, the conclusion of this work will seek to go one step further to argue that by not just comparatively analyzing each thinker's system of thought but by also placing those systems in dialogic negotiation with one another, we can see how the thought of both figures might be able to contribute more effectively—individually as well as collectively—to forming new trajectories for religious reflection and spiritual practice in the contemporary postmodern world.

Chapter 1

COMPARATIVE THEOLOGY, RELIGIOUS DIVERSITY, AND THE QUESTION OF ULTIMATE TRUTH

I. Introduction: The Problem of Religious Diversity for Religious Epistemology and the Church's Dialogical Stance

As this project commences the question still remains as to why a Catholic theological thesis would involve an interreligious component at all, or why one would choose to compare a Catholic "modernist" theologian with a Buddhist "modernist" philosopher rather than simply two Catholic thinkers from the plethora of theologians engaging with modern thought? There are multiple reasons for the selection and framing of this particular project. This chapter, therefore, will briefly seek to investigate the purpose behind embarking on a specifically religiously *comparative* theological project, as well as suggest a process or method for engaging in theological comparison, and also finally present an outline of the unique creative potential that might possibly emerge from a comparative theological project such as this one. Moreover, specifically, this first section will then focus on the purpose of doing a Catholic theology in a comparative and dialogical manner based on a response to the current state of religious diversity in contemporary life and culture through an examination of three significant voices on the subject from within the Catholic Church: the papal encyclical of Paul VI *Ecclesiam Suam*; the Second Vatican Council's "Declaration on the Relation of the Church with Non-Christian Religions," *Nostra Aetate*; and lastly the statements of Pope Francis (then-Cardinal Jorge Bergoglio) on the necessity and parameters of interreligious dialogue in his book, cowritten with Rabbi Abraham Skorka, *Sobre el cielo y la tierra* (*On Heaven and Earth*). Once the need for a dialogical and comparative approach to theology is established, this chapter will then be able to address more effectively the two other significant questions concerning the most appropriate and effective way for doing theology comparatively along with the potential constructive outcomes hoped for through a theologically comparative project. Thus, in the end, the point of this chapter will be to display the unique benefit achieved by placing Schillebeeckx's specifically Catholic-oriented approach to the questions of modernity in dialogue with the Buddhist approach of Gendun Chopel toward the similar issue of formulating a religious understanding capable of not only withstanding but also efficaciously functioning in light of a radical awareness and suspicion toward the limits of human knowledge.

First and foremost, however, possibly the most significant reason for engaging the religious implications of the questions of modern epistemology on faith communities in a specifically *comparative* manner is the fact that one of the most prominent aspects of modernity's epistemologically critical awareness arises not just out of the existence of many competing worldviews and contradictory claims to truth. Rather, it also stems from an increased awareness of the rivaling and relativizing diversity of particularly *religious* worldviews—all of which assert their own rendition of religious ultimacy. As many religious sociologists such as Diana Eck and Robert Wuthnow point out, modernity and globalization have brought about a staggeringly acute awareness among the various religious groups themselves of religious diversity[1] and the reality that identity formation is often constructed polemically through distinguishing oneself by one's differences with others.[2] The Catholic comparative theologian Francis X. Clooney, S.J., eloquently describes this trend when he states, "Diversity not only envelops us, it works on us, gets inside us; if we are paying attention, we see that attentiveness to other religions affects even how we experience, think through, and practice our own religion."[3] Accordingly, Wuthnow further notes how this hyperawareness of both the reality and the effect of religious diversity within society has sparked the desire for "truly pluralistic" responses by religious groups as methods to embrace, ignore, or merely cope with the tensions of religious diversity.[4] Eck reflects this desire for a "truly pluralistic" response to diversity among many modern religious individuals when she proclaims,

> We cannot live in a world in which our economies and markets are global, our political awareness is global, our business relationships take us to every continent, and the Internet connects us with colleagues half a world away and

---

1. Diana L. Eck, *A New Religious America: How a "Christian Country" Has Now Become the World's Most Religiously Diverse Nation*, 1st ed. (San Francisco: HarperSanFrancisco, 2001), 2–3. Focusing on American culture in particular as just one example, Eck here makes an observation that she believes might be startling for many Christians within the ever-increasing context of American religious diversity when she proclaims, "We are surprised to find that there are more Muslim Americans than Episcopalians, more Muslims than members of the Presbyterian Church USA, and as many Muslims as there are Jews—that is about SIX MILLION."

2. For a poignant and concise discussion of this particular point, see Hugh Nicholson, "The New Comparative Theology and the Problem of Theological Hegemonism," in *The New Comparative Theology: Interreligious Insights from the Next Generation*, ed. Francis X. Clooney (New York: T&T Clark, 2010), 53–60.

3. Francis X. Clooney, *Comparative Theology: Deep Learning across Religious Borders* (Malden, MA: Wiley-Blackwell, 2010), 6.

4. Robert Wuthnow, *America and the Challenges of Religious Diversity* (Princeton, NJ: Princeton University Press, 2005), 286.

yet live on Friday, or Saturday, or Sunday with ideas of God that are essentially provincial, imagining that somehow the one we call God has been primarily concerned with us and our tribe.[5]

Again Clooney reiterates Wuthnow's and Eck's observations when he declares,

> Individual religious traditions are under internal and external stress as they are challenged to engage an array of religious others. Some find themselves under siege, threatened by a bewildering range of religious possibilities; some withdraw and demonize their others; some, perhaps too accommodating, begin to forget their identities.[6]

Thus within modern society and culture the notion of "pluralism" has emerged as an ideological response to religious diversity that hopes to maintain the importance of individual and collective religious identities[7] while also attempting to help modern religious individuals and groups wrestle with how the divergent convictions of others play a role in influencing their own religious experiences and understandings.[8] Even more significantly, Wuthnow continues, as a result of this increasing awareness of how these various influences from other religious traditions shape one's own religious experience within contemporary society, religious communities are now beginning to look increasingly to theologians in order to help them make more informed and proactive choices about how to respond to these other religious forces, rather than letting circumstances blindly dictate their responses.[9] According to Clooney, therefore, the version of theology becoming most demanded by the believing public is one where "comparative theological reflection is required" as a means to help believers make sense of their "situation amidst diversity and likewise keep their faith."[10] And as such, echoing the reflections of the sociologist Clifford Geertz, both scholars and the public in general are coming to the conclusion that theological monologues are of less and less value for dealing with this reality of religious diversity, and what is more necessary are internal as well as external theological *discussions* that must be sustained with others.[11]

---

5. Eck, 24.
6. Clooney, 3.
7. Ibid., 7.
8. Wuthnow, xii–xiii.
9. Ibid., xv.
10. Clooney, 3.
11. Clifford Geertz, *The Interpretation of Cultures: Selected Essays* (London: Hutchinson, 1975), 29.

A. Ecclesiam Suam: *Paul VI on the Need for Dialogue with Modern Culture*

Although particularly in recent decades the Church's awareness of religious diversity and its effects on the way believers understand themselves and the nature of their faith might have brought about an even more conscious desire among practitioners for an approach to theology that is dialogical and comparative rather than being self-focused monologues about truth, the church's recognition of a more dialogical approach to the world is certainly not unique to the turn of the twenty-first century. Actually right before the third session of the Second Vatican Council in August 1964 on the Feast of the Transfiguration, Pope Paul VI released a papal encyclical entitled *Ecclesiam Suam* (literally *His Church*)[12] in which emphasis was placed on the necessity of the Church, as the social and "Mystical Body of Christ" in the world [22 & 30], to be consistently in dialogue with contemporary culture. This intention is presented very early on in the document when it proclaims, "The aim of this encyclical will be to demonstrate with increasing clarity how vital it is for the world, and how greatly desired by the Catholic Church, that the two should meet together, and get to know each other" [3]. And although the document clearly defines the boundaries of the potential influence from this dialogue when it cites "Modernism" as "an error which is still making its appearance under various new guises, wholly inconsistent with any genuine religious expression" [26],[13] at the same time it also acknowledges that the "Church must enter into dialogue with the world in which it lives" both in order to communicate its own message to the world [65] as well as to assist the Church in correcting through its own critical self-examination "those flaws introduced by its members" [11]. Therefore, it officially recognizes dialogue as an effective method for "making spiritual contact" with the world as long as it is done with "clarity" (intelligibility), "meekness" (humility), "confidence" ("not only in the power of one's words, but also in the good will of both parties to the dialogue"), and "prudence" (making "allowances for the psychological and moral circumstances of [the] hearer") [81]. Overall, then, when dialogue is approached in this way the goal of the encounter will always be one where "truth is wedded to charity and understanding to love" [82].

For the interests of this discussion then, the most significant contribution this document makes toward the necessity of a particularly *comparative* approach to theology is in its statements regarding the various modes of the Church's potential dialogue. Here it commands that "the Church can regard no one as excluded from its motherly embrace" (with exception only to "those who wish to make themselves

---

12. Pope Paul VI, "*Ecclesiam Suam*," http://www.vatican.va/holy_father/paul_vi/encyclicals/documents/hf_p-vi_enc_06081964_ecclesiam_en.html (2014).

13. Later the encyclical goes on to specifically define a couple of these "guises" of modernism as "Naturalism, which attempts to undermine the fundamental conception of Christianity" and relativism, which "seeks to justify everything, and treats all things as of equal value" and thus "assails the absolute character of Christian principles" [49]. Hence it should not be assumed that the dialogical emphasis of this document somehow implies a "pluralist" attitude toward truth or other religions. That is certainly not the case.

such") [94] and directs it to "take up with great renewal of fervor" all dialogue "conducted with all [people] of good will both inside and outside the Church" [93]. Thus, while it also affirms that these exchanges with all individuals of good will outside of the Church must not lead to "vague compromises" concerning its principles because that might "water down" or "whittle away" an understanding of truth [88], it also acknowledges that voices and participation of individuals outside of its traditional auspices are necessary in the realization of "its mission to foster love, unity and peace among [humanity]" [94]. Hence, it places the Church in a position of not just humility and respect toward those existing outside of its walls but also one of need and interdependence for achieving both its mission and self-purification. In regard to this particular comparative theological project, moreover, it eventually turns to address the mode and need for dialogue with "the followers of the great Afro-Asiatic religions." And although it insists that because of some of the stark differences with these traditions (namely, denying monotheism) the Church "obviously" cannot *agree* with these various forms of religion or "adopt an indifferent or uncritical attitude toward them" as if in some profession of "Relativism," it does nonetheless set the basis for a potential dialogue with these traditions—the boundaries and intentions of which would be further articulated and defined by the Second Vatican Council two years later in 1965 as a part of its "Declaration on the Relation of the Church with Non-Christian Religions" commonly referred to as *Nostra Aetate*.

B. Nostra Aetate: *The Question of Religious Truth in Non-Christian Traditions*

During the last session of the Second Vatican Council the assembly of bishops passed by an overwhelming majority its "Declaration on the Relation of the Church with Non-Christian Religions," *Nostra Aetate* (lit. *In Our Age*).[14] Though quite brief in length, this document is packed with a number of very significant statements concerning the nature of the Church's relationship with religious traditions other than Christianity and its ability to recognize viable truth within them. It acknowledges that members of other traditions look to their own religions in order to seek answers to many of the same "unsolved riddles of human existence" that Christians ask themselves, especially including "what is the ultimate mystery, beyond human explanation, which embraces our entire existence, from which we take our origin and towards which we tend?"[15] And once again, in a manner particularly significant for the comparative basis of this project, it extends *Ecclesiam Suam*'s stance about the need to dialogue with Buddhists by acknowledging some shared "Truths" between the two traditions. For example, it commends Buddhism,

---

14. "Declaration on the Relation of the Church to Non-Christian Religions," in *Vatican Council II: The Conciliar and Post Conciliar Documents*, ed. Austin Flannery (New York: Costello, 1988), 738–42.

15. Vatican II, "Declaration on the Relation of the Church to Non-Christian Religions," 738.

"in its various forms," for attesting to "the essential inadequacy of this changing world" and for proposing "a way of life by which [humans] can, with confidence and trust, attain a state of perfect liberation and reach supreme illumination either through their own efforts or by the aid of divine help."[16] Moreover, it famously goes even one step further than that to proclaim in regard to Hinduism and Buddhism, "The Catholic Church *rejects nothing of what is true and holy in these religions. She has a high regard for the manner of life and conduct, the precepts and doctrines which, although differing in many ways from her own teaching, nevertheless often reflect a ray of that truth which enlightens all [people]*."[17] For this reason, Clooney echoes the shared sentiment of many theologians (both comparative and otherwise) when he proclaims that at its core *Nostra Aetate* represents the Church's "best instincts,"[18] which are ones directed toward nurturing "discussion and collaboration with members of other religions" so as to "acknowledge, preserve and encourage the spiritual and moral truths found among non-Christians, also their social life and culture."[19] And, furthermore, although the Church has certainly failed at times since this document has been issued to live up to its own standard of collaboration, recognition, and acceptance of these other traditions, it is statements like these that reflect the Church's "best instincts," which can serve as the hope and impetus for interreligious theological projects.

C. Sobre El Cielo y La Tierra *(On Heaven and Earth): Pope Francis on the Role and Significance of Interreligious Dialogue in the Discovery and Knowledge of Truth*

One example of these collaborative and dialogical instincts being put to use in an interreligious theological project that has gained a particular notoriety recently is the book of interreligious dialogue between then-Cardinal Jorge Bergoglio and the Jewish biophysicist Rabbi Abraham Skorka (both of Argentina) entitled *Sobre El Cielo y La Tierra (On Heaven and Earth)*. Following Cardinal Bergoglio's election as Pope Francis in late February 2013, many immediately turned to this piece in hopes of gleaning a better understanding of the new pontiff's position and practice toward interreligious dialogue. In many ways what they found was another exposition of the same instincts set forth in *Ecclesiam Suam* and *Nostra Aetate*. In this informative "back and forth" between the bishop and the rabbi, Cardinal Bergoglio bemoans the recent tendency of Christians to succumb to inhospitable attitudes toward the religious Other that stymie the potential benefits from interreligious learning by preemptively condemning the position of the religious Other before actually listening to what he or she might have to say. Instead he contests that the type of dialogue commanded of Catholics in the two

---

16. Ibid., 739.
17. Ibid. Emphases added.
18. Clooney, 17.
19. Vatican II, "Declaration on the Relation of the Church to Non-Christian Religions," 739.

documents previously discussed is "born from a respectful attitude toward the other person, from a conviction that the person has something good to say. It supposes that we can make room in our heart for their point of view, their opinion and their proposals."[20] He stresses that an attitude of dialogue thereby cannot be one focused first and foremost on proselytization and conversion[21] because such attitudes typify a form of "rigid religiosity" that is disguised in doctrines that claim to give answers but "in reality deprive people of their freedom and do not allow them to grow as persons."[22]

Instead he defines the proper attitude of dialogue as one that is grounded in a "notion of humility" (or "meekness") and that asserts the "true power of religious leadership" not in aggression and imposition but in a mentality of service toward the world and others.[23] "No believer," he elaborates, "can limit the faith to himself, his clan, his family or his city. A believer is essentially someone who goes into an encounter with other believers, or non-believers, to give them a hand."[24] Moreover, he affirms that, even though "religious truth does not change," nonetheless it can "develop and grow."[25] As a result, as long as the primary objective of interreligious dialogue remains the discovery and articulation of truth, the religious Other does possess the propensity to expose where Christians have been wrong in their belief and actions, compelling them to confess: "We were wrong in this."[26] Hence for him, the goal of dialogue must not be a globalizing uniformity of thought and belief in which "the richness of each culture is lost" but instead a system of interaction and participation among peoples and traditions that both promotes a sense of communal integration and also helps others maintain their particularities so that they can enrich each other through their differences of perspective.[27]

And therefore, as this project now turns to articulate its own method for engaging in theological reflection through a comparative dialogue with the religious Other, it will seek to do so in accordance with the spirit conveyed by all three of the documents examined above. It will intend to construct an attitude

---

20. Jorge Mario Bergoglio and Abraham Skorka, *On Heaven and Earth: Pope Francis on Faith, Family, and the Church in the Twenty-First Century*, ed., Random House Large Print (New York: Random House, 2013), xx–xxi.

21. Bergoglio and Skorka, 15.

22. Ibid., 93.

23. Ibid., 303. It should be noted, however, that here his promotion of the ideal of "humility" should not be confused with passive acceptance of others' assertions. Although he affirms that he completely agrees with the notion of humility in dialogue, he also prefers to use the word "meekness"—emphasizing that this does not mean *weakness*. Rather for him, a religious leader can be "very strong, very firm" in their beliefs and convictions while at the same time not "exercising aggression" against the other.

24. Ibid., 27–8.

25. Ibid., 160.

26. Ibid., 242.

27. Ibid., 206.

and approach toward dialogue that embodies the spirit of these documents in a few specific ways: first, by formulating an approach that is responsive to the documents' call for the need to dialogue with the religious Other and the world in theological reflection; next, by promoting an openness to the potential truths within other religious traditions (ones not only capable of reflecting one's own assumed understandings but that can actually also assist in pointing out areas in which one has the potential to "develop and grow" in understanding); and finally, by emphasizing the need to maintain the "otherness" of the religious Other by acknowledging certain legitimate differences of belief and perspective along with not attempting to reduce the Other simply to articulating one's own preconceived belief from another perspective. Hence, this project will seek to allow the differences in thought and belief between the two religious traditions engaged to enrich each other's perspective in new, possibly unforeseen ways. Accordingly, it is my belief that the best method for realizing all three of these goals is what I label a "bridge-concepts" methodology for doing comparative theology.

II. "Bridging" Conceptual Differences: Aaron Stalnaker's Innovative Approach to Interreligious and Cross-Cultural Comparison

In his 2006 book of Comparative Religious Ethics (CRE) entitled *Overcoming Our Evil*, the scholar of comparative ethics and philosophy of religion Aaron Stalnaker initiates a methodology for interreligious comparison that utilizes vague comparative concepts, which he labels as "bridge concepts," as a means to allow the distinct and respectively iconic voices of the early Christian theologian Augustine of Hippo (354–430 CE) and the Confucian philosopher Xunzi (312–230 BCE) to converse on the topics of "human nature" and "spiritual exercises."[28] And although, as James Miller mentions in his review of the book for the *Journal of Theological Studies*, Stalnaker's method somewhat resembles Robert Cummings Neville's method of "vague comparative categories" that is used for the "Comparative Religious Ideas Project" out of Boston University,[29] Stalnaker utilizes this approach

---

28. Aaron Stalnaker, *Overcoming Our Evil: Human Nature and Spiritual Exercises in Xunzi and Augustine*, Moral Traditions Series (Washington, DC: Georgetown University Press, 2006).

29. See James Miller, "Review of *Overcoming Our Evil: Human Nature and Spiritual Exercises in Xunzi and Augustine*, by Aaron Stalnaker," *Theological Studies Review* 69, no. 1 (2008): 200–1. Stalnaker himself acknowledges this apparent similarity with Neville's methodological concept in a footnote attached to the original use of the expression "bridge concepts" but does not claim it as the originating source of his distinct terminology. Instead he both acknowledges someone else for the idea (without publication) and also attempts to differentiate his own method from that of Neville's when he writes:

> I owe this way of framing things originally to John Reeder. And although arrived at independently, my "bridge concepts" and Neville's "vague categories" of comparison

in a unique way that I believe might assist comparative theologians in dialogically engaging the religious Other with more clearly defined parameters of what a specifically "religious" comparison might entail as well as allowing the comparison itself to evoke new implications for their respective broader religious traditions while nonetheless remaining firmly grounded in the concrete particularities of two specific (though largely influential) religious thinkers.[30] Stalnaker argues that creatively constructing the dialogue in this way between the systems of thought in two contained, historically situated individuals—rather than abstract and vague ideas as a whole—allows him to effectively make generalizations regarding the religious implications in reference to those thinkers within their traditions that are "much more defensible, and can be more effectively qualified as necessary, than generalizations about whole religions or traditions."[31]

Stalnaker insists that by participating in this form of comparison the religious comparativist might be able to achieve a new amount of constructive insight and implications concerning both the objects of comparison as well as the broader subjects of the analysis. He lists the three main "virtues" he believes this type of comparison might produce as first specifically illuminating "each of the objects compared in new and surprising ways, revealing easily overlooked details or themes"; second, provoking, testing, and developing various theoretical generalizations about the compared objects; and finally, most importantly, helping to "generate new theories about the substantive domain being considered." Moreover, he also holds that this form of comparative method within his own field of CRE "can be just as effective as historical and 'genealogical' studies in bringing to consciousness the full range of consequences of common contemporary ways of

---

seem to function in similar ways in the process of inquiry. Perhaps the main difference is scope: Neville's Comparative Religious Ideas Project aims to bring six different traditions (conceived and articulated in various ways by various authors) into mutual imagined dialogue, and to flesh out their vague categories in the process into a metavocabulary capable of accurately relating all six traditions' claims about the topic marked out by the category. I am less hopeful than Neville and his fellows that this degree of scope will yield rich insights, when compared with more carefully specified and delimited comparisons, but this is only partly a matter of judgment, partly a hunch, and partly a result of my own limitations as an investigator. (See Stalnaker, 26 n.61)

For a more extensive and useful summary of Neville's methodology of "vague comparative categories," see Robert W. Smid, *Methodologies of Comparative Philosophy: The Pragmatist and Process Traditions* (Albany: State University of New York Press, 2009), 141–92.

30. It is this last point on the constructive *yet concretely situated* aspect to his approach where I believe Stalnaker's method particularly distinguishes itself most clearly from Neville's and the Comparative Religious Ideas Project's helpfully constructive and dialogical approach.

31. Stalnaker, 15.

framing ethical issues, and thus calling them into question."[32] It is the assessment of this project that these same implications might be successfully achieved in the field of Comparative Theology through the application of this method—even if necessarily slightly adapted—to a dialogical and comparative approach to doing theological reflection. This section, therefore, will briefly outline the foundations and parameters of a "bridge-concepts methodology," as chiefly formulated by Stalnaker, as the general methodological direction of this current project regarding the religious epistemologies of Schillebeeckx and Gendun Chopel.

However, before one can move to discussing the methodological possibilities and benefits for doing this type of interreligious comparison, Stalnaker calls attention to the fact that the discussion of "religions" in the plural, which is inherent in any interreligious comparison, inevitably generates the problem/question of "what 'religions' are, and how they relate to each other."[33] In his essay "Religion, Religions, Religious" the historian of religions Jonathan Z. Smith also summarizes the crux of this "problem" of defining what religions actually are when he concludes,

> "Religion" is not a native term; it is a term created by scholars for their intellectual purposes and therefore is theirs to define. It is a second-order, generic concept that plays the same role in establishing a disciplinary horizon that a concept such as "language" plays in linguistics or "culture" plays in anthropology. There can be no disciplined study of religion without such a horizon.[34]

Accordingly, Stalnaker uses an idea of "vocabularies of social life" as a functioning way to define what religions are, and therefore the comparativist's object of comparison. Nevertheless, Stalnaker confesses that undoubtedly some will question if such a linguistically based, or "semiotic," method for interpreting religion might intrinsically imply an assumption of theological relativism within scholars' interpretations, "which attempts to cordon off distinct cultures or groups and insist that what each believes is 'true for them.'"[35] Citing historicist (and pragmatist) thinkers such as Rorty, Donald Davidson, Robert Brandom, and Jeffery Stout, Stalnaker seeks to mitigate this concern by formulating a significant distinction between what he terms "conceptual *relativism* and conceptual *diversity*."[36] According to him, conceptual relativism insists that there is no way to adjudicate between competing truth claims and interpretations, and thus commonly "freezes and hermetically seals vocabularies as if they are never used by real people acting in the world."[37] On the other hand, conceptual

---

32. Ibid., 1–2.
33. Ibid., 1.
34. Jonathan Z. Smith, "Religion, Religions, Religious," in *Critical Terms for Religious Studies*, ed. Mark C. Taylor (Chicago: University of Chicago Press, 1998), 281–2.
35. Stalnaker, 5.
36. Ibid., 7. Emphasis original.
37. Ibid., 6.

diversity better handles the differences of interpretation from both within and outside religious communities by a sometimes laborious comparative analysis that helps one determine which interpretation is more plausible, or "accurate," based on its pragmatic ability to help scholars predict religious interactions, to fit into the communities' already existing vocabularies in a way that represents their own interpretations, and to help those communities "cope" with the reality that their own vocabularies create.[38] Furthermore, this sense of conceptual diversity, or "discursive pluralism," better recognizes the reality that humans' identities and their vocabularies are *not* hermetically sealed but rather are constantly in flux—being negotiated on the "untrodden inferential ground" of individual and collective interaction in which their meanings, beliefs, and even self-identifications are being formed and reformed based on the tensions found between their own interpretations of themselves and the interpretations of "outsiders."[39]

Therefore, somewhat similarly to Geertz's sociological interpretation of "culture," I generally agree with Stalnaker's vision of religions as "vocabularies of social life" and for this project choose to interpret the social convention of religion as primarily a "semiotic one."[40] Before forging ahead with this functioning definition, however, it is important to note that I am not suggesting that "religions" are *reducible* simply to language—that would possibly exclude some of the most vibrant and vital elements of various religious traditions, practices, and understandings. Rather, what is intended by viewing religions through a primarily "linguistic" lens is just to say that the scholar of religion, including this comparative theologian, would probably find it extremely difficult—if not outright impossible—to compare religious traditions apart from the study of their use of language and how their linguistic ideas shape the way their followers experience the world. In fact in his book *The Study of Religion in a New Key: Theoretical and Philosophical Soundings in the Comparative and General Study of Religion*, Jeppe Sinding Jensen agrees with this assessment arguing that a semiotic—or "linguistic"—interpretation of religion allows the scholar to analyze religions phenomenologically (and consequently less reductively) while nonetheless still observing it from a wholly historical and human perspective that makes it "possible to generalize, make comparisons and classifications precisely as it is in the study of languages."[41] This new semiotic interpretation of religion can avoid the pitfalls of both classical phenomenologies of religion as well as overly reductive functionalist explanations by grounding its epistemological basis in a conventional philosophy of language rather than in metaphysical assertions or materialistic positivisms.[42] Moreover, such a depiction

---

38. Ibid., 7–8.
39. Ibid., 9–10.
40. Geertz, 5.
41. Jeppe Sinding Jensen, *The Study of Religion in a New Key: Theoretical and Philosophical Soundings in the Comparative and General Study of Religion* (Aarhus: Aarhus University Press, 2003), 27, 86.
42. Ibid., 27.

of religion can also open the door to what Sinding Jensen describes as a "new comparativism" that can utilize the poststructuralist and linguistic turns in philosophy as a means to "drop the disguise of 'neutrality' " in comparison and opt instead to acknowledge the fact that comparisons themselves not only analyze and interpret the meanings and claims of the "religions" they study but indeed participate in shaping and constructing their meanings as well. In this way, the comparativist can recognize that any idea or interpretation of "religion" in the comparison is always still an endlessly "complex" and "impure object" that is nonetheless necessary for interpreting humans' experiences of world.[43]

Accordingly, this project's semiotic interpretation will depict religions (in particular Christianity and Buddhism) according to Ludwig Wittgenstein's theory of "language games" as systems of discourse and thought that help organize particular social interactions and provide the basis for meaning within societies.[44] This "language-game" translation of religion will allow us to observe the various religious sources, theories, and referents of the two thinkers as "objects of comparison" without demanding they correspond to objective realities "out there" in the world.[45] Moreover, it can also use Wittgenstein's related idea of "family resemblances"—the non-essentializing recognition of similarities and connections across language games—in order to justify situating and classifying the thinkers as belonging to larger traditions of religious thought and belief under more general abstractions, such as the diverse communities of "Christianity" or "Buddhism," while maintaining an acknowledgment of the (sometimes *irreducible*) internal dissimilarities of convictions and beliefs between the thinkers themselves, other various practitioners, and even the social institutions that belong to these broader categorizations.[46] This is because, as George Lindbeck explains, such a "cultural-linguistic" perspective regards religion as "first of all a comprehensive *interpretive medium* or *categorical framework*," which makes certain kinds of experiences and affirmations of meaning possible.[47] In other words, the doctrines, rituals, and ceremonies of religious communities provide "languages of faith" that

---

43. Ibid., 38, 42, 72.

44. Ludwig Wittgenstein, G. E. M. Anscombe, P. M. S. Hacker, and Joachim Schulte, *Philosophische Untersuchungen = Philosophical Investigations*, rev. 4th ed. (Malden, MA: Wiley-Blackwell, 2009), 35.

45. Wittgenstein, Anscombe, Hacker, and Schulte, 56, 31.

46. Ibid., 36. Leo Lefebure also briefly discusses this type of use of Wittgenstein's "family resemblances" for the classification of religion, and specifically James C. Livingston's use of the notion for classifying religious groups "based on [their] relationship to the sacred" rather than "any univocal definition of an alleged essence." For this brief discussion, see Leo D. Lefebure, *True and Holy: Christian Scripture and Other Religions* (Maryknoll, NY: Orbis Books, 2014), 13.

47. George A. Lindbeck, *The Nature of Doctrine: Religion and Theology in a Postliberal Age*, 1st ed. (Philadelphia: Westminster Press, 1984), 80. Emphasis added.

form a communal logic by which religious traditions can regulate truth claims by excluding some and permitting others.[48]

Nevertheless, Stalnaker recognizes that even if one applies a linguistic or semiotic viewpoint to the interpretation of religions and their meanings for the purposes of comparison—especially in consideration of his suggestion that a comparative study be firmly grounded in two specific thinkers—in the act of interreligious comparison itself an individual is often, if not always, challenged with the task of having to bring distant theological statements into interrelation and conversation while also simultaneously preserving each thinker's distinctiveness within the interrelation. Stalnaker maintains that the latter goal is easily accounted for through a scholar's "careful analysis of each thinker's distinctive vocabulary," whereas concerning the former and more noticeable problem, successfully achieving this goal consistently proves much more elusive to comparativists. In pursuit of this more difficult goal, nonetheless, Stalnaker suggests a method of "bridge concepts" as containing the potential to effectively traverse any such chasm between religious language games. For him, "Bridge concepts are general ideas, such as 'virtue' and 'human nature,' which can be given enough content to be meaningful and guide comparative inquiry yet are still open to greater specification in particular cases." These "bridge concepts," he continues, differ from the more common notion of theoretically "thin concepts" in both purpose and use. Bridge concepts are not simply abstract concepts found within each thinker that are to be filled in more thoroughly through high levels of scrutiny and analysis but are specifically *chosen* by the comparativist as a means to better "facilitate a particular comparison of a delimited number of objects." And as such, the process for selecting what bridge concepts to use is primarily an *inductive* one that suggests that ideas of comparison are not necessarily based on a thick analysis and discovery of congruent ideas within the systems of two thinkers but rather are more like intuitive hypotheses that will have to undergo "further testing and revision" during the comparison itself.[49]

At the same time, however, because of the base assumption that religions should be compared on the basis of being "vocabularies of social life," these "hypotheses" are also not suggesting that they reflect or reveal any type of "transcultural universal" of experience or understanding that is shared by the individual thinkers being compared or the broader traditions they are serving to represent.[50] Instead, these concepts function more as a "third idiom" openly "projected into each thinker

---

48. Ibid., 19, 59.
49. Stalnaker, 17.
50. To this point, I completely agree with Stalnaker's skepticism toward any assertion by scholars of "deep structures or 'epistemes' that are supposed somehow to determine or explain thought and practice, whether for humanity as a whole, or merely with a single tradition or era" (17). This is because embracing the reality of such "epistemes" would seemingly purport the exact type of problematic structuralism that the use of such a semiotic approach would seek to avoid.

or text to be compared as a way to thematize their disparate elements and order their details around these anchoring terms." Similarly neither are they intended to necessarily reflect the same idea within each thinker. Rather, they are meant to function as terms or labels that might superficially appear to match ideas within both of the thinkers or texts examined, but not necessarily in the same way or for the same purpose. In this way, for example, using one of Stalnaker's bridge concepts of "human nature," one thinker might view human nature as fundamentally "good" but defiled by the influences and corruptions of society and culture, while another might see human nature as originally "good" or "pure" but defiled or obstructed by a spiritual lapse brought about through some primordial action. In this case then, the bridge concept of "human nature" would possibly function to highlight a similarity in the thinkers' assumptions of humans being originally "good" in their nature even though they would significantly disagree on the cause of their defilement. Accordingly, this difference in their belief of an originating cause to "human nature's" defilement might also elicit very distinct ways of speaking about and achieving its restoration: with one suggesting a much more practical cause and rectification oriented around concrete actions of purification within one's own life to distinguish oneself from the corrupting world, and the other insisting on a more abstract cause and cure that requires an imputation of supernatural "grace" to remedy the individual's fallen nature.

In this hypothetical case then, the bridge concept is effective in that it teases out certain underlying similarities in the thinkers' frameworks, and at the same time it clearly displays that they are not speaking about the exact same thing or about it in the exact same way. Thus the purpose of bridge concepts is not to exhibit equivalents within the two "language games" of thought; rather, it is to show a concept that can be applied at least superficially to each thinker's system while also demonstrating how that initial moment of resonance might be hiding even more significant dissimilarities in their assumptions and beliefs. For this reason, Stalnaker holds, bridge concepts will often "work best" if they can correlate to "near-equivalent terms" in each thinker's scheme of thought or writings that are being compared, but still in the end he asserts "this is not necessary."[51] Because these concepts are intended to provide a "third idiom" or "language game" into which the comparativist attempts to translate the prior two vocabularies, the process of using bridge concepts is open to highlighting both the potential similarities and differences behind the individuals' words and thought equally. Hence, Stalnaker contends that they are not meant to produce a separate *common* or *shared* vocabulary between the two thinkers or traditions but merely to assist in the process of creating "comparative relations," or potential instances of perceived linguistic contact, between otherwise distant and distinct positions.[52]

Moreover, since bridge concepts are inductive hypotheses specifically chosen by comparativists themselves from a wide range of useful possibilities, Stalnaker

---

51. Stalnaker, 17.
52. Ibid., 18.

contends that this "bridge-concept" methodology proves more diverse and flexible in its application. In other words, because these concepts are chosen, or even developed, by the comparativist as the most effective means to induce comparative reflection between two objects of comparison based on the scholar's own assessment and purpose, Stalnaker concedes that bridge concepts can and will vary in scope and character.

> Most simply, they can be univocal and strictly limited. More frequently, however, bridge concepts multiply under comparative scrutiny to cover a cluster of related ideas that can be specified more precisely, but that may or may not cohere in any systematic way; in cases of this sort, comparison serves as a prod to conceptual analysis, and it uncovers the complexity and tension in frequently used terms such as "human nature" and "the will."[53]

Stalnaker goes on to explain that these "clusters of related ideas" might incidentally share the "family resemblances" suggested by Wittgenstein in a similar sense as the one discussed earlier for justifying the categorization of disparate language games under the umbrellas of larger "religious traditions." Still he also emphasizes that these resemblances may or may not eventually "cohere in any systematic way." Rather their intention is primarily to invite comparative reflection, which itself can serve "as a prod" to further and deeper conceptual analysis. Hence in doing this, these concepts also assist the readers in eventually freeing themselves from the seductive lure of any initial "intuitive simplicity and obviousness" and in fact actually expose to a greater extent how the "precise constituents" of an individual's thought emerge out of, and logically cohere to, their own distinct sources of particularly complex and historically contingent processes of influence.[54] And it is for this reason that Stalnaker suggests that bridge concepts do not require "full-blown theories" or firm definitions and are more usually employed as minimal or "thin" concepts as opposed to thicker and more complex ones that require less fleshing out of the ideas and can more quickly be deemed as pertaining to a notion or not.[55] Instead by remaining rather vague or "thin" in their possible application, bridge concepts will spur the scholar to have to "disentangle the various strands" of potential meaning or resonance within a particular thinker's system of thought alongside conceivably pushing the comparativist to search for other, better formulations as well.[56]

And finally, along with using a "third idiom" for translation as a potential means to tease out new insights and even more constructive and contextually applicable conclusions, Stalnaker believes bridge concepts can function in a way that will also help comparative scholars conform more easily to Sinding Jensen's ideal of

---

53. Ibid., 35–6.
54. Ibid., 36.
55. Ibid., 49.
56. Ibid., 38.

the "new comparativism" that wishes to "drop the disguise of 'neutrality'" in its analysis and be explicit about the motivations and intentions behind the scholar's choosing of certain concepts for the study. Since it should be openly known, or at least quickly apparent, that bridge concepts are chosen by the comparativists themselves from among a plethora of possibilities, Stalnaker maintains that this method for comparison will also force the scholar to be more explicit about the reasons for their selections and the overarching goals of their project.[57] Hence, he believes that a bridge-concepts methodology is not just conducive to formulating a more explicit discussion about the constructive nature, convictions, and intentions behind a comparison's conclusions, but it also goes much further than previous methods in obliging comparativists to discuss and justify the constructive and determinative decisions that give rise to the comparisons in the first place. In other words, it allows the comparativist to be up-front about how the particular bridge concepts that are selected in order to raise certain desired comparative questions also can lift any veil of "objectivity" that might, whether wittingly or not, assist the scholar in "smuggling in answers ahead of time or focusing on extraneous or misleading issues."[58] Accordingly, I believe the bridge-concepts methodology both opens up a greater creative freedom for the comparativist within the process of doing the comparison itself while at the same time exposing the scholar to a greater scrutiny and accountability for the choices he or she makes in actually doing it. Furthermore these virtues are not only necessary for, and thus confined to, the realms of comparative religions, religious studies, and in Stalnaker's particular case CRE but are ideals that need to be situated more firmly within the field of Comparative Theology as well. Therefore, in the next section the conversation will now turn to examine how incorporating a "bridge-concepts methodology" into Catholic theology might have significantly positive implications for establishing the more open, dialogical, and comparative theological approach as suggested by the prominent sources discussed in the previous section.

IV. Conclusion: Returning to the Problem of Belief in an Increasingly "Relativistic World"

Now that the purpose, method, and goals of this project have been fleshed out in relation to the calls for dialogue within the Catholic Church alongside previous efforts by other theologians to answer that call, it is time to turn to focus on this comparison of Schillebeeckx and Gendun Chopel itself. The next chapter will seek to first both embody and substantiate this comparison on the grounds of religious epistemology by briefly sketching the broad outline of the comparison according to a certain "cluster of ideas" related to questions of religious interpretation, authority, and experience. After this process of contextualization and embodiment

---

57. Ibid., 33.
58. Ibid., 49.

of the thinkers and their ideas, the next three subsequent chapters (3 through 5) will then move to three comparative "case studies" centered on the question of authority regarding religious traditions, the historical founders of those traditions, and an individual's personal religious experiences. Each of these chapters will conclude with a brief comparative reflection that will intend to tease out further questions evoked by the imagined dialogue between the two thinkers on the given topic of that chapter. And finally then, the last chapter will briefly return to these questions after the analysis of the entire comparison in order to attempt to address these concerns and speculate on possible theological responses to these questions from an interpretation of Schillebeeckx's theology in dialogue with Gendun Chopel's epistemological challenges. So in the end, this final chapter will attempt to utilize the construction and assessment of this entire comparative dialogue between Schillebeeckx and Gendun Chopel to suggest how both thinkers might be able to more effectively contribute individually as well as cooperatively to forming new trajectories for religious thought and spiritual practice in the contemporary postmodern world.

Chapter 2

THE "BRIDGE CONCEPT" AND ITS MATERIALS

I. Introduction

Despite the benefits of a revised "bridge-concepts" methodology for this comparative theological project, as laid out in the previous chapter, there are still some lingering issues that must be addressed and clarified before diving into the thick comparative analysis itself. Namely, *what are* the bridge concepts that will be used and, maybe more importantly, *what makes* Schillebeeckx and Gendun Chopel sufficiently qualified to discuss these ideas—let alone speak authoritatively within their traditions. The significance of this task was one of the most properly criticized issues of Stalnaker's project *Overcoming Our Evil* in which he was questioned as to the "direct" connection[1] he perceived between his two subjects, Augustine and Xunzi, and their understandings of the role of "spiritual exercises" in the religious life.

In "Comparison and the Ubiquity of Resemblance," David Decosimo takes Stalnaker and his methodology to task for a number of issues, beginning with the selection of Augustine and Xunzi as seminal voices regarding spiritual discipline within their respective traditions. While acknowledging and praising Stalnaker's overall contribution to the field of Comparative Religious Ethics, Decosimo is utterly unconvinced by Stalnaker's blithe assertion that a serious consideration of the role of spiritual discipline from within the Christian and Daoist traditions naturally "leads directly to Augustine and Xunzi."[2] Consequently, despite whatever interesting insights and contributions his comparison might produce, Decosimo argues that Stalnaker fails to give the reader the "basic norms by which to evaluate the *success* or *value* of the comparison" by failing to justify the "objects of comparison are *appropriate*" for the "clear goal" of the comparative project. Thus Stalnaker never establishes why the overall project is "*coherent* or *makes sense*."[3]

In fact, Decosimo takes his criticism of Stalnaker one step further by not only contesting that Stalnaker never actually justifies the legitimacy of the objects of his

---

1. Stalnaker, 19.
2. David Decosimo, "Comparison and the Ubiquity of Resemblance," *Journal of the American Academy of Religion* 78, no. 1 (2010): 243.
3. Decosimo, 239–40.

comparison[4] but also asserting that there actually "is a significant disconnect or lack of fit between the items selected *for* comparison and the goals the comparison pursues."[5] As such, Decosimo insists that Stalnaker fails to satisfy a "minimalist" criterion for verifying that "other things being equal, it is worth pursuing more rather than less relevant, interesting, and internally coherent comparative work."[6] Furthermore, anticipating Stalnaker's possible rebuttal that the project *itself* bears out the justification of the comparison, Decosimo is resolute that up-front reasoning regarding the selection of objects and their vital relation to the ultimate comparative goal is absolutely necessary for reasonably providing the reader with the ability to adjudicate whether the proposed comparison is a worthwhile investment as well as determining whether the actual comparison itself ultimately succeeds in its goals of thorough comparative analysis and mutual illumination of the thinkers' ideas and systems. Otherwise, as Decosimo specifically chides Stalnaker for doing, the project itself simply becomes a "promissory note" of an eventual comparative payoff that the reader has no assurance of actually ever receiving in the end.[7] With regard to the particular case of *Overcoming Our Evil*, Decosimo deems the final recompense much smaller than originally promised.

Regardless of whatever one thinks about the various criticisms Decosimo hurls at Stalnaker's methodology in his article, on this particular point of having up-front reasoning regarding one's goals in doing comparison, and in clearly justifying the selections of one's subjects in achieving those goals, Decosimo's critique is as accurate as it is biting. And thus, before analyzing the particular instances, issues, or "case studies" of the bridge concept of "religious epistemology" in the thought of Schillebeeckx and Gendun Chopel for my own project, this chapter will seek to lay out the theoretical and philosophical influences on their thought in order to establish both thinkers' "appropriateness" to the topic as well as their relevance to each other regarding the surrounding issues of knowledge, the nature of truth, valid authority, and finally what can be known about ultimate reality.[8] In some

---

4. Ibid., 243: "And while these goals do not necessarily *rule out* consideration of these two, neither, do they *explain* why they in particular have been selected, just what the connection might be."

5. Ibid., 240.

6. Ibid., 252. It should be noted, however, that within this particular critique of Stalnaker's selection of objects of comparison, Decosimo explicitly states that he is not positing a "maximalist" criterion for comparison either. As he explains, "At the other pole, a maximal version would insist that comparativists select as objects and goals of comparison only those that are maximally relevant and interesting and maximally well suited to one another. I am not endorsing the maximal version."

7. Ibid., 249.

8. Although the question of whether the term "ultimate reality" is an appropriate designation for the Buddhist understanding of the truth and nature of reality, in the case of Gendun Chopel's madhyamaka epistemology the classification seems more or less sufficient. Using the classical categories of "Two Truths" theories in Buddhist philosophy, Gendun Chopel would certainly recognize the distinction between contingent or "conventional" truth

ways, the purpose of this chapter will serve primarily as an assurance of the value of the "promissory note" that will hopefully be cashed out at the conclusion. Or put another way, sticking with the "bridge" metaphor, it will supply not the structure and function of the bridge concept itself but rather make the argument for the materials of which this comparative bridge will be built. Thus, it will examine the shared elements on which each thinker's epistemology is founded and by so doing establish both as viable subjects of comparison while also forming the basis of a subsequently closer comparative analysis in the remaining chapters.

Unlike the questionable choice of Augustine and Xunzi for Stalnaker's project, Schillebeeckx and Gendun Chopel present a much more apparent and appropriate topic of comparison in regard to their understanding of epistemology.[9] For example,

claims or knowledge (*saṃvṛtisatyaI*) and the "ultimate truth" or "reality" (*paramārthasatya*) of emptiness (*śūnyatā*)—denying the epistemic validity of the former and acknowledging the validity of the latter when directly perceived by an enlightened mind. Thus even though, according to him, this "ultimate reality" is in fact a "non-affirming negative" or "ultimate absence" that is completely void of conceptuality or valid expression, it can still be rendered "ultimate reality" in a sense more aligned with Keenan's assertion that the Sanskrit term for "ultimate truth" (*paramārthasatya*) "means literally the final, or ultimate, meaning or aim. Perhaps we can understand it as the truth that is the ultimate term or end point of all our questioning and all our thinking." (See Keenan, Sydney Copp, Lansing Davis, and Buster G. Smith, *Grounding Our Faith in a Pluralist World: With a Little Help from Nāgārjuna* (Eugene, OR: Wipf & Stock, 2009), 63.) Similarly the late Zen Buddhist philosopher/comparativist Masao Abe seemingly would concur with this assessment, especially with regard to Buddhist-Christian/Western dialogue, when he explains how the Buddhist notion of "dynamic sunyata" can serve as the "Buddhist Ultimate." (See Masao Abe, "Kenotic God and Dynamic Sunyata," in *The Emptying God: A Buddhist-Jewish-Christian Conversation*, ed. John B. Cobb and Christopher Ives, Faith Meets Faith Series (Maryknoll, NY: Orbis Books, 1990), 27–33.) At the same time, however, it must be noted that this conclusion is not a universally recognized one. For one example of a discussion of the complexity to this issue see Malcolm David Eckel (with John J. Thatamanil) and Neville's engagement of this idea of "ultimate truth" and emptiness in Neville, *Religious Truth*, 69–76, 222. And for a very condensed assessment of this same discussion, also see Smid, 185–6.

9. Despite the apparent appropriateness of comparing these two thinkers on the topic of epistemology, again it must be pointed out that this does not intend to imply that the role of epistemology is identical in the two traditions. For example, Buddhist soteriology tends to see epistemology as the primary locus of the central human dilemma, whereas many Christians (stemming out of the Augustinian and Thomistic readings of the tradition) see the soteriological problem of humanity as only partly epistemological and also related to the fallen will of sinful humanity. (For an excellent discussion of the role and boundaries of epistemology in soteriology from a particularly Augustinian perspective, see Lefebure, *The Buddha and The Christ*, 115–40.) And yet it is also significant that although Schillebeeckx would have been clearly trained in, aware of, and grounded by this Augustinian notion of the epistemological warping of the sinful mind, especially early in his career, Schillebeeckx's emphasis in "Phenomenological Thomism" made him

regarding Gendun Chopel's writings as an adequate subject of epistemological and philosophical analysis and comparison, the Buddhist Studies scholar Donald Lopez points out in his introduction to Gendun Chopel's *The Adornment to Nagarjuna's Thought*, "One can say with some degree of conviction that the overriding theme of the work is the question of the possibility of knowledge."[10] Moreover, Lopez describes *The Adornment*'s style as a highly complex philosophical treatise on the validity of knowledge, which often assumes "a complete knowledge of Dge lugs scholastic vocabulary, especially in the areas of *pramāṇa* and *madhyamaka*,"[11] and thus reminds him "more of the *Philosophical Investigations* than of any Buddhist text [he has] read."[12] Lopez further endorses Gendun Chopel's credentials both as a student of philosophy and as a creative and constructive philosopher when he declares that in *The Adornment* "[Gendun Chopel] presents his *own* middle way [philosophy], one between wisdom and ignorance, certainty and doubt, faith and skepticism—a middle way that calls everything we know into question *because*, rather than in spite of, the enlightenment of the Buddha."[13]

Similarly, Schillebeeckx's theological development in connection with his understanding of the validity of knowledge and authority has been well documented, including most recently as a particularly precise chapter devoted to Schillebeeckx's epistemological development in Daniel Speed Thompson's work entitled *The Language of Dissent: Edward Schillebeeckx on the Crisis of Authority in the Catholic Church*.[14] In fact, although the generic division of Schillebeeckx's theological and philosophical development had been previously outlined in various places elsewhere,[15] Thompson's demarcation of three progressive trajectories within

deemphasize this aspect of his traditional influence and choose to prioritize the more abstract discussion of the epistemological limits of finitude distinguishing creation from its Creator. As will be discussed further in Chapter 3's comparison of "perspectivalism" in both thinkers' systems, later in his career Schillebeeckx would turn to emphasize this element of Christian epistemology through his engagement with and adaptation of hermeneutics and Critical Theory. Still, even in these discussions of the epistemological effect of rampant and unavoidable sinful self-interest, Schillebeeckx speaks more pervasively in terms of these modern theories as his primary vocabulary rather than directly referencing the Augustinian tradition of thought.

10. Donald S. Lopez and Dge dun chos phel, *The Madman's Middle Way: Reflections on Reality of the Tibetan Monk Gendun Chopel*, Buddhism and Modernity (Chicago: University of Chicago Press, 2006).

11. Lopez and chos phel, *Madman*, ix.

12. Ibid.

13. Ibid., xi.

14. Daniel Speed Thompson, *The Language of Dissent: Edward Schillebeeckx on the Crisis of Authority in the Catholic Church* (Notre Dame, IN: University of Notre Dame Press, 2003).

15. See Mary Catherine Hilkert, "Hermeneutics of History in the Theology of Edward Schillebeeckx," *Thomist* 51 (1987): 97–145; Philip Kennedy, "Continuity Underlying Discontinuity: Schillebeeckx's Philosophical Background," *New Black Friars* 70 (1989): 264–77; Stephan Van Erp, "Implicit Faith: Philosophical Theology after Schillebeeckx," in

Schillebeeckx's epistemological understanding will serve—with only some minor tweaking of terminology—as the basis for schematizing both thinkers' philosophy of knowledge. Actually, rather than picturing these divisions as separate, unrelated "categories," Thompson astutely depicts them rather as "concentric circles" that are somewhat distinguishable and yet carry definite overlaps and particular continuities all the way through.[16] For as Philip Kennedy elucidates on this same subject of Schillebeeckx's epistemological delineation,

> in his many writings, he has not in any way or at any time abandoned the most basic and epistemological fundamentals which have informed his theology since the beginning of his career. His philosophical groundwork has changed its outer vocabulary while retaining its inner syntax. What is more, I would even be prepared to argue that the whole of his theology is one of vast commentary on an epistemological premise which is found in a single text of Thomas Aquinas.[17]

Furthermore, this imagery of concentric circles will be helpful for both thinkers in that (as will become apparent in the course of this study) this three-tiered differentiation of both men's thought is somewhat paradoxically and at the same time evidently discernable, yet not easily separable.

Thompson illustrates his schematic for differentiating Schillebeeckx's epistemological thought as focusing around the three concentric circles of Schillebeeckx's perspectivalism through phenomenological Thomism, his hermeneutical turn, and finally his development of Critical Theory and praxis.[18] However, although this schema is incredibly helpful for distinguishing Schillebeeckx's thought in isolation, it will have to be slightly altered and broadened in order to encompass the Buddhist Madhyamaka philosophy of Gendun Chopel. Obviously, first of all, Gendun Chopel had no apparent knowledge of Aquinas, let alone "phenomenological Thomism," and as such the first circle must be generalized to "perspectivalism" in order to portray accurately the strands in both thinkers' philosophical trajectories. From this more ontological perspective, the focus is on the subject and objects of knowledge, and how "knowledge" is always mediated to the knower in a limited fashion by the use of abstract concepts. The second category is basically sufficient as it stands with just the rather small alteration of eliminating the language of "turn" (which in some ways suggests the "linguistic turn" in European philosophy), and emphasizing the traditional hermeneutical

---

Edward Schillebeeckx and Contemporary Theology, ed. Lieven Boeve, Frederiek Depoortere, and Stephan Van Erp (New York: T&T Clark International, 2010), 209–23.

16. Thompson, 13. Cf. Hilkert, "Hermeneutics," 135. Hilkert gives a good example of this observation when she comments, "Underlying the major shift in Schillebeeckx's theological method from a dogmatic to a hermeneutical-critical approach is a fundamental continuity rooted in his constant conviction that revelation occurs in history."

17. Kennedy, "Continuity," 265.

18. Thompson, 13–46.

questions of textual meaning, interpretation, and authority. Accordingly, this section will emphasize the portions of their philosophical perspectives dealing with the issues of context and new experiences, "where knowledge is mediated by historical tradition, present encounter, and future anticipation."[19] Finally, the last category will require the largest overhaul in order to create the desired "third idiom" between both men's thought. Although both thinkers did eventually address the issues of politics and ideology in their later works, nonetheless there is a much more evident theme underneath and within Schillebeeckx's venture into Critical Theory and praxis-orientated knowledge that displays a moment of possible theoretical contact between the two thinkers—namely, the inexpressible and inconceivable nature of each thinker's notion of ultimate reality. Thus, the third section of this chapter will argue that both share a third corresponding circle of "apophaticism," or indirect knowledge of ultimate reality or truth through the negation of ideas or experiences. Furthermore, it is on this point that the other two conceptual divisions build, and from which they flow. In the end, after completing the various comparative "case studies," this notion of *apophatic* knowledge of the Ultimate provides the richest constructive discourse between the traditions of these two thinkers in developing a more useful understanding of "God" or "ultimate truth" in light of the limits of human knowledge. Yet before moving into deep comparative analyses, it will be more useful to lay out briefly the ideas and concepts that will serve as the materials for constructing the "comparative bridge" between Schillebeeckx and Gendun Chopel.

II. Perspectivalism

A. Schillebeeckx's Perspectivalism: The Development of Knowledge and Phenomenological Thomism

As Mary Catherine Hilkert points out in her seminal 1987 article on Schillebeeckx entitled "Hermeneutics of History in the Theology of Edward Schillebeeckx," prior to his first major shift in perspective during the mid-1940s, the main starting point for Schillebeeckx's notion of "ultimate truth," and his subsequent theological reflection on it, was the dogma of the Church and specifically what it "demands of one as a believing Catholic."[20] Therefore, for example, regarding the question of what can be ultimately known about the nature of the Eucharist, Schillebeeckx insisted that "the first question that should be asked" was "What does God's word of revelation in the Church's authoritative interpretation, tell me about the Eucharistic event?"[21] However, as Hilkert astutely points out, even in this early "dogmatic phase" of his thought, Schillebeeckx never confused or identified the conceptual dogma of "knowledge" within the Church with one's own

---

19. Thompson, 13.
20. Hilkert, "Hermeneutics," 99–100.
21. Edward Schillebeeckx, *The Eucharist* (New York: Sheed and Ward, 1968), 19.

encounter of truth through "revelation-in-reality."[22] This was because, simply put, dogma remained utterly relativized in its supposed knowledge and portrayal of truth because "conceptual expression could never exhaust the mystery of God's self-communicating love." Thus, in this section we will briefly examine the early existential and "anthropocentric mode"[23] of Schillebeeckx's thought, which viewed religion as "essentially a personal relation of man to God, of person to person,"[24] and how that translated to a limited epistemology through a particularly "Thomist-inspired" existential phenomenology.[25]

Thompson concisely and helpfully describes the thrust of Schillebeeckx's "perspectivalist" epistemology[26] as revolving around the central thesis that all human concepts about God must be "open to mystery" and as such can depict

22. Hilkert, "Hermeneutics," 100.

23. William L. Portier, "Edward Schillebeeckx as Critical Theorist: The Impact of Neo-Marxist Social Thought on His Recent Theology," *The Thomist* 48 (1984): 341.

24. Edward Schillebeeckx, *Christ, the Sacrament of the Encounter with God* (New York: Sheed and Ward, 1963), 4.

25. Edward Schillebeeckx, *Revelation and Theology*, vol. II (New York: Sheed and Ward, 1968), 5–29. Cf. pp. 157–206: Here in the appendix entitled "The Non-Conceptual Intellectual Dimension in Our Knowledge of God According to Aquinas," Schillebeeckx lays out his argument for his phenomenological reading of Aquinas's epistemology.

26. This phrasing of "perspectivalism" requires one further step of explanation because of its likely association with Friedrich Nietzsche's (1844–1900) much more radical and irreligious philosophical term "perspectivism." Kennedy explains that in some of his earliest articles (both written in 1945), Schillebeeckx had already begun attempting to distance himself from atheistic forms of humanist and existentialist philosophies—"with particular allusion to [Nietzsche]" and his sarcastic and inflammatory criticism of Christianity. At the time Schillebeeckx designated Nietzsche's philosophy of "perspectivism," which rejects there being any epistemological absolute or any singular meaning behind the empirical world (insisting rather that there are always *many* meanings), as religious apostasy and the most significant problem confronting Christians of the time (see Kennedy, *Schillebeeckx*, 57–9). Accordingly, in a way completely distinct from Nietzsche, throughout his career Schillebeeckx's understanding of the "perspectival" nature of all knowledge maintains that there *is* an epistemological absolute (God) behind reality by which individuals can adjudicate truth claims based on those claims' correspondence to it—even if that reality can never be *fully* known due to the intellectual and contextual constraints of interpretation. In fact even after the significant influence of the Frankfurt School and the "hermeneutics of suspicion" on his later thought, Schillebeeckx still wrote an article in which he outright rejects Nietzsche's notion though this time more so because it depicts the assertion of knowledge as simply an act of the will to power and consequently demeans the virtue of "humility." Conversely, Schillebeeckx insists that the virtue of humility is necessary within Christian epistemology and his own version of perspectivalism. (See Edward Schillebeeckx, "Critique Du Monde Sur L'obéissance Chrétienne Et Réponse Chrétienne," *Concilium* 159 (1980): 39.)

the divine reality, albeit always "in a confused but objective way."[27] Similarly, Kennedy further elaborates on Schillebeeckx's influences and intentions about this understanding of knowledge in relation to "mystery" when he portrays Schillebeeckx as seeking "to fuse what he perceives to be an emphasis on freedom in early Christianity with a stress on the powers of human reason found in a good deal of the philosophy of the Enlightenment."[28] And as such, Robert Schreiter correctly observes in the introduction to his own edited volume, *The Schillebeeckx Reader*, that even from the very beginning of his career as a theologian, one of Schillebeeckx's primary concerns was always with "concrete, contemporary Christian experience."[29] In order to highlight this concern and to comprehend what Schillebeeckx understood as valid knowledge, particularly of God, we must turn primarily to a series of his earliest articles that were later published as the two-volume work *Revelation and Theology*. However, before we can move directly to those texts themselves, it is important to have an adequate understanding of the philosophical influences that led him to those discourses in the first place. Somewhat unsurprisingly, as is the case with most burgeoning academics, some of Schillebeeckx's most significant influences were the voices of prominent professors who shaped his early thought. Particularly in the case of his own perspectivalist epistemology, Schillebeeckx's foremost philosophical inheritance came from the influential and yet ironically more obscure and less cited Roman Catholic source—the Flemish Dominican Professor of Philosophy at Louvain, Dominic De Petter.[30]

While under the tutelage of De Petter for three years at Louvain, Schillebeeckx adopted and adapted De Petter's combination of Thomism and modern phenomenology in order to argue that indeed it was possible for humans actually to "know truth" (reach reality) through the "objective but non-conceptual dynamism" between the human mind and being itself.[31] Kennedy describes De Petter's general epistemology as a "post-Kantian theory of knowledge where knowledge is seen as a synthesis involving contributions from a knowing subject and an object known."[32] De Petter argued that this synthesis is the result of the antinomy between concepts and any reality outside of the mind (the "concrete-existential") that is located within the intellectual act itself, thus leading him to deny the ability to obtain true knowledge of any reality behind our concepts, or the "being-in-itself."[33] However, unlike other post-Kantian Catholic

---

27. Thompson, 19; Schillebeeckx, *Revelation and Theology*, vol. II, 176.

28. Kennedy, "Continuity," 265.

29. Edward Schillebeeckx and Robert J. Schreiter, *The Schillebeeckx Reader* (New York: Crossroad, 1984), 8–10.

30. Kennedy, "Continuity," 266.

31. Hilkert, "Hermeneutics," 100 n.9; Schillebeeckx, *Revelation and Theology*, vol. II, 5–29.

32. Kennedy, "Continuity," 267.

33. D. M. De Petter, "Impliciete Intuitie," *Tijdschrift voor Philosophie* 1, no. 1 (1939): 92, 95; Schillebeeckx, Theologisch geloofsverstaan anno 1983 (Baarn: Nelissen, 1983). All

philosophers,[34] he also rejected the notion that all knowledge or concepts were complete abstractions of the mind inherently disconnected from the "thing-in-itself," or in his terminology "the concrete-existential."[35]

Rather, De Petter argued for what he termed "Implicit Intuition"—the "spontaneous"[36] and "purely spiritual experience" between a subject and object in which the object is engaged directly ("without any distance or contrast") on an instinctive level without any "internal stress or intentionality."[37] In other words, it is the initial moment of intuition in every intellectual act when the intellect receives its "most essential meaning" from which concepts can be discovered through "reflective effort." This theory, as Stephan Van Erp explains, allowed De Petter to set up what he believed to be a post-Kantian (hence more "critically conscious") *realist* metaphysics as "an attempt to conquer every dualism between the knowing subject and the known object, despite the difference between reality's concrete particularities and the intellect's abstract unifying constructions."[38] This is because, for De Petter, one's consciousness "expresses that moment in which the intellectual act for knowing" realizes a "purely spiritual experience and perception" that is not yet formulated or processed as a concept, assertion, or "proposal."[39] Therefore, according to De Petter, the problem of valid knowledge was not located in the interaction with or perception of reality as such but rather in the intellectual process of discernment and abstraction.[40]

Hence De Petter seeks to forge a balanced epistemology that rejects a "naïve realism" where the mind is simply a passive recipient of knowledge, as well as a purely "subjectivist" one in which there is an absolute disconnect between the subject and "reality-as-such" so that the mind is viewed as the sole originator of all knowledge.[41] In other words, De Petter wants to create a *"critically* realist" epistemology in which all knowledge, abstractions, and concepts are derived from this fundamental intuitive moment of the "really real," the "concrete-existential," while at the same time remaining incapable of ever completely capturing or expressing that reality through abstract concepts.[42] And accordingly, De Petter further applies this understanding of the perspectival limits of an individual's knowledge into the area of the awareness and knowledge of God. He subsequently concludes, through Thomistic language, that all knowledge of the divine contains

---

subsequent quotes and references from this article are from my own unpublished translation of the original Dutch.
34. Van Erp, 213.
35. De Petter, 92.
36. Ibid., 91.
37. Ibid., 101.
38. Van Erp, 214.
39. De Petter, 95.
40. Ibid., 94.
41. Thompson, 14–15.
42. De Petter, 104. Cf. p. 94.

both positive and negative aspects—a direct grasp on God's reality through implicit intuition and also "the recognition that all human concepts used to express this intuition themselves do not directly apply to God and fall well short of capturing the divine reality."[43]

In his earliest work, then, Schillebeeckx seeks to appropriate this "critically realist" phenomenological epistemology into his own theological understanding of truth and the authority of the dogma of the Church in order to emphasize the very human and individually perspectival nature of the dialogical process of any revelatory encounter between God and humanity. In order to effectively highlight this emphasis in the Christian (and particularly Catholic) theological context, Schillebeeckx attempted to transpose Aquinas's understanding of revelation and faith onto the phenomenological language of De Petter's epistemological system.[44] Hence, Hilkert explains that according to Schillebeeckx, within the intellectual interaction with the divine subject,

> the divine initiative and human response constitute two sides of a relationship of mutual self-disclosure and response (revelation-in-reality). Precisely because the human partner in this dialogue is body-spirit who comes to self-awareness through the concrete mediation of the material world and the "other," the offer of encounter with God (pure spirit) must necessarily be mediated by concrete, visible human history if human beings are to be able to hear and respond to the offer.[45]

By depicting the revelatory experience between God and the human subject in this way, Schillebeeckx was able to satisfy De Petter's philosophical petition to conceive "knowledge" as the synthesis of active intellectual contributions from both the knowing subject and the object known within their existential interaction. Hence, revelation inherently includes both a "concrete-existential" of the divine reality and also a non-conceptual "implicit intuition" of that true reality so that the expressive concepts of that intuition might be, although always insufficient and incomplete, still grounded in the absolute meaning of that reality.[46] Furthermore, this integration of De Petter's system into Aquinas's theory of revelation also established grounds to insist why human beings' words and concepts are still fundamentally vital for the mediation of a truly personal existential encounter with God. As Hilkert elucidates, for Schillebeeckx "only the free choice to unveil one's deepest self through words (which clarify one's intentions and disclose the true meaning behind external manifestations) really 'reveals' the person and allows true communication between dialogue partners as 'centers of freedom.'"[47]

43. Kennedy, "Continuity," 267–8. Cf. Thompson, 14–15.
44. Edward Schillebeeckx, "Revelation-In-Reality and Revelation-In-Word," in *Revelation and Theology*, vol. I (New York: Sheed and Ward, 1967), 33–56.
45. Hilkert, "Hermeneutics," 101.
46. Kennedy, "Continuity," 267. Cf. De Petter, 90.
47. Hilkert, "Hermeneutics," 101–2.

This understanding of the importance and necessity of words and concepts to mediate the initial implicitly intuitive encounter with the intellectual object leads Schillebeeckx to conclude that "revelation-in-reality" and "revelation-in-word" are inseparable aspects of the singular offer of an existential encounter with God. Thus, at least in this early phase of Schillebeeckx's epistemological development, one's implicit intuition of "revelation-in-reality" (the mystery of the encounter with God) must always be mediated through "revelation-in-word,"[48] and as such the "grace" of implicit intuition further opens up a non-conceptual perspective of knowledge through the various faith confessions that nonetheless ultimately *transcends* the limited content of the dogmatic concepts employed.[49]

Depicting the intellectual process of revelation in this way, in which one must openly acknowledge the inherent imperfection or "deficiency" in every intellectual act as De Petter insisted,[50] served as a valuable function in multiple ways with regard to the role and authority of the church in the individual's obtaining of theological knowledge. First of all, as outlined in the paragraph above, it established the inherent necessity of language and concepts in an individual's knowledge of God because of both the limits of the human's intellectual process itself[51] as well as in the very meaning of the idea of full "self-disclosure" of the divine in the intellectual encounter. Second, it established the intrinsic fallibility of those concepts and language in ever articulating the true nature of the divine reality because of the unavoidable antinomy between the individual's intellectual process of abstraction and the implicit intuition of the reality of God in Godself, or "concrete-existential" of God. Thus Schillebeeckx concluded that the theological knowledge encountered in the dogmas of the church could be grounded in the actual reality of God (in the form of a "critical realism") while never allowing them to convey exhaustively, and as such infallibly, the true nature and reality of God.[52]

Finally as a consequence of this understanding, Schillebeeckx could use these two previous principles in order to develop a more robust theory of the historical "development of doctrine" while still nevertheless being able to affirm the church's belief that revelation closed with the end of the apostolic church.[53] This is because Schillebeeckx could now argue that the full reality of the "concrete-existential"

---

48. Ibid., 102.

49. Schillebeeckx, *Revelation and Theology*, vol. II, 167 and 170–1. With regard to Schillebeeckx's language of "grace" in epistemology see Edward Schillebeeckx, "The Non-Conceptual Intellectual Element in the Act of Faith: A Reaction," in *Revelation and Theology*, vol. II (New York: Sheed and Ward, 1968), 30–75. Cf. M. A. Fatula, "Dogmatic Pluralism and the Noetic Dimension of Unity of Faith," *The Thomist* 48 (1984): 422.

50. De Petter, 87.

51. Ibid., 103.

52. De Petter, 88.

53. Edward Schillebeeckx, "The Development of the Apostolic Faith into the Dogma of the Church," in *Revelation and Theology*, vol. I, 63–73. Cf. Scillebeeckx, "The Concept of 'Truth,'" in *Revelation and Theology*, vol. II, 23–9.

of God is, and *must* be, disclosed through the language and concepts of the early apostolic teachings, while at same time acknowledging that these formulations and expressions are always limited by the individual intellectual processes and cultural embeddedness of the believers engaging them.[54] Or as De Petter explained it philosophically, although the consciousness's engagement with the object of knowledge *is* exhaustive in its intuitive actuality, it is still essentially unclear and confused in its intellectual abstraction and expression. Hence, the mind must continually drive itself to a clarifying expression of the actuality of the preconceptual intuitive encounter of the object (God) in itself.[55] Thus no matter how "absolute," "unchangeable," or even "canonically closed" the disclosure of the ultimate truth of God and reality might be in the apostolic teachings of the church, it is still nevertheless expressed by human concepts and languages that inherently contain within them all the imperfections, relativities, historical conditionings, and as such *possibilities of development*, as do all claims to truth possessed by the human mind.[56] As Schillebeeckx himself explained,

> In the modern view, insofar as it accepts an absolute reality at all, reality (as truth) is seen as the never wholly-to-be-deciphered background of all our human interpretations. The ontological basis, as the mysterious source of a still hidden fullness of meaning, remains the same and does not change, but the human interpretation of this basis, and thus man's possession of truth, grows and evolves. This is, however, drawn in one definite direction by this implicit ontological significance, so that the truth is always apprehended more and more concretely, even though it is never completely apprehended.[57]

And so, in the end, Schillebeeckx can insist that although the apostolic teachings could disclose the full reality of God intuitively, at the same time he can still affirm De Petter's assertion that every concept—because of the limits of the intellectual perspectivalism of the individuals engaging them—necessarily falls short of adequately depicting who or what God "is," and thus all portrayals of God are ultimately god*less* in themselves.[58] Therefore, Schillebeeckx's "perspectivalism" allows for what can be accurately described as a justification of the "critically realist" interpretation of knowledge where all conceptions of the object of knowledge (in this case God) are grounded in a full encounter and disclosure of that reality—making

---

54. Edward Schillebeeckx, "Exegesis, Dogmatics, and the Development of Dogma," in *Dogmatic vs. Biblical Theology*, ed. H. Vorgrimler(Baltimore: Helicon, 1964), 129–31. Cf. Hilkert, "Hermeneutics," 104–5.

55. De Petter, 90. Cf. Van Erp, 215–17.

56. Schillebeeckx, *Dogmatic vs. Biblical Theology*, 131.

57. Schillebeeckx, "Concept of 'Truth,'" *Revelation and Theology*, vol. II, 7. Cf. Thompson, 17.

58. De Petter, 92.

discovering or even *constructing* meaning from it ontologically viable[59]—while nonetheless insisting that the inherent limits of the individual human intellectual process as well as the conditionedness of all human expressions make all human possession of knowledge fundamentally "perspectival" and consequently capable of always growing and evolving in precision and clarity. Thus, in this earliest stage of Schillebeeckx's theory, the goal of theology is to bring more conceptual clarity to the inexhaustible reality and containable actuality of the divine reality.[60]

B. Chopel's Perspectivalism: The Impossibility of Knowledge for the Unenlightened Mind

One could argue that in some ways similar to Schillebeeckx's understanding of the perspectival limits to human knowledge, Gendun Chopel also perceives the limits of human knowledge as beginning first and foremost in the inherent incapability of the individual intellects of "common beings." For this reason, he contests, the validity of knowledge cannot be determined based on any form of intellectual consensus regardless of the size of the collective group, because in the end no matter whether a hundred, a thousand, or even ten thousand people agree on the valid existence of an object of knowledge, it is ultimately still a *decision* "about what exists and does not exist, what is and is not," that is being made "in accordance with how it appears to our respective [and limited] minds."[61] At the same time, however, one must also recognize that the claim being set forth here by Gendun Chopel is still nonetheless quite distinct from the more universal claim held by Schillebeeckx that *all* humans are incapable of gaining definitive knowledge by the very nature and function of the human intellect. Instead, as Lopez explains in his commentary on Gendun Chopel's *Adornment*, the expression "common being" is rather significant in Gendun Chopel's declarations of the perspectival limits of the human intellect, for the word translated here as "common being" (Skt: pṛthagjana, Tib: *so so skyes bu*) is a very technical term in Madhyamaka philosophy, which refers specifically to "any being in the universe who has not directly perceived the ultimate truth of emptiness." Moreover, this term is utilized in distinction to the title of "noble ones" (āryan, *'phags pa*), which denotes beings that have directly perceived this reality of emptiness.[62]

Thus, immediately two significant distinctions arise between the perspectivalist epistemologies of Schillebeeckx and Gendun Chopel. First, there is a disagreement

---

59. Hilkert, "Hermeneutics," 105. Cf. Van Erp, 215. Here Van Erp discusses De Petter's theory of the "singularity" or "unity of being."

60. Schillebeeckx, "What Is Theology?," *Revelation and Theology*, vol. I, 124–5.

61. Dge dun chos phel, "Eloquent Distillation of the Profound Points of Madhyamaka: An Adornment to Nāgārjuna's Thought," in *The Madman's Middle Way: Reflections on Reality of the Tibetan Monk Gendun Chopel*, trans. Donald S. Lopez (Chicago: University of Chicago Press, 2006), 48, v. 5.

62. Lopez and chos phel, *Madman*, 128.

as to the source and character of the limits of knowledge formation within the individual. Schillebeeckx insists that this limitation in one's ability to "know" anything as it is in itself is a universally human phenomenon that is caused by finite limitation of the human's natural intellectual process (in particular, the processes of abstraction and discernment), which is then only compounded by the warping effect of original sin on the human mind, whereas Gendun Chopel begins by promptly distinguishing and containing the problem of the intellect's perspectival limits to a certain segment—albeit one containing the vast majority— of the human population. Then subsequently, and possibly more importantly, the perspectivalism in Gendun Chopel's Madhyamaka epistemology significantly deviates from any form of phenomenological Thomism, specifically as embodied by Schillebeeckx and De Petter, in that it insists that for these "common beings" there is no contact with any form of the "really real" (specifically to Gendun Chopel, the ultimate truth of emptiness) behind the individual common being's phenomenological encounter with an object of knowledge. Instead, as Lopez elucidates, for Gendun Chopel "there is no commonality whatsoever between the way things are perceived by the ignorant mind [of common beings] and the way they are perceived by the enlightened mind [of noble ones]."[63] At this point it must be noted, however, that what Gendun Chopel is proposing is not a form of an epistemological dualism between those beings who have an "enlightened perspective" and those who do not. Rather, as we will see in the section on the apophatic elements in his epistemology as well as in its corresponding discussion in Chapter 5 on the nature of ultimate reality in itself, Gendun Chopel argues that the "enlightened" way of knowing is a completely separate form of knowledge that is in actuality not a "perspective" at all. Rather, it is in essence the perspective-less "abiding" within "the inexpressible and the inconceivable" nature of reality from which one can "truly have no assertion from one's own perspective."[64]

In fact, one could maintain that the thrust of Gendun Chopel's epistemological argument as it is laid out in the *Adornment* is to combat the traditional Geluk (*dge lugs*) position, as taught by the famous Tibetan scholastic Tsongkhapa, that it is of the utmost importance to "guard" the validity and meaning of "conventional" (or contingent, limited, and fallible) knowledge and "to preserve the appearances of the world … in the face of the ultimate emptiness of all phenomena."[65] Rather, throughout the *Adornment* as well as his other various writings, Gendun Chopel constantly reiterates the point that the ultimate reality of emptiness completely contradicts any perceived ("conventional") knowledge of the world by the ignorant mind. And therefore, any attempt to link the perceived knowledge of common unenlightened humans to the ultimate (or "really real") truth of emptiness behind all encountered phenomena, or in the language of Tsongkhapa to insist on the "compatibility of the two truths," *is a gross error*.[66] Thus for Gendun Chopel there

63. Ibid., 246.
64. Ibid., 146.
65. Ibid., 245.
66. Ibid., 246.

can be no claim to "valid knowledge" apart from the direct perception of emptiness experienced only by the enlightened mind, and as such any claim to knowledge from the side of the contingent and limited perspective of the unenlightened individual cannot even attest to sharing the same object of knowledge as one who has had a direct encounter with the ultimate truth of all reality—namely emptiness. This is because, as Gendun Chopel explicates in the 210th verse of the *Adornment*, phenomenologically speaking, the object of knowledge observed by the individual is utterly shaped by the perspective from which the individual encounters the object so that when an item, such as the common example of a "pot" in Tibetan philosophical rhetoric, is engaged by two individuals—one enlightened and one not—each person's claim to the nature and truth of that object is fundamentally shaped by the ontological perspective from which they approach and observe that "form."[67] Thus even when an enlightened and unenlightened individual encounter the same immediate "pot" within their experiences of reality, their difference in ontological grounding for the existence of that pot actually changes the form in which the pot takes within their respective minds so that, from the phenomenological perspective, the object of their knowledge is not in reality shared even if superficially they seem to be encountering the same item.[68] And so for this reason, Gendun Chopel repeatedly contends, "to think that the earth, stones, mountains, rocks that we see now are still to be seen vividly when we are buddhas *is very much in error*" for "when you have understood the lack of intrinsic existence, then the way in which earth and stones, mountains, and rocks appear to you and the way they appear to others come to be very different."[69]

Gendun Chopel bases this assertion of the possibility of having various "objects of knowledge" for the same immediately experienced item on a few key epistemological foundations that serve as the source and structure of his perspectivalism. First is his insistence that the intellectual process of the individual mind functions as the primary basis for even one's most fundamental and cursory encounters with reality. Or as he puts it in one of his most famous articles discussing epistemology and modern science, "even the perception of a shape [of an object] does not exist objectively apart from the power of mind or of human language."[70] And therefore as he later concludes in the *Adornment*, "In the end, the knower is mixed with the object of knowledge with which it is of one taste."[71] Accordingly, Gendun Chopel maintains that the perception of the mind permeates every encounter of the individual's "five weak senses," so he insists that to decide that the basis for all objects of knowledge can simply be located within an item's empirical manifestation "is the door to all trouble."[72] Hence, for example, when the Buddha

---

67. Chos phel, "Adornment," 107, v. 210.

68. Ibid., 59, v. 43.

69. Ibid., 52, v. 20. Cf. 75, v. 109; 63, v. 74; Cf. Lopez and chos phel, *Madman*, 142.

70. Lopez and chos phel, *Madman*, 110. On page 119, Lopez further expounds on this claim asserted by Gendun Chopel.

71. Chos phel, "Adornment," 107, v. 211.

72. Ibid., 52, v. 20.

is said to have used "magical powers" in order to fit the entire world within a single atom, Gendun Chopel contends that the Buddha is not using magic at all. Rather, from an ultimate perspective, all distinctions—even basic size, shape, value (good/bad), and existence itself—are constructs of the individual unenlightened mind that are actually projected out onto reality as something universally experienced by ourselves and others.[73] So from Gendun Chopel's perspective, it is our own ignorant minds, and not the Buddha, that are always magically transforming reality in radical ways.[74] Thus he proclaims, "Whatever most people like appears as the truth; whatever most mouths agree on appears as a philosophical tenet. *Inside each person is a different valid form of knowledge*, with an adamantine scripture supporting it."[75] And therefore, no matter how "concrete," "direct," or "immediate" even our most basic empirical encounters with reality might seem, when it comes to determining any object of knowledge "it is merely the discovery of an object that accords with our own [prior] conceptions."[76]

However, since he attests that all experiences of the world—even the most immediate empirical ones—are intrinsically shaped and transformed by the individual human intellect and its inherent constraints by human language, next Gendun Chopel must explain why these transformations of reality by the mind should not be understood as *correctly* perceiving and shaping reality, and consequently establishing valid knowledge. This leads Gendun Chopel to elaborate on his own theory of the soteriological goal of the Buddhist path, and its correlation with the two kinds of "obstructions" that limit and distort the human intellect and thus make valid knowledge impossible for common beings. The first set of obstructions is known as the "afflictive obstructions" (*kleśāvaraṇa, nyon mongs kyi sgrib pa*), which are directly associated with the traditional "three poisons" in Buddhism of desire, hatred, and ignorance. These afflictive obstructions then are the root cause of unwholesome mental states and actions, which subsequently are the source of all suffering in the world. Hence, this first class of obstructions is commonly thought of as that which trap individuals in the cycle of rebirth (*saṃsāra, 'khor ba*) and therefore must be destroyed in order for one to achieve liberation from that cycle.

Next, however, there are the cognitive obstructions, or "obstructions to omniscience," which in his commentary Lopez describes as "more subtle and insidious [than the afflictive obstructions], consisting of predispositions of ignorance that prevent the simultaneous understanding of all phenomena in the universe."[77] The expression for these obstructions literally means the

---

73. Ibid., 54, v. 26. Elsewhere (p. 165), Lopez further explains Gendun Chopel's position by highlighting his training in Geluk scholasticism, and particularly Prāsaṅgika Madhyamaka, which "upholds the existence of external objects, but asserts that each object is *a mere designation*."
74. Ibid., 54, v. 26; Cf. Lopez and chos phel, *Madman*, 135.
75. Chos phel, "Adornment," 63, v. 69. Emphasis added.
76. Ibid., 69–70, v. 93.
77. Lopez and chos phel, *Madman*, 166.

"obstructions to objects of knowledge" (*jñeyāvaraṇa, shes bya'i sgrib pa*), and these obstructions are considered "more subtle and insidious" than their "afflictive" counterparts because whereas the eradication of the afflictive obstructions leads to a purification of one's subjective consciousness, this subjective purification nonetheless has "no visible effect" on the objects of one's experience, and thus from an ontological perspective these objects continue to appear as if they were truly existent in themselves. And so, even after one's subjective consciousness is purified, an element of ignorance persists because one still empirically experiences items as "truly existent" in themselves and thus, in his own terms, the curtain covering over the proper objects of knowledge remains drawn.[78] Accordingly, for Gendun Chopel the ultimate goal of the Buddhist path is to eradicate these obstructions of omniscience, the "obstructions to objects of knowledge," for these prevent one from properly understanding the ontological status of those objects and subsequently keep one from actually ascertaining any "valid knowledge" or experience of reality.[79]

Similarly to this understanding of the nature and function of the two types of obstructions in the intellect of common beings, the final key foundation for Gendun Chopel's perspectivalism in his Madhyamaka epistemology is his rejection of the two commonly accepted forms of "valid knowledge" (*pramāṇa, tshad ma*) within Buddhist epistemology more generally for the minds of the unenlightened—direct perception (*pratyakṣa*) and inference (*anumāna*). Accordingly, valid knowledge through direct perception refers to the "immediate and accurate perception through the five sense organs," whereas valid knowledge through inference refers to knowledge derived from correct reasoning and logic.[80] Lopez explains that from within the Geluk tradition the aforementioned scholastic teacher Tsongkhapa is most famous and revered for his attempt to *harmonize* the concept of "valid knowledge" with Madhyamaka epistemology through constructing a philosophical system "that was simultaneously able to posit a basis of valid knowledge while upholding the doctrine of the emptiness of all phenomena." Tsongkhapa used the work of the Indian Madhyamaka commentator Dharmakīrti in order to conclude that these two forms of valid knowledge were exclusively the source of any reliable claims about the world. Gendun Chopel, Lopez attests, "will have known of this."[81] Gendun Chopel rejects the possibility of valid knowledge for the unenlightened through direct perception based on the fact that "when one analyzes in detail the final basis for any decision, apart from coming back to one's own mind, nothing else whatsoever is perceived."[82]

---

78. Ibid., 206–7. Here Lopez is giving commentary to Gendun Chopel in verse 213.
79. Ibid., 167. Lopez is commenting on verses 106 and 107.
80. Ibid., 128. Cf. Donald S. Lopez, *Buddhism & Science: A Guide for the Perplexed*, Buddhism and Modernity (Chicago: University of Chicago Press, 2008), 114.
81. Lopez and chos phel, *Madman*, 130.
82. Chos phel, "Adornment," 49–50, v. 9.

This basic belief that all knowledge is decisively formed within the intellect of each individual leads Gendun Chopel to conclude that any determination of valid knowledge based on direct perception is simply a *decision* of what should and should not count as correct perceptions based on a majority consensus.[83] In the case of the unenlightened minds of common beings, such a consensus cannot form any basis for valid knowledge whatsoever since it is a determination brought about by a collection of intellects that are fundamentally flawed by the two obstructions.[84] With regard to this problem, Gendun Chopel frequently references the popular analogy within Tibetan philosophical debate of the perception of the white conch shell in the land of the jaundice. According to this example, when encountering a white conch a community plagued with jaundice will perceive it to be yellow through their relevant senses and yet still be wrong from the ultimate standpoint of a clear-sighted person.[85] Moreover, even if that same community were miraculously healed of their afflictive condition of jaundice, their more subtle ignorance regarding the true ontological existence of the conch would still persist. "Therefore," Gendun Chopel later concludes, "it is impossible for there to be a commonly appearing property and subject for the two people with and without bile disease."[86] Thus, according to Lopez, Gendun Chopel insists that the fallibility of the intellect of the unenlightened is not merely a philosophical problem that can be overcome with correct reasoning by the unenlightened mind, rather it is "the defining characteristic of saṃsāra, the beginningless cycle of birth and death" in which all common beings exist, and by which their intellectual perceptions are essentially shaped.[87] "Therefore," Gendun Chopel finally is forced to concede, "as long as we remain in this land of saṃsāra, it is true that there is no other method than simply making decisions, having placed confidence in this mind in which one can have no confidence in any of the decisions that it makes."[88] And thus, "as long as one abides in this world, there is nothing [for the unenlightened mind] to do other than to remain believing in fictions, placing one's trust in fictions, making various presentations on the basis of fictions,"[89] for regarding the knowledge of all of us "common beings" "it comes down to the fact that there is nothing suitable other than a mere decision by this mind of ours, which is itself a source of fictions."[90]

So in summary, Schillebeeckx's epistemology sets forth a perspectivalism that maintains a universal applicability to all humans based on the nature and function of the intellect itself, and yet he attempts to balance this universal finitude with a critical realism that acknowledges the inherent incompleteness and fallibility of all

---

83. Ibid., 47, v. 4.
84. Ibid., 48, v. 5; 63, v. 69. Cf. Lopez and chos phel, *Madman*, 145.
85. Chos phel, "Adornment," 51, v. 13. Cf. Lopez and chos phel, *Madman*, 129.
86. Chos phel, "Adornment," 87, v. 146. Cf. Lopez and chos phel, *Madman*, 205–6.
87. Lopez and chos phel, *Madman*, 130, 163. Cf. Chos phel, "Adornment," 74, v. 107.
88. Chos phel, "Adornment," 51, v. 14.
89. Ibid., 52, v. 19. Cf. 110, v. 221.
90. Chos phel, "Adornment," 51, v. 15. Cf. Lopez and chos phel, *Madman*, 211.

human truth while nonetheless grounding all claims to knowledge in an intuitive apprehension of the "thing-as-such" within the phenomenological encounter. Gendun Chopel's epistemology, on the other hand, falls just short of upholding this universality of intellectual obstruction among humans (confining it instead simply to the large segment of "common beings"), but at the same time insists that for these "common beings" their knowledge is based on a subjectivism in which their intellectual abstractions and conceptions are completely detached from reality as it truly exists. In other words, Schillebeeckx invokes perspectivalism to temper a universal (yet always *critical*) realism, while Gendun Chopel utilizes elements of perspectivalism in order to disassociate the true knowledge of enlightened individuals while "abiding" in the inconceivable and inexpressible awareness of emptiness from the vast majority of subjectivist constructions made by and for unenlightened beings. Despite these differences in construction and function, however, it is nonetheless undeniable that a deep sense of perspectivalism—defined as asserting a constraint on the possibility of knowledge based on the function of the human intellect—is a foundational element in the philosophy of both thinkers on which their epistemologies are built.

III. Hermeneutics of Interpretation

A. Schillebeeckx's Hermeneutical Orientation: From "Revelation-in-Reality" to "Revelation-in-History"

Now moving from the perspectivalist basis of both thinkers' different conceptions of knowledge, Schillebeeckx's epistemology would take its first dramatic turn in the early to mid-1940s during his doctoral studies at *Le Saulchoir* in Étiolles, France (near Paris). Here he was introduced to modern theology particularly through the instruction of a number of the *Nouvelle-théologie* theologians such as Yves Congar, O.P., and *especially* Marie-Dominic Chenu, O.P. As Kennedy observes about Chenu's influence on Schillebeeckx's epistemology during this time, if from De Petter he learned, above all, that "every concept is in fact godless, that is, every concept falls short of adequately explaining who or what God is," then from Chenu he learned that *all* doctrines and dogmas are first and foremost "the fruits of *human* creativity and reflection."[91] Although upon first glance this idea might not seem to depart significantly from what was the eventual outcome of his previous understanding, nevertheless the starting point *would* undergo a radical reorientation in perspective and, by the end, lead to a substantial shift in his understanding of epistemological theory. Under Chenu's guidance in hermeneutical studies, particularly in the areas of semiotics, structuralist theory, and historical-critical studies, Schillebeeckx became increasingly uncomfortable with De Petter's "metaphysics of participation" and "phenomenological Thomist philosophy," which offered a worldview founded on a concept of "absolute Being."

---

91. Kennedy, "Continuity," 268–9.

In fact, he began to view this philosophy as an "ideological superstructure"[92] that is undesirable for a contemporary culture which demands that "the pluralism and historicity of events and ideas should be confirmed rather than transcendentally grounded."[93]

Further stoking this uneasiness, Chenu emphasized to Schillebeeckx that "there is no opposition between God and the world: the world is *meant* to be secular; the world is *meant* to enjoy its independence and freedom because the world is not God!" Hence, in his studies under Chenu, Schillebeeckx's starting place and orientation toward where to begin looking for truth radically shifted from trying to find the reality of God (or "ultimate truth") that is *behind* the historical experiences and encounters with divine revelation (revelation-in-reality) and toward instead viewing the world and human sociocultural history as the primary *locus* for understanding the ultimate truth. Or, as Hilkert more precisely puts it, he shifted his perception of the "fundamental mystery" of truth from being found as "revelation-in-reality" to "revelation-in-history"—or even more specifically "revelation-in-human-experience." Thus, where his earlier methodology "had been to probe the meaning of dogma in order to point towards the deeper mystery of the human encounter with God (revelation-in-reality), now the theological task was to probe concrete human experience in order to locate that same mystery there."[94] As such, the theological task became primarily one of historical hermeneutics in which it is not just sacred texts and dogmas that are interpreted and assessed as disclosing an element of ultimate truth, but rather where the *very reality of history itself* is investigated and interpreted as the source of all knowledge—as yielding its own "echo of the gospel."[95]

Hilkert contends that this newfound perspective toward a theological method led Schillebeeckx to place the revelation of God "not only in the history of the Christian tradition, but also in the 'foreign prophecy' coming from the experience of the contemporary world."[96] Or, as Schillebeeckx himself concisely elaborates, to place "'religious truth' within a horizon that is ever open to shifting and often new cultural environments and ways of thinking."[97] Hence, at this point Schillebeeckx replaced the "metaphysic of participation" found in De Petter's "implicit intuition" with a "metaphysic of *anticipation*" that recognizes that ultimate truth ("being") is constantly in a state of *becoming* in history.[98] Thus he would later argue that a discussion of human experience and knowledge as being entirely historically

---

92. Ibid., 271. Cf. Edward Schillebeeckx, *The Understanding of Faith: Interpretation and Criticism*, trans. N. D. Smith (New York: Seabury Press, 1974), 102–55.

93. Van Erp, 220. Cf. Edward Schillebeeckx, *Jesus: An Experiment in Christology*, trans. Hubert Hopkins (New York: Crossroad, 1995), 618–19.

94. Hilkert, "Hermeneutics," 108. Emphasis added.

95. Ibid., 107–8. Cf. Schillebeeckx, *Jesus*, 619.

96. Hilkert, "Hermeneutics," 107.

97. Thompson, xiii.

98. Van Erp, 218; Schillebeeckx, *Jesus*, 618–19.

situated is fundamental for establishing any adequate context for even beginning to plausibly discuss the nature and reality of "Christian revelation."[99]

Although, as previously discussed, this process of reorientation and training under Chenu occurred in the early to mid-1940s, Schillebeeckx's most explicit discourses regarding the particular influences of hermeneutical theory and historical-critical studies on his theological methodology and epistemological theory emerge much later in his two-volume series on Christology (namely, *Jesus* and *Christ*) as well as the *Interim Report* which followed them and engaged their critics. By the time he had written these three works, however, Schillebeeckx had already critically reassessed this epistemological approach and adapted it into a third "new wave" of his theological method, which we will discuss later. However, as we will see particularly in the hermeneutical case study of Chapter 4, because of the very nature of Christological studies and their inherent correlation with the authority of the earliest canonical texts that include the proclaimed teachings and "history" of Jesus, these three Christological texts will be paramount in understanding Schillebeeckx's most foundational notions of hermeneutics, interpretation, experience, and even history itself.[100]

Accordingly, within this second epistemological "circle" of hermeneutics Schillebeeckx became keenly aware of how all humans come to understand and form their knowledge of the world through *interpretative experience*. Or, as Schillebeeckx himself frankly avers, "we [only] see interpretively."[101] By this statement Schillebeeckx is simply asserting his persevering argument that no one experiences the world, and therefore formulates knowledge, within a "raw" state from which they then make an assessment and interpretation. "Rather, in an irreducible fashion, human experience is co-constituted by interpretation; *interpretation makes real experience both possible and expressible*."[102] Furthermore, Thompson elaborates, "This interpretative act always exists in a dynamic, historical, and hermeneutical circle of pre-understanding or horizon, new experience, and reshaped horizon."[103] In other words, Schillebeeckx began to consider how all knowledge is intrinsically shaped by an individual's prior and present, conscious and subconscious, experiences of the world that always occur within the possibilities and constraints of a specific historical and cultural

---

99. Thompson, 8; Cf. Edward Schillebeeckx, *Interim Report on the Books Jesus & Christ*, trans. John Bowden (New York: Crossroad, 1982), 3–4. Here Schillebeeckx directly discusses the difficulty of "God-talk" in light of contemporary historical-consciousness.

100. Schillebeeckx, *Jesus*, 583. Schillebeeckx himself establishes one of the major themes of his three Christology books when he cites in his volume, *Jesus*, the famous axiom by Gotthold Ephraim Lessing, "Accidental, historical truths can never become evidence for necessary truths of reason."

101. Edward Schillebeeckx, *Christ: The Experience of Jesus as Lord*, trans. John Bowden (New York: Crossroad, 1993), 53.

102. Thompson, 25. Emphasis added.

103. Ibid., 24.

context. Hence, difficulties naturally arise when one tries to determine any form of "valid knowledge" or "meaning" based on texts or past events that arose in a different historical or cultural context than their own.[104] So at this point, Kennedy elucidates that Schillebeeckx felt he had to abandon what had previously been a largely *a*historical theological and epistemological perspective in exchange for a deeply *historical* reading of theology and knowledge.[105]

However in order to understand how during this period Schillebeeckx actually viewed the nature and influence of history on interpretation and the subsequent formation of knowledge, one must first grasp how he understood the concept of *historicity* itself. In his book entitled *Jesus*, Schillebeeckx explicitly summarizes his own definition of historicity using the thought of the famous French historian (and leader within the "*Annales* School" of historiography) Fernand Braudel.[106] According to Braudel, history can be read on three distinguishable yet interconnected planes of cultural change and development.[107] These are the Ephemeral, the Conjunctural, and the Structural planes of history.[108] Accordingly, Ephemeral History, or "fact-constituted history," is generally the most apparent and almost superficial perspective of history that focuses on the rapid and fleeting events of everyday life. Conjunctural History, on the other hand, takes a significantly broader view of history (which Schillebeeckx found most particularly significant) that has a "more profound reach, and is more comprehensive" than the Ephemeral plane, but moves and develops at "a much slower tempo or rate of change" and as such requires observation over a much larger scope of time. Finally, at the level of Structural History the scholar's historical lens must be widened so much that it stretches over centuries and moves so slowly that it can become difficult to distinguish "what moves and does not."[109]

Even at this "Structural" level, however, both Braudel and Schillebeeckx are clear to point out that culture and knowledge are still entirely grounded within history and are still evolving—no matter how slowly. In fact, Schillebeeckx reiterates this point with an illustration of a spinning top. As the top spins on the surface of a table, it appears to be moving rapidly on its own surface while appearing to be stationary on the table. Yet when observed over a longer period of time, the top will be seen as moving, ever so gradually, around the table as well.[110] For Schillebeeckx this is a vital point. Not even "Structural History" can ever transcend the bounds of history itself in order to reach some completely static or timeless "essence" behind reality. Instead, all experience—no matter the perspective from

---

104. Hilkert, "Hermeneutics," 109.
105. Kennedy, "Continuity," 274.
106. Schillebeeckx, *Jesus*, 576–9.
107. Ibid., 578.
108. See Fernand Braudel, *On History*, trans. Sarah Matthews (Chicago: University of Chicago Press, 1982).
109. Schillebeeckx, *Jesus*, 577.
110. Ibid.

which one observes it—takes place in a dynamic and dialectical manner between direct experience and the historical elements shaping one's interpretation of that experience.[111] Hence there are only "more stable" notions of truth and historical interpretation, but no *transhistorical* encounter with reality that can ground and fully adjudicate the validity of our interpretations and knowledge.[112]

As far as his own particular project and intentions, as alluded to above, Schillebeeckx focuses mainly on the Conjunctural level of history, which he agrees is the source of the "epochal horizon of the intellect" as well as the primary basis for the "interpretative models" of experience. This is because, according to Schillebeeckx's channeling of Braudel, Conjunctural History serves as the "intellective horizon" and "spirit of the age" that gives rise to the fleeting thoughts and experiences of the "day-to-day."[113] In light of this "Conjunctural" vision of history, Hilkert contends, Schillebeeckx reshapes his understanding of how truth is engaged within texts. They no longer can be viewed as disclosing truth in their primary, or "literal," discourse but rather in the "historical experience to which the text points."[114] And even more, this principle applies just as much to the "revealed" truth of scripture as it does to Josephus's *The Antiquities of the Jews*. "In other words, our experience always occurs within an already established interpretive framework, which in the last analysis is nothing more than the cumulative-personal and collective experience, a *tradition of experience*."[115] Hence, God must be seen as completely active in and through human history itself and, as such, encountered only as the mystery of the "revelation-in-*history*" at which the classic texts and dogmas of the tradition seek to point.[116]

Later, equipped with the influential writings of Hans-Georg Gadamer and Paul Ricoeur,[117] Schillebeeckx then wrestled heavily with the common "hermeneutical problem of distance," and specifically how one might be able to traverse the unavoidable chasm of time and interpretation that separates the reader from the

---

111. Thompson, 34.

112. Hilkert, "Hermeneutics," 114. It must be noted that here Hilkert gives an excellent discussion of how faith functions as an "almost" transhistorical element in the human consciousness by which one can begin to transcend human historicity by eliciting the realization of the eschaton through the "surrendering" act of faith praxis. Cf. Edward Schillebeeckx, "Towards a Catholic Use of Hermeneutics," in *God the Future of Man*, trans. N. D. Smith (New York: Sheed and Ward, 1968), 42.

113. Schillebeeckx, *Jesus*, 577–8.

114. Hilkert, "Hermeneutics," 113.

115. Thompson, 24. Cf. Schillebeeckx, *Christ*, 30–40 and 50–55; Schillebeeckx, *God the Future*, 20–35; Schillebeeckx, *Interim Report*, 13–19; Schillebeeckx, "Linguistic Criteria," *Understanding of Faith*, 20–44; Edward Schillebeeckx, *Church: The Human Story of God*, trans. John Bowden (New York: Crossroad, 1994), 15–20.

116. Hilkert, "Hermeneutics," 113.

117. For a helpful list and timeline of eighteen intellectual sources for Schillebeeckx's theology, see Philip Kennedy, *Schillebeeckx* (Collegeville, MN: Liturgical Press, 1993), 36–7.

meaning and intention of the author. One way in which he tries to engage this issue is by distinguishing foundational and direct interpretive elements, which instinctively manifest themselves in what appears to be a more "transparent experience," from the more "foreign" second-order interpretative elements that come "from outside [the] experience" but nonetheless play an integral role in the interpretation of it. Still Schillebeeckx concludes that it is ultimately "never possible to draw a clear distinction" between the internal-fundamental and the "foreign" elements of interpretation.[118]

This dilemma of differentiating first- and second-order interpretations eventually leads him to determine that truth, or historically objective knowledge, cannot be retrieved simply by the replication of the contextual past in which the text was composed; rather it could only be deciphered through the process of searching for the truths of the past *in light of* the present context. The key notion on which this appraisal of reality hinged was the concept of "effective history."[119] "Effective history" implies that meaning and truth, "revelation," can only be passed on through the finite cultural expressions of history, and so the truth of sacred texts and dogmas is solely preserved as the process of a "living tradition." The experiential knowledge of the past can only be passed along via renewed experiences in the present, and consequently all expressions being passed from one cultural context to another require *re*interpretation in order to convey the same truth in its new context. Therefore, the "Truth" of Christianity then is not an expression but an *experience* that takes the form of a message in order to cultivate new experiences in the lives of believers today.[120] In other words, as he would discuss in a much later interview, for Schillebeeckx the Christian scriptures too are inherently contextually limited and conditioned, and yet they still serve as the first "local theologies" of the tradition that have shaped the interpretative horizons and faith experiences of believers ever since.[121]

The continuities and contrasts of Schillebeeckx's perspectivalism and his hermeneutical historicism seem to become much more apparent at this juncture. In his early perspectival epistemology of phenomenological Thomism, Schillebeeckx was willing to claim a direct encounter with the "really real" (the "concrete-existential"), even of God, behind the experiences of history. Thus, the breakdown in the correspondence of knowledge rested in the individual's own intellectual deficiencies as a human. Now at this hermeneutical phase of his epistemological development, it appears he no longer believes the human subject can reach behind or beyond the contextual layering of history, but instead he maintains that "truth" can still be engaged within the renewed experiences of "effective history." Hence, the individual's inability to really "know the truth" is perpetuated by the

---

118. Schillebeeckx, *Interim Report*, 13.
119. Schillebeeckx, "Toward a Catholic Use of Hermeneutics," 1–49.
120. Schillebeeckx, *Interim Report*, 50.
121. Edward Schillebeeckx, Huub Oosterhuis, and Piet Hoogeveen, *God Is New Each Moment* (New York: Continuum, 2004), 62–3.

infinite influences of "interpretative elements" that unavoidably craft all of one's perceptions of one's own life experiences and knowledge. Where the problem of discerning valid knowledge once lay in the process of individual intellect, it now rests primarily (though not exclusively) in the external pressures of history that shape all interpretations of experience. But yet some questions still linger. What if in the end the problem did not fall solely on the shoulders of either (or both) of these elements in themselves? What if the problem of valid knowledge—of deciphering "Truth"—was caused by the very nature of ultimate reality or truth in itself? This is the question Schillebeeckx's next epistemological circle sought to ask and to which we will turn in the next section.

B. Chopel's Hermeneutical Orientation: Historical Manifestation as the Source and Limit of the Unenlightened Mind

In one of the few and oft-referenced translated biographies written of Gendun Chopel, Irmgard Mengele opens the introduction to the work by declaring, "Although Tibet even in the 20th century has abounded in brilliant scholars, the savant dGe-'dun-chos-'phel (1903–1951) was the first 'modern' scholar of Tibet."[122] In his own assessment of Gendun Chopel, Lopez understands why this perception has taken shape: "He was an avant-garde intellectual who explored new forms in his prose, in his poetry, in his painting … and he constantly called upon Tibetans to break with the past." However, Lopez continues, if he is to be labeled "the first Tibetan to be counted as a Buddhist modernist," the concept of "Buddhist modernism" as it might pertain to Gendun Chopel first requires quite a bit of exegesis.[123] Most frequently cited as one of the justifications of labeling Gendun Chopel as a Buddhist modernist was his willingness to break with seemingly traditional interpretations of the teachings of the Buddha, particularly with regard to cosmology, in favor of the discoveries of modern science.

Probably the most famous example of this is found in the newspaper article Gendun Chopel wrote in 1938 for the *Tibet Mirror* under the byline of "Honest Dharma" entitled "The World Is Round or Spherical" (*"'Jigs rten ril mo 'am zlum po"*).[124] In this defense of modern truth against traditional Tibetan beliefs

---

122. Irmgard Mengele, *dGe-'dun-chos-'phel: A Biography of the 20th-Century Tibetan Scholar* (Dharamsala, HP: Library of Tibetan Works and Archives, 1999), 1. Cf. Heather Stoddard, *Le mendiant de l' Amdo*, Recherches Sur La Haute Asie 9 (Paris: Société D'Ethnographie, 1985): It should be noted that Stoddard's work, which Lopez describes as "the most complete biography" of Gendun Chopel, displays a slight controversy in the actual date of Gendun Chopel's birth, ranging anywhere between 1895 and 1905. For the purposes of this project, however, we will follow Lopez (and Mengele) who explains that a "recent consensus has placed his birth on August 14, 1903" (Lopez and chos phel, *Madman*, 5).

123. Lopez and chos phel, *Madman*, 248–9.

124. Lopez, *Science*, 58 and 107. Translating Dge dun chos phel, Drang po "'Jigs rten ril mo 'am zlum po," in *Yul phyogs so so'I gsar 'gyur me long*, June 28, 1938, p. II.

of the world being flat, Gendun Chopel calls for the Tibetan community to stop "stubbornly holding on" to the idea of a flat earth by contending that all ancient religions originally believed the earth to be flat until eventually they were "unable to withstand the light of true knowledge" and adapted their traditions accordingly.[125] Similarly, citing Tibetans' own scholastic traditions that questioned the literal interpretation of the Buddha's teachings, Gendun Chopel argues that the Buddha's descriptions of the cosmos were clearly among "the majority of the sūtras" whose teachings were "set forth by the Buddha in accordance with the thoughts of sentient beings" of the time so that contemporary Buddhists can never completely discern "what is provisional and what is definitive" truth within those teachings.[126] Hence, as Jeffery Hopkins points out, since Buddhists already accept the fact that the "Buddha spoke in accordance with what would be comprehensible to his audience,"[127] and moreover since at that time "the words '[the world] is flat' were as famous as the wind,"[128] then Gendun Chopel insists one should be able to conclude that the Buddha knew that the world was round and only taught ideas contrary to that in order for his followers to understand and believe him at the time.[129]

Yet, as Lopez asserts, it is also noteworthy that in his major philosophical treatise of the *Adornment*, Gendun Chopel makes no references and supplies no evidence for his arguments based on his "remarkable encounter with the modern world during his twelve years outside Tibet." And furthermore, Lopez piles on, it is "striking" that for being known as a scholar who had "such a strong interest in history and historical research," in the *Adornment* Gendun Chopel presents an understanding of ultimate truth and enlightenment (the vision and knowledge of that truth) that is radically *trans*historical and *trans*rational "even in Buddhist terms."[130] We will continue to discuss the relevance and relation that a modern understanding has with Chopel's Madhyamaka epistemology more in-depth in Chapter 4's case study regarding the authority of the teachings of the Historical Founders of each thinker's tradition; however, for the purposes of this section let us simply attempt to examine briefly in broad strokes the roles that historicity and hermeneutics play in Gendun Chopel's theories of the interpretative nature of knowledge and the assessment of "true meaning" within the teachings of the Buddha as well as other major authorities within the later tradition.

Part of the reason that Gendun Chopel's transhistorical and transrational understanding of the Ultimate, and one's knowledge of it, is so jarring and problematic for the common reader in labeling Gendun Chopel a "modernist"

---

125. Lopez, *Science*, 58.
126. Ibid., 58–9.
127. Jeffrey Hopkins and Gendün Chöpel, *Tibetan Arts of Love: Sex, Orgasm & Spiritual Healing*, trans. Jeffrey Hopkins and Dorje Yudon Yuthok (Ithaca, NY: Snow Lion, 1992), 24.
128. Lopez, *Science*, 59.
129. Lopez and chos phel, *Madman*, 250.
130. Ibid., 251.

is because, as Lopez clarifies, Gendun Chopel "is not a modernist who exalts the mundane over the transcendent."[131] Rather he appears more in step with modern thinking in the way he seeks to distinguish and disassociate "in the starkest terms" the experiences and claims to truth from within history (in Western philosophical terms the phenomenal realm) from the reality and knowledge of ultimate truth as such (the noumenal realm).[132] Hence, Gendun Chopel is *not* "historically-conscious" in the sense of questioning whether the Mahāyāna sūtras and the tantras should be understood as the actual word of the Buddha (he appears to still accept this wholeheartedly), but rather in the sense that the world as experienced and known by the Buddha is "literally inconceivable" by the historically or "conventionally-shaped" minds of the unenlightened, and as such the teachings of the Buddha in the sūtras must be seen as "actually culture-bound depictions"[133] that "are merely reflections of local human tastes."[134] Thus, Lopez maintains that while the *Adornment* might be judged as a "modernist work" in the style of its construction and its assertion of the "apparently unbridgeable chasm between the conventional and the ultimate," its *content* nonetheless can still be viewed as rather *traditional* from a Buddhist point of view.[135] This is because Gendun Chopel still understands the teachings of the Buddha to be the skillful use of the contextually limited language of the world as a bridge that can compassionately span that apparent chasm of knowledge and somehow lead sentient beings *beyond* the limits of the historical world to an experience and knowledge of the Ultimate.[136] Hence, as Hopkins further elucidates, Gendun Chopel's position is not a manifestation of an absolute "nihilistic relativism" in which there is no truth to be found outside the historically mundane. Instead, it is one that views the Buddha as possessing a comprehension of ultimate truth that exceeds phenomenological perception, and yet also as still skillfully employing that truth with shades of a "cultural

---

131. Ibid., 252. The categorization of "modern" thought is a difficult and complex label in Tibetan philosophy, which had employed arguably similar philosophical assumptions, questions, critiques, and techniques as the "modern philosophy" of the West as early as the twelfth and thirteenth centuries of the Common Era. For an excellent discussion of this complexity and difficulty of categorizing contemporary Tibetan philosophy as "modern," see Janet Gyatso, "Moments of Tibetan Modernity: Methods and Assumptions," in *Mapping the Modern Tibet: Proceedings of the Eleventh Seminar of the International Association for Tibetan Studies*, ed. Gary Tuttle (Andiast, Switzerland: International Institute for Tibetan and Buddhist Studies, 2011), 1–44.

132. Lopez and chos phel, *Madman*, 246.

133. Hopkins and Chöpel, 24.

134. Lopez and chos phel, *Madman*, 252; Chos phel, "Adornment," 52-3, v. 22.

135. Lopez and chos phel, *Madman*, 252.

136. Ibid., 247. For a great explication of the use of *upāya* in the categorization of "definitive" and "provisional" meaning within the hermeneutics of Tibetan philosophy, see Donald Lopez, "On the Interpretation of the Mahāyāna Sūtras," in *Buddhist Hermeneutics*, ed. Donald Lopez, Jr. (Honolulu: Kuroda Institute, 1988) 47-70.

relativism"[137] in order to lead more followers beyond the limits of the conventional to an encounter of the Ultimate, or from the limited delusions of suffering to the tranquil experience of salvation.

One of the most frequently cited examples of Gendun Chopel's contextual understanding of the teachings of the Buddha is verse 23 of the *Adornment*, where even Lopez confesses Gendun Chopel "sounds unmistakably modern" when he proclaims,

> It is known through detailed analysis that the attire of the *saṃbhogakāya* and of the gods is the attire of ancient Indian kings. (283) These are not merely our concoction but are stated in the sūtras. Indeed, they are merely set forth with skillful methods so that the qualities of the buddha level, which in reality cannot appear to our mind, can appear to our mind in order to create admiration and delight within us. For example, if the Buddha had been born in China, it would certainly be the case that the *saṃbhogakāya* of Akaniṣṭha would have a long shiny beard and would wear a golden dragon robe. Similarly, if he had been born in Tibet, there is no doubt that in Akaniṣṭha there would be fresh butter from wish-granting cows in a golden tea churn five hundred yojanas high, and there would be tea made from the leaves of the wish-granting tree. Therefore, all of this is merely the way that we common beings think. Regarding the actual domains of the Buddha himself, the master Candrakīrti said [at *Madhyamakāvatāra* XII.39d], "However, this secret of yours cannot be told." It is certain that it is not suitable to be spoken in our presence, or that even though it were spoken, it is something that we could not understand. If one has just a little faith toward the inconceivable secret of the Buddha, then one should have some slight belief in all these deeds by the Buddha of making an aeon equal to an instant and an atom equal to a world.[138]

The popularity of citing this passage as an example of Gendun Chopel's awareness of the historical and contextual limitations on the teachings of the Buddha should be self-evident. Here, as Hopkins illustrates, he clearly asserts that the various qualities of the Pure Lands described in the Buddhist sūtras are merely "culture-bound depictions" that are used to match the "local human tastes" of the audience originally engaged. Hence Gendun Chopel proclaims that if the Buddha had taught in ancient China, the celestial buddhas and bodhisattvas would look like members of the Imperial Court; if he had taught in Tibet, the "Pure Lands would have wish-granting trees with leaves adorned with cups of buttered tea!"[139] Thus, Lopez further adds, even though Gendun Chopel "never questions for a moment that the Buddha spoke the sūtras, and tantras," nonetheless he also acknowledges that there are many statements in them that refer to realities and ideas that "[common

---

137. Hopkins and Chöpel, 24; Lopez and chos phel, *Madman*, 134.
138. Lopez, *Science*, 53.
139. Hopkins and Chöpel, 24.

beings] cannot conceptually understand." Moreover, Gendun Chopel contends that these "inconceivable secrets" cannot be unearthed through deeper exegesis or even philosophical excavation, but rather stand as continual reminders of the historical and cultural limits of human thought and language and consequently that the truth of enlightenment toward which the Buddha's teachings generally allude "completely contravenes the world."[140]

One of the reasons for the necessity of the contextual limitations of the teachings of the Buddha within his thought is the Madhyamaka philosophical principle of making *assertions for others*. According to the Prāsaṅgika tradition of Madhyamaka, and following the famous statement of Nāgārjuna that the Mādhyamika can have no thesis,[141] one who has experienced the true reality of the emptiness of existence can never actually express the nature of that reality to those who have not directly perceived it (unenlightened common beings) through the assertion of a positive (*cataphatic*) claim (or "thesis") about the world.[142] This is because, as Lopez clarifies, "the person who has perceived emptiness directly perceived only an absence; emptiness is a nonaffirming negative that implies nothing."[143] Gendun Chopel further explains this difficultly in describing emptiness in verse 201 by quoting a commentary (of Padmapāṇi Dge 'dun rgya mtsho) on Tsongkhapa's classic treatise *The Essence of Eloquence That Distinguishes between the Provisional and Definitive Meanings of the Scriptures* (*Drang nges legs bshad snying po*), "A 'nonaffirming negative' is not the non-existence of something protruding; it is that very freedom from the elaborations that you assert."[144] In other words, since all reality is in essence a nondualistic "absence" of any independently existing things, any attempt to describe reality through the forms of distinction that are inherent in language inevitably becomes an "assertion for others" because it immediately places ultimate reality ("emptiness") into a foreign category to which it does not belong—one of dualistic distinctions.[145] Hence, Gendun Chopel affirms that *all* teachings of the Buddha contain two elements of meaning or knowledge within

---

140. Lopez and chos phel, *Madman*, 252 and 246.

141. Lopez and chos phel, *Madman*, 151. For a further discussion of Gendun Chopel's interpretation of Nāgārjuna's Vigrahavyāvartanī, see Donald S. Lopez Jr, "Dge 'Dun Chos 'Phel's Position on Vigrahavyāvartanī 29," in *Buddhist Forum*, ed. Tadeusz Skorupski and Ulrich Pagel (London: School of Oriental and African Studies, 1994), 161–85. Cf. Jan Westerhoff, *The Dispeller of Disputes: Nāgārjuna's Vigrahavyāvartanī* (New York: Oxford University Press, 2010), 61–4.

142. Chos phel, "Adornment," 80, v. 121.

143. Lopez and chos phel, *Madman*, 192. Cf. Chos phel, "Adornment," 94, v. 169. Emphasis added.

144. Chos phel, "Adornement," 104, v. 201.

145. Hopkins and Chöpel, 23–4. Here Hopkins maintains that Gendun Chopel intentionally denies "the law of the excluded middle and holds that reality is indeed beyond all dualistic propositions."

them: "an assertion that must be congruent with the world" (provisional) and what is known in the Buddha's "own mind" (definitive).[146]

Nonetheless, how Gendun Chopel portrays the function and roles of "provisional" and "definitive" meanings within the teachings of the Buddha here too differs from many of his philosophical predecessors. Instead of differentiating between *which* teachings of the Buddha are "definitive" and which are "provisional," Gendun Chopel concludes that *every* teaching of the Buddha "from the minute precepts of the vinaya to final nature of phenomena" contains both the elements of definitive and provisional truth.[147] This is because, as Gendun Chopel insists in verse 186 while quoting Āryadeva,

> "Just as a barbarian cannot be made to understand with another language, so worldlings cannot understand except with worldly [language]." Thus, just as there is no other method to communicate with barbarians than barbarian language, when the Bhagavan discusses the excellent dharma with worldlings— even concerning how to pass beyond the world—there is no other method than for him to speak, leaving that very presentation of worldlings as it is.[148]

Hence, elsewhere he maintains that inherently all linguistic depictions of the ultimate truth of emptiness, even those of the Buddha himself, are in the end "merely fabrications from examples taken from the world and, within that, from the human realm alone."[149] As a consequence of this limitation of language and historical context, all of the teachings of the Buddha contain meanings that are blatantly apparent to the individual, meanings that can be comprehended through inference and deeper reasoning, as well as truths that are "very hidden"—which exceed the bounds of language and context—and can only be grasped by one who has directly perceived the reality of emptiness, a Buddha.[150] Thus, here Gendun Chopel takes a much more pragmatic approach to determining the truth or meaning of a passage in which the "truth" of the Buddha's teachings is decided solely by the outcome it achieves. In other words, the Buddha's teachings all contain limited, "fallible" historical elements to them, yet his teachings can still be understood as "infallible" based on their efficaciousness in producing particular desired results. In this way, he concludes, "It is not necessary to analyze what is provisional and definitive in such [teachings]" because the meaning lies not in their descriptive or logical accuracy but in their ability to produce the most appropriate experience

---

146. Chos phel, "Adornment," 79, v. 120.
147. Ibid.
148. Ibid., 100, v. 186. It should be noted how Lopez points out that here Gendun Chopel cites Chandrakirti as the source for this quote, but in actuality he quotes Āryadeva.
149. Ibid., 52–3, v. 22.
150. Ibid., 79, v. 119. Cf. Lopez and chos phel, *Madman*, 172.

and reaction within the individual.[151] Thus to assess whether a teaching of the Buddha is "provisional" (fallible) or "definitive" (infallible) by logical reasoning or traditional teaching is utterly misguided, because the meaning or "truth" of a passage is ultimately decided "by [one's] own mind" based on the perception of reality it produces within the individual along with one's eventual assessment of that outcome as either beneficial or harmful in achieving one's desired end.[152]

Therefore, in the end, although they arrive at their conclusions through very different means, regarding the role that history, culture, and language essentially play in knowledge formation, there are still many comparable similarities between Schillebeeckx's and Gendun Chopel's epistemologies. Both thinkers view all writings and language as fundamentally saturated with human creativity and the historical layering of interpretation in a way in which this basic historicity at the same time gives rise to and also confines one's ability to ever convey or decipher meaning. Accordingly, both Schillebeeckx and Gendun Chopel insist that to speak within the world is to speak *about* the world so that no expression of meaning, no articulation of truth, can transcend the original context of the speaker or present situation of the reader. Hence, finally, both thinkers eventually attempt to locate the "true meaning" of a text not in any conveyable linguistic assertion in itself but rather in the efficaciousness of an expression (particularly in a text) to generate a new perception within the individual that can help one understand and navigate one's present experience of reality in new and beneficial ways. Moreover, as we will examine in the next section, this non-linguistic, non-conceptual and fundamentally experiential notion of truth subsequently leads both thinkers to approach the issues of truth and valid knowledge through their own methods of negative dialectics.

IV. Apophaticism

A. Schillebeeckx's Apophaticism: Epistemology after the "Death of God"

The final and most generally observed shift in Schillebeeckx's epistemology began to manifest itself in 1967 with the publication of a series of articles in the now oft-referenced book *God the Future of Man*. In this work, especially in the article/chapter "The New Image of God, Secularization and Man's Future on Earth," Schillebeeckx signals a crucial shift emerging from within his epistemological perspective toward theology—namely, what Hilkert describes as "a *fundamental skepticism* with regard to the very possibility of revelation."[153] Schillebeeckx would later attribute this newfound skepticism to at least two very significant intellectual

---

151. Chos phel, "Adornment," 79, v. 119: "If [a person] is to be followed on that, he is said to be infallible. *In general, fallible and infallible simply mean that when you follow [someone], it leads to either benefit or harm.*" Emphasis added.
152. Ibid., 49–50, v. 9; Cf. p. 63, v. 64–5.
153. Hilkert, "Hermeneutics," 107.

and spiritual experiences he had during the mid-1960s. First was a lecturing circuit in North America and Western Europe that brought him face to face with the questions and scrutiny of the American "Death of God" theologians in the United States as well as a number of university chaplains in France who both were being overwhelmingly confronted by the increasing pressures of a perceived radical "secularization" of culture and an antagonistic skepticism toward all metaphysics.[154] Also Schillebeeckx's involvement in the church's Second Vatican Council[155] moreover exposed him to a very new understanding of the nature and transformation of truth and knowledge within a tradition.

Observing the turmoil and even radical change surrounding Vatican II, Schillebeeckx concluded that what he perceived as the living tradition of the church's "effective history" could nevertheless still not function as any guarantor of any truth or knowledge of faith even despite it remaining the vital source of interpretations that could help shape the understanding of present believers' experience of the faith. Instead, Vatican II displayed to Schillebeeckx that any "continuity is therefore only apparent continuity. A certain *break* [with the continuity of the tradition], such as those of Vatican II, is indeed a rediscovery of the deepest tendencies of the meaning of the Gospel."[156] And hence for Schillebeeckx, as Hilkert explains, any claim to truth that still remained confessional, even if grounded in a thoroughly historical hermeneutic, was ultimately insufficient in itself as a form of valid knowledge.[157] This evaluation of the council's significance, Thompson maintains, bestowed on Schillebeeckx "the mandate, impetus, and intellectual freedom to investigate more broadly the problem of the 'understanding of faith'" within the context of an increasingly secularized modernity.[158]

As a result of this new direction of inquiry, Schillebeeckx began to engage deeply with contemporary critical theorists, especially Jürgen Habermas and Gadamer,[159] in the hope of developing a new hermeneutical theory of truth that could still creatively utilize tradition as a source and perpetuation of knowledge while also allowing one the room to critically *break with tradition* when necessary through the use of ideological critique.[160] Hilkert masterfully summarizes the significance of this new dialogue in terms more relevant to our epistemological discussion,

154. Ibid., 107–9.

155. For a more in-depth discussion on Schillebeeckx's role both leading up to and during the council, see Erik Borgman, *Edward Schillebeeckx: A Theologian in His History*, trans. John Bowden, vol. I: *A Catholic Theology of Culture* (1914–65) (New York: Continuum, 2003), 283–365; John Stephen Bowden, *Edward Schillebeeckx: Portrait of a Theologian* (London: SCM Press, 1983), 32–4.

156. Edward Schillebeeckx, "*Theologisch Geloofsverstaan Anno 1983*" (1983): 20. Again, any direct quote of this text is from my own unpublished translation of the original Dutch.

157. Hilkert, "Hermeneutics," 109.

158. Thompson, 23.

159. See note 115.

160. See Schillebeeckx, *Understanding of Faith*, 102–55. Cf. William L. Portier, "Schillebeeckx's Dialogue with Critical Theory," *The Ecumenist* 21 (1983): 20–7.

From his earliest writings he had maintained that no concept can fully describe the reality it intends. In his shift to history and hermeneutics, he emphasized that no historical or cultural actualization of faith can fully realize the eschatological promise of the God of the Future. The insights of critical theorists were to take him further: language and structures of the living tradition are not only inadequate; they may also be repressive distortions of the true mystery.[161]

Furthering Hilkert's point, in the first chapter of his later book entitled *Church*, Schillebeeckx contends that the very term and idea of "God" is so hopelessly laden with ideological distortions that are perpetuated by the religions that use it that it can typically function as the greatest stumbling block to discovering the nature of ultimate reality—especially if one is attempting to do it in dialogue with the pluralism of the contemporary world.[162] And for this reason, during this later period of his third epistemological circle, Schillebeeckx's *theology* becomes much less formal and systematic and, consequently, his new epistemological orientation much more hidden and implicit within his various discussions on a wide range of indirectly related topics.

Part of the cause for those new *in*direct and implicit insinuations of epistemology is that Schillebeeckx's engagement with Critical Theory pushed him more and more in the direction of viewing knowledge, especially of God, through the lens of a negative (or apophatic) approach for engaging and formulating the reality of truth. This new negative outlook toward the truth of reality resulted in a more dialectical understanding of ultimate reality in which the "revelation" or object of truth cannot be manifested directly through one single text, interpretative framework, or concept, but is only alluded to indirectly through the dialogical interaction of many different and even *competing* discourses, theories, and beliefs. Hence where Schillebeeckx had started this journey of searching for knowledge with discovering the "really real" *behind* experience and then later *within* the interpretation of experience, Schillebeeckx now understood the realm of historical experience (of "human freedom") and the realm of ultimate reality (of "divine grace") as running parallel and thus never directly intersecting with each other.[163] And so, inspired by Gadamer's "hermeneutics of good will" and thoroughly challenged by Habermas's "hermeneutic of suspicion," Schillebeeckx sought to form his own dialectic of negative contrasts that could utilize the more blatant untruths, repressive concepts, and false interpretative social structures of human historical existence in order to indirectly form allusions to the truth of an ultimate "Good" driving human existence.[164]

---

161. Hilkert, "Hermeneutics," 118.

162. See Edward Schillebeeckx, *Church: The Human Story of God* (New York: Crossroad, 1990), 1–45.

163. Schillebeeckx, *Jesus*, 633–5. Cf. Kennedy, "Continuity," 276.

164. Schillebeeckx, *Jesus*, 634. For another great in-depth discussion regarding this method of negative dialectics for knowledge of "Truth," see Aloysius Rego, *Suffering and*

This negative dialectic[165] of finding truth in contrast to the apparent *un*truths of history caused Schillebeeckx to challenge his fellow theologians, and all Christian believers for that matter, to look for the ultimate basis of knowledge in the plight of those who suffer.[166] Accordingly, the argument goes that by standing in solidarity with those persons who are most intensely confronted and afflicted by the very things threatening to destroy humanity, people can become indirectly aware of the "truth" of the human existence that they are attempting to preserve. Schillebeeckx labels these dialectically revealing moments of solidarity with the suffering "negative experiences of contrast" and insists that they alone can be the source from which all valid propositional truth might bubble up from beneath the surface of history.[167] Or as Schillebeeckx himself profoundly articulated regarding this negative process of discovering truth in the arbitrary,

> Human beings live on assumptions and hypotheses, on projects and constructs, and therefore from "trial and error". Their plans can always be destroyed by the resistance or intractability of reality that does not always lend itself to rational human anticipations. In the place where reality provides resistance to human designs and thus implicitly neutralizes them, we are in living contact with a reality *independent* of us, one not conceived or created by humans. So one can say that it comes close to us through the alienation and disintegration of what we already achieved and our future plans. It is not the self-evident, but the scandal of an arbitrary reality which becomes the hermeneutical principle for the disclosure of reality. The "negativity" of the resistance of reality that makes us revise earlier insights is therefore productive, it has a special meaning in our experiences of revelation, be it dialectically negative and critical.[168]

Thus, borrowing an idea from the critical theorist Ernst Bloch, he labeled this inexpressible and yet dialectically encountered reality of truth the "*humanum*" of history. The *humanum* of reality can never be directly experienced or completely articulated by human knowledge and concepts, but it manifests itself in the *anticipation* and the *hope* it produces of the possibility that conditions can and will

---

Salvation: The Salvific Meaning of Suffering in the Later Theology of Edward Schillebeeckx, Louvain Theological & Pastoral Monographs (Dudly, MA: W.B. Eerdmans, 2006), 183–7.

165. Kennedy, "Continuity," 271: Kennedy briefly explains Schillebeeckx's relationship to Theodor Adorno in his use of negative dialectics and how Schillebeeckx actually critiques Adorno for allowing the "praxis" of academics to simply be critically theorizing in itself without any other corresponding action. (This topic is discussed in greater detail in Chapter 5.) Cf. Portier, "Critical Theorist," 355.

166. Edward Schillebeeckx, *God among Us: The Gospel Proclaimed* (New York: Crossroad, 1983), 175–9. Cf. Portier, "Critical Theorist," 367.

167. Schillebeeckx, *Understanding of Faith*, 91–2.

168. Edward Schillebeeckx, "Erfahrung und Glaube," in *Christlicher Glaube in moderner Gesellschaft*, vol. 25 (Friedburg: Herder, 1982), 91.

be better in the future than they are in the current moment.[169] Furthermore, this anticipation and hope then becomes a source of *courage* through which one not only can stand with the victims of suffering and oppression but also *actively resist* the dominant forces of untruth and repression in society. Hence again in discussing the nature of this negative knowledge in his *Jesus* book, Schillebeeckx views all "valid knowledge" as fundamentally critical in orientation and always practical in application (*"practical-cum-critical"*).[170] Accordingly he intentionally tries to distance himself from the purely "theoretical" or "hermeneutical" approaches to deciphering knowledge and begins stressing even more the significance of inspired action, or *praxis*, as both the *"disclosive source"* and *"critical test"* of all epistemological inquiry—and especially the knowledge of ultimate truth or "God."[171]

> For the believer the religious interpretation is more easily understood and more reasonable; the non-believer finds the agnostic interpretation more reasonable. But in this context what believers mean by God can also be understood by non-believers. ... The most obvious, modern way to [the knowledge of] God is that of welcoming fellow human beings both interpersonally and by changing the structures which enslave them. Moreover that is *not a purely theoretical or speculative approach* to [the knowledge] of God (ontological foundations or decisionistic proclamations of free subjectivity), but a meta-ethical, viz. religious or theologal, interpretation of a micro- and macro ethical human possibility. It is *no metaphysics of being or of free subjectivity*, but believing reflection on the praxis of justice and love. What we have here is not just the ethical consequence of religious or theologal life; *here ethical praxis becomes an essential component of the true knowledge of God*.[172]

---

169. Thompson, xiii. Here in the foreword to Thompson's text Schillebeeckx gives a helpful and concrete example of this when he proclaims,

> That is why I end with a note of hope. For it is exactly the negative or contrast experiences in the world and church in the twentieth century, with its Holocaust and ethnic genocides, with its experiences of ecclesial "short-circuits" between religious authorities and Christian believers, that arouse an indignation that is the converse of a latent expectation. *It is a hope ... that things can and must be done differently in the world and in the churches."*

Emphasis added.
170. Schillebeeckx, *Jesus*, 621.
171. Edward Schillebeeckx, *Ministry: Leadership in the Community of Jesus Christ*, trans. John Bowden (New York: Crossroad, 1984), 101. Cf. Thompson, 39–41; Kennedy, "Continuity," 270.
172. Edward Schillebeeckx, *Jesus in Our Western Culture: Mysticism, Ethics, and Politics*, trans. John Bowden (London: SCM Press, 1987), 63. Emphases added.

Therefore, the source of "Truth" within the Christian tradition is no longer found in an implicit intuition of the ultimate truth behind conceptual abstractions *or* simply in the *re*-interpretative influences of the past within the new experiences of present, but rather in the continuity of a *critical*-consciousness of faith and a community of *ethical praxis* that inherently shapes one's interpretation and evaluation of "truth" within any given experience. Now of course the exact image of what this critical-consciousness and ethical action will actually look like obviously varies from context to context and situation to situation, yet these instances of *active critical resistance* implicitly "reveal" a very discernable, though never fully expressible, truth of an always-present potentiality for the future. As William Portier articulates in his article "Edward Schillebeeckx as Critical Theorist," here Schillebeeckx somewhat returns to a version of the "critically realist" metaphysic he formed under De Petter. Except this time instead of insisting on direct encounters with truth through the deepest levels of consciousness itself, he now formulates a "*negative* realist metaphysic" in which the individual encounters the "really real" external to oneself only as "glimpses" into the truth of reality through the seemingly meaningless abyss of history.[173] And so although these glimpses are only negative in nature, they nonetheless supply an actual implicit knowledge of a greater transcendent "Truth" *within* the apparent scandal of the "arbitrariness" and "meaninglessness" of history. Moreover, this awareness can then be further cultivated and articulated through the critical reflection on one's own ethical praxis. As such, for Schillebeeckx this *realist* knowledge of truth through the contrast experiences of history—and the subsequent ethical action to resist them—is vital because otherwise even the most emancipative practice runs the risk of being without any actual meaningful content.[174]

Nevertheless, one must remember that any knowledge derived from these experiences, and one's critical reflection on them, still remains only as a *negative* form of knowledge. As Schillebeeckx himself explains, while one might intuitively perceive an allusionary sense of "truth" through the various contrast experiences of history, at the same time the actual "divine Mystery" of potentiality within all history still "repeatedly shatters all our images and representations of God."[175] Thus no conceptual formulation, even those derived from the critical reflection on praxis, can ever fully express the mystery of the ultimate truth toward which it gestures. This is because the truth grazed upon in these historical moments is *eschatological* in its very nature,[176] meaning that the truth of reality is rooted not in a static and eternal ground-of-*being* but instead in the dynamic and indeterminate state of *becoming*, which emerges from the oncoming horizon of the future rather than the receding one of the present-soon-to-be-past.[177] Hence truth is not

173. Portier, "Critical Theorist," 362.

174. Thompson, 41. Thompson quotes a foreword by Schillebeeckx to the German text *Menschheitsgeschichte und Heilserfahrung* by Tadahiko Iwashima.

175. Thomspson, x.

176. Portier, "Critical Theorist," 349.

177. Schillebeeckx, *Understanding of Faith*, 66.

something *revealed* within the expressions of the past, nor *found* in the immediate encounters with the present, rather it is something *done* in the never-fully-realized hope of the potentiality for a better oncoming future. "Truth" then is something that by its very nature can never be completely known until the full realization of the future—the eschaton.

So once again, in conclusion, one is confronted with both deep strands of continuity and radical divergence in Schillebeeckx's epistemological theory. We have shown how in the end Schillebeeckx returned to a "critically realist metaphysic" that was somewhat analogous in intention to his earliest phenomenological epistemology under De Petter. However this theoretical realism notwithstanding, he still retains the acknowledgment that every experience of the present is utterly shaped by the interpretative influences of the past, and moreover that these interpretative elements often actually become the sources of un-truths and oppression. And so, as Kennedy perceptively concludes, for Schillebeeckx any "propositional knowledge of God springs from actions which confirm God's nature as a God who is concerned for humanity."[178] Hence valid knowledge of this "ultimate truth" cannot be extracted from a present encounter of a "really real" behind our conceptions nor is it decipherable from the *re*-interpretations of the past in light of the present; rather it is only felt through the dialectical encounter with reality at the "absolute limit" of human perception, the confrontation of the radical finitude, contingency, and arbitrariness of all history and knowledge, that reveals the unrealized and indeterminate potentiality of the future that drives the individual to *make* the ultimate reality one hopes to find—the eschatological "Kingdom of God."[179]

B. Chopel's Apophaticism: Feeling the Imperceptible, Knowing the Inconceivable

As one reads through the *Adornment*, one of the most apparent themes that continually manifests itself is Gendun Chopel's consistent attempt to offer his readers "a glimpse of the elusive boundary between the universe of things that can be stated and the universe which cannot be spoken because it cannot be thought, the inexpressible realm about which he wrote so eloquently."[180] To this point we have examined two of Gendun Chopel's major epistemological arguments for why it is impossible for those who have not experienced the nondualistic reality

---

178. Kennedy, "Continuity," 276. Cf. Schillebeeckx, *God among Us*, 61. In this passage Schillebeeckx describes the "Yes of God" toward human life and liberation.

179. Van Erp, 221; Schillebeeckx, *Church*, 77–80: Here Schillebeeckx lays out his own version of the "Irony of Atheism" argument where it is in reaching the "absolute limit" of meaning or "the radical finitude" of human limitations that one is opened up to "an experience of God's absolute saving presence throughout his or her life."; Schillebeeckx, *Jesus*, 669: Schillebeeckx discusses his eschatological theology in terms of "Kingdom" language.

180. Lopez and chos phel, *Madman*, 254.

of emptiness—"common beings"—to have any "valid knowledge" based on the two traditional Buddhist conceptions of the sources of knowledge, "scripture and reasoning." In the first section, Gendun Chopel's perspectivalism showed that apart from a completely reoriented ontological perception of reality formed only as the result of an awareness of the nonaffirming absence of emptiness itself (the realization of enlightenment), common beings can never actually comprehend even the proper object of knowledge because it will always be formed through dualistic distinctions, hence making any formulation of knowledge a completely subjectivist construction and, consequently, the ability to establish valid knowledge based on traditional logical reasoning (*yukti, rigs pa*) impossible.[181] Then, examining the historical and cultural layering within the teachings of Buddhist scripture (*āgama, lung*), he determined that within every teaching of the Buddha there are inexpressible, "very hidden" meanings of truth that can never be understood by common beings who are intellectually trapped within the confines of worldly manifestation and contextual depiction. However, at this point one might ask whether, through his repeated stress that emptiness completely contradicts the knowledge of the world, Gendun Chopel has not just set up yet another dualism between the conventionally dualistic propositional knowledge of the world and the ultimately nondualistic wisdom from the perception of emptiness. Moreover, one is left wondering how any common being can ever perceive emptiness, and become enlightened, if one is fundamentally ensnared in conventional thinking? In this section we will briefly examine how Gendun Chopel uses his training in philosophical dialectics in order to overcome both of these challenges through showing the necessary function of conventional knowledge in obtaining the ultimate wisdom of emptiness.[182]

Based on his discussions of the utter limitations of reasoning and scriptural interpretation in forming valid knowledge, there can be little doubt that Gendun Chopel perceives the intellectual chasm between the enlightened and unenlightened to be so great that all "ideas of the world are incapable of going even a little way toward the other side [of ultimate emptiness]."[183] In fact, elsewhere he even goes as far as making such emphatic proclamations as "if one has conviction in the dharma, one must have conviction in the inconceivable state" and "In brief, all those who believe in the Mahayana must also believe in the inconceivable."[184] Earlier in the *Adornment* Gendun Chopel also grounds his strong conviction in the belief of "an inexpressible ultimate" as being absolutely foundational for all Buddhist thought on Śāntideva's famous declaration in the second stanza of the

---

181. Chos phel, "Adornment," 51–2, v. 15 and 19. Cf. Hopkins and Chöpel, 23: Here Hopkins explains that having "no confidence in the depictions of our minds" is also a major theme running throughout the *Tibetan Arts of Love*.

182. Hopkins and Chöpel, 23–4: Hopkins briefly discusses Gendun Chopel's training in dialectics as the source of his conception of emptiness through the limits of logic.

183. Chos phel, "Adornment," 106, v. 206.

184. Ibid., 81, v. 128; p. 68, v. 89.

ninth chapter of the *Bodhicaryatara* that "The ultimate is not within the mind's sphere; the mind is said to be conventional."[185] Here, Lopez explains, Gendun Chopel utilizes Śāntideva's iconic statement to highlight his own certainty that the realms of the conventional and the ultimate are so radically distinct that the consciousness of any unenlightened mind is completely confined to the dualities of dependent origination.[186]

Nonetheless, Gendun Chopel refuses to leave the discussion there. Immediately in the next verse (117) Gendun Chopel alludes to the ignorance of those entangled in the philosophical disputes of the debating courtyards across Tibet when he rebuffs the accusation that the "very expression 'inexpressible' is itself an expression."[187] Gendun Chopel uses this popular rhetorical maneuver to emphasize that anyone making such an argument is still trapped in the dualistic categories of true and false, "cause and effect, whole and part, basis of designation and designated object," and by consequence he attempts to show that all philosophical argumentation and reasoning is still utterly dependent on linguistic logic and therefore ensnared in the confines of the conventional world.[188] At the same time, examples such as this of Gendun Chopel refuting the efficaciousness philosophical debate begin to tip his hand as to how he will eventually attempt to traverse this chasm of reality. If even too much of an attachment to the deconstructive logic of Madhyamaka philosophy can similarly trap the scholastic in worldly dualities that prevent one's entry into the inconceivable realm, then some experience or practice beyond simple philosophical reflection must be necessary for realizing the truth of reality where all these categories are unified.[189]

Yet Gendun Chopel is continually confronted with the dilemma that even enlightened individuals will eventually still have to speak to other unenlightened beings in the world, and as such even one who has directly realized the ontological emptiness of all reality "must involuntarily assert whatever was asserted earlier." The stakes of falling into nihilism by asserting *absolutely nothing* are too high. Hence, he concedes, "when someone who has no such assertions is asked what is out there, he will be bound to say that it is a mountain, it is a tree, and that it is a human."[190] Or as he quips at another point, the fact that Mādhyamikas can have no valid linguistic assertions to make does not mean that they do not speak for their entire lives.[191] Instead, he clarifies, they must attempt to use the "completely obscuring" "mistaken truth" of conventional language[192] in order to expose the unenlightened to the reality of emptiness indirectly through inferential

---

185. Ibid., 77, v. 115–16.
186. Lopez and chos phel, *Madman*, 170–1.
187. Chos phel, "Adornment," 77–8, v. 117.
188. Lopez and chos phel, *Madman*, 171.
189. Ibid., 205. Cf. Chos phel, "Adornement," 67, v. 86.
190. Chos phel, "Adornment," 81, v. 121.
191. Ibid., 64, v. 77.
192. Ibid., 109, v. 218.

understanding. Hence, for the Mādhyamika "valid knowledge and reasoning" are not synonymous with "accurate" per se, but are rather just the linguistic constructions of *un*truth that most effectively push the unenlightened mind into the liminal space beyond the logic of language where common beings might briefly brush up against "a faint comprehending awareness that falls between two uncomprehending awarenesses."[193]

Thus it is not speaking in the conventions of the world that Gendun Chopel finds inherently problematic, rather it is the common misconception by the unenlightened that their words actually refer to anything ultimately that enslaves their consciousness to the realm of saṃsāra. "What [Gendun Chopel] seems to find particularly irksome," Lopez comments, "is that the unenlightened are not content to limit their mind to the conventional world, but seem compelled to make all manner of grandiose statements about the ultimate, about the nature of reality, to give a name to all manner of supramundane qualities, each of which is beyond expression and beyond imagination."[194] An enlightened being can, and in fact *has to*, make statements about the world and even the nature of reality as a way of directing others toward the limits of their conceptual understandings, yet this is not necessarily the same as making "an assertion" about reality. For him, in order for one to "make an assertion" the speaker actually has to believe "from the heart" the meaning of what is being expressed. Hence, much like the teachings of the Buddha examined earlier, the enlightened individual speaks but only in ways that skillfully unmask the limitations of language and push the unenlightened mind beyond word and concept. Words might be concealing in their inherent desire to draw distinctions on an ultimately nondual reality, but Gendun Chopel also maintains a profound appreciation for the potential rhetorical power these same statements may possess in evoking the ultimate when these distinctions inevitably break down.[195]

Accordingly, on multiple occasions, Gendun Chopel references the passage from the Laṅkāvatāra Sūtra where it is believed that the Buddha prophesied the coming of Nāgārjuna as the one who "will destroy the positions of existence and nonexistence"[196] as a way of displaying how the essential purpose of every teaching of all enlightened beings, including the Buddha and Nāgārjuna, "is to disrupt our ordinary conceptions and lead us to an inconceivable state."[197] This is because in verse 94 Gendun Chopel explains that the only way for the "mind of common beings" to recognize the nature of ultimate reality is "from the negative side" through the deconstructive negation of all language, conceptions, and meaning.[198] For example, just as "by understanding the meaning of light, one

---

193. Ibid., 110, v. 221.
194. Lopez and chos phel, *Madman*, 132.
195. Ibid., 159. Cf. Chos phel, "Adornment," 87, v. 147.
196. Chos phel, "Adornment," 85–6, v. 141; p. 98, v. 180.
197. Lopez and chos phel, *Madman*, 197.
198. Chos phel, "Adornment," 70, v. 94.

knows that darkness is very black" or "by understanding the meaning of virtue, one determines that sin is very wrong," so too it is through the use of positive distinctions that one can begin to perceive the nondual and nonaffirming negative of the emptiness of all reality.[199] However, such understanding through the deconstructive negation of the conventional is not limited simply to verbal expressions. Elsewhere Gendun Chopel also invokes the use of tantric practices as having the power to force individuals past the conceptual limitations of their consciousness to the inconceivable state of enlightenment through "reversing the conception of the ordinary" and exposing the arbitrariness of conventional knowledge.[200] Hence, whether by word or by deed, it is only through skillfully exposing the limits of conventional truth, and consequently by "smashing to dust" all "conceptions of the ordinary," that one can begin to encounter the tranquil and blissful reality of the "nonaffirming absence" of all phenomena.[201]

Moving the emphasis away from the philosophical dialectics of the debating courtyard, however, Gendun Chopel once again attempts to bring the focus back to the importance of meditative practice. This time in verse 114 Gendun Chopel explains that it is only after achieving the experience of meditative equipoise (*samāhita, mnyam gzhag*), in which the individual breaks down all conventional distinctions and is confronted by the nondual emptiness of all reality, that one can then achieve true "subsequent attainment" (*pṛṣṭhalabdha, rjes thob*) where the individual can now comprehend the value and necessity of the conventional in unveiling the emptiness of all reality through dialectical tension.[202] It is at this point following that subsequent attainment that the practitioner can now fully grasp the reality that all "negation of truth in the ultimate sense is at the level of the conventional."[203] This means that in light of the nonaffirming negative encountered during meditative equipoise, one then realizes that even the "ultimate category" of "emptiness" is itself *empty* of any true meaning or distinction.[204] Hence, here any sense of dualistic residue within Gendun Chopel's epistemological depiction of reality begins to fall away as he proclaims a standard Madhayamaka trope that for the enlightened being "even ultimate truths exist conventionally; they do not exist ultimately. An ultimate mode of being is unfounded. Even the ultimate is established in a way which is not ultimate. This means that it is conventionally established."[205] Thus, in the end, it is only through the meditation on the invalidity of all conventional knowledge that one is made aware of the inconceivable ultimate reality of the emptiness of all truth, and in doing so realizes there is no basis for an object of knowledge to be found within existence besides the acknowledgment

---

199. Ibid., 98–9, v. 181.
200. Ibid., 69, v. 91–2.
201. Ibid.
202. Ibid., 76, v. 114. Cf. Lopez and chos phel, *Madman*, 169.
203. Chos phel, "Adornment," 87, v. 147.
204. Ibid., 69–70, v. 93.
205. Ibid., 84, v. 137.

of the simple label of "this mere thing" in the immediate phenomenological encounter.[206]

And so finally, once more we find points of comparable contact and contrast in the epistemologies of Gendun Chopel and Schillebeeckx. Both thinkers appear to situate the locus for all knowledge not in some transcendent object that can ever be definitively "known" apart from linguistic and historical manifestation but rather in the realization of the ontological absence of any determinate reality through the subject's negatively dialectical[207] encounter of language and history. Furthermore, both thinkers reject philosophical reflection as being solely necessary for achieving this understanding of reality, and instead both emphasize the importance of another form of action to be taken by the individual in order to comprehend the true nature of knowledge. However, whereas Gendun Chopel discusses tantric and meditative practices as the source for this realization, Schillebeeckx asserts that it is through the hopeful action of liberative praxis that one can ground all claims to knowledge. Also where Gendun Chopel describes ultimate reality in terms of the absence of a nonaffirming negative, Schillebeeckx tends to describe it ("God") in terms of the indeterminate potentiality of the future. Yet as we will see as we move further into this study, for both thinkers the idea of a metaphysic of negative dialectics plays a pivotal role in grounding all claims to valid knowledge.

V. Conclusion: Further Questions Moving Forward

Nonetheless, in many ways this initial examination seems to spark more questions than it provides answers. And in fact, that was the intention of this broad preliminary assessment all along. As stated earlier in the introduction, the overall purpose of this chapter was not to serve as the main comparison itself, but rather as the foundation and justification for the larger comparative project of Schillebeeckx's and Gendun Chopel's thought through the "bridge concept" of religious epistemology. Using the three categories, or "concentric circles," of perspectivalism, hermeneutics, and apophaticism within the broader concept of epistemology allowed us to determine, using Decosimo's terminology, the "appropriateness" of these two individuals as objects of comparison regarding their insights and convictions about the possibility, nature, and source of valid knowledge

---

206. Ibid.

207. Here I am borrowing the idea of "negative dialectics" from the thought of Theodor Adorno in which thought can only have access to the "nonidentical" source of knowledge via conceptual criticisms of false identifications. Such criticisms intentionally point to specific contradictions between what any thought claims and what it actually delivers. Through this process of "determinate negation," those aspects of the object of knowledge which thought misidentifies receive an indirect, conceptual articulation. I will further discuss Adorno's theory of negative dialectics while examining Schillebeeckx's theoretical foundations regarding metaphysics in a later chapter.

from within their respective religious traditions. Hence, earlier I referred to these more focused categories as "the materials" from which the broader "bridge concept" of epistemology can and will be built. However, determining the "raw materials" of a bridge is by far not all that is necessary for its construction. In this case of comparing Schillebeeckx and Gendun Chopel, the topics that seemingly most efficaciously overlap in content and significance within their systems are the central roles that the religious communities, their historical founders, and their understanding of ultimate reality itself serve as authorities and grounds for establishing valid knowledge for the believer within the contemporary world.

Accordingly, in the third chapter we will turn to examine how both thinkers understood the role of their religious communities and their traditions in the individual's formation of knowledge and understanding of truth. Stemming from this chapter's brief depiction of each thinker's religious and philosophical thought, we will frame the discussion of their views regarding the authority of their religious community in the context of observing how two religious clerics (Schillebeeckx a priest within the Dominican religious order, and Gendun Chopel a Geluk Tibetan monastic), both with beliefs in the intellectual limitations of individuals to definitively know anything and both confronted with tensions between their thought and the institutions of their communities, eventually came to such distinct positions concerning the function and authority of religious communities in determining truth. This will lead to a further exploration into the philosophical and theological sources for the perspectivalist elements in each thinker's epistemology and will conclude with a comparative analysis of their own discussions about the perspectival nature of human knowledge in light of the teachings of the religious community. The outcome of the comparison will then, in the final chapter, guide us to assess the benefits of maintaining a perspectivalist element to epistemology in the contemporary world as well as how the perspectivalism in each thinker's philosophy can assist in developing a theory of knowledge that does not threaten to isolate the individual believer from the guidance of and communion with their present religious community and its historical tradition.

The fourth chapter will then turn to focus on the prior descriptions of how both thinkers were influenced by the challenges of modernity and history in articulating the source and nature of knowledge, particularly with regards to the subject of deciphering the meaning of past statements and texts in one's own current context. This will inevitably direct us toward the issues of historical-consciousness and hermeneutics, and above all each thinker's theories for interpreting the teachings and practices ascribed to the historical founders of their religious traditions (i.e., Jesus of Nazareth and Śākyamuni Buddha). By focusing on the sources and influences of their understandings of history and the nature of meaning within ancient texts, we will then be able to evaluate how both Schillebeeckx and Gendun Chopel attempt to overcome the challenges that historicity and the contextuality of all human expressions put on the religious practitioner's ability to accept the words of their historical founders as a definitive source and authority of absolute knowledge. Consequently, after observing the different causes and tactics for approaching the issue of the hermeneutics within their own traditions, in the final chapter we will conclude by discussing the differences in Schillebeeckx's and Gendun Chopel's theories of the authority of the historical founders of their traditions and also how each individual's respective theory shapes the way he eventually depicts the role and nature of that founding figure as well as the nature of ultimate reality itself.

Finally, in the last case study of Chapter 5, we will explore each thinker's discussions concerning what can be actually known about the nature of ultimate truth, and whether, or how, this reality can function as a legitimate basis for determining valid knowledge in the contemporary world. Once again pulling from the background of this previous chapter, we will begin by observing how both men continually and very publicly struggled with their own inabilities to engage, know, or articulate the nature of ultimate reality in itself. Then moving from their own personal spiritual trepidations about discerning the nature of ultimate reality, we will discuss the way in which both thinkers utilized theories from within, and at times even outside, their respective traditions in order to call for a much more limited depiction of ultimate truth through the use of negative dialectics. Subsequently, returning to this issue at the end of Chapter 6, we will constructively combine and contrast their insights regarding the nature and knowability of ultimate truth in order to develop a religious epistemology that is thoroughly critical in its application and yet nonetheless realist in its ontology. Such an approach to epistemology will hopefully help the contemporary believer avoid the problematic nihilism of a purely subjectivist epistemology—which is so rampant in our contemporary "postmodern" world—while still always maintaining and sharpening the practitioner's humility toward discourses on metaphysics through the critical eye of a deconstructive apophaticism.

Thus, in the end, the purpose of this chapter was to display the appropriateness of comparing these two thinkers according to the issue of epistemology despite their distinct theological and philosophical presuppositions. The three ensuing case-study chapters will use the common concerns of the role of religious communities, their founding figures, and their engagement with the ultimate reality of truth itself as a way to further employ this "appropriateness" so as to detect what each thinker might have to say to the other about their particular epistemological theories. Then, overall, the final chapter will hope to discover and highlight how, through the construction and assessment of this imaginary dialogue, Schillebeeckx and Gendun Chopel might be able to contribute both individually and collectively to forming new trajectories for religious thought and spiritual practice in the postmodern world.

Chapter 3

THE ROLES OF INDIVIDUAL INTELLECT AND THE COLLECTIVE INTELLIGENCE OF THE COMMUNITY IN KNOWLEDGE FORMATION

I. Introduction: The Question of Perspectivalism Embodied in a Community of Individuals

The second chapter briefly discussed how both Schillebeeckx and Gendun Chopel each employ a version of philosophical "perspectivalism" in their epistemologies. Defining "perspectivalism" as the belief that "knowledge" is always mediated to knower in a limited fashion because of the constraints of using abstract concepts (or "universals") in describing particular encounters with reality, it then noted how both Schillebeeckx and Gendun Chopel viewed human knowledge as inseparable from the intellectual processes of the individual (particularly in the processes of recognition, abstraction, and judgment of objects of knowledge) so that all human knowledge is incapable of being verified as completely reflective of reality. This chapter will further investigate the nature and scope of this understanding of epistemological fallibility in both thinkers resulting from their perspectival interpretation of knowledge, especially as it pertains to their interpretations of the authoritative role of religious communities and their traditions in the formation of individual knowledge.

In order to do this in a descriptively "thick" way, however, it will do more than engage the materials directly pertaining to the authority of religious communities in their respective works. Rather, it will first turn to the theoretical and philosophical foundations of their perspectivalism from within their religious traditions. In so doing, it will also display the implications of these views on certain theological and philosophical topics and concepts common within their traditions and also how each thinker necessarily sought to negotiate his own reinterpretations of these concepts in light of his epistemological theory. Only then, after probing these prior areas, will the chapter turn to focus directly on the explicit conversations and arguments each thinker had for understanding ecclesial authority.

Finally, in the conclusion it will turn to openly comparing and contrasting all the areas previously discussed between both Schillebeeckx and Gendun Chopel. By briefly laying out both some of the general similarities within the lives and thought of these quite distinct individuals as well as the considerable dissimilarities in their theories and histories, it will set out to raise some broader questions with significant implications on the reader's own understanding of ecclesial authority to be examined further in the final chapter of the work. Hence, in the end the objectives of the chapter are manifold. First, the chapter will seek to add depth and clarity to what each scholar meant by his use of perspectival language in his theories of knowledge along with how they perceived these theories as relevant to the spiritual goals of their religious communities. It will then tie this discussion, along with the discussions of the previous chapter, directly to the eventual outcomes in how each person defined the epistemological authority of his religious institutions and traditions. Lastly, it will utilize the discoveries from these investigations in order to construct the basic parameters for a larger comparative conversation about the nature and role of communal authority in light of contemporary questions regarding religious epistemology. Thus, in the end, the reader should have a better comprehension of the individual thinkers themselves; the origins, nature, and purpose of their philosophical theories of perspectivalism; in addition to the relevance those theories have within their religious traditions and religious epistemology as a whole.

II. Philosophical Sources and Influences of Perspectivalism

A. Schillebeeckx: Dominic De Petter and Phenomenological Thomism

In his own retelling of the events of his colloquium for theological clarifications with representatives of the Congregation for the Doctrine of the Faith (hereafter CDF) in December 1979, Schillebeeckx recounts how he responded to a question asking him to explain his use of hermeneutics in his theology simply with the standard "slogan from St. Thomas": *Quidquid recipitur, ad modum recipientis, recipitur* (whatever is received is received in a way suited to the recipient). Supposedly, the inquisitor (the Dominican A. Patfoort, professor at the Angelicum in Rome) could only reply, "Ah, now I understand … Fine, fine."[1] This simple anecdote is worth mentioning within this current discussion for primarily two reasons. First, it highlights Schillebeeckx's lifelong identification of his theology with his educational grounding in the thought of Aquinas and also how—even after his public separation from De Petter's philosophical positions regarding epistemology and metaphysics in 1966[2]—Schillebeeckx's training in Thomist thought under the guidance of De Petter still played a foundational role in his religious epistemology. Second, it depicts the interestingly dialectical tension within Schillebeeckx's own thought between the epistemological authority of the church and its tradition—even while he himself was being examined by the church for challenging the standard interpretations of traditional theological doctrines and meaning. Accordingly in the next two sections we will investigate how the

---

1. Edward Schillebeeckx and Francesco Strazzari, *I Am a Happy Theologian: Conversations with Francesco Strazzari* (New York: Crossroad, 1994), 32; Schillebeeckx, Schoof, and Catholic Church *Schillebeeckx Case*, 55.

2. For Schillebeeckx's account of his separation from De Petter's form of phenomenology see Schillebeeckx, *Jesus*, 618.

philosophical and theoretical foundations of De Petter's phenomenological perspectivalism shaped and developed Schillebeeckx's theological formulations of revelation and human knowledge of ultimate truth (God),[3] in addition to their far-reaching implications into the development of Schillebeeckx's understandings of the epistemological authority of the church (in the tradition, the episcopate, and the broader community) in the knowledge and faith of the individual.

As Daniel Thompson explains, part of the difficulty in articulating Schillebeeckx's theory of knowledge throughout his career and theological development is that he was never "interested in laying out a purely formal epistemology." Rather, the structures of his epistemological theory can only be excavated, deciphered, and systematized from his many other various theological discussions, particularly revolving around the issues of "revelation and the Christian knowledge of God."[4] Kennedy seconds Thompson's analysis by proclaiming, "Schillebeeckx is a systematic theologian who has never produced a systematic theology. *He is a dogmatician without a dogmatics.*"[5] Moreover, adding to the difficulty, Kennedy explains that if one reads his publications in chronological order, that person will soon be confronted by "a prominent *metamorphosis* at the heart of his work" that complicates any attempt to boil down his thought into a singular formal theory. Nevertheless, Kennedy also insists that Schillebeeckx's "work is of a piece in that his theology's most basic conceptual infrastructure has never changed substantially during the full length of his career."[6] Hence, the purpose of this section will be to attempt to discern and uncover part of that "conceptual infrastructure" that would both develop and shape his emergent theories of individual knowledge and the role of the church in establishing truthful interpretations of personal experience.

In the introduction to his edited volume the *Schillebeeckx Reader*, Robert Schreiter contends that the one concern linking Schillebeeckx's thought throughout his career is understanding how "the concrete, contemporary Christian experience"[7] can unveil the absolute within the relative; the ultimate in the limited.[8] Or as Kennedy phrases it in another way, "It is the quandary of explaining how that which is absolute, called God, or Allah, in the context of religion, can be recognized and *contacted* in that which is limited, historical, and particular."[9] In essence, it is the age-old theological problem of reconciling

---

3. Kennedy, *Schillebeeckx*, 43. Kennedy elaborates on how at this early stage in Schillebeeckx's thought both he and De Petter saw "God" as "the totality of meaning" that is intuitively prehended by the individual in the formation of knowledge. Later on Schillebeeckx, however, would eventually deny that an individual can perceive something of the completeness of meaning.

4. Thompson, 47.

5. Kennedy, *Schillebeeckx*, 83.

6. Ibid., 3.

7. Schillebeeckx and Schreiter, 8–10.

8. Schillebeeckx, *God among Us*, 157. Cf. Kennedy, *Schillebeeckx*, 4.

9. Kennedy, *Schillebeeckx*, 4.

universality and particularity in notions of truth and knowledge from a human, historical perspective.[10] In his 1969 work *God and Man*, Schillebeeckx himself lays out the significance of resolving this dilemma for the contemporary theologian:

> This problem of the actual nature of our knowledge of God may seem academic, but it is nevertheless a matter of "to be or not to be" for religion. For if we know nothing positive about God, not even in an implicit manner, then the life of grace—which is nothing other than intersubjectivity with God—becomes, quite simply, meaningless and without content: people are not concerned about an unknown x, except out of mathematical interest (and in that case the x is ultimately determinable). Deism was at least consistent![11]

Initially with the guidance and help of De Petter,[12] Schillebeeckx would begin his "thoroughly modern philosophical" quest to "determine what can be known indubitably by human beings," and moreover speculate on how that question can and should be linked to the believer's ability "to elucidate the nature of religious knowledge"—religious epistemology.[13]

During his time with De Petter in Louvain,[14] Schillebeeckx became convinced that the starting place of all human knowledge had to emerge from the "givenness of experience." In other words, "People experienced reality, and this was subsequently reshaped, through analysis and synthesis, description, comparison and induction, from a diffuse and disordered whole into synthetic knowledge of the truth."[15] However, as a result of this prioritizing of the individual intellectual process of experience in the formation of all knowledge, Schillebeeckx came to realize that before one could solve the epistemological riddle of universality and particularity, one first had to answer two other central questions of existence: first the ontological and metaphysical questions of the nature of being and reality itself, and second the anthropological question of what it means to be human.[16]

One crucial development out of Schillebeeckx's philosophical training with De Petter was his belief in both the usefulness and necessity of a Thomistically *realist* metaphysic. In other words, as Kennedy describes it, Schillebeeckx and De Petter opted to read all instantiations of Aquinas's approach to knowledge through the prism of phenomenology, maintaining that although "human consciousness is not like a mirror that simply and passively reflects images of reality external to its consciousness," nonetheless any perception or active interpretation of an external

---

10. Ibid., 43.
11. Edward Schillebeeckx, *God and Man*, His Theological Soundings, 3 (New York: Sheed and Ward, 1969), 169.
12. Borgman, 388 n. 94. Cf. Schillebeeckx, *Jesus*, 618.
13. Kennedy, *Schillebeeckx*, 34.
14. Borgman, 40–1. He describes working with Fr. Désiré Mercier on this topic as well.
15. Ibid., 40.
16. Kennedy, *Schillebeeckx*, 33–4.

reality must also actually involve a real object to be perceived.[17] Thus the experience and existence of *reality itself* must take a certain precedence over any expressions of it, so that as Thompson describes, "reality provides a directing, shaping, and interrupting element in [all] human knowledge."[18] Thus the central starting point in their philosophical perspective was the *conviction*, derived out of a particular reading of Husserl's phenomenology, that any notion of "pure objectivity" or "pure subjectivity" is in the end nonsensical.[19] Rather, human experiential knowledge could not originate simply from an object of reality to be encountered, nor a knowing subject to perceive it, but instead depended on the active interaction of the two. Or as Kennedy aptly summarizes the position, "there can no more be a known without a knower than there can be a knower without a known."[20]

Therefore, at this point early on, Borgman explains that De Petter and Schillebeeckx are epistemological *idealists* in that they both believe that in the act of knowing, the subject is in direct contact—albeit intuitively—with reality as such, and yet they are also *not* pure conceptualists.[21] This is the case for Schillebeeckx because the conceptual synthesis of one's intuitive experience of reality and one's expressive interpretation of it—that together *is* knowledge—always inherently leaves a mysterious "something more" than any conceptual formulation of reality.[22]

> The whole thing amounts to the fact that the content of our consciousness makes no sense, cannot be explained in such a way that we do not put at the beginning of it—as something that always remains—an intuition, an experience which comprehends the original whole, which expresses all those perfections in the rational content, synthesizes them in itself in an inexpressible way.[23]

Hence with regard to the knowledge of religious truth, Schillebeeckx always wants to make the distinction between the "real essence of the dogmatic affirmation" and the "secondary aspects" of language and concepts within which the expression is couched.[24] In distinction from the purely subjectivist "modernists" Schillebeekx's perspectivalism views "absolute reality" (which he equates "as truth") as actually contacted by the individual knowing subject, although "in a confused but

---

17. Ibid., 40.
18. Thompson, 50.
19. Borgman, 41–2.
20. Kennedy, *Schillebeeckx*, 42.
21. Borgman, 388 n.94. It is significant to note that despite their similarities, Borgman also observes a distinct and significant difference even early on in their philosophical stances: "Whereas the former above all addressed the *possibility* of the knowledge of God, the latter was above all concerned with the *comprehensiveness* of knowledge of God and thus of the breadth of the awareness of God, philosophy orientated on God and—later—theology."
22. Schillebeeckx, *Revelation and Theology*, vol. II, 167. Cf. Fatula, 421.
23. Borgman, 47.
24. Schillebeeckx, *Revelation and Theology*, vol. II, 25–6. Cf. Thompson, 19.

objective way,"[25] so that one's knowledge of truth can grow and evolve over time as the truth of reality is "apprehended more and more concretely, even though it is never completely apprehended."[26] Thus in the end for Schillebeeckx, from the ontological perspective, "to be" as humans is to be engaged in a dynamic, prehensive experience and relationship with the totality of reality.

In order to address the question of the nature of "being," however, Schillebeeckx must also examine what it means to be *human* from a Christian perspective. Furthermore, in Schillebeeckx's mind the issue of anthropology must begin with understanding the relationship between God and creation. As Schillebeeckx has proclaimed on numerous occasions and in seemingly countless works, for him "creation is the foundation of all theology"[27] for it is "the background and horizon of all Christian belief."[28] As Thompson simply puts it, Schillebeeckx views "creation" as "*the continuing act* of the infinite and transcendent God who establishes and preserves creatures *in their finitude* and is present and immanent to creatures *precisely through* their finitude."[29] Important to note, Schillebeeckx holds that creaturely, and particularly *human*, finitude is not the regrettable result of an original sin or some defect in natural design (what he describes as the problem of "dualism"), nor is it something that must be annulled in order to engage the totality of existence, but rather it is the very thing that places humanity in relationship with ultimate reality (through "the spark of the soul")[30] and affirms its valuation as that which "is good."[31] Thus in his mind, belief in "creation" is *not* so much concerned with giving explanation of the origin of the universe[32] nor with defining or circumscribing the nature of God, but more about the recognition of the manifestation of God permeating all worldly reality.[33] Hence humans, as creatures of divine creation, are at the same time both *limited* in knowledge by their finitude[34] and also *opened* by it to receive the salvation and revelation of

---

25. Schillebeeckx, *Revelation and Theology*, vol. II, 176.
26. Ibid., 7. Cf. 169–71.
27. Schillebeeckx and Strazzari, *Happy*, 47.
28. Schillebeeckx, *Church*, 90. See also Schillebeeckx, *Eucharist*, 147; *Church*, 181; *Interim Report*, 113.
29. Thompson, 48.
30. Schillebeeckx, *Church*, 234; Cf. 77.
31. Schillebeeckx, *Interim Report*, 113; Schillebeeckx, *Church*, 181: 'God is essentially creator, the lover of the finite, loving with the absoluteness of a divine love which is unfathomable to us' (Citing Aquinas, *Summa* Ia, 40–44, esp. Ia, 1, 7, ad 2.).
32. Edward Schillebeeckx, *World and Church* (New York: Sheed and Ward, 1971), 242. Here he proclaims, "God did not first create a primordial atom or a primordial mist, from which the whole world later came into being from within by means of gradual development, without any further activity on the part of God the creator." Cf. Schillebeeckx, *Church*, 229–30 (also see *Church*, 3, 78).
33. Schillebeeckx, *Interim Report*, 114–16; *God among Us*, 94–6.
34. Schillebeeckx, *Jesus*, 669. Also see Schillebeeckx, *Church*, 181.

truth from God only in and through the limited conditions of human language and experience.³⁵ In other words, as Kennedy perceptively describes, "creation" implies that "God's very being involves humanity. Whereas one might be inclined to separate sharply human and divine realities, for Schillebeeckx reality is one and selfsame, and that which is worldly and human is included in the divine."³⁶ And therefore, as the young Schillebeeckx once proclaimed, for one to seek any knowledge of reality is to seek a contact with God implicitly; "where this—implicit—contact with God is not, there is no knowledge."³⁷

This assumption of the full manifestation of God in the finitude of all creation leads Schillebeeckx to categorize the experience of truth, and subsequently the formulation of knowledge, under the fundamental encounter of "revelation-in-reality." Of course, Schillebeeckx further holds that this basic revelation of the truth of reality within the finitude of creation has been manifested in no more perfect way than in the human life of Jesus:

> As an act of God in historical form, the whole of Jesus' human life was revelation. From his dialogue with the Father, the Son entered our human history, which thereby became, because of Jesus' human freedom, definitive saving history ... But the definitive entry of this salvation in Christ into our history can be historically recognized only in the prophetic message of the same Christ, and only by those who believe in this message. It is only through the revelation of Christ's word that the saving significance of the revelation-in-reality which has been accomplished in the life and death of Christ becomes accessible to us historically in faith. It is precisely because salvation offers itself to us as a supernatural reality in the form of an earthly, secular reality—the humanity of Christ—that this saving reality appears as given and as revealed to us in the word.³⁸

For this reason, early in his theological development Schillebeeckx often refers to Christ as the "condensation" (or "perfect encapsulation") of all that is entailed in creation and its ability to manifest the full—though never *fully comprehended*—truth of God in all reality.³⁹ Therefore, in the end, Jesus Christ serves as the exemplar manifestation of human beings as the true "children of God." This potential reality was not exclusive to Jesus—it was there for all human beings—but Christ spelt it out and brought it into consciousness, making it possible for others to fully embrace all that was natural and human.⁴⁰

35. Schillebeeckx, *Revelation and Theology*, vol. II, 7.
36. Kennedy, *Schillebeeckx*, 7.
37. Borgman, 47.
38. Schillebeeckx, *Revelation and Theology*, vol. I, 10. Cf. Schillebeeckx, *Christ the Sacrament*, 25–33.
39. Kennedy, *Schillebeeckx*, 10. Schillebeeckx uses the expression "condensation of creation" in many places throughout his writings.
40. Borgman, 51.

Since the divine discloses itself in the created and contingent reality of history, especially in the figure of Jesus, Schillebeeckx argues that for humans to attempt to "obliterate" the boundary of finitude is "the fundamental sin of idolatry."[41] Rather, "God is concerned to be our God in our humanity and for our humanity, in and with our finitude."[42] Thus, though humans can and should always attempt to develop and grow in their knowledge and comprehension of the truth of God's "revelation-in-reality," they nonetheless should never feel completely satisfied with nor equate their conceptually expressed depictions of reality with the actual truth of ultimate reality. In other words, the reality of God's salvation (revelation-in-reality) always surpasses any individual's attempt to express it (revelation-in-word), and yet it always imparts "a direction and meaning to the transcending beyond the concepts of reality."[43] Furthering this dialectical balance of valuing finitude while also recognizing its limitations, Schillebeeckx again appeals to Aquinas but this time concerning Thomas's concepts of "nature" and "grace." According to this system, "nature" describes the world ("creation") as it is in itself—and particularly human society and culture—as the historical reality in which humans naturally encounter God. Following his reading of Thomas, Schillebeeckx insists that "grace," or humans' actual exposure to the salvific reality of God's truth which Aquinas calls "the light of faith,"[44] does not *destroy* human nature but rather elevates and perfects it. As Schillebeeckx elucidates, "Grace perfects nature in two ways, in a transcendent and in an immanent way; because it makes the human being more than human and at the same time more human, more *profoundly* human."[45] Therefore, even when humans have directly encountered the "grace" of God's revelation-in-reality, they are not lifted out of their finitude to a complete understanding of the nonconceptual truth of reality, but rather instead understand the reality more fully through and within the limitations of conceptual language.

Consequently, Kennedy concludes, Schillebeeckx "is not at all immediately concerned to unravel philosophical enigmas once and for all. His impelling ambition is at once more modest and more pastoral. His works are driven by a concern to help people who find Christian faith either incredible, meaningless, or destructive."[46] Instead of ever attempting to know the full truth of ultimate reality in itself, the ultimate goal of the individual is simply to improve and refine the dialectical unity of one's synthesis between one's preconceptual ("intuitive") encounter with reality and one's conceptual analysis of it.[47] As we turn to the next section and examine the relation of Schillebeeckx's perspectivalism to his

---

41. Kennedy, *Schillebeeckx*, 35 and 88. Cf. Borgman, 60.
42. Schillebeeckx, *Interim Report*, 115.
43. Schillebeeckx, *Revelation and Theology*, vol. II, 20.
44. Schillebeeckx, *Revelation and Theology*, vol. II, 72–4. For a helpful discussion of this passage see Fatula, 422.
45. Borgman, 58.
46. Kennedy, *Schillebeeckx*, 34.
47. Borgman, 65.

understanding of the authority of the church and the religious community, it is this last point that becomes particularly significant. To be clear, in no way is he advocating a pure philosophical skepticism toward truth—as a critical *realist* he still maintains that truth is objectively engaged and drives the conceptual expressions of it—yet the *critical* aspect of his realism causes him to also hold that "it is always dangerous simply to repeat the formulation of faith which was made to a different climate of thought in the past and that if we do so it is hardly possible to speak of a *living* affirmation of faith."[48] Thus, as we will examine shortly in the next section, Schillebeeckx consistently holds that the role of the theologian is a delicate one that must both try to uphold and explicate the significance and content of faith as professed by the magisterium, while also using the insights from one's own experiences and contexts in order to penetrate these facts and drive them to more clearly represent the reality to which they point.

B. Gendun Chopel: Valid Cognition and Dharmakīrti's Epistemological Anti-Realism

In his assessment of Gendun Chopel's philosophical theory of Madhyamaka as laid out in the *Adornment*, the renowned scholar of Buddhist philosophy David Seyfort Ruegg once aptly described Gendun Chopel's thought as "highly individualistic and controversial."[49] Although this depiction is far from unique, with this statement Ruegg places his finger on the pulse of what drives the significance and prominence of Gendun Chopel's epistemology—especially with regard to its appraisal of the role and authority of the Buddhist community (*saṃgha*) in formulating knowledge for the individual practitioner. First, Gendun Chopel's call to a highly individualized theory of knowledge not only questions the authority of the religious tradition but also actually challenges the efficaciousness of religious dogma to shape an individual's perceptions of knowledge, truth, and reality. Citing the "glorious Dharmakīrti" [at *Pramāṇavārttika* I:221], Gendun Chopel himself touted the importance and role of personal reasoning in religious belief and one's understanding of truth, at one point writing,

> "Those who are mistaken about the truth cannot be changed, no matter how one tries, because their minds are prejudiced." The rejection of reason is the most despicable act ... Therefore, whether one either stubbornly says "No!" to the new reasoning [of modern science] or believes in it and utterly rejects the teaching of Buddhism, one is prejudiced; this is nothing more than recalcitrance and will not take you far.[50]

48. Schillebeeckx, *Eucharist*, 25.
49. David Seyfort Ruegg, "A Tibetan's Odyssey: A Review Article," *Journal of the Royal Asiatic Society of Great Britain and Ireland* 121, no. 2 (1989): 306.
50. Dge 'dun Chos 'phel, Thupten Jinpa and Donald S. Lopez. *Grains of Gold: Tales of a Cosmopolitan Traveler*, Buddhism and Modernity (Chicago: University of Chicago Press, 2014), 404. Cf. Lopez and chos phel, *Madman*, 19.

As we will explore in this section, Gendun Chopel's *anti*-realist interpretation of Dharmakīrti leads him to take an extremely personalized theory of knowledge and truth, so that choosing *any* tradition of thought as authoritative for interpreting one's personal phenomenological experience of reality is simply a matter of pledging loyalty to one arbitrary distinction of reality while committing "recalcitrance" against another.

Second, his highly individualistic interpretation of Madhyamaka not only challenges the authority of the religious institutions but also is controversial in its subversive approach to the process of learning against the traditional and cultural norms of his time.[51] For as Dreyfus elsewhere explains, in Tibetan scholasticism most Tibetan thinkers belong to some form of the Madhyamaka school of Buddhist philosophy.[52] And while they might disagree on the exact interpretations of it, for the most part all sects tend to share more in common than disagreements. Hence, what tend to distinguish the various "schools" of Madhyamaka thought within Tibetan scholasticism are differences of mostly "personal and political alliances."[53] And so for this reason, "Great importance is attached to devotion to one's guru and the related idea of a spiritual lineage as a necessary basis for religious practice."[54] Particularly for the Geluk sect (the tradition in which Gendun Chopel was trained and is commonly associated with), its founder Tsongkhapa (1357–1419) stands as the definitive voice and systematic reading of Nāgārjuna's Madhyamaka philosophy as interpreted by the seventh-century Indian commentator Candrakīrti.[55] The

---

51. Toni Huber, *The Holy Land Reborn: Pilgrimage & the Tibetan Reinvention of Buddhist India* (Chicago: University of Chicago Press, 2008), 4–5. Huber insists that scholars can be at least somewhat "certain" that "his detention was motivated by the Tibetan elite's fears of his newly made progressive political connections, and perhaps more so by his out-spoken criticisms against the traditional government and monastic system and the jealousy of enemies he had made within it."

52. For a depiction of Geluk curriculum (especially in contrast to other scholastic schools) see Dreyfus, *Hands*, 238.

53. Dreyfus, *Hands*, 28–9.

54. Ibid., 28.

55. Thupten Jinpa, *Self, Reality and Reason in Tibetan Philosophy: Tsongkhapa's Quest for the Middle Way*, Curzon Critical Studies in Buddhism Series (New York: RoutledgeCurzon, 2002), 9. Also see page 17 where Thupten Jinpa explains how Tsongkhapa attributed "almost all his views on Madhyamaka philosophy to Buddhapālita and Candrakīrti, whom in turn [he] sees as expounding the ultimate standpoint of Nāgārjuna and Āryadeva, the founders of the Indian Madhyamaka school." It is important to point out that Thupten Jinpa contends that "many of Tsongkhapa's views on Madhyamaka were perceived by his peers and subsequent critics as heterodox," and how later scholastics would justify his permutations in Madhayamaka through "a mystical communion he is reported to have had with the bodhisattva Mañjuśrī." As we will see, it is this selective reasoning for adjudicating the differences between thinkers' systems that is so problematic for Gendun Chopel's perception, particularly regarding the elevation of Tsongkhapa over figures such as Dharmakīrti.

Geluk Geshe and longtime English translator to the 14th Dalai Lama, Thupten Jinpa, describes this authoritative place of Tsongkhapa's thought within Geluk scholasticism, "Tsongkhapa's towering stature within the history of Madhyamaka philosophy in Tibet, and perhaps more importantly, given that his writings have assumed an almost canonical status within the dominant Geluk school of Tibetan Buddhism, an extensive exegetical tradition has evolved with respect to reading Tsongkhapa's thought."[56] Thus, Gendun Chopel's use of variant interpretations of Dharmakīrti's ontology and epistemology in order to blatantly and aggressively challenge the teachings and authority of both Tsongkhapa's and Candrakīrti's understanding of the "Two Truths" philosophy would be acutely jarring to Geluk scholastics.

As has been noted in many accounts of Gendun Chopel's scholastic training, at least once (and more than likely multiple times), part of his early scholastic education would have been an in-depth study of Dharmakīrti's *Commentary on Valid Knowledge* (*Pramāṇavārttika*) as the philosophical basis for logic and epistemology that can serve as the gateway to "the Madhyamaka insights" as expounded by Candrakīrti.[57] However in his autobiographical and ethnological investigation of Geluk scholastic training *The Sound of Two Hands Clapping*, Dreyfus points out that while Dharmakīrti's works are a foundational aspect of the Gelukpa scholastic training, they nonetheless tend to be used in a rather polemical way that serves to gradually convince students of what is inherently wrong with Dharmakīrti's epistemological system "and the essentialist assumptions it entails." Hence, its main purpose within the curricula is to give "the most systematic philosophical presentation of foundationalism in Buddhist philosophy," so as to lead "students from unquestioning assent to essentialization to skeptical questioning." In other words, "once the student understands Dharmakīrti's system, which is based on the difference between a reality definable in terms of essence and a projected essenceless conceptual realm, he is shown how this distinction leads to unsolvable difficulties." In this way, rather than serving a mainly authoritative role in Geluk epistemology, Dharmakīrti's system is meant to teach through *antithesis* by exemplifying "the type of problems encountered by any highly systematic and foundationalist thought." This subsequently is intended to lead students to the Geluk interpretation of Candrakīrti's Madhyamaka view—which, although considered the "crowning achievement" of the Gelukpa tradition, is likewise thought to be too "radical and difficult to grasp" on its own.[58]

Hence, coupling Gendun Chopel's extensive education in Dharmakīrti's epistemology with the fact that he is reported to have translated the entire *Commentary on Valid Knowledge* from Sanskrit to English during his time in India,[59] it seems apparent that Dharmakīrti's epistemology played a significant role

---

56. Jinpa, 2.

57. Georges B. J. Dreyfus, *The Sound of Two Hands Clapping: The Education of a Tibetan Buddhist Monk* (Berkeley: University of California Press, 2003), 238.

58. Ibid., 237–8. Cf. p. 282.

59. Lopez, *Science*, 106. This text now is non-extant.

in Gendun Chopel's own thought. This is particularly evident in Gendun Chopel's use of elements of Dharmakīrti's language regarding ontology and epistemology throughout his writings. Even more glaring, however, is the specific way in which Gendun Chopel interprets and incorporates Dharmakīrti's system into his own construal of epistemology and Madhyamaka. Gendun Chopel decidedly emphasizes the "non-realist" aspects of Dharmakīrti's thought in his attempt to preserve coherence between it and later Madhyamaka interpretations of reality. This is controversial not only in *what* it does but also in *how* it does it. By adopting elements of a Dharmakīrtian-based anti-realist ontology, and thus an inherently more individualized perspectivalist epistemology, Gendun Chopel not only challenges the standard interpretations of Geluk epistemology within Prasaṅgika-Madhyamaka philosophy, but he also does it in a way that is seemingly intentional in highlighting the problems with authoritative lineages of interpretation (i.e., Candrakīrti, Dzong-ka-ba, Tsongkhapa, etc.).[60]

Before attempting to assess Gendun Chopel's personal positions on ontology and epistemology, one should at least first briefly inquire into what is meant by the term "epistemology" in the Tibetan context and the Indian texts from which it arises.[61] In his study of Dharmakīrti's epistemology *Recognizing Reality*, Dreyfus tackles this question by observing that "Epistemology" as a field in the West is often defined as "a branch of philosophy that systematically investigates the nature, scope, presuppositions, basis, and reliability of knowledge."[62] Moreover, as he expounds on the topic elsewhere,[63] in the Western tradition of epistemology "knowledge" is often demarcated as "justified true belief." Dreyfus contends,

---

60. Dreyfus, *Hands*, 238.

61. Georges B. J. Dreyfus, *Recognizing Reality: Dharmakīrti's Philosophy and Its Tibetan Interpretations*, Suny Series in Buddhist Studies (Albany: State University of New York Press, 1997), 285. Cf. Dreyfus, *Hands*, 282: "[For Candrakīrti] Usual philosophical categories such as ontology and epistemology are part of the problem, not the solution."

62. Dreyfus, *Reality*, 285.

63. Ibid., 309. Here Dreyfus notes an important caution about the study of Buddhist philosophy through the Western philosophical paradigm:

> I believe that we, as modern Buddhist scholars, must be careful in our use of labels such as pragmatist, empiricist, or deconstructivist. These descriptions are of limited use for the comparativist, for they do not delineate eternal sides in the philosophical conversations of humankind. More modestly, they describe thinkers who have a substantial shared tradition of common references, concerns, and the like and who are historically connected. For example, it makes sense to describe Pierce, James, Dewey, and Rorty as pragmatists because of their common background and concerns. A term such as pragmatist is most useful not as a doxographical description, but as a description of a historically embedded tradition of inquiry. The task of the comparativist is precisely to bridge thinkers who do not share such a continuity.

"Buddhist epistemology goes essentially in the same direction."[64] He explains that the early Indian Buddhist philosophers too were concerned with defining knowledge, or at least "the Indian equivalent," along the lines of a correct, or "right," cognition (*pramā*) that is achieved through valid means (*pramāṇa*).[65] Hence, according to Dreyfus, for both the prominent Western and Buddhist systems "a well-grounded belief or cognitive event can be accepted as knowledge." Thus, in the eyes of most Geluk scholastics, Tsongkhapa's most celebrated achievement was his harmonization of Dharmakīrti's anti-realist and foundationalist understanding of the two valid *means* to knowledge (*pramāṇa*)[66]—direct perception (*pratyaksa*) and inference (*anumana*)—with the later realist epistemology of Candrakīrti which serves as the basis of interpretation for the Prasāṅgika-Madhyamaka philosophy. As Lopez tersely puts it, "[Gendun Chopel] will have nothing of this."[67] In other words, whereas Tsongkhapa wants to reconcile the traditional epistemology of Dharmakīrti with a—albeit tempered—realist Madhyamaka ontology, Gendun Chopel prefers to attempt to preserve Dharmakīrti's anti-realist language in tension with Madhyamaka by rejecting *any* valid means (*pramāṇa*) to conventional knowledge.[68]

As mentioned in the previous chapter, Lopez astutely observes that the "single theme that runs through [the *Adornment*]" is Gendun Chopel's objection to Tsongkhapa's "concern to uphold the validity of the conventional ... in the face of ultimate emptiness of all phenomena that seems to motivate much of [his] work." In this way, Gendun Chopel's main point, "reiterated again and again" in the *Adornment*, is that the ultimate reality of "emptiness" completely contradicts the world, and therefore any notion of the compatibility of the "two truths" (conventional and ultimate) "is a gross error."[69] Gendun Chopel seemingly bases this conviction on an anti-realist reading of Dharmakīrti's epistemology in which all thought and language are powerless in depicting reality because of the inherently "distorting nature" of mental concepts. As such, all concepts are incapable of providing "an accurate vision of reality" and rather are only useful as pragmatic constructs to establish agreed upon practices. This line of reasoning is apparent in Gendun Chopel's argument early on in the *Adornment* when he states in verse 4,

> All of our decisions about what is and is not are just decisions made in accordance with how it appears to our mind; they have no basis whatsoever. Therefore, when we ask, "Does it exist or not?" and the other person answers, "It exists," in fact, we are asking, "Does this appear to your mind to exist or not exist?"...

---

64. Dreyfus, *Reality*, 297.
65. Ibid., 285–97.
66. Ibid., 289–93. Cf. Lopez and chos phel, *Madman*, 128–30.
67. Lopez and chos phel, *Madman*, 130.
68. Ibid., 24.
69. Ibid., 245.

In the same way, everything that one asks about—better or worse, good or bad, beautiful or ugly—is in fact merely asked about for the sake of understanding how the other person thinks.[70]

In other words, Gendun Chopel's epistemology follows a Dharmakīrtian anti-realist position that rejects a correspondence theory of truth, "at least as understood in the metaphysical sense."[71] This means that although he believes reality to be "out there" and experienced by the individual,[72] following the Dharmakīrtian anti-realists, he also wants to distinguish between the direct perceptions of individuals engaging *particular* realities—which are "real"—and any notion of "universals" in reality, which are "conceptual and linguistic constructs" used to interpret and categorize our perceptions.[73] Gendun Chopel illustrates this position in verse 24 using the example of "the magical powers and abilities of the Buddha." According to his logic, the stories of the Buddha being able to fit whole worlds into single atoms shows no special ability of the Buddha at all. Rather it is simply our minds that are the magicians, for it is with our own minds that we construct the universal concepts of "atoms" and "worlds"—establishing the latter as extremely vast and the former as "the smallest material form." Therefore, it is only the reification of our own mental constructs that makes the ability to fit the latter into the former seemingly impossible.[74] Thus, when it actually comes to understanding "the empty nature of reality," Dreyfus concludes that in this "Dharmakīrtian" version[75] of anti-realism "concepts can be used only in a self-canceling way."[76]

---

70. Chos phel, "Adornment," 47–8, v. 4.

71. Dreyfus, *Reality*, 310.

72. Ibid., 297. Dreyfus explains that this is why he would still classify Dharmakīrti as a "foundationalist," because "he holds that both forms of knowledge must be grounded in reality," despite his anti-realism.

73. Dreyfus, *Reality*, 443.

74. Chos phel, "Adornment," 53–4, v. 24.

75. Dreyfus, *Reality*, 82. Dreyfus does recognize that this convenient label of a "Dharmakīrtian" system is also problematic for at least two reasons. First, because of the distinct commentarial interpretations of him that make one standard reading difficult, if not impossible to discern. More importantly, however, Dreyfus contends the greater difficulty in determining a "system" within Dharmakīrti's thought is the significant ambiguity within his own thought, especially regarding the nature of existence.

76. Dreyfus, *Reality*, 310 and 446. In these two passages Dreyfus elaborates on the notions of "realism" and "anti-realism" in Indian Buddhist philosophy. He defines realism as insisting that reality is intelligible to thought and language. Later he juxtaposes this view of realism with "anti-realism" by discussing anti-realism's rejection of "universals." In this way, "it attempts to explain the existence of commonality without presupposing the existence of anything other than the individual objects with which we are acquainted. This economical explanation appears quite satisfactory on the ontological level, for it does not require the intervention of entities that are not parts of common experience."

In fact, according to Dreyfus it is actually the later *realist* Tibetan readings of Dharmakīrti's thought, such as Tsongkhapa's, that represent a real "paradigm shift within the epistemology of this tradition." And although Dreyfus contends that these later realist readings of Dharmakīrti are not completely without justification (he argues in consort with Thupten Jinpa that such a reading is based in an attempt to resolve major epistemological and soteriological problems raised by anti-realism),[77] these reinterpretations of his thought nevertheless change the foundations of Dharmakīrti's epistemology and ontology by suggesting that objects of knowledge are not "bare particulars" but rather "elements of an articulated cognitive order that *partly* reflects reality."[78] This seems to be the fundamental problem within the standard Prāsaṅgika-Madhyamaka position from Gendun Chopel's perspective. Hence, instead of trying to reconcile Dharmakīrti's epistemology with Candrakīrti's Madhyamaka ontology by emphasizing Dharmakīrti's foundationalism and raising the ontological status of conventional reality (as he perceives Tsongkhapa to be doing), Gendun Chopel attempts to uphold Dharmakīrti's foundationalism while completely undercutting the ontological status of conventional reality and, subsequently, its status as "truth" through valid cognition. In other words, Gendun Chopel seeks to affirm Dharmakīrti's "foundational mode of epistemology," which insists that the "validity of a cognition" is determined by the ontological status of its object, by pushing to *lower* the status of conventional reality within the Madhyamaka ontology—and therefore applying a notion of anti-realism to all conventional "truth."

This manifests itself in Gendun Chopel's thought with his complete rejection of "conventional truths" as being valid cognitions, since they have no correspondence with ontological reality. In this way, Gendun Chopel seems to believe that he can maintain Dharmakīrti's perceived rejection of a correspondence theory of truth while at the same time clearly establishing the ontological status (and subsequent epistemological validity) of "ultimate truth" in contradistinction to the unestablished (and epistemologically invalid) nature of conventional truth claims. Moreover, in doing so, Gendun Chopel believes he actually better preserves the "middle way" approach between eternalism and nihilism that Madhyamaka philosophy purports to intend. One example of this is shown in verse 43 of the *Adornment*, when he discusses the invalidity of the cognition of a pot in light of its ontological status of being empty.

> Even if [the view nothing exists] were produced [by the refutation of the validity of all "pots and pillars"], because he knows explicitly that the pot is something to be seen and something to be touched, the thought is spontaneously produced that "this pot is something that appears to me. However, it does not exist at all in the way that it appears." Such a thought is the Madhyamaka view of the composite

---

77. Dreyfus, *Reality*, 378. Cf. Jinpa, 150.
78. Dreyfus, *Reality*, 377–8.

of appearance and emptiness, which understands that although things appear, they do not exist in the way that they appear. How is this nihilism?[79]

Again, what Gendun Chopel seems to be combating with this statement is Tsongkhapa's conviction that, as Thupten Jinpa describes it, "maintaining the reality of this world is crucial for spiritual liberation; denial of this dimension constitutes falling into nihilism, which according to Tsongkhapa, can only lead to spiritual downfall."[80] Tsongkhapa holds this position because, from his perspective, preserving the identical nature of the two truths ontologically is the only way possible to bridge the chasm of bifurcation and unify them in one's vision of ultimate reality. In other words, it is only by recognizing the apparent "valid existence" of conventional reality, which is defined as lacking "intrinsic existence," that one is exposed to that absence of "intrinsic existence" in all phenomena. Consequently, the "valid existence" of conventional realities actually embodies and exposes their own ontological emptiness so that "their emptiness is their conventional reality; their conventional reality is their emptiness."[81] In the section entitled *Special Insight* (*Lhag mthong chen mo*) of his monumental work *The Great Treatise on the Stages of the Path of Enlightenment*, Tsongkhapa uses the example of one's notion of the "self" to articulate this relationship. In one particular passage, Tsonkhapa argues that only when one accepts the apparent (conventional) validity of "a self in the sense of the object our simple, natural thought 'I am'" can the idea of "a self conceived in terms of an intrinsic nature that exists by means of intrinsic being" be negated by reasoning.[82] Another example of this, this time from his *Illumination of [Candrakīrti's] Thought* (*dBu ma dgongs pa rab gsal*), is his exposition of Candrakīrti's famous image of the "snake-rope" in the *Madhyamakāvatāra* (Tibetan, 'dBu-ma-la 'Jug-pa). Here using Candrakīrti's words and logic, Tsongkhapa argues that although both a directly perceived "pot" and the perception of "a snake imputed onto rope" can be considered similar to the extent that they are both "conceptual constructions," still, as Jan Westerhoff exegetes, "this does not mean that they are on a par in all respects." This is mainly because of the efficaciousness of validly establishing the conventional reality of a "pot" for smooth communication with others that can then later be deconstructed logical reasoning. On the other hand, the same does not hold for a "snake-rope." Because there is no common object determined by mutual observers (with one asserting it as a "snake" and the other a "rope"), then there is no effective way to push the elementary experience of either individual to break down its apparent existence into a lack of *intrinsic* existence. Thus in Westerhoff's words, Tsongkhapa

---

79. Chos phel, "Adornment," 58–9, v. 43.
80. Jinpa, 169.
81. The Cowherds, *Moonshadows: Conventional Truth in Buddhist Philosophy* (New York: Oxford University Press, 2011), 37.
82. Jinpa, 71. Cf. 159.

concludes, "It is more advantageous if we do not construe the rope as a snake and abstain, for example, from issuing unfounded snake warnings."[83]

In response to Tsongkhapa's two-step reasoning where the valid establishment of conventions leads to their negation and the realization of emptiness, Gendun Chopel simply posits that "If that is the meaning of the union of the two truths, *how sad*."[84] This is because, according to Gendun Chopel, if one attempts to unify the two truths by validating conventional knowledge, then once one has experienced the direct perception of emptiness the conventional objects would still have to appear to the mind of the observer (even if only in a recognized illusion-type state). In this way, any vision of emptiness within an individual's state of "meditative equipoise" would still inherently include a dualistic perception of reality (even if ultimately that dualism can be deconstructed by reasoning).[85] As such, he argues that Tsongkhapa's "union of the truths" is not a union of conventional and ultimate truth at all. Rather, it is the union of two *ultimates*—"the ultimate of fools" and "the ultimate of the wise."[86] What Gendun Chopel seems to be specifically rejecting here is Tsongkhapa's reading of Candrakīrti that even "the ultimate truth—emptiness—is an external negation, a mere elimination of any intrinsic existence in things and of any conceptualization."

If this is the case, Gendun Chopel perceives Tsongkhapa and Candrakīrti as overemphasizing the domain and authority of the *conventional* realm in the unification of the two truths. For according to this line of thinking, Gendun Chopel believes one is led to conclude that ultimately "conventional truth is the only truth that there is," because even "ultimate truth" is a conventional construct that is made valid by its ability to infer the absence of intrinsic existence in all things, even the idea of emptiness itself.[87] Gendun Chopel, on the other hand, wants to achieve the unification of the two truths through seemingly the complete *inverse* of this reasoning. Rather than positing the conventional realm (including the *concept* of emptiness) as all that is "merely existent," and which implicitly entails the lack of intrinsic existence ("ultimate truth"), Lopez explains that Gendun Chopel wants to preserve the validity of an "ultimate realm" by undercutting the validity of the conventional realm and any conceptually based truth claims. Hence through a thoroughgoing deconstructive skepticism of valid knowledge based on conventional constructs, Gendun Chopel believes that the individual can eventually perceive what he terms as "an inexpressible ultimate"—"an ultimate not in name only, or a nonconventional ultimate."[88] Thus, rather than unifying the two truths of the conventional and ultimate through validating a certain elementary status of the conventional that subsequently implies the ultimate, Gendun

---

83. Cowherds, 205–7.
84. Chos phel, "Adornment," 93, v. 168.
85. Ibid. Cf. Lopez and chos phel, *Madman*, 192; Cowherds, 50.
86. Chos phel, "Adornment," 98, v. 180. Cf. Lopez and chos phel, *Madman*, 198.
87. Cowherds, 25–6.
88. Chos phel, "Adornment," 77, v. 115.

Chopel wants to invalidate all conventional conceptuality with the belief that it will lead to a nonconceptual intuition of ultimate truth that instead implies the conventionality of all language.[89] For this reason, Gendun Chopel determines, "if one has conviction in the dharma, one must have conviction in the inconceivable state."[90] So as long as one tries to validate the inherent distinctions formed by conventional truth claims based in language (including even the concept of emptiness itself), conventional conceptuality will still persist in some way and, therefore, the ultimate nonconceptual realm of reality is never actually perceived.[91]

In the end then, it must be noted that even this debate shows how Gendun Chopel and Tsongkhapa still agree on at least one foundational point of Madyamaka philosophy: "the emptiness of emptiness." Both want to establish that the mental concept of "emptiness" does not match the actual ontological reality (or "truth") of emptiness. Similarly, both maintain that even the category of "ultimate truth" is "established in a way that is not ultimate. This means that it is *conventionally established*."[92] Where they differ, however, once again is in how each one arrives at this conclusion and why. Tsongkhapa wants to uphold the epistemological validity of conventional objects of knowledge, at least at an elementary level. Thupten Jinpa explains that this serves a primarily soteriological purpose. For Tsongkhapa, by validating *some* forms of conceptual knowledge,[93] "his emptiness can serve as the content of [an enlightened being's] liberating gnosis." This is because, in his system "there is no difference" between the nonconceptual awareness of enlightenment and the inferential cognition of emptiness through conventionally established truths such as "emptiness" itself. To put it a little more concisely, the negation of the intrinsic existence of the conventional *is* the cognition of the emptiness of intrinsic existence.[94]

For Gendun Chopel, on the other hand, such thinking entraps the mind in the realm of conceptual distinctions and conventionality, and thus prevents it from ever perceiving the truly nonconceptual state of ultimate reality through meditative equipoise. Consequently, rather than positing some conventional concepts as "valid knowledge" because they help expose the absence of intrinsic existence, Gendun Chopel wants to negate all forms of conventional knowledge in order to expose the individual to an *intuition* of the nonconceptual nature of ultimate reality. Thus, for Gendun Chopel, to be a Mādhyamika (a follower of Madhyamaka

---

89. Ibid., 70–1, v. 96. Cf. Lopez and chos phel, *Madman*, 162.

90. Chos phel, "Adornment," 81, v. 128.

91. Ibid., 84, v. 137.

92. Ibid., 84, v. 179. Cf. Lopez and chos phel, *Madman*, 179.

93. Jinpa, 65. Tsongkhapa argues that "knowledge, like other conventions of our lived world experience, cannot be defined outside the bounds of the framework of conventional validity." Hence for Tsongkhapa, citing Candrakīrti, worldly convention can be labeled as "valid knowledge" as long as it fulfills the basic condition of being unmistaken with respect to its object.

94. Jinpa, 61.

philosophy) literally means to have "no thesis," because in the end all language "has no real bearing on reality, let alone any intrinsic, objective referential ground."[95] In fact, Gendun Chopel claims that his position is nothing more than the exposition of Śāntideva's famous quote from the second stanza of the ninth chapter of *The Entrance to the Boddhisattva Deeds* (*Bodhicaryavatara*): "The ultimate is not within the mind's sphere; the mind is said to be conventional."[96] Hence for him the answer is not to differentiate valid from invalid conventional truths in order to properly use conventions to inferentially perceive the ultimate, indeed such differentiation *is the problem* that keeps the mind trapped in the conventions of saṃsāra. Instead, the goal must be to deconstruct all conceptual and linguistic propositions as invalid claims to truth, so that one is constantly confronted by the mental construction of perceived reality and hence can gain an indirect awareness of the nonaffirming negative that is the ultimate truth.

III. Perspectivalism Applied to Communal Knowledge

A. Schillebeeckx: Individually Fallible Knowledge, Collective Truth

In a way somewhat similar to the difficulties of decoding a "formal epistemology" within Schillebeeckx's thought as we discussed in the last section, when it comes to formulating an explicit "ecclesiology" one is confronted with many of the same challenges. This is particularly true in the sense that Schillebeeckx rarely speaks theologically about the church as a dogmatic category apart from its relation to many other elements of his theological reflections—namely its dialectical relationships with Jesus and the contemporary world. Thus Thompson elucidates that especially in his later period following Vatican II, Schillebeeckx intentionally never constructs "a systematic doctrine of the Church."[97] Nonetheless, Thompson also argues there are still some prominent "suggestive directions" that Schillebeeckx lays out for understanding the nature and role of the church in experience and formulation of truth for the individual. Specifically for Schillebeeckx, to discuss the nature, authority, and relationship of the church to the individual believer in the formation and formulation of personal faith is to discuss one arm of the dialectical and non-antithetical "structure of mediation" for the individual to encounter the truth of God's reality within history, "revelation-in-reality."[98]

Hence throughout his thought, even the church's dogmatic professions of faith never stand as the pristine and transhistorical expressions of the meaning or truth of the reality of God within existence in which one is supposed to conform all other interpretations of experience. Rather the formulation of church dogma is

---

95. Ibid., 28. For Gendun Chopel to have "no-thesis" really means not to believe what one says in one's own heart.
96. Chos phel, "Adornment," 77, v. 116. Cf. Lopez and chos phel, *Madman*, 170.
97. Thompson, 84.
98. Thompson, 73–4.

only one aspect of the historical, limited, and contextual formulation of the truth of reality that emerges from the interaction between an individual's encounter of that reality within one's own personal experience of history, within the message of Jesus's proclamation of truth within his own experience of history, and also within the collaborative interpretations of experiences by the community of believers over time.[99] Thus one can argue that the two-fold structure and basic role of Church tradition within Schillebeeckx's thought, which he lays out early on in his career, remains operative over its entire development. As he explains in his article entitled "What Is Theology?" (originally published in 1958), Church tradition serves two important and necessary roles in the formation of the believer's faith knowledge: first, it helps legitimize and give a basis to the "entire objective, true, and speculative value" of the use of human concepts and language as a credible "objective projection"[100] to the nonconceptual "*mystērion*" of revelation-in-reality. Second, and more importantly, it also serves as a constant reminder that any doctrine or confession of faith both mediates and yet is also always transcended by the actual nonconceptual object of theological reflection.[101] Therefore, even as Schillebeeckx's theories of the nature of knowledge and truth evolve over time, one can also see how Schillebeeckx consistently holds that the role and authority of the church remain both as an *ecclesia docens* (a teaching church) as well as "first and foremost an *ecclesia discens*" (a learning church) with regard to "*sensus plenior*" (fuller meaning) of the nonconceptual nature of reality.[102]

This dialectical relationship of epistemological learning notwithstanding, the question must still be asked as to the basis of how the church maintains *any* authority concerning claims to knowledge over the individual experiential interpretations of reality by believers themselves, particularly if church doctrines are believed to be just as limited and fallible as individual human interpretations. In some of his earliest writings concerning the church, Schillebeeckx answers this question with a concept of sacramentality. In other words, the church's teaching authority regarding belief and practice stems from its connection to the quintessential revelatory event of Jesus of Nazareth.[103] The church's doctrines and practice are linked to this original event through the apostolic testimony and teachings of it,[104]

---

99. Schillebeeckx, *Revelation and Theology*, vol. I, 130–1. Cf. Schillebeeckx, *Understanding of Faith*, 47–9; *Christ*, 808.

100. Schillebeeckx, *Revelation and Theology*, vol. I, 124–5 (see n. 72). Here Schillebeeckx explains that by his use of the word "objective" he intentionally wants to "completely dissociate [himself] from the 'intellectual dynamism' of Maréchal."

101. Schillebeeckx, *Revelation and Theology*, vol. I, 125–30. See Fatula, 419, for an excellent and concise summary of this idea. Cf. Schillebeeckx, *Revelation and Theology*, vol. II, 169–70.

102. Schillebeeckx, *Revelation and Theology*, vol. I, 17–18.

103. Schillebeeckx, *Sacrament*, 15. Here he defines Jesus as the "primordial sacrament" of God.

104. Schillebeeckx, *Revelation and Theology*, vol. I, 25–32.

and it is by this apostolic succession of authoritative interpretation Schillebeeckx contends that the church continually renews and transmits the truth of reality from within Christ's salvific revelation through the practice of the sacraments. Hence in one of his most recognized works from that early period, *Christ the Sacrament of the Encounter with God*, he argues that the power and authority of the church rest in its dissemination of the sacraments not as simply objects or practices ("things") but as "encounters of men on earth with the glorified man Jesus by way of a visible form."[105] Thus elsewhere he concludes,

> Revelation in word and deed is not handed down within the church in a mechanical way, like a dead thing passed on from hand to hand. It is, on the contrary, essentially linked with its living subject, the church, consisting of the living people of God headed by ecclesiastical office, both of which are under the guidance of the Spirit of the heavenly Lord. The entire church is subject to tradition—the church which prays and lives in faith, hope, and love, the church which celebrates the liturgical mysteries, the church which is apostolically effective in its office and in its people and the church which reflects on its faith.[106]

Therefore during this early period, and especially leading up to and immediately following Vatican II, Schillebeeckx chose to refer to the church as the "sacrament of the world" in that it mediates explicit encounters with the salvific truth of God ("revelation-in-reality") through the liturgical events of the sacraments. Or as Thompson precisely summarizes,

> The dialectic of revelation in reality and revelation in word matches the sacramental dialectic, so to speak; the sacraments are visible and verbal signs through which the believer encounters in the present the saving reality of God. In both cases the word brings the reality of salvation to its fullest possible expression, but in both cases this word, however God-directed, authentic, and necessary, still falls short of capturing conceptually and linguistically the working of God in human history. Salvation as experienced by the believer retains a certain *priority over the expression* of this experience in the language of revelation.[107]

In this way, Schillebeeckx can insist that the church is authoritative in its understanding of truth, because it serves as the conduit by which believers encounter "a positive intellectual content that *directs* us *objectively* towards God's own mode of being." Nonetheless, since both the church's sacramental events (revelation-in-reality) and doctrines (revelation-in-word) simply serve as mediations of individuals' *encounters*, still the "noetic value of our knowledge of

---

105. Schillebeeckx, *Sacrament*, 44.
106. Schillebeeckx, *Revelation and Theology*, vol. I, 19.
107. Thompson, 53. Emphasis added.

God is therefore situated in a projective act"—although one that is at the same time given "a precise *direction*" in which "we reach out for God" by its relationship to the ultimate reality it discloses. Consequently, Schillebeeckx can also preserve his conviction that all "so called 'concepts of God' really define an intelligible content that is, however, *open to the mystery*."[108] So in this way he is able to maintain his desired dialectical tension between the explicit limits and implicit value of finitude that surfaces in his understanding of creation.[109] This is because the role and authority of the church can rest within the contingencies of historical context and finitude[110] by being the sole mediator of one's full encounter with the totality of reality through the sacramental participation in the Christ event.[111]

Maintaining this tension allows for Schillebeeckx to uphold that the church's authority of truth is "infallible" because the source of its truth claims is grounded in the direct encounter with God that it provides in the lives of believers. And yet by prioritizing the truth of one's experiential encounter with revelation-in-reality through the event of the sacraments over any expression of doctrinal revelation-in-word, he also is able to distinguish between dogma as the infallible *expressions* of reality and their conceptual content that is limited by human language and ideas.[112] Thus, for Schillebeeckx, the teachings of the church can at the same time be both *infallibly true* and also *conceptually inadequate*, requiring "a true development of doctrine" that continually serves to construct and clarify the doctrinal concepts that express the ultimately nonconceptual truth of God.[113] At this point then, Schillebeeckx subsequently understands the role and purpose of theologians as being vitally important while also very limited. Theology is inherently human and, therefore, always limited and never itself "revelation." As such, the main function of theology is to make the reality of revelation more "*credibile prout intelligibile*" ("credible as intelligible") within the lives of believers,[114] and yet it is much less—if at all—about challenging the authority of church teachings (whether in dogma or doctrine).[115]

---

108. Schillebeeckx, *Revelation and Theology*, vol. II, 175. Emphases added.

109. Schillebeeckx, *Church*, 78; Cf. Schillebeeckx, *Revelation and Theology*, vol. II, 161–2.

110. Schillebeeckx, *Sacrament*, 15, 40–5, 47–8. In these passages Schillebeeckx pronounces Jesus as the "primordial sacrament" of God, while also developing how after Christ's death God did not abandon the human structure of bodiliness as the means of encounter between humans and Godself. In this way, the church sacraments function as effective signs of grace, because the Church is the primordial sacrament of Christ himself in the world.

111. Ibid., 47–54.

112. Schillebeeckx, *Revelation and Theology*, vol. I, 57–83.

113. Ibid., 78–83.

114. Ibid., 101.

115. Ibid., 162. At this point Schillebeeckx still maintains the real yet *limited* authority of theology in challenging the church; Cf. 82–3.

However, starting in the later phases of his theology, in the late 1960s shortly following Vatican II, Schillebeeckx began to become much more skeptical about the inherent priority of authority that he had previously recognized in the institutional hierarchy of the church. As a result, he began to view dogmas and doctrines less as the assurance and conduit of the nonconceptual truth of reality encountered by believers, but rather as the product of the historical process of translation of the collective encounters with reality by individual believers in faith. Although we will discuss the role of hermeneutics and historical consciousness in his theological development with more detail in the next chapter, it is significant to note that this confrontation with the awareness of the historical limitations and weaknesses of the church led him to begin to understand the role of the theologian within the church to be not only one of preservation and clarification of the "deposit of faith" contacted by the church teachings but also one of participation in the "continual process of renewal and purification" of its teachings and practices toward the possibilities of the future.[116]

> Every dogma must have an orientation towards the future and be open to the sphere of the future. This has consequences for our conception of dogma itself, since truth then becomes, for us now, something whose fullness belongs to the future; to the extent that its content is already realized, it discloses itself essentially as a *promise*. The present, itself a sphere of interpretation of the past, must be caught up in a sphere of promise, or the past will not be seen clearly for what it is. What is ultimately and primarily in question here is conceiving both the present and past as open-ended orientated towards a new reality—what is still come. Dogma thus becomes the proclamation of the historical realization of God's promise, which of its very nature implies an openness to the future and to new historical realizations.[117]

Hence whereas he had previously argued that the communal authority of the church rested in a "theology of the sacrament as encounter," Thompson explains that in his later theology Schillebeeckx places a "greater emphasis on the autonomy and concrete historicity of human beings" and, as a result, his understanding of the direct activity of God in the church is far less discernible—whether in its teachings, practices, or the sacraments.[118] Accordingly, his earlier idea of the "salvific knowledge of God" as experienced through sacramental encounter (revelation-in-reality) begins to yield itself to a belief in the cooperative presence of God in the historical overcoming of evil and suffering by humanity.[119] Therefore, by the end of his theological career Schillebeeckx explicitly challenges the understanding

---

116. Edward Schillebeeckx, *The Mission of the Church* (New York: Seabury Press, 1973), 12; Cf. Thompson, 108, for a further helpful discussion of this topic.
117. Schillebeeckx, *God the Future*, 36. Emphasis original.
118. Thompson, 92.
119. Ibid.

of the institutional church as possessing a definitively "formal authority," instead highlighting how it in fact has often become ineffective in conveying truth because it "obscures its own truth, especially the liberating freedom of Jesus Christ, through the form of its authoritarian and hierarchical mediation."[120]

Despite this major adjustment in his attitude toward the church hierarchy and its authority, it is still important to notice some essential foundations that continue to show through his entire theological corpus: namely, the intrinsic merit of finitude as the *locus* of any encounter with reality; the centrality of Jesus's life, ministry, and message in interpreting one's experience of reality; the necessary—yet always inadequate—role of linguistic and conceptual expression of ultimately nonconceptual knowledge; and most importantly the dialectical nature of the church's authority as a tradition and as a contemporary community. Although the way in which they are conceived and applied may vary significantly from his earliest writings, by examining these most basic principles one can see how Schillebeeckx's philosophically perspectival orientation persists in shaping his understanding of the limits of the authority of religious communities throughout his career and theological development.

The first major principle that persists from his early training in philosophy and theology is his conviction that the limitations of contingency and finitude, particularly as they pertain to knowledge, are not flaws resulting from some primordial sin but instead the characteristic that makes all creation essentially "good," because it is our awareness of our contingency that keeps us within the presence of the "Wholly Other."[121] Or as Schillebeeckx explains it, "for the believer, non-divine finitude is precisely the place where the infinite and the finite come most closely into contact. From this close contact of the secular and the transcendent, the infinite and the finite, there arises, as mystics say, the spark of the soul; there all religion takes fire."[122] Similarly, the historicity and contingency of humans, as creatures of God's creation, are not things that need to be transcended but rather are elements of existence to be enriched and cultivated through their encounters with ultimate truth in the historical experiences of reality. Hence, Schillebeeckx insists, "salvation from God never consists in the fact that God will save us *from* finitude and *from* all that it involves ... [Rather] enjoying and delighting in the secular things of this world, the humanity of man, is enjoying and delighting in what is divine in God."[123]

Kennedy points out that Schillebeeckx's affirmation of the goodness of finitude did not just remain there; however, beginning in the second half of the 1960s Schillebeeckx "became convinced that reality is characterized by an *illimitable*

---

120. Schillebeeckx, *Church*, 214–15. Cf. Schillebeeckx and Strazzari, *Happy*, 50–1.

121. Schillebeeckx, *God among Us*, 93.

122. Schillebeeckx, *Church*, 234. Here Schillebeeckx uses the idea of "limit situations" in order to discuss how the breakdown of our conceptual language and ideas is precisely the place where the individual can become acutely aware of the nonconceptual infinite.

123. Schillebeeckx, *Interim Report*, 115.

pluralism." This means that reality is so complex that it cannot be described or understood by any single human. This is because reality is not static, but an open-ended and dynamic process.[124] Thus, Schillebeeckx's conviction about the essential and inescapable finitude and fallibility of all human knowledge and experience became even *more* central to his thought and formed the basis of his eventual conclusion that it is the universal "pre-linguistic" experience of "being utterly constrained by finitude" that is itself the encounter of the reality of God ("truth") and the basis of all human knowledge and action (both of believers and non-believers).[125] Therefore, Schillebeeckx contends that one can never separate God's action of salvation in history from human actions of liberation and social justice, for the *immanence* of God is found precisely in the historical experiences of human beings that expose and accentuate their limitations and mortality.[126] As we will discuss later, this is why Schillebeeckx utilizes the concept of the *humanum* as the hope for the constant potentiality of a better existence for humanity—over against the evil and suffering of the world—as the place where individuals come into closest—albeit still partial—contact with the ultimate truth of reality.[127] Hence, at this point, Schillebeeckx begins to shift from speaking of the "object of knowledge" (or "the truth of reality," namely God) in the abstract terms of the "intuitive apprehension" of the universal within the particular, to using the language of the experience of truth not as the existential encounter of reality but as the experience of *anticipation* and *hope* found within the limitless potentialities of human action within the particularities of history.[128] Thus, the active "teaching" role of the church to the world and believers becomes less associated with passing down of dogmas and doctrines and more with functioning as a living sign of a "heavenly humanism," in which the church through the liberative message of Jesus and its own liberative efforts in the world offers humanity an existence that is situated within the confines of history and yet is able to hope and anticipate a potential reality beyond the present condition.[129]

Second, as a result of his emphasis on God's being as encountered and involved in the hopeful and liberative praxis of humanity, Schillebeeckx is also naturally able to maintain the centrality of the ministry and message of Jesus as central to the church's epistemological authority in the world. As Schillebeeckx himself elaborates at one point,

---

124. Kennedy, *Schillebeeckx*, 35.
125. For probably Schillebeeckx's most focused discussion of religious pluralism see Marc H. Ellis and Otto Maduro, *Expanding the View: Gustavo Gutiérrez and the Future of Liberation Theology* (Maryknoll, NY: Orbis Books, 1990), 182–6.
126. Schillebeeckx, *Church*, 78, 8.
127. Edward Schillebeeckx, *The Church with a Human Face: A New and Expanded Theology of Ministry* (New York: Crossroad, 1985), 34–9.
128. Schillebeeckx, *Church*, 6.
129. Schillebeeckx, *World and Church*, 10–15.

> In other words, the church is a movement of eschatological liberation with the aim of bringing together all men and women in a single unity, in a single peace, peace among them, peace among the peoples, peace with the environment. Ecclesiology therefore derives from the eschatological message of Jesus.[130]

In this way, Schillebeeckx upholds his previous assertion that Jesus might still be considered the "condensation of all creation" in its utterly historical finitude, as long as his embodiment of the truth of all reality is viewed as existing in only one of many possible contextual and limited forms. Hence, Jesus's message and actions within the sociohistorical context of ancient Palestine "proportionally display"[131] the message and service of the church most present to the world in order to reinterpret and reactualize the hope of Jesus's praxis within the contemporary context.[132]

Therefore, Thompson concludes, the figure of Jesus still serves as "the source, norm, and guiding presence" of the church's interactions with the world.[133] And as such, Schillebeeckx upholds not only that the authority of the church in conveying the truth of reality fundamentally rests in its origin as the outcome of the Jesus's authoritative life story but also in its ability to rearticulate and translate that story into the various different sociohistorical contexts of the present world. Thus ecclesiology is fundamentally dependent on Christology because of the church's role to realize and evoke the hope of Jesus's message for the liberative renewal of all humanity from suffering—and subsequently mediate encounters with the ultimate truth of reality—within the diverse contexts of history.[134] It is the church's task to act in praxis according to what he terms the "*sequela Jesu*" (following of Jesus) in order to preserve the human "*anamnesis*" (remembrance) within every period and context of history. As we will see shortly, however, it is also the memory preserved through praxis that must allow the church to be criticized and even corrected by both believers as well as the world at large if and when it strays from embodying the spirit of his message and praxis.[135] This perception also then allows Schillebeeckx to sustain his conviction that the church's authority rests in its function as a "sacrament of dialogue," as both a "teaching church" (*ecclesia docens*) and at the same time a "learning church" (*ecclesia discens*), in open communication with the experiences of the world.[136]

Nevertheless, third, within this relationship of dialogue with the world Schillebeeckx still does want to protect the church's role and authority as a "teaching church" as part of its dialectical authority over interpretations of the truth of

---

130. Schillebeeckx, *Jesus*, 47–8.
131. Schillebeeckx, *Understanding of Faith*, 55–72.
132. Schillebeeckx, *Jesus*, 56–7; Schillebeeckx, *Anno 1983*, 14–15.
133. Thompson, 73.
134. Schillebeeckx, *Understanding of Faith*, 60–1.
135. Ibid., 226–8.
136. Schillebeeckx, *God the Future*, 123.

reality. He attempts to do this by maintaining the church's vital role of opening up the tradition to "a horizon of possible experience also for us now."[137] This horizon of "interpretive experience" provided by the tradition however cannot in itself ensure an "authentic" experience or knowledge of truth by faith. Rather, the unavoidable conditions of human historicity still make a complete epistemological comprehension of reality, even through faith, ultimately impossible.[138] Instead of positing "an unchangeable formula" of belief (or "even a homogenous one") the tradition and office of the church is to provide a "referential framework"[139] through which believers "structure" their lives and praxis according to the "*analogia fidei*" (analogy of faith) between Jesus's original message and the present context. Thus in numerous places Schillebeeckx redefines the notion of "authority" in the tradition of the church as simply its limited yet necessary ability to elicit the consciously critical and liberatively productive experiences of humanity through its prior traditions of experiences emerging out of Jesus's message.[140] Nonetheless, this "apostolic tradition" of the church is not necessarily bound exclusively to the church as an institution or teaching office, but also includes the present communities of believers themselves and their localized ministries and praxis.[141]

In fact, Schillebeeckx wants to take the perspectival limits on the church's linguistic expressions of the nonconceptual truth of reality one step further by insisting that there is *no* static or constant "deposit" of faith to be encountered and conceptualized. Instead the exact object of knowledge, "the content of salvation," cannot be defined at all, rather it can only be engaged *in*directly through the experience of hope that the intuitive sense of the *humanum* brings forth in individuals that there is possibility of a fuller humanity still yet to come.[142] Or as Schillebeeckx summarizes it himself,

> The object of Christian faith is, of course, already realized in Christ, but it is only realised in him as our promise and our future. But the future cannot be theoretically interpreted, *it must be done*. The *humanum* which is sought and which is proclaimed and promised to us in Christ is not an object of purely contemplative expectation, but also a historical form which is already growing in the world: at least this is what we have to do, in the perspective of eschatological hope. Christianity is not simply a hermeneutic undertaking, not simply an illumination of existence, but also a renewal of existence, in which 'existence' concerns man as an individual person and in his social being.[143]

---

137. Schillebeeckx, *Anno 1983*, 5.
138. Schillebeeckx, *Understanding of Faith*, 58.
139. Ibid., 62.
140. Schillebeeckx, *Christ*, 29, 36–40, 817–21.
141. Thompson, 114.
142. Schillebeeckx, *Christ*, 790.
143. Schillbeeckx, *Understanding of Faith*, 66.

Hence the community's authority as a "teaching church" is to assist in formulating a sense of a "communal unity of faith" (a *sensus fidelium*) through a consciously collective understanding of "orthopraxis" in the present circumstances based on the broader witness of the traditional actions of the church as a whole.[144] By asserting this contention, Schillebeeckx argues that he is simply extending the church's traditional measurement of orthodoxy of "*lex orandi, lex credendi*" in which the church's actions and practices dictate their beliefs about the nature of God in relation to creation.[145] This principle notwithstanding, however, Schillebeeckx also recognizes that because the institution of the church is social as well as spiritual, it can and often does act as the result of self-interest and ideological distortion, and thus all its actions cannot be trusted as self-authenticating and must be liable to criticism from within and without.[146] For this reason, it is the obligation of believers (particularly theologians) and non-believers alike to constantly attempt to expose the ideologically laden language and actions of the church in order to reauthenticate the correspondence of its actions to the hope of the future that Jesus professed continuously.[147]

In line with this recognition of the need of theological and sociological critique of the church is the final and most important principle of Schillebeeckx's understanding of the ecclesiastical authority of the church regarding knowledge, namely the importance of dialogue and correction between the institution and its members. From very early on in Schillebeeckx's thought he acknowledged and discussed the necessary balance between the "hierarchical church" and the "lay apostolate" in the formulations of the truths of faith.[148] Following the Vatican II's teaching of *Lumen Gentium*, Thompson avers that Schillebeeckx emphasizes an even greater "basic commonality of membership which precedes any hierarchical distinction or any office" and argues for an even closer commonality between the laity and clergy.[149] This is at least partially because, whereas earlier in his theological understanding of Thomas he once tended to consider sin as an all pervasive *atmosphere* in the world which distorted human experiences and interpretations of reality,[150] later on in his theology[151] he became acutely aware of the church's simultaneous existence as an earthly and sociological reality comprised of sinful people whose actions and teachings often emerge out of self-interest and the

---

144. Schillebeeckx, *Ministry*, 101.
145. Schillebeeckx, *Understanding of Faith*, 72.
146. Ibid., 137–8. Cf. Schillebeeckx, *For the Sake of the Gospel*, 136–9.
147. Schillebeeckx, *Anno 1983*, 17.
148. Schillebeeckx, *Sacrament*, 48–9, 168–9.
149. Thompson, 112. Cf. Schillebeeckx, *Church*, 216. Here Schillebeeckx argues for a church with "no real *hierarchy.*"
150. Borgman, 60 (see n. 140).
151. This would be mostly the result of his interactions with more historically conscious theologians such as Chenu and Congar (who we will discuss more in the next chapter) and the critical theorists of the Frankfurt school (who we will discuss in Chapter 5).

oppressive distortions of philosophical ideologies.¹⁵² As result, Schillebeeckx concludes that the role of the church in the authoritative formation of knowledge is a dialectical one between the teaching offices of the institution and the "grassroots" interpretations and proclamations of local communities.¹⁵³

Under the guidance of the Holy Spirit, the entire community—clergy, theologians, and lay believers—necessarily participate in a collaborative discernment between all the participants of the community. Schillebeeckx never denies the legitimate need for the institutional hierarchy of the church—particularly in regard to the sacramental importance of the liturgy¹⁵⁴—rather he simply wants to ground its authority within the dialectical process of shaping while being shaped by the beliefs and convictions of believers on the ground.¹⁵⁵

> On the one hand, that tradition of faith is a religious tradition of meaning *with transformative, renewing and liberating, and finally saving power.* The meaning-disclosing tradition of faith is at the same time a summons to a well-defined, practical way of life. However the specific-characteristic of what is named 'liberation' can also be filled in within the different great traditions, those traditions promise through their own disclosure of meaning and salvation and liberation to human beings: *truth* concerning life-as-human-beings. Ultimately it is a matter of the flowing together of two stories: the story of the evangelical tradition of faith and our personal and communal story of life.¹⁵⁶

This process of the constant regulative exchange back and forth between the formal institution and the grassroots voices of its participants serves to produce a situation where no particular experience of human liberation is ever reified as a universal ideology applicable to all, but rather must be articulated, negotiated, and *re*negotiated throughout the historical life of the church. In fact, in order to further protect this regulative balance, Schillebeeckx even contends that the institutional structure of the church should be a purely democratically elected system of the local parishes.¹⁵⁷ Moreover, in some of his latest works, Schillebeeckx began

152. Schillebeeckx, *World and Church*, 151; Schillebeeckx, *Sacrament*, 203–5.
153. Schillebeeckx, *Church*, 216.
154. Schillebeeckx, *Christ*, 836:

> As long as there is still a real history of suffering among us, we cannot do without the sacramental liturgy: to abolish it or neglect it would be to stifle the firm hope in universal peace and general reconciliation. For as long as salvation and peace are still not actual realities, hope for them must be attested and above all nourished and kept alive, and this is only possible in anticipatory symbols.

155. Thompson, 112.
156. Schillebeeckx, *Anno 1983*, 7.
157. See Schillebeeckx, *Church*, "Towards democratic rule of the Church as a community of God" (Chapter Four), 187–228. Cf. Schillebeeckx, *Understanding of Faith*, 71, for his proposed structure and function of critical communities.

calling for the establishment of "Critical Communities"[158] within local churches as formal regulative bodies to the centralized institutional church so as to evoke as much critical dialogue between the institution and laity as possible.[159] Therefore, through balancing the sacramental activity and praxis of the institutional church, the individual interpretations and proclamations of theologians simultaneously engaged with the tradition and contemporary society, and the collective voice and effective acceptance of the laity, Schillebeeckx hopes to both mitigate the sinful tendencies that distort claims to knowledge through ideological self-interest by all humans and the institutions run by them as well as assist individuals in their encounters with the truth of the world.[160]

B. Gendun Chopel: The Impossibility of Comprehending Valid Knowledge for Unenlightened Beings

By most accounts, shortly before his imprisonment by the Tibetan government in 1946,[161] Gendun Chopel dictated a series of teachings intended to "leave a contribution," and hence explicitly give meaning to his life, by showing "to Tibet an [essential] characteristic of both *Madhyamaka* [and] *Pramāṇa*."[162] A few years later immediately following his death, these dictations were compiled and published under the title *Eloquent Explanation That Combines the Profound Key Points of the Middle Way into Their Essence, An Adornment for Nagarjuna's Thought* (*Dbu ma'i zab gnad snyingpor dril ba'i legs bshad klu sgrub dgongs rgyan*).[163] As discussed earlier, unlike Schillebeeckx who never formally laid out a systematic explanation or defense of his epistemology, and as both the above quote and the title of this piece clearly suggest, Gendun Chopel's single most significant textual contribution to his tradition was actually a treatise of an epistemological critique as well as defense of Madhyamaka philosophy. In general, this work comes across much more as a series of lectures and often-disjointed teachings that at times meander off into personal gripes and tangential quips than a tightly structured systematic treatise. However, at the same time, over the course of the entire piece Gendun Chopel manages to present a generally coherent articulation of his own theory of the "two truths" and an impactful argument for a reinterpretation of the Geluk understanding of the (im)possibility of knowledge, particularly from the perspective of unenlightened beings. And although at times its tone can

---

158. Portier, "Critical Theorist," 357 n. 29.

159. Schillebeeckx, *Ministry*, 1–3; Schillebeeckx, *Human Face*, 1–12 (esp. 10); Schillebeeckx, *Church*, xv.

160. Schillebeeckx, *Understanding of Faith*, 70.

161. Lopez, *Science*, 107.

162. Mengele, 65–6. It should be noted that there is a slight debate over exactly when the text was dictated, with Stoddard (238) and Lopez (3) giving their own slightly varying accounts as well.

163. Lopez and chos phel, *Madman*, 121.

vacillate between the extremes of profound piety[164] and "biting satire," Lopez reminds the reader that in the end its overall content is still a "highly traditional" attempt to preserve religious meaning within the Tibetan Buddhist tradition.[165] In this way, Lopez astutely interprets Gendun Chopel's approach to the Geluk scholastic tradition as "not simply one of radical skepticism. Rather, it is a *pious skepticism* that seeks, however vaguely, to define a path to enlightenment [for the individual]."[166]

Moreover, as Lopez also asserts, considering the religious and philosophical tradition within which Gendun Chopel existed, "it is highly doubtful that he would have regarded the *Adornment* as in any way innovative, in any way modern." Rather, as we will see somewhat in this current section and certainly in more depth in the next chapter, Gendun Chopel would probably deem the *Adornment* as an age-old argument just formulated in a necessarily new idiom, or what he would describe as an "assertion for others."[167] And so, in the most straightforward sense the *Adornment* is far from Gendun Chopel's attempt to separate himself once and for all from the Tibetan Buddhist (specifically Geluk) tradition, but is in fact his own attempt to recapture the meaning of Nāgārjuna's traditional Madhyamaka through putting forth his own interpretation of it. Yet, as Lopez reminds us, when it comes to Gendun Chopel's self-positioning within the tradition there is nonetheless still a controversial or "highly charged" element to his presentation even within the very title of the piece. This is because his claim simply to be imparting an "adornment to Nāgārjuna's thought" actually says more to the Tibetan reader than the English translation seems to imply. In Tibetan, Lopez expounds, the term "thought" (*dgongspa*) actually more closely reflects the idea of "intention" rather than what most English speakers mean when they discuss "the life and thought" of a famous philosopher.[168] Thus in that brief clause Gendun Chopel seems to be revealing much of his mentality about his own relationship with the tradition. In some ways he is clearly asserting that he *knows* and is explicating what was Nāgārjuna's *true intention* within Madhyamaka all along, and in others he is also claiming "to beautify and highlight the body of Nāgārjuna's mind" by constructing an "adornment" to what Nāgārjuna actually said.[169]

The text's attempt at the delicate balance between traditional piety and substantive critique might be no more evident than in the first few poetic verses of the entire piece. Traditionally these initial lines function as an opportunity for the

---

164. Chos phel, "Adornment," 115, v. 247. Lopez (*Madman*, 219) explains that Gendun Chopel's rhetoric in this final verse of the text, particularly the appeal to Mañjusrī for protection which was a standard epithet of Tsongkhapa, "suggest that [Gendun Chopel] did not regard the *Adornment* as an anti-[Geluk] tract, as so many would see it."
165. Lopez and chos phel, *Madman*, 252.
166. Ibid., 246.
167. Ibid., 245.
168. Ibid., 123-4.
169. Ibid., 124.

author to claim his devotion to his teachers, the community, and also the Buddha himself, almost assuring the reader of the author's sincere devotion to the dharma and its teaching by the tradition before continuing with the exposition. Gendun Chopel, on the other hand, begins with the well-known story of Devadatta's assassination attempt of Śākyamuni Buddha in order to highlight and critique what he perceives as the inadequate response of the Buddha.

> To the sharp weapons of the demons, you offered delicate flowers in return. When the enraged Devadatta pushed down a boulder [to kill you], you practiced silence. Son of the Śākyas, incapable of casting even an angry glance at your enemy, what intelligent person would honor you as a friend for protection from the great enemy, fearful saṃsāra?[170]

Moreover, in the following two stanzas he proceeds to mock "the assembled philosophers" whose devotion to the Buddha leads them to naïvely declare him "the lord of the dharma, the supreme lion of speakers" by baiting them to observe how "the sweet honey of the *true* transmission" can emerge from his own "heart of meager knowledge." Similarly, his omissions of praise for his own teacher and any lineage of transmission for his wisdom are significant. Instead he simply asserts his own interrogative reflection on his uncertainty of whether his glorious wisdom is "innate or acquired." These examples seem to further express the tenuous relationship he has toward the tradition that is a repeated motif throughout the text. Indeed, it illustrates his desire to place himself firmly within the tradition, while at the same time completely disassociating himself from any specific lineage or tradition of teaching deemed authoritative by it.

This paradoxical balance in Gendun Chopel's thought between his desire to be recognized as firmly established within the tradition while at the same time harshly critiquing the formal lineages of authority within the tradition is probably nowhere more thoroughly embodied than in his writings and actions during his travels in India. During this time of his self-described "exile" in India, Gendun Chopel became increasingly severe in his criticisms of the monastic institution and its use of tradition while at the same becoming more and more "obsessed with his legacy" in the eyes of his fellow Tibetans out of a fear that any alleged heterodoxy would illegitimate his voice among his "fellow countrymen."[171] In this regard, Ruegg observes, Gendun Chopel would all too often seem to be "his own worst enemy," as he took an ostensibly insatiable delight "in disconcerting and shocking those round him by his non-conformist behaviour and his paradoxical or radical pronouncements." As a result, "during his lifetime Tibetan opinion appears to have been divided about [him]."[172] In fact, even today many prominent Tibetan scholastics and leaders have written and upheld serious formal critiques

---

170. Chos phel, "Adornment," 47, v. 1.
171. Lopez, *Science*, 126.
172. Ruegg, 308.

of Gendun Chopel, and specifically the *Adornment*.¹⁷³ Yet in the end, Ruegg continues, his desire to protect a vaunted legacy within the Tibetan community has been almost fully realized, as in the last few decades many of his disciples have been rather successful in rehabilitating his memory and defending his often-radical ideas and behavior as displaying the ultimate wisdom of an enlightened being. Consequently, Gendun Chopel has achieved the status of "a kind of hero and even a cult-figure" among contemporary Tibetans who view him as a symbol of the potentiality for progressive reinvigoration to the tradition over against an obstinate traditionalism within the institutions.

His legacy within the tradition and the minds of contemporary Tibetans notwithstanding, the question still remains as to *how* his supposed perspectivalism caused, aided, and/or enforced his particular attitude and mistrust of the tradition. Once again this question immediately leads us back to his interpretation of Dharmakīrti's system as a fundamentally anti-realist assessment of conventionality and knowledge in multiple ways. First, if Gendun Chopel chooses to reject the validity of conceptual universals based on this Dharmakīrtian anti-realism, then there might be no better example of linguistic conceptualization projected out as universals than doctrinal affirmations. It is for this reason that Gendun Chopel defines "belief" as an ignorant "force of habit" that involuntarily compels the individual to engage conventional objects,¹⁷⁴ and perhaps why he would not even discuss the meaning of "faith"—instead simply concluding that "faith" must be a feeling derived out of a personal sense of conceptual affinity.¹⁷⁵ Instead as an anti-realist, what Gendun Chopel seems to prioritize is direct personal experience, or "direct perception."

According to this anti-realist line of thinking, direct perception is the engagement with reality that is "epistemologically and psychologically free from concepts," however once one tries to express or even personally conceptualize that contact with bare reality it no longer becomes knowledge from perception but rather moves to the distinctions of "apprehension" which are formed by "inference" according to the preferences of one's own mind and ensnare the individual in dualities and conventionality.¹⁷⁶ This is why he argues in verse 34 of the *Adornment* that if one is to take the nonaffirming negative of emptiness seriously then "one must accept that all our decisions are fabrications of the mind, with no basis whatsoever." Consequently, *all* concepts including even the traditional Buddhist teachings of "existence and nonexistence, is and is not, purity and filth, good and bad, Buddha and sentient being, heaven and hell, and so on" must ultimately be refuted.¹⁷⁷ Thus, Gendun Chopel repeatedly says that absolutely

---

173. Stoddard, 351; Ruegg, 309; Lopez and chos phel, *Madman*, ix.
174. Chos phel, "Adornment," 60, v. 49.
175. Mengele, 67.
176. Dreyfus, *Reality*, 443–5, 337. Cf. Tom J. F. Tillemans, *Scripture, Logic, Language: Essays on Dharmakirti and His Tibetan Successors*, Studies in Indian and Tibetan Buddhism (Boston, MA: Wisdom, 1999), 156.
177. Chos phel, "Adornment," 56, v. 34.

any attachment to concepts or conventional logic, even traditional beliefs such as the nature of buddhahood and depictions of the various forms of the Trikāya, is "incapable of going even a little way toward the other side."[178] Rather, Lopez explains in his commentary on the text, the truth of reality encountered by the individual through direct perception is simply "a negation that implies nothing [conceptually] positive in its place."[179]

Second, Gendun Chopel's experience of resistance to some of his positions, in particular his Dharmakīrtian anti-realism, by traditionally minded Buddhist thinkers caused him to question the validity of the authority of tradition generally. One example of this type of argument by Gendun Chopel is verses 32 and 33 of the *Adornment*. Here in a thinly veiled reference to Dharmakīrti and his non-realist language regarding the knowledge of reality, Gendun Chopel asserts that phrases such as "inexpressible," "inconceivable," and "free from elaboration" are used by both the Buddha ("in the sūtras") as well as the revered Nāgārjuna just as much as "earlier Tibetan scholars" (i.e., Dharmakīrti); however, the latter are mockingly deemed "fools and nihilists"—or at best ignorant because at the time in which they spoke the "finer points" of "the Foremost Lama" (Tsongkhapa) had not yet appeared—whereas for the former, the assumption simply is that "there are no errors in the thinking of the Bhagavan himself." Thus using specific quotes from the Buddha, Gendun Chopel mockingly gests that according to their logic "the way that the Buddha himself taught the doctrine is something that lacks fine points."[180] Gendun Chopel's criticism of this perceived hypocrisy is clear and direct. As he chides his critics in the very next verse,

> Therefore, if the earlier Tibetans and the Buddha are to be refuted, refute them equally. If they are to be affirmed, affirm them equally. Please do not be deceitful, turning your tongue in various ways and worrying about whether or not people will criticize you.[181]

Such blatant hypocrisy in the judgment of the traditional authorities and institutions who evaluate, and essentially rank, the validity of claims from within the tradition (such as Tsongkhapa's supersession of Dharmakīrti) in Gendun Chopel's mind only serves to further illustrate his larger point that for "common beings" no opinion of any majority—not "some hundred people," not "a thousand or ten," not "all humans," nay not even "all the common beings of the three realms"—can serve as an authority on the validity of any knowledge. This is because any claims or adjudications of "truth" are "merely decisions in accordance with how it appears to [common beings'] respective minds."[182] Accordingly, as exemplified in the previous

---

178. Ibid., 106, v. 206.
179. Lopez and chos phel, *Madman*, 203.
180. Chos phel, "Adornment," 55–6, v. 32.
181. Ibid., 56, v. 33.
182. Ibid., 48, v. 5.

example of the Buddha and "earlier Tibetans," collections of common beings do not even assess the significance of assertions equally within the tradition. Instead, "the more people there are who agree, the more the point they agree upon becomes of great significance and importance. Contrary views are taken to be wrong views, mistaken perceptions, and so on."[183] Thus, a statement by the Buddha that might undermine the Gelukpa interpretation of Tsongkhapa's Madhyamaka is regarded as periphery and simply the use of "skillful means" (*upāya*) based on the ignorance of his audience, while Dharmakīrti's use of the same statement may be judged as the fundamental flaw to his system and the reason why his thought must be surpassed. Gendun Chopel illustrates this point in verse 7 by citing Candrakīrti's commentary on Āryadeva's *Four Hundred Verses* (*Catuḥśataka*). In this passage, the famous disciple to Nāgārjuna asserts the provocative question: "Therefore, why is it incorrect to say the whole world is insane?" Candrakīrti's equally famous response to this verse is the story of a king who is informed by an astrologer that in seven days there will be a rainfall whose water will cause anyone who drinks it to go insane. According to the story, all the king's subjects drink the water and subsequently are driven to insanity, except for the king who had heeded the caution of the earlier sage. In the end, however, since the king is the only individual not affected by the tainted water all the people of the kingdom determine that it is the *king* who is insane. In response, "not knowing what else to do," the king eventually gives in to the social pressure of his subjects and drinks the contaminated water, "whereby he came to agree with everyone else."[184] Therefore, in the next verse Gendun Chopel concludes,

> Thus, due to the single great insanity from our having continually drunk the crazing waters of ignorance from time immemorial, there is no confidence whatsoever in our decisions concerning what exists and does not exist, what is and is not. Even though a hundred, a thousand, ten thousand, or a hundred thousand of such insane people agree, it in no way becomes more credible.[185]

Moreover, in verse 9 he continues by extending the implications of this universal delusion of "common beings" ever further down the branches of traditional lineage, now to include the traditional "roots" of the teachings of Nāgārjuna and even the Buddha as well.

> One may think: "We concede that our decisions are unreliable, but when we follow the decisions of the Buddha, we are infallible." Then who decided that the Buddha is infallible? If you say, "The great scholars and adepts like Nāgārjuna decided that he is infallible," then who decided that Nāgārjuna is infallible? If you say, "The Foremost Lama [Tsongkhapa] decided it," then who knows that

---

183. Ibid., 47, v. 4.
184. Ibid., 49, v. 7.
185. Ibid., 49, v. 8.

the Foremost Lama is infallible? If you say, "Our kind and peerless lama, the excellent and great so and so decided," then infallibility, which depends on your excellent lama, is decided by your own mind. In fact, therefore, it is a tiger who vouches for a lion, it is a yak who vouches for a tiger, it is a dog who vouches for a yak, it is a mouse who vouches for a dog, it is an insect who vouches for a mouse. Thus, an insect is made the final voucher for them all. *Therefore, when one analyzes in detail the final basis for any decision, apart from coming back to one's own mind, nothing else whatsoever is perceived.*[186]

Here Gendun Chopel not only challenges but also blatantly satirizes the notion of lineage that serves as the foundation of traditional authority within Tibetan Buddhism in the most direct way. According to the traditional Buddhist tropes, the Buddha is always described as the "lion of the dharma" and Nāgārjuna a tiger. So then mirroring the order of the parallel lineage listed immediately prior, that means Tsongkhapa is depicted as a yak (not exactly flattering) and the lineage deteriorates from there.[187] This is not only a slight to the "Foremost Lama" of all Geluk teaching, but the further denigration of the conduits of tradition to filthier animals including vermin is a more pronounced jab at the current authorities of the tradition during his time. Besides the rhetorical dig embedded in analogy portrayal, however, it's the larger point he is making in this verse that actually packs the more powerful punch. That is, the power and authority of traditional teachings are ultimately rendered impotent because in actuality it is the decision and power of one's own mind that grants the authority to any conceived lineage of teaching in the first place. Thus, the weak and limited perception of an insect ends up authorizing the perspectives and claims of all the other animals in an obviously backward system of "authority." Gendun Chopel draws this conclusion for if "when one analyzes in detail the final basis for any decision, apart from coming back to one's own mind, nothing else whatsoever is perceived," then he recognizes a complete illogical circularity to the Tibetan logic of traditional authority at this point.

He succinctly illustrates this conundrum later in verse 64, "Analysis by reasoning depends on founders; the founders are established [as such] by the power of reasoning; if I can decide on my own, whom should I follow? If I cannot decide, on whom can I rely?"[188] In other words, he intuits a "chicken-or-the-egg" enigma with this type of reasoning. If traditional teachings establish the definition of proper reasoning but at the same time it is through proper analysis that one can determine the authoritative teachings, then how can the conclusion of either authority or reasoning be anything more than a creation of the individual's own mind? Therefore, Gendun Chopel feels compelled to conclude that any external authority given to the tradition—whether lineages of transmission, scriptural

---

186. Ibid., 49–50, v. 9. Emphasis added.
187. Lopez and chos phel, *Madman*, 131.
188. Chos phel, "Adornment," 63, v. 63. Cf. Lopez and chos phel, *Madman*, 148.

authority, or even the Buddha himself—is an arbitrary creation of one's mind that is at best superficially shared conviction agreed upon by ignorant beings.[189] Or as he summarizes in verse 69, "Whatever most people like appears as the truth; whatever most mouths agree on appears as a philosophical tenet. Inside each person is a different valid form of knowledge, with an adamantine scripture supporting it."[190]

So then, one might ask, if one cannot determine valid reasoning or the authority of teaching because of the circularity of its logic, then how is it possible to ever arrive at enlightenment, which is beyond the conceptions of "reasoning" and "tradition" according to which "the path" is based? To this, Gendun Chopel has a simple response. "Again, in order to progress to a place beyond the world, it is certain that *one must pass beyond the thoughts and expressions of the world*. Thus, from a position that does not agree with the entire world and does not accord with its thinking, one must proceed to the level of a noble being."[191] What he means by this is that to achieve enlightenment, one must use language, concepts, and logic of conventional "knowledge" and teaching so as to deconstruct their meaning and expose the inherent arbitrariness of their assertions. In this way, Lopez exegetes, the "goal" is to reach a point where "one must stop believing in one's own thoughts" and where all ideas, concepts, and language are refuted and rejected "until one has no assertions of one's own."[192]

> In brief, in order to destroy another's position or the position of the world, there is nothing [to be done] other than to destroy these positions of existence and nonexistence. The Buddha said, "He will be called by the name Nāga and he will destroy the positions of existence and nonexistence."[193]

Once again, it seems Gendun Chopel wants to use unconventional methods to arrive at a thoroughly traditional position.[194] As Dreyfus explains, generally speaking, Geluk Scholastic thought professes that "truth cannot be imparted dogmatically but needs to be appropriated by each person individually. It cannot be captured immediately and certainly not in simple statements, but must be understood through a process of inquiry that involves a certain open-endedness."[195] Hence citing the Buddha's famous prophesy of the coming of Nāgārjuna, Gendun Chopel argues that it is only through the personal use of conceptual language and

---

189. Chos phel, "Adornment," 99, v. 182; Cf. 75, v. 109.
190. Chos phel, "Adornment," 63, v. 69.
191. Ibid., 99–100, v. 185. Emphasis added.
192. Lopez and chos phel, *Madman*, 208; Chos phel, "Adornment," 108, v. 214.
193. Chos phel, "Adornment," 98, v. 180.
194. Jinpa, 30. Thupten Jinpa explains that ultimately Tsongkhapa rejected the "no-thesis" view as nihilistic, and therefore the Prāsaṅgika position is not a true "no-thesis" understanding.
195. Dreyfus, *Hands*, 278.

teachings in a self-destructive manner that one can expose their inherent ambiguity and arbitrary meanings that the individual can arrive at an experience of reality that is "beyond the thoughts and expressions of the world." As such, traditional teachings may not be "true," and certainly not "valid knowledge," but that does not mean they cannot be useful. Rather, they can serve the purpose of being mutually deconstructive and, in that sense, ultimately exposing. Accordingly, for Gendun Chopel the value of the tradition, including even the Buddha's teachings, rests in its ability to "disrupt our ordinary conceptions and lead us to an inconceivable state."[196] Hence, the authority of the tradition is not in what it *affirms*, but rather in what it *does*. And so, in the end, for Gendun Chopel it is actually because one radically rejects the epistemological authority of the religious community and its tradition that one can be the true Mādhyamika that the tradition venerates. As Donald Lopez professes, this is how Gendun Chopel arrives at his own version of the middle way. One that strives to negotiate between the extremes of "wisdom and ignorance, certainty and doubt, faith and skepticism—a middle way that calls everything we know into question because, rather than in spite of, the enlightenment of the Buddha."[197]

IV. Conclusion: Comparative Observations and Questions for Further Reflection

So far in this chapter we have examined the ways in which both Schillebeeckx and Gendun Chopel understood the nature of, and their own relation to, their respective religious communities and the traditions that accompany them—particularly with regard to the authority of truth claims. In the process we have exposed a number of cursory similarities across the areas of their biographical histories, their theoretical and philosophical orientations, as well as their visions of the role of religious communities in the formation and formulation of individuals' knowledge, both personally and theoretically. What remains more noteworthy for our purposes, however, is probably a closer parsing of the often stark contrasts between the scholars' positions, and at least some initial speculation as to how these differences might have served to produce such drastic disparities between the final outcomes of each thinker's personal standing within and theoretical opinions of their own respective traditions. Thus, in conclusion, this final section will be dedicated to further probing the comparison of the different perspectival orientations to both Schillebeeckx's and Gendun Chopel's epistemologies, and thus hopefully unearthing a second level of comparative analysis that focuses on the differences in the similarities and similarities in the differences between them. The overall goal of this final section then will be to utilize this comparative analysis in order to tease out the larger questions and broader challenges raised by

---

196. Lopez and chos phel, *Madman*, 197.
197. Ibid., xi.

both thinkers' understandings that can then function as a basis for a constructive synthesis in the final chapter.

To this point in our study, at least superficially, it is in the area of their biographical histories where these two thinkers display the most obvious overlap despite the radical differences in the historical cultures and contexts. For example, we have already discussed how both were raised in devoutly religious households that began teaching them in religious intellectual and spiritual life from very early ages. Furthermore, we highlighted how both thinkers began training in scholastic education since adolescence and how both reached the highest levels of theological/philosophical education within their respective traditions (although only one, Schillebeeckx, formally completed that education). Moreover, for both individuals it was during this period in their initial academic formation that each one was confronted with the burgeoning philosophical, cultural, and scientific possibilities and challenges confronting their religious traditions in Western modernisms. And although the visions for the role that modern philosophy and science should perform in their own religious traditions' conceptions of knowledge and truth would certainly vary, nevertheless their general reactions and conclusions derived from their interactions with Western modernity remain somewhat analogous. Neither saw modernity as inherently threatening to the truth claims of their communities, and subsequently neither saw the "truths" of their communities as in an "either/or" relation to the claims of modern philosophy and science. At the same time, neither saw the claims and thought of their own religious communities as completely isolated from, nor consequently theoretically immune to or unaffected by, the often seemingly contradictory propositions of other traditions including modernity. As a result, both believed that "alien" traditions (whether religious or nonreligious) could have a significant function in the formulation of religious truth within their own traditions.[198] Similarly, both thinkers attempted to recapture and utilize earlier philosophical elements from within their tradition in order to reinterpret and challenge the common beliefs of their communities, and particularly scholasticisms, at the time. Finally, at least in part as a consequence of their somewhat similar mentalities toward modernity, during their lifetime both thinkers' positions were quite controversial within their particular forms of scholasticism, and accordingly the ideas of both figures garnered polemical reception within their community.

Nevertheless, it is the stark *differences* in their personal narratives that are probably more interesting and also more useful in framing the major questions that emerge out of this initial comparison. While by all accounts both men were raised in religiously pious households, Schillebeeckx also grew up surrounded by a firm anticlericism that early on forced him and his family to wrestle with the balancing of an acceptance of communal religious identity and a sharp institutional criticism.

---

198. Both thinkers had extensive interactions with other religious traditions, philosophies, modern histories, and science. We will discuss these encounters more in the following chapters.

Gendun Chopel, on the other hand, was raised within a family with deep clerical ties to the religious institution of his tradition. Whereas Schillebeeckx insisted that he remained firmly within the Catholic tradition of Christianity throughout his life however, Gendun Chopel nonetheless experienced an at least partially forced transformation of religious identity and communal belonging through his transition from the Nyingma sect to the Geluk sect of Tibetan Buddhism. And although scholars should not overstate this historical reality in Gendun Chopel's personal development and beliefs, it still must also be noted that such a transition certainly *could have* shaped his personal feelings toward and commitment to his eventual community.

Additionally, although both thinkers displayed clear resistance to perceived forms of "traditionalism" within their scholastic communities, and despite the fact that both individuals chose to work under scholars whom they discerned as like-minded in their attitudes toward that traditionalism, the eventual outcome of those mentoring relationships are possibly quite revealing in their distinctions. On the one hand, Schillebeeckx found a personally challenging yet philosophically compatible partner in De Petter who assisted him in formulating theories that he believed might mediate traditional religious claims and the philosophical challenges of modernity. Even though he would eventually disavow the most significant theories that emerged from this collaboration, this interaction of philosophical exchange and development clearly had a profound impact on Schillebeeckx's theological and philosophical engagement with his tradition and set him on a continual trajectory of mediation and dialogue between other intellectual traditions and his own throughout his career. On the other hand Gendun Chopel's relationship with Geshe Sherab can only be described as (quite publically) tumultuous and definitely not living up to his initial expectations. Moreover, this relationship appears to serve rather easily as a microcosm of most of Gendun Chopel's personal relationships, where he is often clearly influenced by his various personal encounters with other specific thinkers but rarely maintains long-term friendships, or even dialogical exchanges, with them. Simply put, over and over again one observes instances that display a disposition in Schillebeeckx's personality to be a "bridge-builder," whereas it seems with an almost parallel frequency Gendun Chopel's personality shows a strong propensity toward burning down all relational "bridges."

This is especially put on display during the later part of their respective careers and lives in which both individuals experienced intense formal resistance and scrutiny from the institutions of their religious communities, and yet the apparent outcomes of these instances of formal opposition appear to be radically variant. Schillebeeckx would maintain his clerical vows and, although he would undoubtedly remain a controversial and even polarizing figure within the academic circles of his tradition, he would nonetheless die as a generally beloved member of the Dominican Order. Conversely, as we have previously discussed, Gendun Chopel disrobed from his monastic vows rather early on in his life while yet clearly remained cognizant of his reputation among the Tibetan community. And still, in the end, Lopez describes his state following his imprisonment by the Tibetan religious and political institution as one of an utterly "broken man," suffering from alcoholism and writing numerous poems reflecting a sense of loneliness, regret, and despair.[199] Yet whereas Schillebeeckx remained firmly a member of his community and order but also remains a divisive thinker in Catholic theological circles to this day, Gendun Chopel—despite voicing deep-seated feelings of isolation and regret toward the end of his life—today has taken on the wide-ranging status of a "cultural hero or even cult-figure" among his fellow Tibetans. We will examine the factors that might have contributed to this resurrection in his image later in the next chapter. However, for the purposes of this chapter, the larger question surrounding the significance of the discrepancies in these two biographical outcomes remains. It is a question of how much the differences between each thinker's conception of epistemological perspectivalism and their resultant understandings of the epistemological authority of their religious communities might have contributed to their standing within their traditions at their deaths. Thus, there is still an overall question then as to whether an epistemological perspectivalism in the understanding of religious truth can be employed in a way that can protect the individual from relativistic individualism and/or communal isolation.

At this point, therefore, once again we are confronted with some significant similarities and differences that begin to emerge between what we are classifying as "perspectivalism" in the epistemologies of both Gendun Chopel and Schillebeeckx. This means that both thinkers fundamentally reject any notion of a naïve representational realism when it comes to knowledge. Consequently, for both any conceptual knowledge is also essentially tied to, and therefore intrinsically limited by, the individual's cognitive processes, making it subsequently relative to that individual's experiential and imaginative perspective. Any formulation of knowledge must be, at least in part, the result of the cognitive construction of our individual intellects and therefore constrained by the limits of our personal history, context, empirical perception, and individual predilections. Thus, both want to depict their own respective visions of ultimate reality as being inherently *non*conceptual in nature, and therefore both understand linguistic truth claims as at least partially[200] unable to interpret and convey individuals' phenomenological encounters with reality. Hence, to some degree both thinkers want to describe the individual's encounter with reality at best in terms of a nonconceptual *intuition* of ultimate truth. But nonetheless, some glaring differences remain.

Maybe the most evident difference between them is their understanding of whether truth claims actually correspond to the reality they seek to articulate.

---

199. Dge 'dun Chos 'phel and Lopez, *Forest*, 93: "In my youth, I did not take a delightful bride; In old age, I did not amass the needed wealth. That the life of this beggar ends with his pen, This is what makes me feel so sad"; p. 107: "In the jungle where the frightful roar resounds Of the stubborn tiger drunk on the blood of envy, The honest little child is left all alone. May the wise think of him with compassion."

200. Schillebeeckx partially; Chopel completely.

As a realist, even though certainly a "critical" one, Schillebeeckx believes that not only are truth claims actually connected to the reality they are interpreting, but also they can at least in some ways be adjudicated over others by how well they correspond to the reality that is apprehended—essentially establishing "higher" forms of knowledge. Whereas for Gendun Chopel, as a ("Dharmakīrtian") *non-realist*, all linguistic and conceptual interpretations of reality are completely divorced from, and in fact irreparably distorting of, ultimate reality so that the best the individual can do is intuit the nature of ultimate truth by negating what it is not. Consequently, Schillebeeckx sees the world's status as "contingent" in relation to ultimate truth—its "finitude"—as the source of its value, and thus something to be protected and maintained; in contrast Gendun Chopel sees the contingent as that which must be negated and extinguished for a true encounter and knowledge of reality to be achieved. And although one could argue that later on Schillebeeckx eventually moves closer to Gendun Chopel's position of gaining knowledge through negation with his notion of "negative experiences of contrast," his steadfast commitment to a form of—an albeit deeply consciously critical—epistemological realism nevertheless remains as the foundational means for determining the nature, source, and value of human knowledge.

Therefore, once again major questions persist between the two systems. Does Schillebeeckx's conception of a *critically* realist perspectivalism in epistemology truly maintain a consistent "middle way" between the philosophical extremes of realism and idealism? In other words, can Schillebeeckx's "critically realist" epistemology sufficiently take seriously the contingency (or in Gendun Chopel's language, "conventionality") of all truth claims in a way more akin to Gendun Chopel's non-realist idealism with regard to conventional truth? Similarly, however, does Gendun Chopel's conventional awareness actually avoid the extreme of nihilistic relativism that he seems so adamant to distinguish his own position from? Does Gendun Chopel's distinction between the unenlightened conventional knowledge of "common beings" and the ultimate knowledge of enlightened beings truly solve the problem of mediating eternalism and nihilism?

Moreover, as we then observed in the last section, it also became apparent how both of these thinkers' philosophical orientations, alongside their biographical personalities and contexts, led them to use their notions of the perspectival nature of all knowledge in radically distinct ways for determining the role and authority of their religious communities in the formulation of truth and the formation of knowledge. As a result of their two different understandings of perspectivalism, it is clear that both Gendun Chopel and Schillebeeckx wanted to limit the authoritative role of their religious institutions and the traditional teachings they profess. Nevertheless in what way, and to what extent, each thinker sought to limit this epistemological authority of the traditional community varied quite significantly. For Schillebeeckx the balance should rest in a dialectical interplay between the epistemological authority of the institution (as a "teaching church") and the locally contextualized voices of particular practicing communities and individuals, especially theologians (as a "learning church"). Thus the institutionalized teaching and understanding of the tradition is ideally directed and authorized by the collective voice of localized communities and even individual practitioners, while those voices are also constantly checked, evaluated, and reformed by the broader community of voices within the larger institutionalized church. Gendun Chopel, on the other hand, seemingly wants to even further decentralize the epistemological authority within the community to each individual mind. Hence, for him the role of traditional teachings is not to assist in the construction of valid knowledge for individuals but rather to function in a more self-deconstructive manner that constantly exposes the individual follower to the limits of conceptual and linguistic—"conventional"—knowledge. Only then is the individual intellect capable of intuiting the "very hidden" knowledge of reality to which the traditional teachings allude.

One of the possible reasons for this distinction in the way each thinker uses his perspectival epistemology in determining the authority of the claims of their religious community is the difference in how they perceive the connection between soteriology and epistemology. Earlier on in his development Schillebeeckx actually understood the relation between one's knowledge and one's soteriological standing in a way more similar to Gendun Chopel. At this early phase for Schillebeeckx, sin is understood as a more passive condition, or "atmosphere," encompassing the entire created order. Therefore, to know the ultimate truth of God is to know the salvific presence of God in all creation, that is, the way he often equates the expressions "revelation-in-reality" with the "revelation-of-salvation." Similarly, as we observed, for Gendun Chopel the invalidity of the knowledge of common beings is directly tied to the ignorant (or delusional) state of the unenlightened mind. And in this way, Gendun Chopel seems to uphold a much more passive understanding of the condition of ignorance that in many ways parallels the earlier Schillebeeckx's notion of an "atmosphere of sin." Hence, Gendun Chopel believes that if the individual can overcome the delusional tendency of reifying conceptual projections then one can directly experience the "nonaffirming negative," or the "absence," that is the ultimate truth of emptiness. As we also noted, Schillebeeckx later on adopts a much more active conception of the sinful distortion of truth, instead emphasizing the power of ideologies to distort concepts of knowledge within both societal institutions and individuals. As a result of this new awareness of the active distortion of knowledge for self-interested gain and exploitation, Schillebeeckx shifts a suspicious eye toward both the motives of the institutional church as well as individual believers in the formulation of knowledge and depiction of ultimate truth. And for this reason, Schillebeeckx wants to use the dialectical exchange of knowledge between the teachings of the larger institution and the more localized experiences of individual voices as a way to balance epistemological authority between the individual and the community, essentially checking the power of either one and hopefully mitigating the potential for exploitation and oppression. Turning toward Gendun Chopel then, one must wonder why he chooses to emphasize one aspect (delusion) of "the three poisons" over the other two (greed and hatred)? Accordingly, how might a more balanced discussion of the factors distorting the knowledge of common beings change his depiction of ignorance from a very passive to a more active, or intentional, condition of the mind? Would this possibly at all change his individualist persuasion regarding knowledge and the perception of the enlightened realm?

And so, finally, we are confronted with the most important question arising from the comparison of this chapter: considering the accepted inherent limits of the individual intellectual perspective on the possibility of knowledge assumed by both thinkers, how can a community of individuals with personally fallible conceptions of knowledge be a conduit of the infallible reality of ultimate truth? However, in this discussion we have also observed how the purpose and authority of the lives and teachings of the historical founders of each thinker's tradition (namely, Śākyamuni Buddha and Jesus of Nazareth) are inseparable from their personal understandings of the authority of the community. Therefore before we can turn to engaging this question of communal authority in the final chapter, we must first comprehend how each thinker construes the epistemological authority of the historical founder of his community. And it is to this question we must now turn to in the next chapter.

Chapter 4

THE ROLE OF THE HISTORICAL FOUNDERS OF RELIGIOUS TRADITIONS IN SHAPING AND CONVEYING RELIGIOUS KNOWLEDGE, MEANING, AND TRUTH FOR CONTEMPORARY BELIEVERS

I. Introduction: The Problems and Possibilities of Deciphering Knowledge of Ultimacy from within Particular Historical Contexts

In the preceding chapter we investigated how both Schillebeeckx and Gendun Chopel understood all knowledge to be perspectival in nature, and compared and contrasted how this conclusion shaped their conception of the role and authority of religious traditions in formulating one's knowledge of reality. This chapter will now turn to examine the ways in which both thinkers' systems of thought were introduced to and challenged by encounters with new cultural paradigms for adjudicating truth, and particularly how these new engagements with modern methods of research and cultural questions reshaped their epistemological understanding of the authority of the historical founders of their religious traditions. Highlighting how both men were significantly influenced during times spent abroad from their home countries, it will observe how during these periods each individual's philosophical theories and religious beliefs were evidently transformed by new encounters with modern methods in historical, philosophical, scientific, and hermeneutical studies. After analyzing both thinkers' traditional and theoretical foundations for conceptualizing a theory of the nature and capability of theological truth to transverse variant historical and cultural contexts, it will then turn to analyze their own personal articulations of the nature of religious meaning and authority as pertaining to the historical founders of their tradition. Finally it will then conclude by comparing and contrasting the analogous points of contact between Schillebeeckx's and Gendun Chopel's thought on this topic. This will result in a new series of broader questions to be raised concerning the soteriological nature and function of knowledge that will then be addressed in the final two chapters.

II. Theological and Theoretical Sources of Hermeneutics

A. Schillebeeckx: The Problems and Potential of Radical Historicity in Theological Knowledge

It is not coincidental or insignificant that the clarifying questions in his colloquium with the CDF in December 1979 centered on Schillebeeckx's two Christological texts—namely *Jesus* and *Christ*—published during that decade.[1] This is because, as Thompson offers, although Schillebeeckx has "written copiously on many topics since the time of his 'clear break' with De Petter in 1966, the 'Christological trilogy' has been the backbone of his mature work."[2] Kennedy concurs with this assessment insisting that Schillebeeckx's "Christological writings serve as an *epistemological crucible*" through which he "unravels problems associated with the cognitive intentionality of the Christian faith" as opposed to attempting to "clarify God's knowability" by means of a predominantly philosophical discourse.[3] This is because even though the central theme of Jesus's *humanity* was present in some of his earliest works in Christology since as far back as his brief doctoral studies in Paris under Chenu, starting in 1966—when he began formally teaching hermeneutics at Nijmegen—Schillebeeckx began to publicly speak about Christology as the key for a Christian understanding of the knowledge of God (or "revelation") in light of the radical historicity of the human subject. Nonetheless, despite the transition from phenomenological to historical and hermeneutical categories of epistemology at that time, Leo O'Donovan insists that Schillebeeckx's new emphasis on Christology was simply his own attempt to preserve his critical-realist Thomist epistemology while embracing the mounting philosophical

---

1. See *The Schillebeeckx Case*, 112, 117. It should also be noted that questions were also open to his *Interim Report* which he published in response to the criticisms and questions of the *Jesus* and *Christ* books raised by other theologians. Also, it is significant to point out that the nature of the questions was to address and discuss "only what [was] objectively expressed in the texts, and not the subjective intention of the author."

2. Thompson, 84.

3. PhilipKennedy, *Deus Humanissimus: The Knowability of God in the Theology of Edward Schillebeeckx*, Ökumenische Beihefte Zur Freiburger Zeitschrift Für Philosophie Und Theologie 22 (Fribourg, Switzerland: University of Chicago Press, 1993), 288. Shortly after this passage Kennedy helpfully lays a brief sketch of the various stages in Schillebeeckx's Christology. He correctly emphasizes that even in his "early period" (due to the influence of Chenu and Congar) Schillebeeckx's focus was still mainly on the humanity of Jesus as the "primordial sacrament" of God within history. However, as Kennedy further elaborates, during his time at Nijmegen, particularly following the Second Vatican Council and when teaching hermeneutics there in 1966, he began reexamining his Christology in light of historical-critical methods and biblical studies. By the late 1960s he had begun to incorporate studies in Critical Theory in order to specifically respond to "a particular post-enlightenment view of human reason which denied that a historical particular can yield knowledge of that which is universal" (297).

challenges of historicity: "Schillebeeckx's real master here is still probably Thomas Aquinas, whose theological realism he is transposing into a critical and practical historical language."[4]

And yet Thompson also astutely observes that this "translation" of Aquinas is "also a transformation as well." In other words, Schillebeeckx "does not simply cover the inner syntax of thought with new philosophical terminology, but he also makes substantial shifts in content"[5] as a result of engaging the pressures of modernity that he perceives are causing a "present-day crisis of faith."[6] Kennedy hypothesizes that these new "pressures" manifest themselves in Schillebeeckx's work by his preoccupation with "four philosophical themes" throughout his later Christologically laden theological epistemology. These themes are: the linguisticality of humankind, the historicity of human existence alongside the resolute recognition that *meaning* and *truth* are inherently *historical*, the priority of the future in relation to the past and present in conceiving of truth, and finally a priority of praxis over theory in the conception of knowledge.[7] In this section we will examine how Schillebeeckx attempts to incorporate a multitude of philosophical and theological perspectives in order to uphold the possibility of theological knowledge despite the modern challenges of "newness, change, and crisis" confronting contemporary believers.[8] Thus, in the end, it will set up the final section of the chapter in which we will discuss how and why Schillebeeckx believed Christology could best solve the riddle of preserving "universal truth" within "historical particularity."

As noted earlier in his biography, immediately following the conclusion of the Second World War Schillebeeckx became convinced that theology must be focused on answering the pressing philosophical and existential questions and crises confronting one's current cultural context. This sense of conviction was only heightened by his studies with the theologians of the "*Nouvelle Théologie*"— particularly Chenu and Congar—during his time in Paris. However, these theologians also emphasized and added a new component to Schillebeeckx's consciousness and concern for culture, namely a *historical* consciousness.

---

4. Leo O'Donovan, S. J., "Salvation as the Center of Theology," *Interpretation* 36 (1982): 196. Cf. Kennedy, *Deus*, 297. Here Kennedy contends that Schillebeeckx's "entire theological corpus" is "preoccupied" with "explaining religious knowledge."

5. Thompson, 23.

6. Schillebeeckx, *God the Future*, 4. Cf. Schillebeeckx, *World and Church*, 94, where he in fact heightens his language by describing it in terms of the "supreme crisis" of contemporary faith.

7. Kennedy, *Deus*, 154.

8. Ibid., 158. It should be noted, however, that earlier Kennedy also cautions that the indisputably multidisciplinary nature of his later theology should nonetheless "not be taken as an indication that he has thoroughly studied each discipline he refers to in his writings. Often he simply makes random selections of phraseology from a particular author without embracing the author's system of thought" (149).

Therefore in outlining what he demarcates as the "second circle" of Schillebeeckx's epistemology, Thompson comments that "one of the greatest differences" between the first two circles of Schillebeeckx's epistemological development is his "more thoroughgoing embrace of the radical historicity of the human subject in the second."[9] By "historicity," Hilkert elaborates, Schillebeeckx means the problem that "All human experience and understanding occur within a specific historical and cultural context. The hermeneutical problem arises when one tries to understand a text or an event which arose in a different historical or cultural context."[10] Thus here Schillebeeckx's emphasis in approaching the difficulty of acquiring knowledge of God transitions from one centered on mediating the "subject and object dichotomy" within all conceptual knowledge (the focus of his early "perspectivalism") to one focused primarily on formulating universal knowledge despite the integral linguistic and historical nature of all human existence.

The challenge of historicity then for Schillebeeckx is a challenge of *newness*, the fact that events and words spoken (or written) in the past can never be encountered directly by an individual in the present, but instead always occurs in a *new* context, culture, and perspective. Thus, despite Schillebeeckx's move away from the purely phenomenological approach of De Petter, his new venture into historical consciousness still confronted him with the fact that historicity by its definition implies that humans' knowledge is essentially still limited by the concrete historical and cultural contexts enveloping them. And therefore, all human knowledge remains fundamentally *perspectival* (although understood in a new way).[11] As a result of this observation, especially during the 1960s Schillebeeckx began to dialogue with the work and theories of many contemporary philosophers, particularly Martin Heidegger, Hans-Georg Gadamer, and Paul Ricœur, among others,[12] on "the problem of 'universal' history"[13]—the question of whether, and if so *how*, any universal meaning or truth can be known *through* the particularity of history and context.[14] In other words, if the theologian accepts that human beings are fundamentally "co-constituted by their location in time

---

9. Thompson, 32.

10. Hilkert, "Hermeneutics," 109.

11. Where in previous chapters I defined "perspectivalism" as the limits of human knowledge based on the natural limitations of the human cognitive process itself, now—while maintaining that all knowledge is limited to individual *perspective*—the basis for Schillebeeckx's understanding is grounded in the limitations *imposed* on the individuals based on the external burden of historicity and the contextuality of all expressions of meaning.

12. For more useful (though not comprehensive) and loosely chronological lists of the various intellectual and philosophical influences and sources see Kennedy, *Schillebeeckx*, 36–8, and Kennedy, *Deus*, 147.

13. For a discussion of this "problem of 'universal' history" see Schillebeeckx, *Jesus*, 612–16.

14. Schillebeeckx, *Jesus*, 592.

and culture" and if "language and history are not simply expressions of human experience of knowledge, but [also] the very framework that makes experience and knowledge possible,"[15] then how can the Christian faith speak universally to all (or even *any*) individuals even though it "is never entirely dissociated from a historically conditioned view of man and the world"?[16] Or as he would elsewhere explain the conundrum, if "the conceptuality which belongs to our thinking, and hence to our understanding of the faith, is subject to our situation in history," then how does one theologize about a Universal Truth in light of the fact that "the real content of human knowing and believing is the ever present *mystery* of promise—the mystery which is not uttered, which is everywhere reaching towards expression but in itself is never thought."[17] Therefore, as Kennedy aptly summarizes Schillebeeckx's concern, if "any message from God (Scripture) is expressed in a specific historical situation in the past" then how can that message of that past become "a norm for today where the Christian faith is experienced in a markedly different historical situation"?[18]

This question of historical newness for the interpreter of any expression of knowledge or faith inevitably leads Schillebeeckx to yet another problem, this time the reconciling of continuity and change within historically situated expressions of faith and conceptions of universal knowledge. For Schillebeeckx the recognition of the problem of constantly *new* historical encounters with a text or an expression of meaning inherently leads to a *hermeneutical* problem of the gap between expressions of truth (i.e., "texts") and the receivers of those expressions ("readers"). Beginning very early on under the guidance of Chenu and Congar with their focus on the "*ressourcement*" movement, Schillebeeckx began to hold firmly that for any individual to hold a "literal repetition" of a text or expression of theological truth from the past was actually being unfaithful to the meaning of that expression because a change in—or "translation of"—meaning is always necessary to account for the newness of context. As Schillebeeckx himself elaborates, "Understanding must change in changing situations, otherwise the same thing cannot continue to be understood ... The past will remain unintelligible to us if we do not incorporate its meaning into our contemporary existential experience. If we do not do this, we shall not understand what the past really has to say to us."[19] In other words, unless there is an interpretative *change* in meaning ("translation") in order to account for the constant newnesses of concrete human historical existence, then the possibility of deriving any universal meaning from past expressions of faith is lost.

Nonetheless, Schillebeeckx is not calling for a complete "*laissez-faire*" approach to deciphering meaning from within history either. Rather, by employing semiotic and structuralist readings of literary theory, he wants to uphold the normative

---

15. Thompson, 27.
16. Schillebeeckx, *The Mission of the Church*, 26.
17. Schillebeeckx, *God the Future*, 40. Emphasis original.
18. Kennedy, *Deus*, 176-7.
19. Schillebeeckx, *God the Future*, 31.

status of texts themselves at least in the sense that they *do* play a pivotal role in demarcating the boundaries of possible meaning within any given context. However the text itself should never be understood as the literal expression of meaning but rather only as the portal through which one encounters the reality that the text gestures toward. This is because, following the lead of Ricœur, Schillebeeckx understands truth to be a fundamentally *multifaceted* reality, one that can never be known in a purely separated form but is always manifested within the guise of a historical particularity. Here he views it necessary, therefore, to make a distinction between the "intrinsic dogmatic affirmation" of a text (i.e., Sacred Scripture) and its current "moment of presentation." Yet, at the same time these two realities of meaning, though distinct, remain inseparable so that the essential meaning of a text "is *never* given as a pure datum, but is always concealed *within* a historical mode of expression."[20] Or again in line with Gadamer and Ricœur, for him it is impossible for anyone to perceive and know truth in a "raw" state, rather all human knowledge and experience is inevitably interpretative. In fact, he maintains, it is this interpretative nature of all encounters with and knowledge of reality that makes those experiences both meaningful and expressible.[21] Still, on the other hand, the moment a person conceptually expresses any particular understanding of reality (whether written or spoken) that expression is imbued with "the imperfection, the relativity, the possibility of development, the historical conditioning which goes with all truth as possessed by men."[22] And accordingly, any depiction of knowledge, theology, or faith has intrinsically left the "storm-free zone" of ahistorical certitude and is rightfully left vulnerable and subject "to the exigencies of critical rationality."[23] The "essential implication" of this, he concludes, is that we can only comprehend the "biblical word of faith" through a contextually appropriate "reinterpretative understanding of faith."

Despite his conviction that individuals "cannot grasp the biblical text directly 'in itself,' as though we, as readers or believers, *transcended time*," still as a Christian theologian Schillebeeckx wants to maintain that the Christian believer must take the biblical text itself as the point of one's departure toward discovering its meaning. The interpreter still must also go beyond the texts and their contextually situated meanings in order to enquire "about the *reality* to which the texts intentionally or unintentionally bear witness."[24] Thus, in the end according to Schillebeeckx,

20. Kennedy, *Deus*, 178–9. Emphasis original.
21. Schillebeeckx, *Jesus*, 53. Cf. Schillebeeckx, *Interim Report*, 13.
22. Schillebeeckx, *Dogmatic vs. Biblical*, 131.
23. Schillebeeckx, *Jesus*, 32.
24. Schillebeeckx, *God the Future*, 33. While generally accepting this reading of Schillebeeckx's hermeneutical theory, however, it should be noted that Hilkert maintains that the text itself is not the only guide to determining its meaning, particularly when addressing scripture and dogmatic statements of faith. Hilkert insists that for Schillebeeckx the actual activity of "the *Holy Spirit* … in and through the Christian community (or communities) is key to understanding his critical hermeneutical method." (See Hilkert, "Hermeneutics," 126.)

the task confronting the contemporary theologian (or believer) is to mitigate the inevitable and fundamental occurrence of *change* within the meanings of various expressions of ultimate truth by at the same time effectively showing how any interpretation and experience of that meaning "is never wholly strange to us":[25] that it maintains at least a "present echo" of the historically inspired meaning it originally sought to convey.[26]

Whereas to this point the conversation about the problems that Schillebeeckx perceived were confronting contemporary theology has revolved around the concerns of history ("newness") and the possibility of meaning within that developing history (change), still maybe the most significant concern emerging out of Schillebeeckx's historical and hermeneutical consciousness is his acknowledgment of the fundamental role that the interruption of *crises* plays in our understanding and conception of knowledge. This is because, for him the interruption of crisis unmasks not only the meaningful or "sensical" elements of history but also the reality of "non-sense" and "meaninglessness" within history. Hence distancing himself from a purely "Hegelian" conception of historicity, Schillebeeckx insists that in counterbalance to any historical formation of meaning or truth within history there is "a different meaning" that is always also ignored—a "historical scrap" of meaning that "slips between the meshes of the rational system" of any given context.

> There is, in point of fact, unmeaningful history; there is non-sense in our history: violence, lust for power, coveting at the expense of others, enslavement and oppression—there is Auschwitz, and goodness knows what else in the private sphere and in our own personal life. All of that does indeed fall outside the "logos" which the historian looks for in history—so much the worse for the varieties of concrete historical experience!

Hence, Schillebeeckx holds that there are always at least two competing narratives in the retelling of history: "the meaning discovered (by dispensing with a lot of reality) by the Hegelians and the possible 'different meaning' (which would take into account all the 'non-sense')." And thus, for him, the sheer existence of these multiple "histories" for the contemporary interpreter of meaning inevitably results in an "absurdity, that is, in the elimination of all true history."[27] In fact, later he would even up the proverbial ante on this conclusion when he asserts, "Finitude or contingency mean that man and the world hang by themselves in a vacuum, above absolute nothingness."[28] Accordingly, Kennedy argues that it is this recognition of the threat of "meaninglessness" and "absurdity" within history by Schillebeeckx that primarily drives the focus of his theological orientation and gives his theology

---

25. Schillebeecx, *Jesus*, 576.
26. Schillebeeckx, *Christ*, 43.
27. Ibid., 614.
28. Schillebeeckx, *Interim Report*, 114.

"a certain intellectual ferment and sense of urgency" beginning in the mid-1960s.[29] This is because, epistemologically speaking, it signals the most "overt" shift in Schillebeeckx's terminology when referring to the knowledge of God. Sometime after he had begun lecturing on hermeneutics at Nijmegen in 1966, Schillebeeckx began to significantly alter his language and categories for understanding "the knowability of God" from terms such as "conscious ignorance" and "implicit intuition" (à la De Petter) to a resolute determination to approach meaning and ultimate truth in terms of "negative contrast experiences" and through the lens of suffering.[30] Or as he summarizes this point, "Logos, meaning, and facticity, the occurrence of meaninglessness, injustice and suffering, are interrelated in a tension which cannot be resolved theoretically."[31]

Hence as a result of the exposure to the atrocities of both World Wars and the many other manifestations of egregious oppression and suffering imbued in human history, Schillebeeckx notes that the modern culture of the twentieth century had become rightfully suspicious of *all* monological systems of interpretation and knowledge, *including Christianity*. "The consequence of this," he later writes, "is that a theologian, or even a group of theologians working together, has no more than a *limited* and *one-sided* view of the totality of the reality of faith, both qualitatively and quantitatively."[32] And as a result of this newfound realization, theologians must now learn to speak of "Truth" and the "knowledge of God" in a context where "pluralism is simply inevitable and, in this sense, impossible to overcome."[33] Hence the end goal of theology can no longer be the monolithic (and socially *dangerous*) "discovery" and assertion of a definitive understanding of ultimate truth, but rather a dialogical participation with the Other so that "the place ... where truth may possibly be found is human-being-as-possibility-of-communication."[34] For this reason, in his later theology Schillebeeckx argues that primary addressee of theologians should no longer be the "ecumene of the Christian faith" but rather the much broader "ecumene of suffering humanity."[35]

This new emphasis on the plight of suffering humanity combined with his incredulity toward purely theoretical approaches to deciphering meaning leads Schillebeeckx to determine that the "the basic hermeneutical problem of theology, then, is not so much the question of the relationship between the past (scripture and tradition) and the present, but between theory and praxis."[36] In this way, any supposed knowledge of ultimate reality, or "new concept of God," can no longer come as the a priori precursor for any valid claim to truth, rather any notion of

---

29. Kennedy, *Deus*, 159.
30. Ibid., 150.
31. Schillebeeckx, *Church*, 174.
32. Schillebeeckx, *Understanding*, 51.
33. Schillebeeckx, *Understanding*, 50–4 (51).
34. Schillebeeckx, *Jesus*, 614.
35. Schillebeeckx, *Future of Liberation*, 186–8.
36. Schillebeeckx, *Understanding*, 67.

truth can only "come indirectly to light" through the pragmatic activities of the individual interpreters themselves. This means that the adjudication of any truth claim, or any "reinterpretation" of a prior meaning, can only be determined by the nature of the *activity* it produces in those encountering it.[37] Even more importantly then, Schillebeeckx's insistence that the problem of truth and historical meaning can be resolved solely in a plural, dialogical, and nontheoretical manner means that the locus of all interpretations of meaning and claims to truth are not only innately historical and anthropocentric but also fundamentally social and deeply political.

In light of these three major concerns of newness, change, and crisis for determining the nature of any "universal truth" and what he perceives as the factors prompting those issues, now let us return to examining these problems and specifically how Schillebeeckx seeks to reconcile and overcome (or assuage) them within his own religious epistemology. The problem of "newness" or "historicity" for Schillebeeckx clearly must serve as the starting point for discussing the formulation of his new historically and hermeneutically conscious approach to religious epistemology for a few significant reasons. The first, and possibly most prominent reason, is the fact that even in the later stages of his career Schillebeeckx sought to maintain his belief in the interdependent relationship between individuals' knowledge of ultimate truth (revelation) and their sapiential, social, and spiritual betterment and fulfillment (salvation). Schillebeeckx's increased awareness of the strains of historical newness—historicity—forced him to attempt to reconceive and ground this interdependent relationship in a more tangible and concrete way that could account for the irreducible complexities of human history. As he explains this new situation, historicity unavoidably exposes the contemporary believer to the dilemma that "we do not possess the absolute which acts as an inner norm to our faith in an absolute way; we possess it only within our historical situation."[38] Thus, any formulation of knowledge always emerges through the complex interactions between the simulants of historical influences, new experiences, and future anticipation.[39] However his rejection of any "unhistorical or supra-historical" form of knowledge notwithstanding, Schillebeeckx also wants to reject the idea that adjudications of truth from within any particular historical context are completely relative or arbitrary either. Rather, Schillebeeckx argues that it is necessary to maintain in essence what I label a "tempered fallibilism." In this fashion he seeks to strike a dialectical balance where historicity injects suspicion to any universal, or supra-historical, claim to truth while at the same time also making comparisons and assessments regarding such claims possible through a standard of historical "evidence" for any instantiation of "truth."[40] Thus it not only

---

37. Schillebeeckx, *God the Future*, 184.
38. Ibid., 39–40.
39. See note 131.
40. Schillebeeckx, *Jesus*, 589–90.

limits (or even eliminates) the possibility of articulating any direct knowledge of ultimate truth but also makes all functional knowledge possible.

In order to maintain this "dialectical and nonantithetical" vision of history as viable, Schillebeeckx must find an understanding of history that can recognize the constant development of contextual "newness" while also preserving space to account for various trajectories of noticeable similarity from one historical context to another. As was discussed earlier in Chapter 2, Schillebeeckx found his inspiration for answering this question from the French *Annales* school of historiography—and in particular the historian Fernand Braudel. By devising a scheme for interpreting historical newness and similarity using three distinct "planes" of history—the Ephemeral, the Conjunctural, and the Structural—Schillebeeckx is able to formulate an interpretative model of history in which novelty and symmetry can be held in a tension of complexity across these three planes which "are neither separably procurable nor parallel." Instead historicity is simply an abstraction attempting to depict the "criss-crossing" planes of influence and difference within history, which nonetheless resembles a sense of unity when examined over greater lengths of time.[41] Similarly influential on Schillebeeckx's conception of historicity was Thomas Kuhn's seminal work *The Structure of Scientific Revolutions*. Here Kuhn presents a theory of scientific knowledge where various "paradigms" or "interpretive models" throughout history provide the categorical and conceptual basis for all knowledge within those contextual moments. Nevertheless, Kuhn argues that every one of these paradigms will eventually be overthrown in "paradigmatic revolutions" whereby "all meaning already attained has to be 'translated' anew."[42] With both of these models, therefore, Schillebeeckx hopes to formulate an approach to the difficulties of historicity that can both recognize historical and contextual "newness" as an unavoidable reality and yet also not as utterly debilitating to the potential appraisal of knowledge within one's present context.

By appropriating a synthesis of Kuhn's and Braudel's systems of knowledge and historicity, Schillebeeckx is also able to integrate more seamlessly a Gadamerian conception of the "fusion of horizons" into his method of hermeneutical epistemology. Accordingly, within his hermeneutical method Schillebeeckx seeks to "design a *historical* frame of reference which is distinct from our *present* frame of reference and thus to become conscious of the other as different within the fusion of the two spheres (since historicity is one great evolving process)—that is understanding the past."[43] Therefore, "historicity" does not necessarily have to imply *incommensurability*; rather it eliminates the possibility of absolute historical symmetry without demanding an outright *a*symmetry of historical meaning. For Schillebeeckx this distinction is particularly important because he believes it allows him to uphold that the Christian scriptures (previously

---

41. Ibid., 576–9 (esp. 578).
42. Ibid., 580. Also see Kuhn, *The Structure of Scientific Revolutions*.
43. Schillebeeckx, *God the Future*, 29. Emphasis original.

described as "revelation-in-word") are an actual mediation of the ultimate truth of reality without denying that its language, structure, and even literary motifs are nonetheless culturally conditioned to the core.[44] In fact, in a noteworthy and telling moment of an interview much later in his career, Schillebeeckx elaborates on the significance of this point by insisting that the Christian scriptures *do* convey a meaningful interpretation of the truth of reality, while at the same time not doing so in a fundamentally *superior* way to any more contemporary theological expression of it. Instead, as he assesses it, the Christian scriptures do validly constitute a basis of knowledge, but only as the first among many "local theologies" that came both before and after their authorship.[45] And thus beginning with his hermeneutical evolution in the later 1960s, Schillebeeckx began to take a keen interest in the historical study of the sources and context of the New Testament scriptures. His interest now, however, would not be to decipher clear metaphysical categories of "truth" for comprehending the historical figure of Jesus, but rather forming meaning out of the "historically conditioned, localized and limited" retelling of Jesus's *story*.[46]

Even if a Braudelian conception of historicity alongside a Gadamerian method of historical differentiation and synthesis could assist Schillebeeckx in overcoming the problem of contextual *newness*, still these viewpoints did not necessarily resolve the other apparent tension of *change* in expressed meanings over time—whether of scripture, doctrine, or philosophical theology. As previously mentioned, Schillebeeckx's deep venture into hermeneutical studies had exposed him to yet another difficulty in validating any interpretation of reality. It unveiled that the hermeneutical problem of interpretation was not just one of historical distance but was also just as significantly one of humans' ontological condition—a state of being that permeates any interpretation of reality and meaning.[47] That is, Kennedy clarifies, the only element that can truly ever guarantee a "*continuity* between past expressions of faith and contemporary reinterpretations of faith is the *reality itself* referred to by *both* past and present formulations of faith."[48] Any determination of what this reality actually is, however, for Schillebeeckx can be labeled as nothing more than "ambiguous" at best. This is because the very structure of revelation (at the very least as it is perceived within the Christian tradition) naturally produces a "hermeneutical circularity" where contemporary interpretations are hypothesized based on the prior expressions of scripture (or dogma, theology, etc.), which in turn themselves are interpretations of even further prior expressions, experiences, and encounters of reality ad infinitum. In short, "the answer is to some extent

---

44. Schillebeeckx, *Christ*, 631–4.

45. Schillebeeckx, Oosterhuis, and Hoogeveen, *God Is New*, 59. Cf. Schillebeeckx, *World and Church*, 167.

46. Kennedy, *Deus*, 319, 311.

47. Schillebeeckx, *Understanding*, 38.

48. Kennedy, *Deus*, 184. Emphasis original.

determined by the question, which is in turn confirmed, extended or corrected by the answer." And so, individuals

> can never escape from this circle, because [they] can never establish once and for all the truth or the content of the word God. There is no definitive, timeless understanding which raises no more questions. The "hermeneutical circle" thus has its basis in the historicity of human existence and therefore all human understanding. The interpreter belongs to some extent to the object itself that he is trying to understand, that is, the historical phenomenon. *All understanding is therefore a form of self-understanding.*[49]

As a result of this conundrum, Schillebeeckx follows the lead of Wolfhart Pannenberg in contending that the question of truth must be disentangled from the question of "meaning" or "significance." For although "a totality of meaning embracing all experience does indeed at the same time coincide with the revelation of truth," still such a totality of meaning "by definition" cannot be known because any formulation of meaning "does not allow any experience outside itself" and its present situation.[50] Consequently, the *meaning* of any expression of reality can be determined and adjudicated based on its relevance and applicability by the interpreter of any present moment, while the *truth* of a statement—its correspondence to reality itself—can never be fully determined. Hence, Schillebeeckx concludes, "A modern theologian ... may feel *secure* as a believer and yet *hesitant* as a theologian—in this, he is respecting the mystery."[51] Schillebeeckx believes he can affirm a viable continuity of *meaning*—whether in the New Testament's transmitted experience of grace and salvation[52] or, for example, in the shared existential encounter with the Eucharist[53]—while preserving the mystery of ultimate truth by insisting on the necessary *reinterpretation* of that reality in order to make it communicate that meaning within a new context. Accordingly for Schillebeeckx, all religious knowledge contains both positive and negative components: a relatable and pragmatically verifiable *meaning* that speaks to the individual believer within one's particular context, and the mysterious truth of reality that always eludes confinement to the historical layers of interpretation.

By differentiating between the realities of ultimate *truth* and historical *meaning* in this almost dichotomous manner, Schillebeeckx believed he could maintain a commitment to the continuously experienced meaning of religious practice by believers across the spectrum of history and tradition, while at the same time also preserving the vital principle that "the real content of human knowing and believing is the ever present mystery of promise."[54] In consequence, he also began

---

49. Schillebeeckx, *God the Future*, 7–8. Emphasis added.
50. Schillebeeckx, *Church*, 173.
51. Schillebeeckx, *God the Future*, 19. Emphasis original.
52. Schillebeeckx, *Christ*, 32.
53. Schillebeeckx, *God the Future*, 34.
54. Ibid., 40.

to rearticulate the purpose and function of theology not as the dissemination of the metaphysical facts of all reality (the divine) but rather as the "reflection on, and articulation of, the mystery of faith as lived and experienced within concrete human history."[55] This new persuasion on the goal and nature of his own work and its general field was probably no more dramatically and emphatically enunciated than in his article "The New Image of God, Secularization and Man's Future on Earth," originally published in 1968 as *"Het nieuwe Godsbeeld, secularisatie en politiek"* for the Dutch *Tijdschrift voor Theologie (Journal of Theology)*.[56] Here he avers that the true hermeneutical problem confronting theology is not an undiscernable, unsalvageable truth lost in the past but instead the innately indeterminate mystery of the future—a future rife with interruptions, crises, and new voices, all of which can fundamentally change our conceptions of meaning and truth in unforeseen and profound ways.[57] As such, in this article he begins to reframe traditional notions of God's transcendence in terms of this future mystery.[58]

Presenting new titles to this indeterminate ultimate reality of God then, Schillebeeckx chooses to speak of God in more eschatological language such as "the [always] Coming One," "the One who is *our future*," and (in a clear play on the theologies of Martin Luther and later Karl Barth) no longer the hidden "wholly Other" but now the one manifested "as the 'wholly New.'"[59] This shift in theological language is significant because it represents not just an alteration in *rhetoric* but also a more foundational modification of *content*. For if ultimate reality ("God") can only be spoken of in terms of the future, then its openness and persistent vulnerability to the unforeseen interruptions of history (e.g., crisis, suffering, unknown "Others") make it intrinsically elusive of any theoretical definition. Moreover, as Hilkert elaborates, on this point "the insights of critical theorists [particularly Jürgen Habermas and Ernst Bloch] were to take him further: language and structures of the living tradition are not only inadequate; they may also be repressive distortions of the true mystery."[60] And so, a question still remained in Schillebeeckx's mind. Since any purely theoretical formulation of "truth" or a "totality of meaning" should not just be viewed with conceptual

---

55. Hilkert, "Hermeneutics," 115.
56. Schillebeeckx, *God the Future*, x. Cf. pp. 167–203.
57. Ibid., 172–3.
58. Ibid., 181.
59. Ibid.
60. Hilkert, "Hermeneutics," 118. It should also be noted, however, that Schillebeeckx certainly did not adopt a "Critical Theory" approach to hermeneutics wholesale. For his own further elaboration on the benefits, as well as the clear shortcomings, of Critical Theory, see Edward Schillebeeckx, "New Critical Theory" and "The New Critical Theory and Theological Hermeneutics," in *The Understanding of Faith*, 102–55 (127–8), as well as Edward Schillebeeckx, "Critical Theories and Christian Political Commitment," in *The Language of Faith: Essays on Jesus, Theology, and the Church*, Concilium Series (Maryknoll, NY: SCM Press, 1995), 71–82.

circumspection but also with political suspicion, then how can any theologian or believer convey any knowledge of truth in a nontheoretical way? And moreover, how can *other* believers assess the validity of an individual's expression of that truth? Schillebeeckx's response to these remaining theological quandaries is as direct as it is innovative:

> The *identity* of the new concept of God with the original Christian message will have to come indirectly to light in the activity of Christians themselves. If a reinterpretation of the Christian message produces an activity in which its identity with the Gospel cannot be discovered, this interpretation cannot be a Christian interpretation. It will therefore be apparent that there is a special kind of *understanding* which is appropriate to statements about faith—such statements, after all, have nothing to do with ideology. Hermeneutics consisting of the very practice of Christian life are therefore the *basis* for the concrete exegesis of ancient, biblical or magisterial texts.[61]

As the above passage displays, Schillebeeckx began to lean on the works of other contemporary theologians such as Pannenberg, Jürgen Moltmann, and Johann Baptist Metz[62] in order to emphasize "the basic hermeneutic problem" as the gap "between theory and practice" rather than "the relationship between past and present" as the most significant challenge to modern theology.[63] Because of historicity and interpretative change, he understood the question for contemporary religious epistemology as no longer being how knowledge can capture the totality of historical meaning but instead how articulations of knowledge could be open to an *anticipation* of new meanings inevitably caused by the crisis-ridden inbreaking of the future. For him, it had been all but proven impossible to formulate a positive, transhistorical, and transcultural expression of meaning that could not be altered by the unanticipated breach of new experiences.[64] However, despite the fact of unavoidable particularities in context and meaning, Schillebeeckx held that humans still shared at least one common experience of reality, namely the constant threat of humanity's destruction, extinction, and meaninglessness within history. Accordingly this perpetually existential threat looming over human history, he argues, is often manifested in particular, contextual instances of profound suffering,

---

61. Schillebeeckx, *God the Future*, 184.
62. Kennedy, *Deus*, 156–7. Kennedy provides a list of helpful resources focused on elaborations of the particular ideas of influence from these thinkers' systems on Schillebeeckx's thought. See Christoph Schwöbel, "Wolfhart Pannenberg," in *The Modern Theologians*, ed. David F. Ford, 2 vols. (Oxford, 1989), I, 257–92 (267); Richard Bauckham, "Jürgen Moltmann," *The Modern Theologians*, I, 293–310 (294); and for Metz, Dermot A. Lane, *Foundations for a Social Theology: Praxis, Process and Salvation* (Dublin: Paulist, 1981), 9–18.
63. Schillebeeckx, *Understanding*, 66. Cf. p. 117.
64. Schillebeeckx, *Church*, 755.

oppression, and hegemony within every culture. Borrowing from Habermas and Bloch, therefore, he names the particular instantiations of this common threat "negative experiences of contrast," which function against the hope of a potentially fulfilling future (i.e., the *humanum*).[65] Hence as opposed to formulating accurate theoretical definitions *of* reality, the only reasonable solution to this dilemma had to be an engagement in a critical, adaptive, and ad hoc "hermeneutic of praxis" that stressed a primacy of movement toward desired future outcomes *in* reality that could help avoid and alleviate this hovering threat of possible absurdity.

Therefore, as we will discuss in more detail in the next chapter with regard to Schillebeeckx's apophatic appropriation of Critical Theory, Schillebeeckx saw an "ethical praxis" orientated toward the indeterminate future as the source of an almost spiritually mystical "cognitive access" to the truth of all reality, God.[66] In other words, for him praxis becomes the sole mediator of a real encounter with the truth of reality—or, as he phrases it, an actual "deposit of faith"—that is not experienced as an object of knowledge in reality but instead the *promise* of a potential truth and meaningfulness in our reality which we ourselves help create.[67] "The conclusion is then," Schillebeeckx declares, "that the thematization of universal meaning can be accomplished meaningfully only with a practical-critical intention, i.e. in a perspective in which a bit of meaninglessness is done away with, step by step, through human action."[68] And in his mind there might be no better example of the historical construction of meaning through ethical-praxis than the nontheoretical, liberating, and "practical prolepsis" of future potentiality in Jesus's message of the oncoming "Kingdom of God."[69] Thus, it is to this particular application of his new hermeneutical epistemology that we will investigate in the later section of this chapter on Schillebeeckx's understanding of the authority of Christianity's religious founder.

B. Gendun Chopel: The "New Old World" of Buddhist Hermeneutics

Right from the outset, there are striking similarities and dissimilarities that stand out between how Schillebeeckx and Gendun Chopel epistemologically engage the topics of historical and hermeneutical consciousness within the contexts of their religious traditions and their own systems of thought. Like Schillebeeckx, Gendun Chopel left his home country toward the end of his academic training in the scholastic tradition of his religious order (however for a much more significant period of time) and was starkly confronted by modernist challenges to the traditional Buddhist interpretations of scripture and history, as well as to many of its broader religious claims to truth in light of a modern historical consciousness.

---

65. Schillebeeck, *Understanding*, 65.
66. Kennedy, *Deus*, 291.
67. Schillebeeckx, *God the Future*, 37.
68. Schillebeeckx, *Church*, 175.
69. Ibid., 176.

Therefore as a result of these exposures, both men wanted to find a way to maintain the viability of the truth claims of their religious traditions despite being confronted by modernist inclinations to disprove and relativize universal religious assertions of knowledge, narratives, and history. What makes Gendun Chopel's encounter with hermeneutics somewhat distinctive to Schillebeeckx's, however, is that within his Tibetan Buddhist tradition of philosophy there was already an established method of hermeneutics through which Gendun Chopel felt he could appropriately address these concerns. So whereas Schillebeeckx felt the need to incorporate a somewhat "alien" system[70] of contemporary modern hermeneutics into his Catholic theological method, Gendun Chopel seemed to want to *re*interpret the traditional hermeneutical system prevalent in much of Mahayana Buddhism in order to reconcile some issues quite similar to Schillebeeckx's. In the introduction to possibly one of the best-known volumes of collected essays on the topic, the editor of *Buddhist Hermeneutics*, Donald Lopez, explains that the hermeneutical endeavor of bringing the past into an experience of present is nothing new for Mahayana Buddhism (and certainly including Gendun Chopel's Geluk Tibetan philosophical tradition).

> If the goal of Mahāyāna philosophy is to bring oneself and others to the experience of enlightenment, which is nothing more or less than a repetition of the experience of the Buddha, then the attempt to establish the intention of the author, the goal of what Gadamer terms the Romantic endeavor, has strong

---

70. I acknowledge that modern hermeneutics did not arise within a historical vacuum but in fact its origin has actually been ascribed by some to the biblical criticism of Friedrich Schleiermacher (see Friedrich Schleiermacher, *Hermeneutics and Criticism and Other Writings*, Cambridge Texts in the History of Philosophy (New York: Cambridge University Press, 1998)), and so to describe modern hermeneutics as an "alien" system to Christianity might be slightly misleading. However, I choose to use the term "alien" to note how the contemporary iterations of modern hermeneutics that Schillebeeckx is utilizing do not claim the traditional Christian standards of interpretation as their own, and therefore most of its terminology, discourse, and evaluation would be seen as "foreign" to much of the prior Christian traditions of interpretation. For one of the most influential theories concerning Schleiermacher's relation to the rise of modern hermeneutics, see Wilhelm Dilthey, Rudolf A. Makkreel, and Frithjof Rodi, *Hermeneutics and the Study of History*, Selected Works / Wilhelm Dilthey (Princeton, NJ: Princeton University Press, 1996). Also, for another seminal discussion about where both Schleiermacher and Dilthey fit in the lineage of modern hermeneutics, see Palmer, *Hermeneutics*. Further complicating this "alien" distinction, moreover, Schillebeeckx's use of modern hermeneutics is often (particularly in the *Jesus* and *Christ* volumes) explicitly employed in a direct response to Rudolf Bultmann's largely influential writings on the existential interpretation of the New Testament. For an excellent overview on Bultmann's "demythologizing" hermeneutic of interpretation see Rudolf Bultmann, *The New Testament and Mythology and Other Basic Writings*, trans. Schubert M. Ogden (Philadelphia: Fortress Press, 1984).

soteriological overtones for the Buddhist. In this respect, the discussion of the intended audience of a given teaching is not merely a device by which one can relegate one's opponent to the audience of a provisional teaching. Rather, it is a means by which the interpreter attempts to find his own place among the circle surrounding the Buddha.[71]

Similarly in his own history of the origins of the doctrine of two truths within Mahayana Buddhism, *Echoes from an Empty Sky*, the History of Religions scholar—and Christian-Buddhist comparativist—John Buescher concurs with Lopez's above assessment. In fact Buescher argues that the doctrine of two truths, which we have already seen is the catalyst for Gendun Chopel's own epistemology, actually emerged primarily out of the Buddhist exegetical dilemma of interpreting their own scriptures, "particularly in abstracting the Buddha's highest teaching from the mass of his discourses." "In this sense," he continues, "the doctrine covered much of the same ground as another early distinction—between scriptures that were literal or definitive, and those that were figurative or required interpretation."[72] Thus, according to this line of argument, not only did Gendun Chopel's philosophical tradition embrace and provide him with an orienting framework for approaching the question of whether knowledge, meaning, and truth can be encountered through the particular historical teachings of a prior thinker (especially a religious founder) but indeed it also organically tied to such questions and, therefore, in at least some ways *had* to be dealt with by Gendun Chopel in order for him to lay out a meaningful and communally resonant Madhyamaka epistemology.

Moreover, for Gendun Chopel not only was an engagement in hermeneutics inherently necessary for a robust Two Truths theory within his Tibetan tradition of Mahayana Buddhism but indeed his philosophical tradition also provided the four foundational rules, or "refuges"/"reliances" (skt. *pratisaraṇa*), for doing textual interpretation—especially regarding the teachings of Śākyamuni Buddha. In fact, during his time in Sri Lanka he wrote that possibly the greatest connection linking "the Mahāyāna of the north and the Hīnayāna of the south" was their common recognition of "the four seals that define a view as being that of the Buddha." Indeed, for him this was one of the most sacred and profound connections across the various Buddhist traditions that "everyone needs to respect."[73] In his seminal article on the widely influential Mahayana sūtra the *Catuḥpratisaraṇasutra* (Sūtra of the Four Refuges) entitled "La critique d'interprétation dans le bouddhisme" (later translated into English as "Assessment of Textual Interpretation in Buddhism"),

---

71. Donald S. Lopez, *Buddhist Hermeneutics*, Studies in East Asian Buddhism (Honolulu: University of Hawaii Press, 1988), 7.

72. John B. Buescher, *Echoes from an Empty Sky: The Origins of the Buddhist Doctrine of the Two Truths* (Ithaca, NY: Snow Lion, 2005), 7.

73. Dge 'dun Chos 'phel, Jinpa, and Lopez, *Grains*, 346.

the late Belgian priest and influential scholar of Buddhism Étienne Lamotte[74] lays out these four principal concerns for the authority of textual interpretation:

> (1) the dharma is the refuge and not the person [skt. *puruṣa*—meaning the individual, historical teacher]; (2) the spirit is the refuge and not the letter; (3) the sūtra of precise meaning [*nītārtha*] is the refuge and not the sūtra of provisional meaning [*neyārtha*—that is, requiring interpretation or inference]; (4) (direct) knowledge is the refuge and not (discursive) consciousness.[75]

Accordingly, as Buescher later would observe while commenting on Lamotte's prior article, "The contrasts within these four 'reliances' suggest that within the diversity of appearances which offer contradiction and inconsistency, it is both possible and necessary for the Buddha's disciples to extract the pure kernel of truth. This was the goal of interpretation."[76]

Hence, this section will briefly expound on the ways that many Buddhists traditionally appropriated these "reliances" of interpretation and more specifically how these traditional understandings served as the foundation for Gendun Chopel's own epistemological hermeneutics. This will set up the discussion in the subsequent section of this chapter as to how Gendun Chopel employed this hermeneutical framework himself with regard to conceiving the epistemological authority of the historical Buddha (Śākyamuni)—albeit with his own modern or historically conscious twist. Thus after firmly establishing the traditional orientation to Gendun Chopel's line of questioning on the matter, we can then turn primarily to a few of Gendun Chopel's more practical pieces on this topic that he wrote during his twelve years traveling and researching in South Asia (primarily India and Sri Lanka). This will then allow us to examine how he attempted to reinvent these principles so as to ensure viability of the philosophical epistemology of his more culturally isolated community back in Tibet as well as his own. In this way, we will be able to better understand why Lopez declares that Gendun Chopel "discovered a new old world" during his time in India that both ensconced him in the value of the traditional tenets, practices, and historical sites of Indian Buddhism and at the same time embedded in his thought the conviction that Buddhism would cleverly have to find new ways to engage the persistently encroaching paradigm of Western modernity if it hoped to "abide together" with it for the next "ten thousand years."[77]

---

74. Originally published as Étienne Lamotte, "La critique d'interprétation dans le bouddhisme," *Annuaire de l'Institut de Philologie et d'Histoire Orientales et Slaves*, vol. 9 (Brussels, 1949), 341–61. Later it was translated into English as Étienne Lamotte, "Assessment of Textual Interpretation in Buddhism," in *Buddhist Hermeneutics*, Studies in East Asian Buddhism, ed. Donald S. Lopez Jr., trans. Sara Boin-Webb (Honolulu: University of Hawaii Press, 1988), 11–27.

75. Lamotte, "Assessment," 11–12. Cf. Buescher, 25–6.

76. Buescher, 26.

77. Dge 'dun Chos 'phel, Jinpa, and Lopez, *Grains*, 6, 407.

At least on the surface, the first "refuge" discussed by Lamotte in his article—"the dharma is the refuge and not the person"—might seem to be the most easily accessible and readily adaptable to a Western audience. This is because, at least as Lamotte reads it, this guideline suggests that adherence to any doctrine cannot be dependent on simply human authority alone, "however respectable, since experience shows that human evidence is contradictory and changeable; adherence should be based in personal reasoning (*yutki*), on what one has oneself known (*jñāta*), seen (*dṛṣṭa*) and grasped (*vidita*)."[78] Hence, a basic reading of this rule might seem to resonate with a Western counterpart who would value experimentation and experiential validation to any truth claim over a simple submission to the proclamations of a predetermined authoritative teacher. Therefore, it would seem easy for many Western thinkers to accept the *Bodhisattvabhūmi*'s conclusion (v. 257) that "By relying on reasoning and not on a person's authority, one does not deviate from the meaning of reality, because one is autonomous, independent of others when confronted with rationally examined truths."[79] However if one is reading all of these statements as doing away with a sense of reverence and devotion to the historical Buddha in exchange for a purely experientially verifiable orientation to deriving religious truth, that individual would be sorely mistaken and subsequently probably quite disappointed in much of the philosophical rhetoric of Gendun Chopel and others. The reason for such disappointment would be because, unlike Schillebeeckx who we will see wants to strip away suprahistorical "titles" that assert unparalleled revelatory authority from the historical figure of Jesus of Nazareth in order to show the more "pragmatic" authority of his life and teachings, Gendun Chopel among many other Buddhist philosophers incorporates in the prologues to most of his philosophical writings ornate overtures to Śākyamuni, as well as other Buddhas and Bodhisattvas, proclaiming his reverence, devotion, and dependence on the Buddha for understanding the revealed truth of the dharma. And in this way, to the untrained reader these declarations might seem to contradict this first principle completely.

However Malcom David Eckel explains in his book on the interconnection between religious philosophy and spiritual practice in Bhāvaviveka's conception of Madhyamaka, *To See the Buddha*, that this Western misconception typically derives from an almost implicit understanding of the dichotomous relationship between any idea of a universal truth (read dharma) and any particular historical manifestation or proclamation of that truth (i.e., the historical Buddha). In the Mahayana mindset however, Eckel illuminates, the relationship between the particular and the universal is viewed as interpenetrating rather than dichotomous.

---

78. Lamotte, "Assessment," 12 (referencing *Majjhima* I.265). Lamotte does also provide one caveat to this principle, however; citing the *Bodhisattvabhūmi* (v. 108) he explains that in the case of the spiritual novices or beginners who do not have the ability to judge reality and interpretation on the basis of their own insights yet, "faith in the master's word is a provisional necessity."

79. Lamotte, "Assessment," 12.

For example, Eckel shows using Bhāvaviveka's text *The Verses on the Essence of the Middle Way* how this revered Buddhist philosopher depicted this relationship between the universal dharma and its particular manifestation in Śākyamuni Buddha. "[We] consider [the Dharma Body] to be the Tathāgata's Body because it is not different in nature from [the Tathāgata] and because it is the reality that [the Tathāgata] has understood. And [we] do not [consider] it to be anyone else's [body] because [others] do not understand it."[80] Accordingly, Eckel contends, "For Bhāvaviveka, the concept of Emptiness and the concept of the Buddha were inseparable: to see Emptiness was to see the Buddha, and vice versa."[81] In fact, referencing the "Perfection of Wisdom" tradition (*Prajñāpāramitā*) within Mahayana Buddhism, Eckel utilizes the idea of the various "bodies" (*kāya*) of the Buddha to display the complex and ambiguous interconnection and dependence of this relationship.

> *Kāya* can mean not only the physical body, like *śarīra* and *ātma-bhāva*, but also "body" in the sense of "combination" or "collection." This further meaning makes it possible to speak of the Buddha's body as a "combination" of virtues or as a "collection" of teachings. When the different meanings of the word *kāya* are combined with the different meanings of the word *dharma*, it is possible to speak of the Buddha simultaneously as the physical entity that consists of the Dharma (a physical text), a combination or collection of the Dharma (the teaching), and a combination of *dharmas* (virtues or qualities) that are the Buddha's distinguishing characteristics.[82]

Furthermore, with some of his own unique interpretations and conclusions notwithstanding, Eckel proceeds to exhibit how this basic conception linking any historical manifestation of the Buddha to the ultimate dharma of emptiness itself is not peculiar to Bhāvaviveka's Madhyamaka philosophy alone but in fact is prominent across many of the various strains of Madhyamaka thought and even other Buddhist philosophical schools beyond it. Hence, one can begin to see that the conviction that "the dharma is the refuge and not the person" does not mean that the dharma is separable or even completely *divorced* from the historical teacher, but rather that the test of a teaching's dharmic authenticity does not rest in its association with the historical teacher *alone*. Instead it simply implies that a teaching's truth is dependent on its ability to assist the individual in seeing reality as it really is—empty. Thus, its authority does not rest in its ability to transcend the historical Buddha but actually in its ability to allow the Buddha to be seen by the present-day Buddhist practitioner and philosopher.[83]

---

80. Malcolm David Eckel, *To See the Buddha: A Philosopher's Quest for the Meaning of Emptiness*, 1st ed. (San Francisco, CA: HarperSanFrancisco, 1992), 46, 170.
81. Ibid., 3.
82. Ibid., 99–100.
83. Ibid., 142–7.

Moreover, Paul Harrison's various pieces on the Buddhist theory and ritual practice of *buddhānusmṛti*—"usually translated into English as 'recollection,' 'remembrance' or 'commemoration of the Buddha,' 'calling the Buddha to mind,' or 'meditation on the Buddha'"[84]—also provide an excellent example of the ambiguous and interpenetrating relationship between the historical manifestations of the Buddha and the encounter of ultimate dharma. Now admittedly the literature regarding this practice of *buddhānusmṛti* does not typically reflect directly on discussions of visualizations of Śākyamuni Buddha but rather focuses more toward extant buddhas such as the buddha Amitābha through the famous recitation of the *nembutsu* (Japanese; Ch. *nien-fo*).[85] Nonetheless Harrison suggests that this practice, which he describes as "pre-eminent" across Mahayana literature, provides a substantial insight into the interconnection between realizing the dharma (namely, emptiness) and visualizing the qualities and even "physical attributes" of the Buddha through "an imaginative evocation of his presence by means of structured meditative practices."[86] This is because no matter which buddha a person concentrates on to evoke the *samādhi* of an empty experience (skt. *śūnya*), it is believed that "all Buddhas everywhere resemble the historical Buddha in that, by and large, they follow the same course, undergo the same experiences, acquire the same attainments, and perform the same services to the beings in their sphere of influence."[87] Accordingly, Harrison contends that this practice functions "by collapsing the I with the Thou, by placing the process of identification with the 'deity' in the forefront of the practitioner's consciousness"[88] and as such displays how for many Mahayana Buddhist practitioners and philosophers the prioritization of "dharma" over "teacher" is not the separation of dharma away from the teacher but in fact the exact opposite. Instead, it is actually *through* their ability to visualize, and therefore to access, the Buddha that "practitioners are assured of the constant possibility of hearing the dharma, and thus authentic *buddhavacana* may be brought into the world at any time."[89] Thus, what these two examples show is that the rule of "the dharma not the person" is not a rejection of the particular in preference of the universal, rather it is the insistence that the validity of a teaching cannot be based solely on it being a profession of the Buddha himself but must be based on a particular teaching's ability to cultivate the experiential realization of the dharma in the current receiver.

84. Paul Harrison, "Commemoration and Identification in *Buddhānusmṛti*," in *In the Mirror of Memory: Reflections on Mindfulness and Remembrance in Indian and Tibetan Buddhism*, ed. Janet Gyatso (New York: SUNY Press, 1992), 215.

85. Paul Williams, *Buddhism: Critical Concepts in Religious Studies*, 8 vols., Critical Concepts in Religious Studies (New York: Routledge, 2005), 85–6.

86. Ibid., 86–7.

87. Ibid., 88, 93. Cf. Harrison, "Commemoration," 222–3.

88. Harrison, "Commemoration," 227.

89. Paul Harrison, "Mediums and Messages: Reflections on the Production of Mahāyāna Sūtras," *Eastern Buddhist* 35, no. 2 (2003): 124.

This distinction between prioritizing the experience of the dharma in a teaching over the simple authority of the historical Buddha himself leads directly into the second of the four reliances of interpretation—the focus on "the spirit not the letter." By raising the point of how the visualization of the qualities and even the historical manifestation of the Buddha himself are inseparable from an encounter with the ultimate dharma, we are then left wondering why the hearer of the Buddha's teachings cannot accept them as authoritative based on their connection to the Buddha alone. Lamotte elucidates the answer to this question as conveying that from a traditional Buddhist perspective although the ultimate meaning of any teaching of the Buddha is "single and invariable," still the literal form and exact wording of a given teaching ("the letter") is "infinitely variable" so that even "the four noble truths which were expounded in Vārāṇasī have only one acceptable meaning, but they can be explained in an infinity of ways."[90] In other words, since the Buddha can use an infinite amount of expressions, analogies, and images to lead the hearer to an encounter with the dharma, if one holds too literally to the words of his teachings themselves as the basis for experiencing and understanding this reality, that individual risks reifying and projecting his or her own conventional devices of language and conceptual constructs onto the meaning of the teaching rather than truly seeing the dharma as it really is—the nonaffirming absence of emptiness. Or as Lamotte tersely frames it, "The letter indicates the spirit just as a fingertip indicates an object, but since the spirit is alien to syllables (akṣaravarjita), the letter is unable to express it in full. Purely literal exegesis is therefore bound to fail."[91]

Citing the *Majjhima Nikaya* ("Collection of Middle-Length Discourses" of the Buddha), Lamotte theorizes that this rule was basically intended to counteract the tendency among monks who fail in their monastic duties because they would seek simply to memorize the various teachings of the Buddha without actually attempting to *understand* their meaning. For this reason, in the *Majjhima* the Buddha chides some of his followers explaining, "There are some foolish men who learn the *dhamma, suttas, geyas,* and so on by heart but once they have learned it by heart they do not examine the meaning in order to understand the texts."[92] Similarly, Lamotte uses an iconic passage from the much revered (and also at times quite impervious) *Laṅkāvatārasūtra* to expound on how the "spirit is alien to syllables" and as such incapable of being expressed simply through "the letter" of (or by a "purely literal exegesis" of) a text:

> O Mahamati, the son and daughter of good family should not interpret the spirit according to the letter since reality is not connected with syllables *(mraksaratvdt*

---

90. Lamotte, "Assessment," 13.
91. Ibid., 15.
92. Ibid., 14, quoting *Majjhima* I, 133. Cf. Buescher, 52. Here Buescher explains how the motif of the "fool" who fails to see the true dharma beyond the particular (because that individual reifies the conventional as the ultimate) is prevalent across Buddhist literature.

tattvasya). One should not act like those who look at the finger: it is as if someone pointed out something with his finger to someone else and the latter persisted in staring at the fingertip [instead of looking at the object indicated]; similarly, just like children, foolish worldlings end their lives as attached to that fingertip which consists of the literal translation and, by neglecting the meaning indicated by the fingertip of literal interpretation, they never reach the higher meaning. It is as if someone were to give some rice to children, for whom it is the customary food, to eat but without cooking it; whoever were to act in such a way should be considered foolish, since he has not understood that the rice must first be cooked; equally, the nonarising and nondestruction [of all things] is not revealed if it has not been prepared; it is therefore necessary to train and not to act like someone who thinks he has seen an object merely by looking at a fingertip. For this reason, one should try and reach the spirit. The spirit, which is in isolation, is a cause of nirvāṇa, while the letter, which is bound up with discrimination favors saṃsāra. The spirit is acquired in the company of educated people, and through learning, one should be conversant with the spirit and not conversant with the letter. To be conversant with the spirit is a view which is alien to the discussions of all the sectaries: it is not lapsing into it oneself and not making others lapse into it. In such conditions, there is a learning of the spirit. Such are those who should be approached by someone who seeks the spirit; the others, those who are attached to the literal interpretation, should be avoided by those who seek the truth.[93]

In the case of Gendun Chopel, this fundamental suspicion of language and the *literal* interpretation of any text or teaching of the Buddha provide him with one way of reconciling classical Buddhist texts with the challenges posed by modern historical criticism. Hence it does not necessarily matter if "the letter" of Buddhist texts can withstand the scrutiny of critical historical examination (in fact some might say that Gendun Chopel is often all too quick to concede such debates to Western criticism), because as he would later insist in the *Adornment*: "When we carefully examine all of these assumptions that we hold about supramundane qualities, they are merely fabrications from examples taken from the world and, within that, from the human realm alone."[94]

Nonetheless in a way somewhat similar to the first reliance, Lamotte also cautions that this proscription of *subordination* of "the letter" to "the spirit" should not be mistaken to mean that the *Catuḥpratisaraṇsūtra* intends to completely deny the relevance and importance of "the letter" either. Although the spirit must always take precedence, the best teachings of "the good doctrine" are ones that are perfect in their spirit and in their letter—this is the sign of "a good monk, a good instructor and a student."[95] Thus he cites the *Sūtrālaṃkāra* in order to exhibit

93. Lamotte, "Assessment," 15.
94. Chos phel, "Adornment," 52–3, v. 22.
95. Lamotte, "Assessment," 13–14.

how a good exposition of the dharma by the Buddha is "good in the beginning, in the middle and at the end: the meaning is good (*sāttha*) and the letter is good (*savyañjana*)."⁹⁶ So according to the *Sūtrālaṃkāra* one can assess the value of a teaching by determining if the meaning is good "because it applies to conventional truth and absolute truth, and that its letter is good because the phrases and syllables are intelligible."⁹⁷

Likewise in his own article in the same volume, Lopez reminds the contemporary scholar not to conflate the prioritization of the spirit over the letter within Buddhist hermeneutics with modern Western notions (such as he argues in Gadamer) of an inherent relativity and boundless potentiality of future meaning in the words of a given text. He explains that—unlike the process we have already observed in Schillebeeckx's emergent methodology—for the Buddhist interpreter, "the discovery of the true meaning of the text is not the infinite process that Gadamer envisions; the horizons of the Buddha and the interpreter are not even imagined to exist separately." In other words, the experience of emptiness *transcends* the limits and boundaries of historical and conventional depiction, and as such one does not need to *make* meaning out of a passage of the Buddha's teaching "through a conversation with the text" but rather the Buddha's teachings should elicit the singular universal meaning of the dharma in the current hearer. And so, as we will see in Gendun Chopel's discussion of the authority of the Buddha in light of modern science, he is resolute that there is no need for some form of a Gadamerian "fusion of horizons."⁹⁸ Even if the prioritization of the spirit over the letter does not simply relegate the letter to irrelevance and obscurity, nevertheless Lopez reflects elsewhere that the claim of there being teachings that match in accuracy according to both the spirit and the letter in contradistinction to those which do not still "raises a number of fascinating questions about when and where the words of the Buddha are to be taken at face value, and when they should be declared merely provisional, questions that the tradition has struggled with for two millennia."⁹⁹ It is to these questions we turn in our discussion of the third refuge of Buddhist hermeneutics.

From very early on within the development of the Buddhist tradition, even as early as the Sarvāstivādins, interpreters of the sutras were confounded by the apparent difficulty of interpretation that "the Blessed One uttered words which were not in accordance with the meaning (*ayārtha*), that sutras spoken by the Buddha were not all precise in meaning (*nītārtha*) and that the Buddha himself said that certain sūtras were indeterminate in meaning (*anītārtha*)."¹⁰⁰ Much

---

96. Ibid., 13.

97. Ibid. Citing *Sūtrālaṃkāra*, 82.

98. Donald S. Lopez Jr., "On the Interpretation of the Mahāyāna Sūtras," in *Buddhist Hermeneutics*, Studies in East Asian Buddhism, ed. Donald S. Lopez Jr., trans. Sara Boin-Webb (Honolulu: University of Hawaii Press, 1988), 65-7.

99. Lopez, *Science*, 70.

100. Lamotte, "Assessment," 16.

later in the *Madhyamakāvatāra* (VI.44) the revered Madhyamaka philosopher Candrakīrti explained the primary source of this conundrum:

> Even though the Buddha is free from the view of self (*satkāyadṛṣṭi*),
> He teaches [using the terms] "I" and "mine."
> In the same way, although things lack intrinsic nature,
> He teaches that they exist as an interpretable meaning.[101]

Therefore, Lopez quips, rather than endure the "inconvenience of expunging all nouns such as 'I,' 'myself,' 'oneself,' and 'person,' from the common parlance," Buddhist commentators had to cipher a way to accommodate for the Buddha's wide use of such language while at the same time not undercutting his teaching authority.[102] Consequently alongside the development of the doctrine of two truths, which attempted to reconcile the apparent (conventional) existence of objects with an ontological viewpoint of ultimate emptiness, another pair of cardinal terms was also employed to distinguish between the scriptural passages whose meaning is "definitive" (*nītārtha*) and the ones whose meaning requires "interpretation" (*neyārtha*).[103] As Dreyfus explains, such a system of hierarchy for interpretation was necessary to narrow the boundaries of a text's polysemy and thus avoid any type of hermeneutical relativism by not granting all possible competing interpretations of a text with equal validity.[104] And thus, with the exception of the early Mahāsāṃghika school which insisted that *all* teachings of the Buddha were definitive (*nītārtha*), most Buddhist exegetes would use this twofold system of "definitive" and "provisional" (or "requiring interpretation") classifications as one of the most fundamental guidelines of exposition.[105]

In his iconic text the *Mūlamadhyamaka-kārikā* (*Fundamental Verses of the Middle Way*), which is widely considered the foundation of all Madhyamaka philosophy, the most revered Buddhist philosopher Nāgārjuna provided the basic demarcation between these two categories of scriptures: scriptures of "precise meaning" were ones whose "allegations are obvious and easily understood," whereas scriptures of "provisional meaning" are "those which through skillful means (*upāya*) say things which at first sight seem to be incorrect and which demand an explanation."[106] Therefore, simply put, scriptures that can be read literally without contradiction are definitive while ones requiring an explanation to reconcile contradictions are provisional. Or as Lopez aptly condenses it, "If the statement is what the Buddha meant, it is definitive. If it is not, it is interpretable."[107]

---

101. Lopez, *Hermeneutics*, 62.
102. Ibid., 61.
103. Cowherds, 5.
104. Dreyfus, *Hands*, 192.
105. Lamotte, "Assessment," 16.
106. Ibid., 17–18.
107. Lopez, *Hermeneutics*, 59.

As one can imagine, however, developing common criteria to determine which texts can be read completely literally would prove to be a completely different matter, with each various school tending to "take literally the doctrinal texts which conform to its theses and to consider those which cause dilemmas as being of provisional meaning."[108]

Nevertheless, generally speaking most schools within the Mahayana tradition began to equate "provisional meaning" with sūtras associated with the first "turning of the wheel of doctrine"—namely the Four Noble Truths and especially the doctrine of no-self (anātman)—while "definitive meaning" was aligned with any teaching of the doctrine of emptiness (śūnyatā). Lamotte provides a passage from the Samādhirājasūtra as a prime example of this orientation: "Whoever knows the value of texts with a precise meaning knows the [precise] way in which emptiness has been taught by the Sugata; however, wherever there is a matter of an individual, being or man, he knows that all those texts are to be taken as having a provisional meaning."[109] Still the disputes could certainly not end there. Texts such as the Laṅkāvatārasūtra and Saṃdhinirmocana (both associated with the "mind-only," Yogācāra school) asserted themselves as a "third turning of the wheel of doctrine" and ipso facto the true and absolute definitive teaching of the Buddha—although not without contestation from Madhyamaka detractors.[110] What is particularly relevant to our discussion of Gendun Chopel's epistemology, however, is the fact that somewhat in concert with these Yogācāra views (which he repeatedly shows a proclivity toward in his own appropriation of Madhyamaka) Gendun Chopel also seems inclined to push the division of "definitive" and "provisional" meanings beyond the teachings of emptiness and everything else. Rather than prioritizing a new hierarchy of *texts* such as the Yogācāra ones just discussed, however, Gendun Chopel followed a system of demarcation more in line with some tantras of the esoteric Vajrayāna tradition (another school of thought he was well versed in and clearly sympathetic toward). The unique position taken within some of this literature, which Gendun Chopel found especially appealing within his own epistemology, is that the two labels of "definitive" and "provisional" can be "applied to *one and the same passage*" so that any teaching of Buddha can be said to contain both nītārtha and neyārtha, definitive and provisional meanings.[111] Similarly in accordance with his own epistemological conviction of the impossibility of "the very notion of valid knowledge for unenlightened beings," Gendun Chopel contends that "short of

---

108. Lamotte, "Assessment," 19.

109. Ibid., 18–19.

110. Lopez, *Hermeneutics*, 54–8. Lopez gives one particular example of Candrakīrti's Madhyamaka rebuttal to such assertions of Yogācāra in the *Madhyamakāvatāra* (VI.95).

111. Michael M. Broido, "Killing, Lying, Stealing, and Adultery in the *Kālacakratantra*," in *Buddhist Hermeneutics*, Studies in East Asian Buddhism, ed. Donald S. Lopez Jr., trans. Sara Boin-Webb (Honolulu: University of Hawaii Press, 1988), 72.

becoming enlightened oneself" there is no way to parse the provisional and definitive meanings of a passage, because the Buddha only used all language as a skillful means for the sake of his audience. Therefore, all linguistically based assertions are by definition "merely provisional" and can only be "definitive" if they enable nondiscursivity.[112]

And so, once again we can see how Gendun Chopel's reframing of one of the four "reliances" of Buddhist hermeneutics quite naturally flows into his conception of the next one. This time it is the irreconcilable mixture of the linguistically provisional meanings and the direct experiential definitive meaning within all teachings of the Buddha that shape his own understanding of the last "refuge" of interpretation: "direct knowledge is the refuge not discursive consciousness." Although we will examine this final branch of his hermeneutics in greater detail in the next chapter concerning his conception of the epistemological authority of direct religious experience, let us briefly here discuss its relevance in Gendun Chopel's formulation of the authority of the historical Buddha. For Gendun Chopel, the fourth and final refuge of direct knowledge over discursive thought and expression takes a clear precedence above all the others in his epistemological hermeneutics. Following the tact of the *Bodhisattvabhūmi* (v.257), he seems to adopt its assertion that

> The bodhisattva attaches great importance to the knowledge of the direct comprehension [of the truths], and not to mere discursive consciousness of the letter of the meaning, which [consciousness] arises from listening and reflecting. Understanding that what should be known through knowledge arising from meditation cannot be recognized only through discursive consciousness arising from listening and reflecting, he abstains from rejecting or denying the teachings given by the Tathāgata, profound as they are.[113]

It is only the direct apprehension of the knowledge of all reality through the conscious awareness of the nonaffirming absence of ultimate emptiness that can be in any way recognized as a "definitive meaning" and therefore "valid knowledge." Hence, such passages affirm Gendun Chopel's conviction that the only way by which one can understand the epistemological authority of the historical Buddha is to be led by the Buddha to a "transcendental and undefiled" encounter with reality that "confers on the ascetic the quality of the holy one."[114] Therefore, in accordance with his reading of Dharmakīrti, any use of language (even the Buddha's) cannot be seen as a valid source of knowledge separate from an existential encounter with

---

112. Lopez, "*Vigrahavyāvartanī* 29," 173–4.
113. Lamotte, "Assessment," 23.
114. Ibid., 24.

emptiness. In this way, any statement or teaching of the Buddha can only be taken as a reliable *indicator* of the Buddha's *intention* and not as definitive proof of his meaning or argument.[115] This is because according to common interpretations of Dharmakīrti, linguistic assertions are not "self-validating," meaning that "[discursive] thought can never be directly in touch with real individuals. It is limited to its own constructs." Thus, they require inference in order to determine meaning indirectly through mental constructs, and as such can at best "inform us of the speaker's subjective intentions."[116] And so, Gendun Chopel views the historical Buddha's authority as not located in the words and syntax of his teaching but in his efficaciousness to bring individuals to an existential encounter with the truth of reality through his words and being. Hence, Gendun Chopel believes he upholds Nāgārjuna's proclamation that "The Buddha did not teach any doctrine, [a]nywhere to anyone" but simply orientates them to an experience of the Ultimate themselves.[117]

In conclusion, then, as we turn to how each of these thinkers specifically applied his epistemological hermeneutics to his conception of the authority of the respective historical founders of their traditions, once again we can observe similarities in their conclusions despite the seemingly antithetical presuppositions to their hermeneutical methods. In the end, both Schillebeeckx and Gendun Chopel want to move away from an understanding of authority that situates the truth of a religious founder in his particular, contingent use of words and imagery (and the texts that convey them) and instead relocate it in an openness to a nondiscursive reality beyond the historical purview. As this preceding section displayed, however, Gendun Chopel's hermeneutical method toward achieving this goal of relocating the Buddha's authority can be said to have done so through a more identifiable *re*interpretation of the categories of traditional Buddhist hermeneutics. Schillebeeckx, on the other hand, admittedly sought to bring new or "alien" methods of modern hermeneutics—albeit ones he saw as congruent or at least compatible with traditional Christian understandings—into his Catholic theological method. As we will observe in the following sections, this distinction in their approaches would bear a great effect on their depictions of the founding historical figures of their tradition, especially in regard to how they adhere to previous conceptions of those figures from within their respective traditions. Therefore, with that said, it is to this observation and discussion that we now must turn.

---

115. Dreyfus, *Hands*, 252.

116. Dreyfus, *Reality*, 294–6. Cf. Tillemans, *Scripture*, 41–2. Here Tillemans synthesizes quotes from the *Svārthānumānaparicccheda* of Dharmakīrti's famous *Pramāṇavāttika* (his commentary on Dignaga's *Compendium on Valid Cognition*) to exhibit this point.

117. Lopez, *Hermeneutics*, 48.

III. The Problems and Potential of Universal Truths within Particular Teachings

A. Schillebeeckx: Jesus's Story as the Experience, Teaching, and Action of "Revelation-in-Reality"

As I mentioned in the introduction to the section on his incorporation of hermeneutical and historical consciousness into his theological method and understanding, Schillebeeckx's Christology is definitely the most suitable illustration of the full effects of these consciousnesses at work within his own religious epistemology. This is the case despite the fact that practically *all* scholars of his work would agree that his Christology can only be labeled as an "evolving" element of his thought throughout his career (as really one could say for his entire corpus). The reason for this sense of continuity in spite of the apparent evolution nonetheless is because from even some of his earliest reflections on the topic going as far back as his first years lecturing at Louvain, his Christological method has always underscored a primacy of Jesus's humanity for interpreting his universal and historical significance. In fact, Kennedy insists, throughout his Christological development and in the midst of every one of his Christological "crises of faith," Schillebeeckx believed he consistently returned to a fundamentally *Thomistic* hermeneutical principle that he was taught in his earliest years as a student— namely the necessary preeminence of the actual reality *believed in* over any conceptual expressions of that reality in forming one's knowledge.[118] Accordingly one could easily argue that even though his answers to the theological questions he believed to be most imperative throughout his career certainly "evolved," nonetheless the central theological question itself did not. It is the persistent struggle to explain "how human beings can make cognitive contact with God, or, otherwise expressed, how universal meaning can be known through historical particularity."[119] And for him, there can be no greater exemplar of locating the universal through a "historically particular intermediary" for Christians than in their founding figure of Jesus.[120]

Schillebeeckx's choice then to make Christology the "epistemological crucible" of his system (to borrow Kennedy's phrase) was neither arbitrary nor artificial. Instead, as highlighted in the previous section on his influences and foundations, the question of Jesus's authority as a preceptor of truth remains naturally grounded in his dialectical understanding of the knowledge of ultimate reality as at the same time both "revelatory" (emerging out of an encounter of that reality itself) and "salvific" (crucial to humanity's sapiential, social, and spiritual betterment)—even though his understanding of this relationship becomes increasingly complex and historically situated over time. Hence, in this section we will examine how throughout its development Schillebeeckx's Christology, and subsequently

---

118. Kennedy, *Deus*, 295.
119. Ibid., 286.
120. Schillebeeckx, *Jesus*, 592.

his understanding of Jesus's epistemological authority, persistently sought to answer three axiomatic questions concerning the nature of knowledge: its source ("revelation"), the dialectical tension between one's encounter of it and one's expression of it (i.e., "revelation-in-reality" versus "revelation-in-word"), and finally its implications on a broader human spirituality. By investigating his shift to a historically focused Christology "from below," his narratival reinterpretation of the implications of Jesus's life for humanity, as well as his reconstruction of the role of theology for Christians in light of the continuous mystery and hope of Jesus's message and actions, we will be able to better appreciate how for Schillebeeckx the historical figure of Jesus of Nazareth can be at the same time *crucial* for a Christian articulation of knowledge while also not exclusively necessary for a general human understanding of ultimate truth and existential meaning.

Even from some of his earliest theological reflections on the nature and significance of Jesus, Schillebeeckx held that any understanding of Jesus's universal import could not be done apart from a particular focus on his humanity and historical life. There is no doubt, moreover, that this sharp focus on Jesus's personal history would only intensify throughout the progression of his Christology and career as Schillebeeckx's own historical consciousness would ever-increasingly protrude to the forefront of his thought. As discussed in the previous section, assisted by the hermeneutical influences of Gadamer and Ricœur as well as the historiographical interpretations of Braudel and Kuhn, Schillebeeckx became persuaded by the argument that all knowledge is inseparably conjoined to the historical context of knower, and in particular with the "interpretative models" or "paradigms" prominent at that time. In this way one's knowledge is always simultaneously grounded in an absolute reality, which is its source and serves as an "inner norm" of its validity, while at the same time the knower also never possesses that reality in itself but always through the guise of the current historical situation, or "interpretative horizon."[121] The conditions regarding our knowledge of Jesus of Nazareth are no different. Although our interpretive understanding of Jesus is still built against a background of other interpretive concepts and influences, nevertheless Schillebeeckx maintains that for Christians there is no more "concentrated" manifestation of the epistemological conditions of universal knowledge within a particular expression of history than in the message and actions of Jesus of Nazareth.

However, to say that Jesus's humanity is *singularly* important in Schillebeeckx's Christology would certainly be an overstatement. Rather the humanity of Jesus only seemed to be the crux of Schillebeeckx's project because it is precisely where the Christian interpretation of Jesus becomes most scandalous. It is scandalous because the firm assertion of Jesus's humanity for Christians inevitably also results in the assertion that through this particular historical Palestinian something about the nature and totality of all reality is revealed. As a result, early on in his career Schillebeeckx would discuss at length about the difficulty of formulating a

---

121. Schillebeeckx, *God the Future*, 40; *Jesus*, 585–90.

conception of the "hypostatic union" in Christ—the divine and human natures in one person—in a way that did not convey a sense of a final Christological dualism within the contemporary philosophical idiom. His solution, which he would uphold throughout his Christological development, was to assert a "Hypostatic *Unity*" (rather than union) in the person of Jesus of Nazareth. In short, Jesus is essentially *one*—one indivisible human being through whom the ultimate reality of God is encountered and revealed.

Hence it is this specific investment in cordoning off any possible sense of duality from an understanding of Jesus that leads Schillebeeckx—especially beginning in the latter half of the 1960s—to both promote and also philosophically constrain the potential of historical-critical methods for approaching the New Testament with regard to the historical person of Jesus.[122] For him, a deep historical understanding of the context and data regarding the biblical narrative can certainly help add nuance and depth to the exegetical interpretation of the text. In this way, it provides boundaries for any possible interpretation and allows the text (as much as it can) to speak more for itself. In other words, while he certainly finds the historical-critical interpretation of data significant and helpful in his own exegesis of Jesus's *story*, he nonetheless rejects any Harnackian idea of an unassailable "kernel" of truth that can be discovered by shucking away all of the "historical husk." On the other hand, however, Schillebeeckx also acknowledges that his selection of a more historical-critical approach to biblical exegesis is still "only one of many possibilities" selected particularly to fit his own "pastoral intention" of dogmatic "translation." And in this sense, he admits it relativizes his entire project.[123] Therefore, Kennedy situates Schillebeeckx squarely within the camp of the "New Quest" for the historical Jesus as opposed to the "Old." This is because, simply put, Schillebeeckx recognizes the impossibility of ever historically reconstructing the "earthly Jesus" as he actually was in his time, but still sees a profound value in reimagining a "historical Jesus" (based on historical and archeological data) in order to serve one's own pragmatic purpose for exegesis.[124]

Yet he argues his own interpretive exegesis—"relative" as it might be—does have "its own right to existence," a right that is proven in the pragmatic ("pastoral") value of its contribution. In Schillebeeckx's case, this pragmatic value was a fundamental shift in Christological method away from using dogmatic confessions of faith (read Chalcedon) as the starting point for one's own understanding of the significance of Jesus (Christology "from above"), to one instead where such confessions are the "point of arrival that follows a search for the identity of Jesus which begins

---

122. See Kennedy, *Schillebeeckx*, 106–8, for an excellent and concise summary of Schillebeeckx's sources for his historical-critical assessments of the New Testament. In this passage Kennedy points to Schillebeeckx's 1972 article *"De toegang tot Jezus van Nazaret"* ("Access to Jesus of Nazareth") as the premier example of the depth to which he sought and used historical-critical methods in his Christological exegesis.

123. Schillebeeckx, *Jesus*, 36–40 (esp. 40).

124. Kennedy, *Deus*, 319. Also see Schillebeeckx, *Interim Report*, 29.

with the earliest historical interpretations of Jesus" (Christology "from below"). Accordingly, in his later more historically conscious Christology "he concluded that Jesus is the primary focus of Christian faith, whereas 'Christ' is somewhat secondary in that the notion of Christ is a faith-inspired, human, theoretical construction: in short, it is a title."[125] And although there is nothing inherently wrong with the Christological titles in and of themselves, Schillebeeckx believes that such presuppositions to interpretation account for at least part of the reason for the dilemma of "hermeneutical circularity" discussed earlier—where an answer is derived from a question that presupposes the answer. Instead Schillebeeckx explains that he wants to hold the notions of "faith seeking understanding" (*fides quaerens intellectum*) and "understanding seeking faith" (*intellectus quaerens fidem*) together in tension within his Christology, so that understanding is not simply used as a mechanism to justify one's faith but in fact might organically emerge out of one's own encounter with the historical figure of Jesus of Nazareth.[126] As a result, Schillebeeckx seeks to distance himself from some of his own earlier proclamations of Jesus as the inbreaking of "the infinite" into history, and later in his career instead chooses to speak of Jesus as the one who "raises the issue of God in an age which in most if not all sectors of its life appears to do without God."[127]

Pulling back from the particulars of his Christological argument for a moment then, one can now begin to see the full implications of Schillebeeckx's epistemology in his eventual outworking of his Christological development. For example, Schillebeeckx's focus on establishing a Christology "from below" highlights his conviction that all knowledge can only originate out of an existential encounter with reality, and in particular *historicized* reality; as such "revelation" can only be an "unveiling" of a possibly hitherto unrecognized element of reality from within the particular linguistic and historical contexts of an individual's experience. In other words, ultimate truth is never encountered in an unmediated way that directly bypasses linguistic and categorical constriction. Instead, revelatory language and expression can always only *in*directly point to the truth of all reality,[128] and as such can at best only convey "God" through a "mediated immediacy."[129] It is for this reason that in his later works he would insist that the salvific nature of the revelatory knowledge of the "hidden God" can only be understood as a "this-worldly reality." Therefore, he asserts that it must be proclaimed that there is "no salvation outside the human world."[130] And so, because of the historically contingent nature of all knowledge, Schillebeeckx upholds his firm belief that all religious knowledge contains both positive and negative components—those cataphatically proclaimed

---

125. Kennedy, *Deus*, 295–6.
126. Schillebeeckx, *Jesus*, 33.
127. Ibid., 636.
128. Schillebeeckx, *Christ*, 810–17.
129. Ibid., 814–17.
130. Schillebeeckx, *Church*, 6–13 (12).

in human language and constructs and those apophatically eluding those same elements.

Similarly within Schillebeeckx's Christology, the figure of Jesus both unveils as well as veils one's potential knowledge of reality. Simply put, the person of Jesus affirms a truth about the nature of ultimate reality ("God") through the medium of historical and human contingency, while at the same time imposing limits on what can be known about the reality because of the constraints of his contextual manifestation in history—thus somewhat "relativizing" its potency.[131] As a historical person therefore, Jesus himself is both the source (or interpreter) of the knowledge of reality and also the object of interpretation for individuals today. Hence, Jesus is the embodiment of Schillebeeckx's epistemological dialectic of interpretation: he brings forth a knowledge of reality to its fullest possible historical expression, and yet he inevitably falls short of depicting that reality in and of itself due to the historical constraints of language and conceptuality. Moreover, one can argue that his use of Christology to convey the necessity of the transmission of knowledge through a radical conception of historicity leaves Schillebeeckx's most deep-seated question still unresolved. That is the question of how universal meaning can be known through historical particularity. Or, as he summarizes this dilemma Christologically,

> So religious faith in Jesus of Nazareth, a person appearing within our human history, is problematical for me if the personal relation of this historically localizable individual with the "Creator of heaven and earth," the universal factor cementing all that lives and moves—the living God—is not clear to us. Enthusiasm for "Jesus of Nazareth" as an inspiring human being I can appreciate—at the human level, that is quite something in itself! But it entails no binding invitation, can bear no stamp of the universally human, unless it can be shown that "the Creator," the (monotheistic) God of Jews, Muslims, Christians and so many others, is personally implicated in this Jesus event.[132]

Therefore just as Schillebeeckx acknowledged a distinction between the problem of "newness" (historicity) and that of "change" (the development of meaning) over time, this distinction also persists in the development of his Christology. As the above quote displays, despite his acknowledgment that the revelation of absolute reality could only come in a contextually particular form (i.e., Jesus), Schillebeeckx nevertheless still recognizes it as difficult, if not impossible, to justify an assertion of a universally applicable *meaning* based solely on an affinity to a particular manifestation of truth. In this way it is actually not merely Jesus's historical existence nor even the actual words, message, and activity of the "earthly Jesus" per se that can convey an universal meaning of history across the various contexts and theological interpretations. The universal significance of Jesus's actions and

---

131. Schillebeeckx, *Dogmatic vs. Biblical*, 133–6.
132. Schillebecckx, *Jesus*, 31.

message cannot be contained in a theological postulate nor in some theoretical participation in (or "implicit intuition" of) the totality of reality by which he can be the hermeneutical key to understanding in every context. Rather the universal applicability of the interpretation of Jesus's historical life for epistemological purposes rests in the narratival telling of his *story*. It is a story that is grounded in specific historic events and a particular cultural context, but nonetheless as a *story*—as an interpretive *retelling*—it can contain pertinency greater than some of its historical parts.[133]

Thus for Schillebeeckx, in the retelling of a story a text's "meaning" not only *can* but indeed unavoidably *does* carry an evocative surplus of potential meaning that exceeds even the intention of the speaker or author. Utilizing Metz's theological reflection on Aquinas as an example, Schillebeeckx argues that a text can contain "a datum" that is "really present" in the words and expression of its pages that at the same time was beyond the author's thematic consciousness. Hence, the concern of a reader is not so much the resembling of historical facts in order to discover the *intended meaning* of the author but instead to ask what is "the *reality* to which the [text] intentionally or unintentionally bear witness."[134] In fact, Schillebeeckx goes as far as to quote Heidegger's axiom in proclaiming that often "What is not thought is the supreme gift that any thinking has to give."[135] Schillebeeckx presents one such example of how meaning can exceed the immediate intention of an author, indeed even the originating experience itself, in his lengthy discussion of the "resurrection experience" in the first book of the Christological trilogy. Here he draws distinctions between the actual events surrounding the death and resurrection of Jesus, the interpretive experience of those events by the disciples themselves (based on the surplus of meaning of the events), and the interpretive expression of those events in the New Testament text (exemplifying the surplus of meaning within the authors' interpretative experience of those events). Moreover, he concludes, this textual narrative of the events in question actually spurs more historical interpretations based on its own surplus of meaning.[136]

Therefore Schillebeeckx insists that in the story of Jesus of Nazareth, this evocative surplus of meaning is typically manifested by a sense of hope that inspires the hearer not with a specific prescription of action or postulate of belief but rather by forming a "narrative-practical structure" of faith that promotes an evolving and shifting sense of "orthopraxis" that is capable of anticipating new embodiments of meaning and expression in different concrete situations.[137] This approach to understanding the theological meaning of the "Jesus narrative" typifies what makes Schillebeeckx's theology and Christology highly unique and yet even

---

133. Schillebeeckx, *Church*, 177–8.
134. Schillebeeckx, *God the Future*, 32–3.
135. Ibid., 33.
136. See Schillebeeckx, *Jesus*, 320–97. For another interesting example of Schillebeeckx's conception of this see Kennedy, *Deus*, 319.
137. Schillebeeckx, *Church*, 178.

more highly controversial. The goal in his Christology is not an attempt to uncover historical proof or even an interpretative retrieval of dogmatic Christological affirmations of the tradition within history, nor is it to use historical data to "unmask" the real "happenings" of the life of Jesus. Instead, it explicitly intends to investigate the origins of the Jesus narrative in order to chart its progression of meaning throughout a historical narrative so as to open it up to new potential interpretations and applicability based on its continued surplus of meaning. Or, as he explains this process elsewhere,

> The entirety of prior experience becomes a new framework for interpretation or "horizon of experience," within which we interpret new experiences. At the same time, new individual experiences subject this predetermined framework to interpretive critique and correction, or allow earlier experiences to be seen in a new context. In other words, our experience always occurs within an already given interpretive framework, which in the end is ultimately nothing other than the cumulative-personal and collective experience, a tradition of experience.[138]

This understanding of tradition is precisely why Schillebeeckx believes one can rightfully consider the New Testament as the first among many "local theologies" because the biblical expression of the events surrounding Jesus's life is a series of linguistic and conceptual interpretations that seek to *construct* meaning and that have continually proven to provide both the impetus and openness to *new* interpretations and constructions of meaning from age to age.[139] In fact, he believes that it is the church's and believers' failure to recognize this "openness of meaning" within the "tradition of interpretation" that causes most of, if not all, the "Christological crises" in contemporary theology. When believers, whether individually or collectively, attempt to dismember the surplus of meaning in the Christological narrative with the scalpels of idiosyncratic philosophical terminology or outmoded dogmatic formulas, they are often left with an incomprehensible expression that neither matches the creedal formulations they intend to emulate nor speaks to the interpretative horizon of "modern men and women." For him, it is precisely this interpretative disconnect caused by linguistic reification of doctrine that is the source of all the Christological searching and heated debates in contemporary theology.[140]

Moreover, this demand for constant reinterpretation and emphasis on the persistent "more" in potential meaning also leads to one of the most significant points of his Christology: the fact that *no* Christological interpretation of Jesus can be final. That is, all interpretations of Jesus and the Christ narratives are simply that—*interpretations*. They are readings based on one's own limited perspectival

---

138. Schillebeeckx, "Erfahrung und Glaube," 80.
139. Schillebeeckx, *God the Future*, 38–9.
140. Edward Schillebeeckx, *Jesus in Our Western Culture: Mysticism, Ethics, and Politics*, 1st British ed. (London: SCM, 1987), 46.

horizon of experience, bound by the constraints of one's own language and shaped by one's exposures to prior traditions of interpretation.[141] Just because Christians have found a particular relevance and responsiveness to the meaning they believe they have encountered in the Christ narrative does not mean that they know or understand "him" in a way unique from the other standard epistemological conditions for forming knowledge. In fact Schillebeeckx contends that Jesus's existence as a culturally conditioned and contextually situated human himself serves only to further underscore the fact that we only know about Jesus through the same limited means of all our knowledge; that there is always a lingering mystery at the heart of our knowledge of reality that can never be exhausted. And as result, there must be a plurality of interpretations, perspectives, and experiences in order to even begin to explore the fullness of this mysterious hole in all claims about reality. Indeed, for this reason Schillebeeckx reminds us that when it comes to interpreting the meaning and formulating any knowledge of the figure of Jesus, "*Anagkè stènai* ['we must stop']: sometimes it is high time—and tide!—for keeping silent in reverent adoration, and for critical recollection of the great tradition of *theologia negativa*. After all that we do know of him [Jesus], in the end we do not know who God is."[142] In other words, Schillebeeckx's Christology fully corresponds with the foundational theme of his entire theological epistemology: knowledge is *dialectical*. Our understanding of the person of Jesus both reveals something about the nature of the reality we existentially encounter through him (whether textually, emotionally, or spiritually), while also remaining linguistically and conceptually incapable of ever exhaustively capturing the essence of that reality—thus at the same time both revealing and concealing, unveiling and veiling.

Nonetheless, if in the end Schillebeeckx wants to assert and maintain a primacy of openness to possible new interpretations to the narrative of Jesus of Nazareth by stipulating that no one interpretation is ever *final*, then one might wonder if and how it can still justly be said that Jesus's narrative holds a *universal* significance. Schillebeeckx's response to this concern is both simple and provocative. For him, the "universality" of Jesus's story does not imply an exclusivity of relevance or significance. Rather if Jesus's story can be understood as a fully realized symbol of "concentrated creation"[143]—an embodiment of humanity's ontological relationship with reality—then it can serve as a "parable of God and paradigm of humanity."[144] The implication of his use of the terms "parable" and "paradigm" is significant here. He is not saying that Jesus's story gives a specific answer to the struggle of existence and search for truth that is applicable to all contexts and situations. He is not saying that Jesus's story provides a theoretical or metaphysical conception of the nature of the universe or our existence. Rather, what he *is* saying is that Jesus's story articulates a common question confronting humanity regarding the

---

141. Schillebeeckx, *Jesus*, 668–9.
142. Ibid., 669.
143. Schillebeeckx, *Interim Report*, 126–8.
144. See section title in Schillebeeckx, *Jesus*, 626.

purpose of our existence and the possibility of there being a meaning to our lives in the face of crisis, evil, and enduring conflict. Jesus's narrative is a common human one of "negative contrast experiences," in which he like the rest of us tries to make meaning of his life despite experiences of pain, suffering, oppression, and an impending sense of mortality. It is a story of maintaining the hope that our lives can have purpose despite our limitations, challenges, and finitude. And most importantly, as such it is an exemplar of *how* to construct that sense of purpose and meaning to our lives by pursuing actions ("praxis") that help instill that sense of hope in others who are suffering.[145] Since this story of overcoming the suffering and crises of existence is not uniquely his own but a more fundamentally human narrative however, then Jesus cannot be the sole arbiter of its meaning. Schillebeeckx would maintain that not only *can* others share in this experience but also in fact others *do* share in this narrative every day, particularly those who are facing social oppression.[146] In this way, Jesus can provide a norm of orientation for the Christian life—"faith in search of historical understanding"[147]—and yet, because that is only one possible interpretation of his story among many, his narrative can remain available to a broader human applicability as essentially a human life in search of historical understanding.[148]

Accordingly, Schillebeeckx holds that Jesus's narrative does not provide a singular, definitive answer to the question of the "total meaning of history" among the "divergent ideologies ... in the 'common market' of world history," but instead more accurately orients the believer or interpreter toward the idea of an "anticipation of a total meaning amid a history still in the making." In other words, it is a "hypothesis" of historical meaning, "of which the cognitive value—and so the value as reality or truth—will have to 'appear' from its being tested on the material of our human experiences in history."[149] In this sense Schillebeeckx's Christology reflects his epistemological emphasis that we previously discussed regarding an openness to the future and new conceptions of knowledge resulting from the interruptions of new experiences of crisis and suffering. Thus the "truth" behind any interpreted *meaning* of Jesus's narrative is not yet fully realized or established but is still in the making. Hence it is the "practical structure" of praxis itself that at the same time both mediates the "truth of reality" while also *creating* that very truth through overcoming the causes of human suffering.[150]

It is for this reason then that Schillebeeckx insists that especially in the case of Christians (those claiming to "follow" Jesus), "Resistance to all forms of evil

---

145. Schillebeeckx, *Christ*, 809. While acknowledging the Western (Greek) predisposition to this expression, here Schillebeeckx describes this sense of hope that is both conveyed and instilled by Jesus's story as a sense of "God for us." Cf. Schillebeeckx, *Interim Report*, 29.

146. Schillebeeckx, *Interim Report*, 112–19.

147. Ibid., 29.

148. Schillebeeckx, *Jesus*, 638–9. Cf. Schillebeeckx, *Understanding*, 40.

149. Schillebeeckx, *Jesus*, 618–19.

150. Schillebeeckx, *Church*, 176–7.

and suffering, in whatever guise they appear to us, is then the pre-condition for (if not actually the hidden reverse side of) an authentic faith in God and sincere confession of Christ."[151] This is the meaning and purpose of Jesus's message of the coming "Kingdom of God" in Schillebeeckx's mind. He interprets Jesus's teachings of the oncoming "Kingdom of God" as the reality that can and will eventually be made by individuals following the general orientation of his praxis: a reality resultant from being an advocate for the suffering, the poor, and social pariahs (i.e., the "divorced, homosexual, heretic, married priest!"[152]) and built upon actions that seek to liberate the oppressed and overthrow the power and structures of societal oppression.

> For Jesus, the praxis of the kingdom of God seems to be alternative action, in contrast to what people are usually inclined to do in our society. Jesus does not defend people who do evil, but he does go and stand beside them. He unmasks the intentions of those who are zealous for God and justice when they do not act for the salvation and well-being of others, but to the detriment of human beings, men and women.[153]

In this sense, according to Schillebeeckx the authority of Jesus's story, message, and actions is not any assertion of a theoretical postulate of knowledge.[154] Alternatively it is an orientation of *orthopraxis* in which one is directed "towards the grace of the future" by making the truth of all reality anew according to the image of an emancipated and liberated existence for all humans.[155] Thus Jesus's epistemological authority does not reside in his ability to supply answers or information about the nature of reality as much as it is to open up individuals to a possible experience of and participation in a future reality in the making. Or as Hilkert summarizes it, Schillebeeckx views the Jesus narrative as an imperative to shift the intention of theology from "faith seeking understanding" to "faith-praxis seeking critical historical understanding."[156] And so now, it is to this dialectical experience of encounter with and participation in the mysterious reality of the future that we will turn to discuss in the next chapter.

---

151. Schillebeeckx, *Jesus*, 616.
152. Schillbeeckx, *For the Sake*, 18.
153. Ibid.
154. It should be noted here that Schillebeeckx also strongly warns against reifying particular actions as fundamentally "liberative" and rightfully cautions that an orientation toward Jesus's praxis might mean that same action though liberative and "world renewing" in one context might not necessarily be in another. Thus, he acknowledges that the mantra of liberative orthopraxis can be misused similarly to reified theological abstractions. Hence, all actions must be critically evaluated anew in every context. See Schillebeeckx, *Christ*, 774–5.
155. Schillebeeckx, *God the Future*, 38.
156. Hilkert, "Hermeneutics," 138.

B. Gendun Chopel: Trusting the Inexpressible

> The Bhagavan sat cross-legged in unmoving equipoise
> In the forest on a broad-topped mountain.
>   May the profound truth that he saw
> Become manifest to all migrators.
>
> That state is not an object of words, minds, or analysis
> By these creatures of three realms.
> May the state of peace where the Sugata has gone
> Be swiftly found.
>
> Gendun Chopel[157]

It is certainly not uncommon to find many poems written by Gendun Chopel much like the one above. What is so striking about this particular poem is how it incorporates his adoration for the historical Buddha into a reflection on his own philosophical epistemology. One could say what is even more arresting about this poem, however, is that he wrote it during his travels in India where he was deeply confronted by modernist challenges to the authority of the Buddha—challenges that he seemed to take seriously and engage thoroughly with mixed results. Once again as we have previously observed on a number of occasions, for Gendun Chopel—in some ways quite similar to Schillebeeckx—one of the most significant philosophical catalysts came from his travels abroad (mainly in India and Sri Lanka) where he was introduced to new philosophical challenges to his traditional religious beliefs particularly through the methods of Western modernity and science. Hence in the introduction to his translation of Gendun Chopel's "travel journals" (although they are much more than that), Lopez describes Gendun Chopel's time traveling in India as the discovery of "a new old world" in which his traditional trainings were constantly exposed to new forms of learning—"from philosophy to linguistics, from poetics to iconography, from the monastic code to tantric practice, from mythology to history."[158] And yet, again much like Schillebeeckx, Gendun Chopel did not shrink away from the criticisms and insights of modern culture and academia but engaged and (at least somewhat) embraced them in order to produce a contemporary Buddhist philosophy that could account for these inevitable encounters with "modern scholarship, modern travel, modern geography, modern archaeology, modern science, modern religion, and modern love."[159]

In many ways Gendun Chopel seemed to thrive (at least intellectually) in response to the many new modernist discoveries he came across while traveling in India. His contrarian propensities were often even further stoked by his encounters

---

157. Dge 'dun Chos 'phel and Lopez, *Forest*, 35.
158. Dge 'dun Chos 'phel, Jinpa, and Lopez, *Grains*, 6.
159. Lopez, *Madman*, 13.

with the disciplines of critical historiography, archeology, and even the modern scientific methods. Lopez points out that throughout his "journals" and other writings while in India, Gendun Chopel does not hesitate to criticize, "sharply, and often humorously," his fellow countrymen for their "love of the fantastic" and rampant historical misinformation. "Over the course of the seventeen chapters," Lopez continues, "he bursts one myth after another—'We need not take so seriously this bad tradition that excites all the fools'—while beseeching his readers not to be angry with him for doing so."[160] Nevertheless, his adherence to the Buddhist tradition and devotion for Śākyamuni Buddha persisted throughout all of these years of travel and new exposures. Actually, rather than finding the modern Western worldview as a threat to his religious convictions, Gendun Chopel actively sought to adopt and incorporate much of the research and methods of historical scholarship in order to compose his own Buddhist narrative of history and meaning.[161] And as a result, in many of his writings during this time one can find an interesting blend of the devotionally traditional alongside the cynically modern—all in an attempt to ground the tradition he loved firmly in reality so that it might withstand the ever-increasing winds of change. Hence, despite his antagonistic posture toward his own tradition at times, he would also plead with other Tibetans for them not to misunderstand his intentions.

> My concern for the dharma is not less than yours. For that reason, do not dismiss my statements with only the wish to attack me. If one does not want the tree trunk of the [Buddha's] teaching and these roots of our Buddhist knowledge to be completely uprooted, one must be far-sighted.[162]

Accordingly it is probably in his writings during this period more than any other that Gendun Chopel discusses most extensively and provocatively his own response to the challenges of the Buddha's authority and teachings that inevitably emerged from his own Buddhist interaction with a modern Western worldview. Therefore in this section, we will briefly transition away from our reliance on Gendun Chopel's purely philosophical treatise, the *Adornment*, and instead refocus our examination on his other writings mainly composed during his travels in India where he speaks more extensively on this specific topic. With these sources as an investigative base, we will revisit the categories of Buddhist hermeneutical interpretation that we discussed as Gendun Chopel's philosophical foundation in the earlier section, in order to observe how Gendun Chopel both reimagined and maintained his understanding of the authority of the historical Buddha in light of new insights and concerns. In the end, this will allow us to briefly compare and contrast his philosophical notions within this new form of Buddhology with the development of Schillebeeckx's Christology so as to observe how modern historical research

---

160. Dge 'dun Chos 'phel Jinpa, and Lopez, *Grains*, 4.
161. Ibid., 12.
162. Ibid., 407.

affected both of their own conceptions of their historical religious founders in similar and dissimilar ways. Moreover, this will then set up in the conclusion of this chapter a brief space in which we can speculate on questions that the systems of these two very different thinkers might raise for each other. This can serve as the starting point for a further comparative dialogue between the two thinkers about the role and authority of the historical founders of religious traditions in the final chapter.

Gendun Chopel opens the first chapter to his travel journals with the traditional format of a poem called the "expression of worship" (Tib. *mchod brjod*) in which he both praises and professes his personal devotion to the Buddha, the one for whom the work is written. Unlike the more satirical and ironic poem that we have already observed in the *Adornment* where he appears to question the Buddha's epistemological authority in the conventional world, however, in this piece he begins with a much more traditional adoration for the Buddha.

> I pay homage with body, speech, and mind and go for refuge with great reverence at the lotus feet of the Blessed One, the perfectly awakened Buddha.
>
> You destroy the world of darkness with wisdom's wheel of light, profound and clear.
>
> You step down upon the peak of existence with the feet of the samādhi of liberation and peace.
>
> You are endowed with the mind of stainless space unsullied by clouds of elaboration.
>
> May the sun, the glory of all beings, rain down goodness upon you.[163]

He then proceeds to describe his travels in terms of a holy pilgrimage whose spiritual benefits "cannot be known through investigation at home in bed." Moreover, he insists that his time in India is intended to help "those who enjoy the flavors of meaning ... [f]rom the learned treatises of ancient times ... complete the branches of learning."[164] In other words, he is declaring his travels and research are not just a pilgrimage for his own spiritual betterment but also one for the spiritual development and growth of all interested Tibetans. And although this rhetoric might seem odd as the opening for a text that continues on to *question* many of the traditional teachings, lineages, and sacred histories of Buddhism—even more by an individual criticized as a "sophist" (a non-devout "mere lover of words") by many of his peers—in fact such statements of adoration and praise for Śākyamuni Buddha consistently appear throughout most of his writings. Indeed, what he seems to be assuring his readers in this passage (and the many others) is that despite the rather "demythologized" reading of the Buddha and Buddhism he is about to advance, his intentions remain grounded in a profound devotion to the figure of the Buddha and his subsequent teachings.[165]

163. Ibid., 29–30.
164. Ibid., 30.
165. Dge 'dun Chos 'phel, Jinpa, and Lopez, *Grains*, 13.

In actuality, one could argue that all of Gendun Chopel's devotional language, visualizations, and even painted depictions[166] of the Buddha serve as a quite sincere embodiment of the first "refuge" of Buddhist hermeneutics—a reliance on the dharma, not the person. For even though he often praises the Buddha with honorific titles such as the "reliable refuge that never deceives" and "a body made of thousands of virtuous deeds, worthy of the world's worship" to whom he constantly bows himself before, still these praises are never allocated apart from the pragmatic function this figure and these visualizations seek to achieve—the turning of one's mind to the "essential sacred dharma," the recognition of the "emptiness of [one's] own mind."[167] Hence in Gendun Chopel's practices and affirmations of devotion one can see how he emulates the philosophy of spiritual practice professed by Bhāvaviveka we discussed earlier in which one visualizes the Buddha as a means of standing in the "absent presence" of emptiness itself. Or as he describes it, "When you look directly at the perceiver itself, [y]ou will see your own inexpressible face."[168] Likewise, in a practice very similar to *buddhānusmṛti*, he will visualize the attributes and qualities of Śākyamuni, such as "the wheels on the soles of his feet" and the "Marks of his mastery of method and wisdom," as a means of being led "from the path of world conventions [t]o the sphere beyond the world."[169]

In his journals this conviction causes him to notice and reflect on the somewhat seemingly foreign practice of some Indian Buddhist traditions that—in a "quite amazing" fashion—never make any depictions of the Buddha himself but instead substitute his image with footprints, an empty saddle, or even an empty throne.[170] Gendun Chopel protests that this practice should create "a sense of surprise in the minds of many thoughtful people" because various texts within the vinaya not only do not prohibit images depicting the Buddha but also actually positively speak about illustrations of the "Teacher."[171] Thus, although one can be sure that the meaningful and symbolic intention of such artists is certainly not lost on Gendun Chopel, at the same time he seems to argue that such actions are misplaced. Because for him, not only is the visualization of the traditional images, titles, and qualities of Śākyamuni important and useful for cultivating an awareness of "the one door of entry into the realm of peace"—"the two truths: profound doctrine,

---

166. During his time, Gendun Chopel was almost known more for his artistry than his research or philosophical writings. It is well documented that upon disrobing from his monastic vows, he often helped provide for himself by selling his sketches and paintings. For an excellent examination of the wide variety of his collection of paintings, including depictions of the Buddha, see Donald S. Lopez, *Gendun Chopel: Tibet's First Modern Artist*, 1st ed. (Chicago: Serindia, 2013).

167. See the series of poems in Dge 'dun Chos 'phel and Lopez, *Forest*, 27–33, for such examples.

168. Dge 'dun Chos 'phel and Lopez, *Forest*, 29.

169. Ibid., 37.

170. Dge 'dun Chos 'phel, Jinpa, and Lopez, *Grains*, 82.

171. Ibid., 83.

and stainless path"[172]—but also he believes it is a practice that can actually unite "the Mahāyāna of the north and the Hīnayāna of the south on the basis of the four seals that define a view as being that of the Buddha."[173] And therefore, in distinction to Schillebeeckx whose encounter with modern philosophy and historical studies caused him to want to shed the a priori acceptance of traditional honorific titles of Jesus of Nazareth as the foundation of his authority, Gendun Chopel seems to insist the opposite. Instead, for him, even though he is more than willing to acknowledge and accept the historical "errors" within traditional documents and texts of the Buddha, these titles and images still must serve as the primary "doorway" to an encounter with the truth of all reality. Thus, in the end, these honorific titles and proclamations of adoration toward Śākyamuni cannot be separated from the true dharma itself. In this way, they do not obscure or prevent one from seeing and understanding reality as it truly is, but are indeed necessary devices for efficaciously lifting the practitioner beyond the historical, contingent, and "conventional" conceptualizations of reality—"calming all illusions of meaningless saṃsāra"[174]—and toward the path of true buddhahood, the recognition of the dharma of emptiness.

Yet at the same time his anti-realist philosophical conviction that the unenlightened being can have absolutely no valid knowledge of reality because their thinking is unavoidably ensnared in the conventional also serves to stoke Gendun Chopel's historian impulses and causes him to persistently want to unmask the unbeneficial reification of language and history by Buddhists in many of their texts. In fact, all of his extensive historical research and works of translation only further confirmed to him that knowledge is fundamentally elusive to those stuck in a conventional worldview. Accordingly, he is both quick and assiduous in challenging many of Tibetan's traditional histories of Buddhism, such as Lhodrak Namkha Gyelpo's (Tib. *lho brag nam mkha' rgyal po*) *History of Buddhism*, for lacking historical "objectivity" and promoting inconsistencies by declaring one definitive understanding of history and prophecies while also maintaining that "a single diamond word [of tantra] has at least two or three different meanings."[175] Similarly, he chides his fellow Buddhists for engaging "in minute analysis of such things as whether [the Buddha] was born in the year of Horse," while also insisting that it is "inappropriate" to cling too tightly to conventional language and the use of historical dates.[176] For him, if one understands the difference between prioritizing "the spirit" and "the letter" of teachings and texts, then exposing the faults of language and concepts with historical and scientific research should not "trample on the hearts of so many [Tibetans]."[177]

172. Dge 'dun Chos 'phel and Lopez, *Forest*, 31.
173. Dge 'dun Chos 'phel, Jinpa, and Lopez, *Grains*, 346.
174. Dge 'dun Chos 'phel and Lopez, *Forest*, 27.
175. Dge 'dun Chos 'phel, Jinpa, and Lopez, *Grains*, 346.
176. Ibid., 361.
177. Ibid., 31.

As Hopkins explains in the introduction to his translation of Gendun Chopel's work *The Tibetan Arts of Love* (an attempt at a Tibetan version of the *Kāmasūtra*), Gendun Chopel's "wide travels gave him a sense of cultural relativism that most of his fellow Tibetans lacked."[178] Harmoniously however, Hopkins also reminds Gendun Chopel's readers that this cultural relativism does not equate into a general attitude of "nihilistic relativism." In other words, Gendun Chopel's historical, archeological, and philological research did not cause him to reject a belief in "Buddhahood" but rather simply confirmed to him that the Buddha always spoke in "culture-bound depictions" that would be comprehensible to his audience.[179] Dreyfus's assessment of Chopel's Geluk training in Madhyamaka only operates to confirm Hopkins's analysis here. Dreyfus explains that within the Tibetan scholastic tradition, which Gendun Chopel went through the highest levels of training in, one is taught "the cornerstone of that universe is emptiness," and as consequence the ability of traditional texts to expose their readers to the reality of "emptiness" is taken as a way to "confirm the soteriological validity of the grand narratives of the tradition."[180]

Therefore, Gendun Chopel has absolutely no reservations about unmasking and dismantling the many "culture-bound," conventional fallacies within traditional texts and depictions of the Buddha. For example, he readily points out in his research how many images of Śākyamuni Buddha are actually eerily similar, if not identical, to those of Amitābha Buddha and even "the teacher of the Jains" in a completely relativizing manner.[181] Conversely, he also seems to take pleasure in comparing and contrasting the starkly distinct images of the historical Buddha he finds within the larger Buddhist tradition across regional boundaries.[182] Furthermore, he seems to point out wherever he can how Buddhist scriptures contradict their own narratives, contradict any reasonable sense of historical time and place, confuse dates of the Buddha's birth with the construction of statues, as well as share common literary sources with various scriptures of the Jains.[183] For him, all of these uncoverings in no way delegitimize the authority of the historical Buddha, they simply assist in confirming that the Buddha's conventional use of "skillful means" (*upāya*) goes all the way through his teachings without remainder. In fact, the inherent fallibility of conventional language, concepts, and dating exposed by these new methods can actually themselves function as new "expedient means" (*upāya*) of revealing the truth of the emptiness of all reality to contemporary Buddhists and non-Buddhists alike.[184] For this reason, he proclaims, "to be excessively proud and continually assert that even the smallest details of all

---

178. Hopkins and Chöpel, 24.
179. Ibid.
180. Dreyfus, *Hands*, 242.
181. Dge 'dun Chos 'phel, Jinpa, and Lopez, *Grains*, 81.
182. Ibid., 84.
183. Ibid., 83–4, 92, 361, 325, 145.
184. Ibid., 131; Cf. 410.

explanations in our scriptures are unmistaken seems attractive only temporarily; it is pointless stubbornness."[185]

All the examples just mentioned notwithstanding, probably Gendun Chopel's most forceful and provocative criticism against religious views that he believes require "that one rely only on the letter" is laid out in his extended discussion regarding the relationship between religion and science in the concluding chapter of his journal.[186] He begins this passage with the rather strong proclamation that "Generally, the intelligence of the Europeans in every kind of worldly pursuit is superior to ours [Buddhists] in a thousand ways." Still at the same time he also admonishes them for "putting the empty [words of their] scriptures" into practice in ways that only seek to gratify the desires of their "hearts filled only with self-interest" (and especially "sexual lusts") so that they are incapable of using, or even realizing, the value of their conventional systems of knowledge toward an ultimate knowledge of emptiness.[187] Nevertheless, despite this larger criticism of Europeans he goes on to give his own brief history of the development of science in the West in order to show how it has arisen to the perch of being the dominant source of knowledge so that all religions of the West must find a means to coincide with it or else face extinction by admitting that their beliefs are "utterly false."[188] He then utilizes a brief biographical account of the Russian woman Helena Petrovna Blavatsky (1831–1891), founder of the Theosophical Society, as a means to illustrate how a religion that seeks not to contest the findings of modern science, but in fact wishes to embrace it, can "impress everyone" in the West.[189] No matter how strong of an example of the Theosophical Society however, Gendun Chopel contends that, because of the deep-seated suspicion of the conventional and "the letter" already existent within its own tradition, there is no better religion to engage and correspond with modern science than Buddhism. In fact citing various examples of how the Buddha anticipated the discoveries of everything from light waves, "video machines," radios, telescopes, and some rudimentary elements of quantum mechanics ("objects not persisting" in time), he then even proceeds to prophesy that "in the future the religion of the Buddha will be the religion of science, that is, a religion of reason, and other religions will be religions of faith."[190]

Nonetheless if we were to assume that Gendun Chopel believes that modern science actually has captured the true realities of existence (i.e., emptiness) we would be mistaken as well. Rather he explains that the "ladder of science," like all other "ladders" of "the letter," will eventually have to be abandoned in order for individuals to travel "even further beyond" in realizing the "nature of reality."[191]

185. Ibid., 406.
186. Ibid., 404.
187. Ibid., 397.
188. Ibid., 398–404.
189. Ibid., 402–3.
190. Ibid., 405.
191. Ibid., 404.

In other words, when Gendun Chopel states that "science can serve as the foundation" for every aspect set forth in the teachings of the Buddha, what he really is proclaiming is that the claims of science are the new expedient means by which Buddhists can achieve, as well as bring others to, an experience of the truth of emptiness in the current context. Hence, for him modern science has not discovered any form of valid "truth" within the conventional realm—that would be impossible. What it has discovered is a method to deconstruct linguistic and conceptual truth claims in a way that seems to correspond to the pragmatic orientation of the Buddha's teachings. For this reason he admits that Buddhists will have to adjust and reframe "the letter" of their claims continually in order for Buddhism to appear to fit continuously with the proclamations of science—similar to how "the strings of a bow ... must be reset again and again whenever they become too lax."[192] He views this constant reframing not as deceptive or even as undue to Buddhism, but actually as an exemplar imitation of the very practice and teaching of the Buddha himself. Thus he believes Buddhists should be thankful for this new skillful device that can advance the Buddha's cause. At one point in conclusion, he even goes as far as to beseech his fellow Tibetans and Buddhists, "Please pray that the two, this modern reasoning of science and the ancient teaching of the Buddha, may abide together for ten thousand years."[193] This is because Gendun Chopel acknowledges that by coinciding with modern science Buddhism will be able to direct individuals to the pragmatic "spirit" of the Buddha's teachings, even if the "letter" of those teachings must consistently change.

Similarly, another great example of how the Western scientific discourse had an effect on Gendun Chopel's depiction of the authority of the historical Buddha is the short essay he wrote in 1938 for the *Tibet Mirror* under the byline of "Honest Dharma" entitled "The World Is Round or Spherical" ("*'Jigs rten ril mo 'am zlum po*").[194] This article in particular illustrates how Gendun Chopel reimagines the third "rule" of traditional Buddhist hermeneutics—the distinction and prioritization of the "definitive" (*nītārtha*) teachings of the Buddha over the "provisional" (*neyārtha*) ones—in his own distinct way. In this brief argument he firmly admonishes his fellow Tibetans for continuing to hold on too tightly to what he perceives as an outmoded cosmology (one that maintained that the world was flat) simply because the Buddha had taught such in scriptures that were deemed "definitive."[195] Because of his conviction that all language and concepts require the

---

192. Ibid., 407.
193. Ibid.
194. For a complete translation of this essay see Lopez, *Science*, 58–9.
195. One could certainly argue that there is a noticeable parallel between Gendun Chopel's argument here and Bultmann's distinction between the New Testament worldview of the scriptural writers and the demythologized existential interpretation of the New Testament's meaning. For concise versions of this argument see the articles "New Testament and Mythology" (1941) and "Science and Existence" (1955) in Bultmann, 1–43, 131–44.

use of invalid conventional constructs based in human consciousness and history (i.e., *saṃsāra*) in order to be able to communicate, Gendun Chopel holds that for anyone to assert that any given teaching of the Buddha could be considered *literally* true is problematic. First of all, he protests that saying the world is not round simply "because the Buddha stated that it is flat" is unhelpful in any discussion with non-Buddhists because they do not presuppose the Buddha's authority, "and thus [such an argument] does not do a pinprick of damage" to any assertion they make to the contrary. Additionally, even in discussions among Buddhists themselves who *do* accept statements of the Buddha to be potentially authoritative, he points out that arriving at a consensus on whether a specific teaching of the Buddha can ever be determined as "definitive" (*nītārtha*) is nearly impossible. This is because even Buddhists recognize that "the majority of the sutras were set forth by the Buddha in accordance with the thoughts of sentient beings" and so one can never be certain what elements are provisional and what are definitive in a teaching. Lopez insists that based on his extensive academic training Gendun Chopel certainly knew that one can find detailed instructions on how to differentiate between the categories of meaning, but likewise he would have also been aware that "the various schools of Buddhist philosophy differ both on what those instructions are and on what constitutes the Buddha's own view." And for this reason, he "professes a certain agnosticism" as to making such a determination.[196]

Moreover, Gendun Chopel inquires: if Buddhists can accept that the Buddha spoke provisionally about "matters of great importance, such as emptiness and the stages of the path to liberation" (which they do), then why on this particular matter would they contend that his teaching was not just simply in accord "with the customs of time and place?" This would seem especially the case about this teaching, he continues, since "at that time, throughout all the world, the words '[the world] is flat' were as famous as the wind." Thus he challenges them with the rhetorical rebuttal, "Even if the Buddha had said, 'it is round,' whose ear would it have entered? Even if he had said so emphatically, it would have no purpose, even if he had demonstrated it with his miraculous powers." Accordingly later on in the *Adornment* he would further develop this point by asserting that the only consistent way to approach the teachings of the Buddha is to assume that the "skillful method of the Sugata must be applied in the same way from the minute precepts of the vinaya to the final nature of phenomena." And as such, one must also assume that every teaching of the Buddha contains both "provisional" and "definitive" aspects: "an assertion that must be congruent with the world, and the teacher's own mind."[197] For this reason he then also asserts, "It is not necessary to analyze what is provisional and definitive" because both can be found in any examined teaching. Instead therefore the ideas of "*fallible* and *infallible*" really are only assessments of pragmatic value, whether or not they are effective in achieving a desired end.[198] The authority of the Buddha's teachings then has little to do

---

196. Lopez, *Science*, 62.
197. Chos phel, "Adornment," 79, v. 120.
198. Ibid., 78–9, v. 119.

with their actual correspondence to the nature of reality but instead *everything* to do with whether they assist in bringing the hearer into a better awareness and understanding of the inexpressible, empty reality of existence. Hence he concludes the essay by pronouncing, "If all of us would believe in this world that we see with our eyes rather than that world that we see through letters, it would be good."

This interpenetrating and non-antithetical approach to conceiving of "provisional" and "definitive" meanings in the Buddha's teachings then leads directly into his understanding of the final "refuge" of Buddhist hermeneutics that "direct knowledge is the refuge and not discursive consciousness." During his time in India Gendun Chopel had become frustrated with the pervasive strains of religious literalism in both Buddhist and non-Buddhist religious traditions alike throughout the subcontinent. At one point he even goes as far as to lament, "All the people [here in India] still believe these tales and, carrying such texts in their hands, dispute facts established by direct perception and inference."[199] For him, such blind acceptance of *any* scriptural claim is the absolute height of epistemological folly. Fittingly then while himself acknowledging that he cannot even be certain of its authentic Dharmakīrtian authorship, Gendun Chopel proceeds to quote from the respected *Pramāṇavārttika* to further support his point—declaring that an acceptance of "valid knowledge derived from words" only causes individuals to become more "rigid" in their thinking and controlled by the "unbearable demon of doctrine."[200] Thus he believes he is in accordance with "the glorious Dharmakīrti and his disciples" in maintaining that the function of scriptures and the use of language generally are *not* to be able to "refute or establish" one assertion of truth over another. Instead their purpose is just the opposite: scriptures function actually to "prevent the development of certainty about one thing over another" so as to expose their inherent limits of contingency, falsity, and emptiness of meaning.[201] As such, many elements of a text can in effect be completely "erroneous" in various ways (including its historical claims and even inferential logic) and yet still be unmistaken in its ability to convey the "profound wisdom" of "emptiness, dependent origination, and so on."[202] Hence, according to him, being able to verify the truth or falsity of claims within the teachings of the Buddha does not ultimately matter. Rather what matters from an epistemological standpoint is a teaching's pragmatic ability to present individuals with an experience of the deepest qualities of Buddhahood that have no extension in space and time, that cannot be seen or touched.[203] Therefore, somewhat analogously to our prior discussion of Schillebeeckx's Christology, Gendun Chopel understands the authority of the historical Buddha as not resting in "the letter" of his message, nor

---

199. Dge 'dun Chos 'phel, Jinpa, and Lopez, *Grains*, 152.

200. Ibid., 152–3.

201. Ibid., 153.

202. Ibid., 153–4.

203. Here I am borrowing language from Eckel's discussion of the scriptural image of the "Silent Buddha" in Buddhist literature. See Eckel, 68.

in the determination of a definitive "meaning" that is verifiable in every historical context, but instead in the Buddha's ability to orient the receiver toward an experiential understanding of the true emptiness of all reality through his message and actions. And so, in yet another way somewhat similar to Schillebeeckx, it is to the question of how one can derive authoritative knowledge from the direct experience of the dharma—what he terms the "inconceivable state"—that we must turn to next and in the final chapter of our comparative analysis.

IV. Conclusion: Comparative Observations and Questions for Further Reflection

In conclusion, then, this chapter sought to examine the ways in which both Schillebeeckx and Gendun Chopel wrestled with and responded to challenges confronting the authority of the teachings and lives of their religious traditions' historical founders (Jesus of Nazareth and Śākyamuni Buddha respectively) posed by modern society and culture. Noticing how both men were significantly stimulated during time spent abroad from their home countries, we observed how during this time they were presented with new encounters of modern methods in historical, philosophical, scientific, and hermeneutical studies that had a deep effect on both men philosophically and theologically. Moreover, we perceived how both thinkers seemed to share some analogous responses in epistemological orientation as a result of their exchanges with the modern concerns of historical contingency and hermeneutical separation. Despite any sensed commonalities, however, we also identified some significant divergences both in the methodological approaches as well as the eventual theological outcomes of their thought. This section, therefore, will briefly seek to review both some of the major similarities and differences between these two individuals' hermeneutical theories of epistemology, particularly toward how they shaped each thinker's understanding of the religious authority of past historical figures and teachings. Thus, we will finish by using this process of comparison as a means to then further flesh out some of the lingering pertinent theological questions still remaining as a result of our comparative analysis. These questions will then serve to direct us to the topic of the following chapter regarding the nature and authority of religious experience and also provide the foundation for a possibly more constructive synthesis of the two thinkers' positions in the final chapter.

As already mentioned, either toward the end of or immediately following their formal academic training in their religions' scholastic tradition, both Schillebeeckx and Gendun Chopel traveled out of their home countries in order to gain contact with new cultures as well as to learn new methods for developing their theological and philosophical epistemologies. And although neither individual actually went beyond the broader geographical and cultural climates of their own continent—both rather choosing to travel to a closely neighboring country—nevertheless both journeys proved to be equally momentous in both exposure and intellectual influence. During his brief time in Paris (less than two years), Schillebeeckx worked alongside the theologians of a growing movement of the time referred to as the "*Nouvelle Théologie*," who sought to incorporate contemporary studies in literary theory, hermeneutics, and historical-critical methods of exegesis as a means to reappropriate, evaluate, and translate texts of the past into contemporary philosophical discussions and idioms. These new approaches to theological method had a profound effect on Schillebeeckx, who as a result began to formulate his own more historically conscious theology that could effectively address the contemporary concerns of existentialism, secularism, philosophical pluralism, and Critical Theories. Gendun Chopel's travels abroad, on the other hand, were for a much more substantial length of time (about twelve years) and were probably a much more significant cultural shift in perspective. During his time in British-colonized India, Gendun Chopel was not only confronted with many different competing religious traditions and historical data contradicting the religious claims of his own tradition, but he was also confronted with the completely alien culture of Western modernity, particularly regarding methods in science and historical research. Regardless of the apparent tensions that the Western worldview might have placed on Gendun Chopel's Buddhist interpretation of reality however, we observed how he saw it as both necessary and also pragmatically efficacious to attempt to uphold his Buddhist perspective in a way that could coexist with the claims of Western science and historiography. Moreover, we witnessed how the recognition of the contextual nature to all assertions of knowledge and the historical limitations to all interpretations of universal claims to truth caused both thinkers to not abandon but to rather in effect *relocate* the epistemological authority of the religious founders of their respective traditions from being situated in the words of the specific teachings or the verifiable historical accuracy of their actions to being based upon the pragmatic efficacy of their teachings and narratives to produce new "true" experiences of reality to their past, present, and future followers.

Nonetheless, how they arrived at their analogous new orientations for imagining religious authority were quite different. In light of the challenges of historical-critical studies Schillebeeckx believed it necessary to learn and understand the person of Jesus from a truly *historical* perspective—apart from any presupposed traditional honorific titles such as "Savior" or "Christ"—as a means to reconstruct the meaning and significance of his life's story to have any soteriological efficacy in his modern Western context. Whereas Gendun Chopel, on the other hand, seems to take the exact opposite tact by utilizing the recitation of and meditation on the traditional titles and depictions of the Buddha as expedient devices for cultivating an encounter with the truth of reality. Furthermore where Schillebeeckx actively sought to bring a larger plurality of voices and philosophical perspectives in the traditional theological hermeneutics of the past in a deliberate attempt to do away with a hegemonic depiction of truth, we illustrated how Gendun Chopel attempted to reimagine the traditional "rules" of Buddhist hermeneutics by solely utilizing elements within his own tradition in innovative ways. The resultant outcomes of these two distinct approaches could be labeled as almost antithetical. While Gendun Chopel's philosophical emphasis (one of a radical epistemological anti-realism) appears more hostile to the more traditional limited-realist epistemology of the Geluk tradition, at the same time his depiction of the figure of Śākyamuni Buddha remains rather traditional in style and content. Conversely, Schillebeeckx's (critically) realist epistemological foundation coincides rather effectively with traditional Christian understandings of knowledge and ontology, and yet his eventual Christology appears in ways to be a much more radical reimagining of the nature and role of the figure of Jesus. Hence, in the end, for both men their growing consciousness of historicity, linguistics, and contextual influences on the interpretations of meaning caused them to be deeply suspicious of locating "truth" in the linguistic and conceptual elements of human cognition. And still, they arrived at this analogous conclusion through seemingly opposite methods and with distinctly variant results.

Once again, however, in the overall assessment of our analysis we are left with a number of interesting and more general questions to answer moving forward. First of all, our discussion of how each thinker endeavored to discuss the nature and authority of their religious leader in different ways as a means to preserve their soteriological efficacy in a new contemporary context raises the question of whether—and if so, *how*—new formulations of traditional terms and ideas can impact the possible relatability and effectiveness of those figures to speak to one's own religious community either positively or negatively. Can reimagining the nature and role of such prominent figures as Jesus of Nazareth or Śākyamuni Buddha within their respective tradition actually hinder the soteriological potential of those figures by rendering their message and even their very person unrecognizable to the rest of the tradition? Accordingly, do such figures require an authority fundamentally distinct and superior over any other individual within their tradition's understanding of history? Need they be the *exclusive* authority on knowledge in order to remain soteriologically meaningful within their religious traditions? And finally, we discussed how both thinkers looked to assert the authoritative knowledge of their religious leader in an experiential encounter with truth rather than a conceptual, linguistic, or propositional understanding of ultimate truth. Yet the question still remains as to *what* exactly individuals in the present actually learn from the founders of their religions in the past. Moreover, what does it mean to claim "knowledge" to be experiential rather than cognitive? We will return to the first few questions regarding the effect that one's understanding of the nature and authority of religious leaders can have on those figures' soteriological potency in the final assessment of the concluding chapter. But it is to the last two questions surrounding the nature and authority of personal experience that we will first turn to in the next chapter.

Chapter 5

THE ROLE AND AUTHORITY OF PERSONAL EXPERIENCE IN THE APOPHATIC KNOWLEDGE OF ULTIMATE REALITY

I. Introduction: How Can Experiential Knowledge Be Both Authoritative and Ultimately Negative in Nature?

The last chapter's assessment of Schillebeeckx's and Gendun Chopel's understandings of the epistemological authority of the historical founders of their respective traditions left one wondering how it is possible for "true knowledge" to be primarily experiential in nature as distinct from being conceptually or linguistically based. This chapter, therefore, will now investigate how both these individuals articulated their own understandings of the essentially experiential nature of all valid claims to knowledge of the ultimate truth of reality. Accordingly by focusing on how both men conceived of the relationship between a knowing subject and an encountered object of knowledge it will observe how both Schillebeeckx and Gendun Chopel believed they had constructed their own philosophical "middle way" between the positivistic objectivisms and the relativistic subjectivisms caused by the "subject-object dualism" prominent in much of modern philosophy. After an initial analysis of both thinkers' traditional and theoretical foundations for grounding all knowledge as emergent out of a dialectical interplay between positive or "cataphatic" affirmations about reality and a fundamentally negative or "apophatic" experience of reality itself, it will then turn to examine each thinker's own personal explanation of how an utterly negative awareness of reality can serve as the authoritative source for experiential knowledge and religious belief. Then once again, following the program of the previous two chapters, it will conclude by comparing and contrasting the analogous points of contact between Schillebeeckx's and Gendun Chopel's thought on experiential knowledge. This will set up a concluding observation that will be carried over into the constructive assessment in the final chapter.

II. Theological and Theoretical Foundations of Experiential Knowledge and Apophaticism

A. Schillebeeckx: The Ethical, the Mystical, and Experience in the Modern World

As noted in the previous chapter, in the years immediately following Vatican II (and in particular 1966) Schillebeeckx underwent a profound mutation in his theology based heavily on his studies and lectures in the subjects of hermeneutics and subsequently Critical Theory, as well as travels and conversations in North America and western Europe, that forced him to reconsider the limitations of knowledge in terms of history and interpretation. This realization compelled him to make his now famous "clean break" with De Petter's epistemology of phenomenological Thomism and essentially "to speak of a new view of reality." Thus, where the matrix for understanding Schillebeeckx's early epistemology was a relatively simply one, what Kennedy describes as a "bipolar" Thomistic phenomenology, in the wake of his studies and encounters during 1966 Schillebeeckx's epistemological sources began to vary much more wildly as "his later writings graft ideas culled from ordinary language philosophy and its reaction to logical atomism and logical positivism; speech-act theory; semiotics; synchronic structuralism; Saussurian, Chomskian and Jakobsonian linguistics; phenomenological and practical-critical hermeneutics; universal pragmatics of speech; and finally, poststructuralism and deconstruction." Most importantly for this chapter, however, during this time his exposure to the writings and theories of the famed "Frankfurt School" of neo-Marxist interdisciplinary social theory persuaded him to introduce "arguments from various forms of social theory, literary theory, the sociology of religion and the sociology of knowledge, Marxism, Critical Theory, political studies, and psychology" into his theological approach. Hence, Kennedy summarizes, Schillebeeckx's later thought from that point on becomes much more notably "multi-disciplinary." Although, as we will see with many of the topics in this chapter, Kennedy also notes that this newfound breadth of references "should not be taken as an indication that he has thoroughly studied each discipline he refers to in his writings. Often he simply makes random selections of phraseology from a particular author without embracing the author's system of thought."[1]

Yet despite this new and complex matrix for interpreting his epistemology, Kennedy also keenly observes that the foundational "epistemological axes" of Schillebeeckx's thought still remain the same. The first axial plane is "a superintending ontological postulate which stems from Aquinas's doctrine that *a unique relation* exists between a divine Creator and contingent creatures"; the

---

1. Kennedy, *Deus*, 147–53. To this last point, for example, later Kennedy explains how despite the pervasive influence and heavy use of Critical Theory in his later thought, in actuality Schillebeeckx's understanding of Critical Theory is primarily (if not *exclusively*) derived from Albrecht Wellmer's survey on the subject and a handful of works published by Habermas in the 1960s and early 1970s (see p. 195).

second is that "the locus of a divine-human nexus is *negative*: something of the Mystery of God's Transcendence is mediated through negativity."[2] As a consequence of the first plane, Schillebeeckx maintains the conviction that human (creaturely) knowledge of ultimate reality (creator God) can only be obtained in correlation with a complex and multifaceted empirical encounter of reality so that "truth" is never obtainable through a pure abstract separateness.[3] And the second causes him to insist at the same time that the reality of historical particularity means that any "universal knowledge" can only be apprehended *negatively* because language inherently contains "projective elements" so that one's knowledge always comprises non-ultimate elements derived from the individual's experiential and interpretative background.[4] In order to understand Schillebeeckx's conception of the authority of personal experience, therefore, one must first understand the prominent themes in his thought concerning the nature of one's encounter with reality, the role of humans in constructing knowledge or truth, and the correspondence between knowledge and reality through negativity. Hence, this section will briefly discuss and define what Schillebeeckx philosophically understands "experience" to mean (encounter) and how that serves as the authoritative root for the ethical actions (human participation) that create new "realities" of truth, and subsequently the mystical (negative eminence) components to all knowledge those actions expose. This then will allow us to return in the later section to unpack how he himself actually reappropriates these notions explicitly in terms of theology and faith.

Although in his later thought Schillebeeckx provides no explicit definition for the oft-used term "experience," there are a couple of notions regarding the idea that seem to remain consistent throughout the development of his thought. First is that experience is fundamentally tied to a notion of revelation, in this sense all experience is *revelatory* experience. For Schillebeeckx one foundational element of his epistemology that seems to remain the same despite various changes in the appearance and structure of his theory is that the *locus* for one's knowledge of ultimate reality ("revelation") is in the contingent, empirical world of history. At the same time, however, he absolutely rejects any notion of an empirical *positivism*—any notion that "truth" can be *discovered* simply through a "one-dimensional surface observation"—in his theory of knowledge.[5] Earlier in his career, following the phenomenology of De Petter, he attempted to articulate non-positivist theories of meaning and truth by fusing any notion of meaning with the limitations of the activities of human consciousness. After the mid-1960s he continues to attempt to formulate a non-positivist epistemology; however, in his later articulations this non-positivist conviction is based in the use of modern hermeneutics that insists that empirical experiences indeed are the *locus* of knowledge while also upholding that they at the same time contribute a *limiting* factor to the formation

2. Ibid., 145–6.
3. Ibid., 179. Cf. Schillebeeckx, *Western Culture*, 65.
4. Schillebeeckx, *Church*, 16–20.
5. Kennedy, *Deus*, 154.

of knowledge because they are "always already interpreted—albeit implicitly—and loaded with theory."[6] As such, experience is not a one-directional phenomenon in which reality simply presents itself to a passive receiver, rather it is fundamentally a *dialectical* process between moments of non-cognitive, prereflective perceptions and ones of cognitive, reflective (or interpretative) comprehension.[7] And in this sense, Kennedy highlights, the closest Schillebeeckx ever comes to concisely defining "experience" in his later thought is by once referring to it as an "always interpreting perception."[8] Or as he phrases it in the second volume of his trilogy, *Christ*, while "experience" means "learning through 'direct' contact with people and things" it is also at the same time "*the ability to assimilate [those] perceptions.*"[9]

Hence within the moment of "experience," the agent's perception and interpretation are interwoven in an "irreducible" fashion so that the totality of any "experience" already contains elements of both perception and interpretation in a way that makes purely transparent experiences impossible—rather to perceive is to interpret and vice versa.[10] Or as he tersely puts it, "we see interpretively."[11] Thus he insists, "[We experience] actively, with [our] whole being and having, and contributions of object and subject can never be distinguished with complete exactitude."[12] In this way, Kennedy points out that the entirety of Schillebeeckx's later epistemology attempts to function as a "countermeasure to subjectivism," which "is marked by a Cartesian dualism that supports an image of human beings according to which they have interior and exterior sides."[13] Schillebeeckx laments the "close-knit subjectivity" of modernity promulgated by Kant and prevalent in modern society and philosophy, which seeks to distinguish between the interpreted experience ("phenomenon" or *Gegenstand für mich*) and "the thing in itself" ("noumenon" or *Ding an sich*), because it inevitably *over*emphasizes the contribution of an individual's subjectivity, thereby occluding any notion that experiential knowledge can be grounded in reality itself. And as a consequence, this mentality prevents experiences from garnering any potential for a new epistemological authority. Instead, Schillebeeckx pushes back on any sense of "Kantian rationalism" by maintaining that humans are not "pure subjects" that simply give "meaning to" and constitute an external reality.[14]

However, Schillebeeckx is also not advocating for a completely positivistic "subjectless" world either. He maintains that it could lead, for example, to a "scientific positivism" that harbors its own configuration of Western rationalism

---

6. Schillebeeckx, *Christ*, 50.
7. Schillebeeckx, "Erfahrung und Glaube," 89–90.
8. Ibid., 84. Cf. Kennedy, *Deus*, 262–5.
9. Schillebeeckx, *Christ*, 31. Emphasis added.
10. Ibid., 33. Cf. Schillebeeckx, *Interim Report*, 25.
11. Ibid., 53.
12. Ibid., 32.
13. Kennedy, *Deus*, 223–4. Cf. Schillebeeckx, *Church*, 68.
14. Kennedy, *Deus*, 225–6.

by asserting the "positivistic instrumental reason" of science as "the only cognitive access to reality" and consequently discounting all other epistemic possibilities.[15] Schillebeeckx believes this type of "(neo-)positivism" by preemptively rejecting any "senseless [cognitive] activity" (i.e., "religious symbolic thought") stymies any social, psychological, ethical, or religious dimensions to knowledge. Consequently, this causes "whole areas of our humanity to die out or become stunted, and precisely in so doing [alienating] man from himself,"[16] because "an immeasurable part of reality has disappeared from the horizon of our possible experiences."[17] Accordingly, he defiantly contends that the figurative, poetic, and metaphorical expressions of knowledge found in "religious language" must be seen as no less a possible articulation of the truth and nature of reality than any scientific reasoning. This is because, as he persists,

> The sciences themselves are a child of their time, and down to their own internal autonomy, rightly acquired in a battle against patronizing religious traditions, they reflect the sickness, the relativity and the blindspots of their time. Therefore science is no more a purely objective form of knowledge than other forms of knowledge; moreover it does not have any credentials on the basis of which it may at least legitimately perform this dominant role that it in fact possesses in our Western society as a monopoly, and does so at the expense of many other forms of non-scientific cognitive approaches to reality.[18]

Rather he contends that by grounding epistemology in a "relational ontology" in which the whole of humanity is a configuration of mutually dependent individuals that both individually and collectively exist within a constant dialectical interchange between an encounter with reality itself and the interpretive assimilation of those various encounters, one can remain in tension between these two extreme poles of positivism and subjectivism. This reinforcement of the "dialectical relationship" of all knowledge between interpreted perception and an objective reality that pushes back and gives shape to these perceptions unveils a fundamentally nondualistic element to Schillebeeckx's epistemology. As Thompson simplifies it, "All objects, subjects, events, ideas—all experiences, in short—exist only within a network of irreducible, continually dynamic, and mutually informing relationships."[19] Moreover Schillebeeckx asserts this relationship is at its essence also thoroughly "nonantithetical," meaning that in his thinking "unity is not created by the overcoming of some fundamental opposition but by the *reestablishment* of the irreducible and cooperative relationships which make up all reality, including the very nature of God." It is in this sense, Thompson continues, Schillebeeckx

---

15. Ibid., 228. Cf. Schillebeeckx, *Christ*, 58.
16. Schillbeeckx, *Christ*, 58.
17. Ibid., 805.
18. Schillebeeckx, *Church*, 3.
19. Thompson, 12.

distinguishes his own dialectical epistemology from the earlier "Hegelian or Marxist dialectics of historical opposition and overcoming, and a Barthian dialectic of transcendent Otherness opposed by human self-delusion and disobedience."[20]

Furthermore, this new form of an ontologically relational epistemology also allows Schillebeeckx to give an account for the diversity of conflicting truth claims, especially in the case of religious pluralism. Since knowledge is grounded in an experience of reality itself and yet is also infused with interpretation to its core, then Christians can maintain a viability to their truth claims (since they are founded in a realist experience of reality) while also recognizing that they "do not have a monopoly of the truth" over against "Jews, Buddhists, Hindus, [and] Muslims."[21] This is because individuals (as well as communities of individuals) formulate knowledge of truth based on their own actual interactive encounter with reality while at the same time also instantaneously and inseparably interpreting that engagement with reality through a multiplicity of institutions, traditions of explanation, and worldviews.[22] Thus in accordance with his non-antithetical construal of ontological relation, religious differences do not need to be overcome, reconciled, or synthesized into one essence of experience or truth, but actually can be seen as reflecting the irreducible pluriformity and multidimensionality of reality itself.[23] And as such, the nature of truth can be seen as inherently dialogical—located in the ability of human beings to communicate across variant experiential interpretations of reality.[24] So in his own words, because of the dialectical and non-antithetical nature of existence—the irreducible pluriformity and complexity of reality itself—a pluralism of knowledge "is simply inevitable and, in this sense, impossible to overcome."[25]

Because of his desire to maintain that the nature of being exists as this series of irreducible, plural, and cooperating relationships, Schillebeeckx associates his epistemological system with the "critical negativity" of Theodor Adorno (1903–1969). In 1938 Adorno joined Frankfurt's *Institut für Sozialforschung* (Institute of Social Research) and quickly became one of the major architects of Frankfurtian Critical Theory. As a thoroughgoing historicist and contextualist with regard to the formation of knowledge, Adorno insisted that "all truth is relative to history and that the process of history is not identical with truth in any ontological or metaphysical sense." Moreover, as a critical theorist, he regarded the core of Marxism as its use of dialectical thinking in order to analyze society critically rather than construct metaphysical systems of truth. However in contradistinction to the dialectics of Hegel and Marx, Kennedy elaborates, "the distinctive feature of Adorno's understanding of dialectics was *negativity*"—his disavowal of the

---

20. Ibid., 12–13.
21. Schillebeeckx, *Christ*, 79.
22. Schillebeeckx, *Church*, 50.
23. Schillebeeckx, *Jesus*, 590–1.
24. Ibid., 614.
25. Schillebeeckx, *Understanding*, 51.

positive goal of Hegel's dialectics by rejecting Hegel's final step of the "negation of negation." Instead Adorno emphasized his own "principle of nonidentity," which rather than reconciling opposites until objects of knowledge fit "into their concepts without leaving a remainder" actually views as its goal to display "the untruth of identity": the fact that the concept never exhausts the thing conceived. In other words, instead of using dialectics to resolve "opposing rational views" (a thesis and antithesis) into one final synthetic unity of truth, Adorno sought to take any supposed "unity" simply as the basis for another thesis that must be deconstructed by another antithetical postulate ad infinitum.[26]

Consequently, this system of negative dialectics was particularly appealing to Schillebeeckx for his own epistemology for two major reasons. First, because he saw it as readily translatable to his own "nonantithetical" conception of reality in which the goal too was not a conceptual synthesis of understanding but to indicate and establish reality as consisting of irreducibly complex relationships of interdependence that are integrally resistant to any singular, monological conception of truth. And second, because he believed it resonated with strands of Catholic spirituality (namely, the Thomistic-Carmelite and Dominican traditions) that were founded on the *via triplex* (the three steps of spirituality: affirmation, negation, and eminence), which we will return to shortly. However, as Kennedy stresses, there was at least one significant difference between negative dialectics as Adorno conceived it and the way Schillebeeckx appropriated the term for his own system. For Schillebeeckx, as opposed to Adorno, the never-ending process of dialectical negation could produce a *positive* result in one's understanding of reality or truth. Although he agrees with Adorno that a dialectical process of negation correctly exposes the relative limits of our knowledge and existence, still Schillebeeckx also argues that this unmasking of the "relative limits" of our existence ultimately implies "an absolute limit" that provokes within humans the realization that "they are not masters of themselves."[27] And so, in other words, the dialectical process of critical negativity exposes the reality of humanity's radical finitude in all aspects of existence but at the same time that experience of radical finitude also unveils a dependency (contingency) on a reality that is outside of human control so that individuals are confronted by the fact that humans are completely in relation to an unknown ultimate reality itself. In this way, as he summarizes it elsewhere, "The boundary between God and us is our boundary, and not that of God."[28]

Furthermore, because an experience of ultimate dependence can break through especially within those experiences that negate our conceptions of truth and disclose the relative limits of our existence through all human forms of alienation and suffering (both individual and social),[29] the epistemological authority of

---

26. Kennedy, *Deus*, 234–8. Cf. Portier, "Critical Theorist," 348.
27. Schillebeeckx, *Church*, 98.
28. Schillebeeckx, *Interim Report*, 115.
29. Schillebeeckx, *Christ*, 814.

new experiences rests in their ability to present "unpredictable" content that cannot be seamlessly integrated into one's thought through an already existent interpretative schema or in their ability to present new data that jars or disrupts one's intuitive process of interpretation and forces the individual to stop and think again.[30] Indeed, it's actually through reality's *resistance* to any ultimate dialectical synthesis or unification in a way that continually "surprises" humanity by opening individuals up to "unexpected, new ways of perceiving" their own existence that humans most closely feel and encounter reality itself.[31] Thus, one could say that for Schillebeeckx the "revelatory" authority of new experiences is not to be found in the unveiling of unforeseen metaphysical datums but in the surprising failure of human conceptions to encapsulate all the elements of lived experience.

> On our side we have to experiment, make conjectures, and frame hypotheses, i.e. "reflect," if reality is to reveal itself to us as that which is confirmed, corrected, shattered and constantly given new direction by what we contrive. The permanent resistance of reality to our rational inventions forces us to constantly try new and untried models of thought. Truth comes near to us by the alienation and disorientation of what we have already achieved and planned. This shatters the so-called normativeness or the dogmaticism of the factual, of what is "simply given" … [however] the "negativity" which makes us revise earlier insights as a result of the resistance offered by reality is productive; it has a quite special positive significance as a "revelation in reality," even though it may be dialectically negative and critical. People learn from failures—where their projects are blocked and they make a new attempt, in sensitive reverence for the resistance and thus for the orientation of reality.[32]

Hence, Schillebeeckx concludes, experiences are not "authoritative" by what they "merely express" about reality but rather even *more so* in the conscious discovery of how they obstruct it.[33] And for Schillebeeckx, these indirect disclosures of reality through the rational and critical investigation of the possibilities of "suppression" within our interpretive perceptions are primarily manifested in two ways: in the political (or "secular") realm through ethical action and in the spiritual realm through the "mysticism" of unknowing. And so, it is to these elements of experience we will now turn.

Seemingly quite quickly after Schillebeeckx began studying and teaching hermeneutics at Nijmegen in the latter 1960s, he became convinced that taking a purely hermeneutical approach "such as Gadamer's based simply on a study of the humane sciences" would not suffice for theology. This was because, according to him, "Christianity does not merely throw light on man's existence, it aims above

---

30. Ibid., 32. Cf. Kennedy, *Deus*, 265.
31. Schillebeeckx, *Christ*, 35.
32. Ibid.
33. Schillebeeckx, *Church*, 17–18. Cf. Kennedy, *Deus*, 273.

all to renew that existence."³⁴ As such, the source of any "communal unity and conviction" regarding the reality of existence rests not in a "previously given" understanding of faith or "orthodoxy" but in the Christian process of orthopraxis, or "right doing," that provides "the unity of the same faith and same profession of faith ... even if it is theologically divergent and pluralistically expressed."³⁵ Moreover, besides allowing for a "unity of faith" and common purpose among the diverse beliefs of Christians themselves, Schillebeeckx believed that an emphasis on praxis could allow for Christians to speak across the borders not just of their own tradition but also religious thinking altogether in order to work together with thoroughly secular, humanist, or even atheist individuals who might not understand or accept blatantly Christian terminology. As a result of this ontologically relational approach to epistemology, Schillebeeckx maintains that the "absolute limit" of human existence that indirectly manifests the nondual and non-antithetical nature of ultimate reality at a certain level can prompt interpretations that are "both Christian and secular."³⁶ This is because for him the idea of "ethical praxis" can be defined in a general sense simply as "everything which has as an explicit object the humanization or furtherance of human beings as human beings."³⁷ Hence, one can further interpret the source and function of this broader category of "ethical praxis" in terms of a "mystical" or "religious" experience as "an intensive form of experience of God or the love of God" or conversely in terms of a purely "secular" or "political" one as "an intensive social commitment."³⁸

One of Schillebeeckx's favorite illustrations of the possibility of a dually authoritative experience of the truth of reality across the "religious"–"secular" divide is his story of the sacrificial soldier. According to this example, a soldier of an army under dictatorial rule is ordered "on penalty of death to shoot dead an innocent hostage, purely and simply because the hostage is, for example, a Jew, a Communist or a Christian." However, the soldier refuses to follow the order "on grounds of conscience." Schillebeeckx explains that despite the fact that as a result of this resistance both the hostage and the soldier will ultimately be executed, a greater good about the nature of reality is revealed: a faith in the greater potential of humanity to resist immorality and evil. Hence to the religious believer and "humanist" alike, one can interpret this occurrence as a display of "the hope of the ultimate victory of good" within reality.³⁹ In other words, this instance of self-sacrifice in the resistance to evil, through the "relative limits" of mortality and injustice, presents the believer and atheist alike with an experience of the "absolute limit" of human potential within reality that is common to all.

34. Schillebeeckx, *Understanding*, 67.
35. Ibid., 68.
36. Ibid., 40.
37. Schillebeeckx, *Church*, 91–2.
38. Schillebeeckx, *Western Culture*, 71–2.
39. Ibid., 58–60.

And therefore, the ethical praxis of justice in its resistance to, and even an apparent *failure* to prevent, evil and injustice reveals an element of the ultimate truth of reality: the impermanence of social structures of power and oppression, and even more so the potential for humans to both change and inspire others to change the structures that enslave them.[40] Schillebeeckx believes that this understanding of the transreligious authority of new experiences of ethical "praxis" to reveal an awareness and a knowledge about reality is not only beneficial to Christians for achieving their end goals but also in accordance with the heart of their very message. Quoting a biblical passage (1 Jn 4:12) he proclaims this way of thinking to be an exemplar of the Christian belief, "No one has ever seen God; if we love one another, God abides in us and his love is perfected in us."[41]

Still the question could be asked as to what Schillebeeckx actually *means* by the term "ethical praxis" and how it differs from simply ethical theories of right conduct. This is mainly because, despite his frequent use of the term, Schillebeeckx rarely actually defines it. In fact, probably his most direct explanation of his understanding of the term comes in a parenthetical aside where he simply expounds on "praxis" as "actual conduct."[42] However, what we can know is Schillebeeckx's newfound emphasis on "praxis" over theory is traceable to his studies in the early Critical Theory of Jürgen Habermas at the start of the 1970s. According to Kennedy, Schillebeeckx particularly found a resonance with Habermas's rebuke of the Gadamerian tradition of philosophical hermeneutics in light of the recognition of the pervasive role of "cognitive interests" within all interpretations and assertions of knowledge.[43] Moreover, Schillebeeckx had "an unmistakable satisfaction" with Habermas's theories about the indivisible relation between one's knowledge of reality and one's activities within that reality. For Habermas, Kennedy elaborates, "praxis" is a "twofold complex" that combines "*work* (or instrumental action) and *interaction* (or communicative interaction)" that simultaneously both discloses the nature of reality and also critically tests its own and other theoretical expressions of truth.[44]

Accordingly, Schillebeeckx uses this notion of "actual conduct" as both the source (the experiences out of which reflection and interpretation are produced) and the judge (the experiences from which interpretations are applied and critically evaluated) of truth in that by participating in "ethical praxis," and thus exposing the seemingly fixed social structures of society to be in fact undetermined and changeable, one not only unmasks the various social interests and power plays driving assertions of truth but also asserts the viability of an alternative interpretation of reality that once might have appeared impossible or irrational.[45]

---

40. Ibid., 63.
41. Ibid., 64.
42. Schillebeeckx, *Jesus*, 60. Cf. Kennedy, *Deus*, 262.
43. Kennedy, *Deus*, 174–5.
44. Ibid., 277–82 (esp. 281).
45. Schillebeeckx, *Understanding*, 117.

In other words, it embodies the function of negative dialectics by concurrently presenting an "antithesis" to those assertions about reality that perpetuate *de*humanization and oppression—thus disclosing the "nonsense" behind any singular depiction of reality—while also leaving bare the complex, irreconcilable, and ambiguous elements of reality that contain the potential and hope of newness alongside limitations and contingency. For this reason, Schillebeeckx acknowledges that a critical assessment of experience ("theory") also *precedes* any actual action of praxis in this dialectical reciprocation between perception and reflection and yet, as the originating source and governing judge of the validity of theoretical expression, the "actual conduct" of praxis must always be given a *primacy over* theory itself.[46] Consequently, Schillebeeckx consistently maintains that it is indeed "ethical praxis" that provides the possibility for a mystical cognitive access to God through reflection on how it paradoxically uncovers both reality's dialectical and non-antithetical nature and at the same time its persistent elusiveness to human conceptions.

Whereas Schillebeeckx believes it is both possible and desirable to define ethics in more general transreligious terms, such as any activity focusing on humanization, when it comes to defining his own understanding of the "mystical" authority of new experiences he is much more willing to speak in standard Christian theological terms. For example, he explicitly defines "mysticism" as "an intensive form of experience of God or love of God" or "an intense form of experience of this element in faith which binds us with God."[47] This is because for him mystical experience is particularly a *reflective* act that seeks to utilize traditions of language and thought in order to interpret and articulate one's encounter with the "absolute limit" of reality ("God"). This is what makes the cognitive assertions of theology and faith still grounded in a realist understanding of epistemology. Hence the exact terminology used to express this encounter with the "radical finitude" of humanity and its utter dependency on a reality beyond itself might vary in scope, but nonetheless such articulations are still founded on an actual encounter with reality. By establishing experience as a possible source for an authoritative knowledge of ultimate reality in this way, Kennedy explains that Schillebeeckx is essentially casting aside any Kantian mistrust of the "epistemological capacities" of a personal mysticism to uncover reality as it is in itself.[48] Schillebeeckx believes he can do this precisely because his relational ontology rejects Kant's dichotomous distinction between "appearances" (phenomena) and the reality itself (noumenon).

As opposed to Kant's epistemological foundations for knowledge, Schillebeeckx holds that human knowledge of ultimate truth is possible despite the limitations of finitude and history because of what he terms "the mediated immediacy" of experience. In other words, as contingent creatures humans are certainly confined to forming knowledge through the resources and contents of the created world

---

46. Schillebeeckx, *Ministry*, 101.
47. Schillebeeckx, *Western Culture*, 72, 66.
48. Kennedy, *Deus*, 222.

(i.e., history, empirical experience, interpersonal relationships, etc.); however, as the *creator* on which all contingent existence is based and sustained God imbues the temporal and finite reality of creation. Thus, although he would agree with Kant that humans as creatures can never encounter reality directly in itself, he at the same time rejects by definition the consequential conclusion reached by others that the reality that sustains all contingent existence ("God") can be epistemically divorced from the very thing it is perpetuating (creation). Thus he elaborates,

> If by talking of the death of the "immediacy of God," one means that man has *no unmediated* relationship with God, then I fully agree. However, things look different if we consider this same, i.e. mediated, relationship from the other side, for in my view there certainly is an unmediated relationship between God and us. The objection that immediacy on only one side of a mutual relationship amounts to an inner contradiction is untenable in this particular case. What we have here is not an inter-subjective relationship between two persons—two mortal men—but a mutual relationship between a finite person and his absolute origin, the infinite God. And that has an effect on our relationship to God. In other words, we are confronted with a unique instance, an instance in which the immediacy does not do away with the mediation but in fact constitutes it. Thus from our perspective there is *mediated immediacy*.[49]

According to Schillebeeckx, therefore, even if humans are incapable of encountering reality directly in an unmediated fashion that does not necessarily imply the same is true for reality itself. Indeed, Schillebeeckx insists the exact opposite to be the case. The fact that humans are consistently reminded that concepts of truth are fundamentally limited and fallibilized by their mediation through the contextual, historical, and even biological limits of existence and thought can in actuality become the source of a mystical awareness of something beyond the confines of language, time, and space.[50] Or put somewhat differently, it confronts human beings with the fact that our experiences are inseparable from our interpretive concepts and yet in doing so also gestures toward something persistently elusive of them.

In this way, the reflective experience of interpreting our actions that continually reveal to us the boundless yet unknown elements of reality becomes an authoritative source for an understanding about the nature of reality itself. However rather than being rooted in a speculative abstraction of a universal "thing," this authoritative awareness is based on the perception of a "disintegrating source-experience" in which the condition of all our concepts and understandings being inescapably bound to the contingent factors of historical existence reveals something about the ultimately inexpressible nature of reality.[51] And it is for this reason, he asserts, that

---

49. Schillebeeckx, *Christ*, 804–10 (esp. 809). Emphasis original.
50. Kennedy, *Deus*, 222.
51. Schillebeeckx, *Church*, 72.

the great mystics of history refer to this experiential knowledge culled from "the highest peaks of mysticism … as 'dark nights' (John of the Cross) or, even more daringly, as 'dark light' (Ruysbroeck)." There is an immediacy felt with an ultimate reality beyond our conceptions, but it is only sensed indirectly through a mediation of pure negativity—"revealing itself as a black hole or, as Thérèse of Lisieux says, 'like a wall.'" Paradoxically, he insists however, an "authentic" experience of mysticism although intuited as a "mediation of negativity" in the end manifests itself not simply as an absolute "nothingness" but rather as a "'nothingness' of overdefined 'fullness' which cannot be embraced in concepts or images."[52]

Therefore, this is where once again Adorno's negative dialectics come clearly back into play. Schillebeeckx perceives a correlation between Adorno's dialectically negative movement between concepts (hypotheses) and the anomalous experiences that remain outside these concepts, and the process of the *triplex via* in the Catholic mystical tradition. Citing specifically his own Dominican tradition of spirituality in the vein of Meister Eckhart (1260–1327) then, Schillebeeckx lays out a method for continually "shattering" our "earlier images of God" while also maintaining that the potential for "new possibilities will come to life." The *triplex via* somewhat resembles Adorno's negative dialectics in that the believer begins with a hypothetical "use [of] names and images of God (conceptions of faith). For example, they say that God is good, God is future, God is liberator." This step in the dialectical process of the *triplex via* is the *via affirmativa* (way of affirmation). However, in the use of such language human beings are inevitably challenged—in Schillebeeckx's case especially through the ethical application of "actual conduct," or praxis—by the way in which "the positive predicates of God say more about ourselves and our expectations than about God" because of the way reality apparently resists all our conceptual categorizations. This then compels believers to "also deny God these names which [they] rightly assign to [God]." That is the *via negativa* (the way of negation). Schillebeeckx comfortingly affirms that humans "are right to do this" because "the dynamic of the reality of God" persistently proves itself to be beyond our control in both thought and action. Still, he warns, this process of negating one's epistemological (hypo)theses of ultimate reality should not be done simply "in order to make God anonymous or even fall into a meaningless silence." Rather through this process of negation the believer as a consequence should be opened up to at least the positive truth of reality that it in the end contains an "inexpressible" and perpetually "mysterious quality." This experience of a truth of reality *through* the recognition that our concepts and language constantly fall short of their target of expression is the final element of mystical knowledge, the *via eminentiae* (the way of eminence).[53]

This is where one can once again really begin to see a resemblance with Adorno's system of negative dialectics: it is in Schillebeeckx's epistemological process of taking a postulate depicting reality and deconstructing it with the

---

52. Ibid., 70.
53. Ibid., 76–7. Cf. Schillebeeckx, *Christ*, 810–11.

antithetical elements in the results of the theory's ethical application in "actual conduct," which in turn presents the individual with an eminent experience of reality's mysterious qualities. These new experiences of the mysterious inspire new theoretical conceptions that must then be tested in the application of "ethical praxis" that uncovers the antithetical elements of its results, which then again lead to new experiences of mystery and so on in perpetuity. Hence theory precedes praxis, but is also necessarily subject to praxis as its critical source and evaluator. And thus, this process of knowledge gleaned from new "mystical" experiences both reflects and challenges Adorno's system of negative dialectics. On the one hand, it agrees that the goal of dialectics is enduring negation of theoretical postulates of knowledge rather than discovering a "true theory" through synthesis. But, on the other hand, Schillebeeckx disputes Adorno's contention that there can be no positive result from the dialectic. Instead he maintains that reality's ability to surprise us continually with unexpected outcomes and challenges to our depictions of it can actually become the source of an experience of *hope* that might be "surprised by the constantly unexpected, but never disappointed!" Borrowing from Ernst Bloch, he labels this hope as the *humanum*—an indeterminate hope of a better existence and understanding of reality that never can be expressed in positive fullness.[54] However as a result of this emergence of hope from an experience of negative eminence Schillebeeckx asserts that one can say, "The truth of religious language and the confidence of hope derive from the same source as the constantly recurring new element which surpasses all religious conceptions and expectations."[55] And so, his dialectic of negation most significantly *differs* from Adorno's in the fact that Schillebeeckx asserts that it provides humans with a true, real encounter with reality itself so that—although we must only articulate it "in a stammering way"—it nonetheless is *actually* based in reality itself and not just our conceptions of it.[56]

The upcoming later section on Schillebeeckx's epistemology of experience, therefore, will return to these new conceptualizations of encounter (experience), ethics (human participation), and mysticism (negative eminence) to examine how Schillebeeckx translates these ideas in expressly Christian theological language and categories. More specifically, it will display how Schillebeeckx conceives of the epistemological authority of new religious experiences within Christian theological knowledge as being located primarily in "negative contrast experiences" (encounter), "orthopraxis" (ethical action), and experiences of undefinable hope or *humanum* (apophaticism, or negative eminence). Before we can do that however, first let us turn to Gendun Chopel's sources and understanding of Madhyamaka theories of experiential knowledge to see if there are any possible correlates in his thought to those just discussed.

---

54. Schillebeeckx, *Jesus*, 622.
55. Schillebeeckx, *Christ*, 57.
56. Schillebeeckx, *Church*, 77.

B. Gendun Chopel: The Problem of Experiential Knowledge within an Anti-Realist Epistemology

When assessing Gendun Chopel's theory on the authority of experiential knowledge in comparison to Schillebeeckx's epistemology, what immediately stands out is the obvious difference between the two thinkers' systems in that Gendun Chopel's epistemology is firmly embedded in an anti-realism that drastically alters his conception of experiential authority within epistemology. This stands directly in opposition to Schillebeeckx whose fundamentally *realist* epistemology by definition almost demands an accounting of an experiential authority within knowledge. What is particularly interesting in this comparison, however, is how at the same time each thinker arrives at an understanding of the role of experience for informing or "unveiling" an awareness and knowledge of ultimate reality that is necessarily *negative* in nature despite approaching the issue from seemingly antithetical viewpoints. Hence this section, then, will examine how Gendun Chopel utilizes an anti-realist conception of experiential knowledge in order to assert an inescapably negative depiction of ultimate reality.

However such a close examination of Gendun Chopel's theory of experiential knowledge is certainly not without its challenges, not least of which is the fact that his main epistemological treatise that we have so often observed to this point, the *Adornment*, does not discuss many of the basic ideas behind topics such as knowledge (*pramāṇa*) and even Madhyamaka philosophy itself but rather assumes the reader will already have a complete knowledge of the Geluk scholastic vocabulary.[57] At the same time, Lopez explains that in the *Adornment* Gendun Chopel does not hesitate in targeting those same "sacrosanct domains" of Geluk scholastic philosophy as the focus of his attack. This especially pertains to the topic of valid knowledge (*pramāṇa*).[58] The famous Geluk scholastic philosopher Tsongkhapa is revered in that branch of Tibetan Buddhism for setting forth a system "that was simultaneously able to posit a basis of valid knowledge while

---

57. Lopez and chos phel, *Madman*, ix. Lopez also points out that much of the style and argumentation of the *Adornment* also embodies as well as assumes an awareness of "the logical choreography of the debating courtyard," which is crucial in understanding the purpose and function of Buddhist dialectics.

58. See Dreyfus, *Reality*, 285–7. Dreyfus explains the complications with identifying "knowledge" with *pramāṇa*. According to him, in classical Indian philosophy "knowledge" typically carried a twofold understanding of "right cognition" (*pramā*) and "its means" (*pramāṇa*). Dreyfus parses these two words: the root word *ma* literally means "to measure or cognize," and the prefix *pra* indicates "excellence or perfection." Therefore, he concludes, "the word *pramā* designates a state of being factually aware of something, and should be literally translated as 'knowledge event,'" whereas with "the adjunction of the suffix *ana*" the word *pramāṇa* makes it more literally to signify "the means or instrument of bringing about the knowledge event (*pramā*)." Hence, according to the Western conception of the authoritative "modes of knowledge," *pramāṇa* appears to be a closer fit than *pramā*, which has more to do with the thought itself.

upholding the doctrine of the emptiness of all phenomena" through his own version of a ("moderate") realist epistemology.⁵⁹ According to Tsongkhapa, one can reconcile this paradox of knowledge by distinguishing "between two distinct domains of [epistemological] discourse, namely, that which pertains to the reality of our everyday world of convention, and that which pertains to the ultimate ontological status of things and events."⁶⁰ This in essence separated epistemological claims to "valid knowledge" into two distinct categories: the practical and communicative ("contingent") knowledge of the conventional world and the non-linguistic, nonconceptual knowledge of the ultimate truth of reality itself linked with attaining buddhahood. As we have already repeatedly observed this point, Lopez establishes that Gendun Chopel "rejects such a harmony outright" and instead in the *Adornment* ventures to preserve a consistent system of "two truths" (*madhyamaka*) through a radically anti-realist epistemology based on the fundamental "rejection of the ability of benighted sentient beings to think or speak accurately about anything, most of all the enlightened state."⁶¹ Hence, this section will seek to examine the three traditional Geluk categories for objects of comprehension (*prameya, gzhal bya*) among the phenomena of the universe—the manifest (*abimukhī, mngon gyur*), the slightly hidden (*kimchid-paroksha, cung zad lkog gyur*), and the thoroughly hidden (*atyartha-parosha, shin tu lkog gyur*)⁶²—that contribute to any knowledge derived from experience, whether by direct perception or inference.⁶³ Subsequently, this will then serve as the basis for us to analyze Gendun Chopel's own reinterpretation and appropriation of these categories for determining the authority of experiential knowledge within his own epistemological system in the later section.

Before substantially discussing the nuances and differences between the various viewpoints informing and influencing Gendun Chopel's own epistemological approach to experiential knowledge, first it would probably be helpful to recapitulate the broader outlines of the arguments for what is at stake in this discussion (as briefly discussed earlier). A foundational text in the Geluk epistemological curriculum is Dharmakīrti's *Commentary on Valid Knowledge* (*Pramāṇavārttika*).⁶⁴ In this work, the Indian philosopher Dharmakīrti "attempts to provide a viable system of logic and epistemology within an anti-realist framework that embodies the basic Buddhist principles of impermanence and selflessness."⁶⁵ Accordingly, Dharmakīrti sets up an epistemological system based on the

---

59. Lopez, "*Vigrahavyāvartanī* 29," 169. Cf. Dreyfus, *Reality*, 445.
60. Jinpa, 42.
61. Lopez, "*Vigrahavyāvartanī* 29," 169.
62. Daniel Perdue and Byams-pa-rgya-mtsho Phur-bu-lcog, *Debate in Tibetan Buddhism*, Textual Studies and Translations in Indo-Tibetan Buddhism (Ithaca, NY: Snow Lion, 1992), 179.
63. Dreyfus, *Reality*, 78. Cf. Perdue and Phur-bu-lcog, 178–9.
64. Dreyfus, *Hands*, 238.
65. Dreyfus, *Reality*, 443.

strict dichotomy between the perceptual and the conceptual viewpoints. Thus Dharmakīrti in essence establishes a duality of dichotomies: an epistemological one where perception encounters "real individual things as they are" and inference creates conceptual constructs of "universals" to identify and categorize those "real individual things"; and another ontological one where "reality" is attributed to the realm of "individuals" and where the realm of "universals," or "conceptual and linguistic constructs," are not. Hence, the result is a foundationalist yet anti-realist epistemology where reality is actually encountered (perceived) but all language and concepts are constructs divorced from that reality as it is in itself.[66]

Later Tibetan thinkers, however, such as Tsongkhapa, perceived this dichotomy to be too strong and consequently preventive of the "union of two truths" that is believed necessary for the conventional to serve its necessary soteriological function of bringing individuals out of a conventional understanding and to an ultimate "liberating" awareness of emptiness ($śūnyatā$). If one were to accept this other system as the case, they argue, it would inevitably lead to nihilism—an untenable position within Buddhism. In an attempt to overcome this soteriological dilemma then, Tsongkhapa sought to strike a balance between the "ontological bifurcation (unbridgeable gulf)" seen as presented by Dharmakīrti's system and a naïve realist "conflation between appearance and reality." Hence, as mentioned just above, he developed a system of epistemology divided along "two distinct domains" of the "everyday" experiential realm and the ultimate realm of emptiness. "As a valid parallel," Thupten Jinpa expounds, "valid propositions pertaining to the first can be said to be conventional truths, while those that pertain to the second are ultimate truths." Or as Tsongkhapa himself writes in the *Lhag mthong chung ngu* (*Abridged Special Insight*), "Each of these inner or outer phenomena has two, two natures, namely, its ultimate nature and its conventional nature."[67] The result of this is that from within the perspective of the "ordinary world" objects of knowledge can be said to be either "veridical" or false based on an undeluded conventional consciousness, whereas from the enlightened perspective of an "*ārya*" the distinction of "true" or "false" is in the end empty of an actual meaning.[68] In this way, Tsongkhapa can claim a realist epistemology in accord with an object's ontological referent.

As will become apparent in the later section on his own system of thought, Gendun Chopel insists almost the exact opposite. For him, the problem with Dharmakīrti's conception of conventional epistemology is not that his anti-realist stance dares too close to becoming nihilistic by proposing an overly large a chasm between the conventional and ultimate realms, but rather that his anti-realism does not go far enough. Accordingly, Gendun Chopel is persistent that "the enlightened state [is] the privileged locus of [epistemological] authority and scathingly lampoons those who would assert that the unenlightened mind can have

---

66. Dreyfus, *Hands*, 237–8. Cf. p. 282.
67. Jinpa, 149–51.
68. Ibid., 154.

any valid knowledge."⁶⁹ And as one can imagine, such a radical and polemical anti-realist stance would greatly impact his understanding of authoritative knowledge derived from empirical experiences of the world.

According to Tsongkapha's system of Prāsaṅgika-Madhyamaka (which is the pervasive view within Geluk scholastic philosophy), although one can claim a "realist" conventional epistemology where a claim can be assessed as "valid" or "invalid" knowledge based on whether "it fulfills the basic condition of being unmistaken with respect to its object" within the existential framework of one's "lived world experience,"⁷⁰ the ultimate reality of emptiness means that ontologically one must remain "nominalist" in that worldly conventions and knowledge cannot attain the ultimate dimension of phenomena. Thus for him, epistemically speaking, a claim to conventional knowledge, such as "there is water in that jar," can be determined as "true cognition" (*pramāṇa*) based on its verification according to the rules of worldly convention as opposed to a mirage that is both conventionally and ontologically nonexistent.⁷¹ In this way, Tsongkhapa believes he can maintain the epistemic authority of existential experiences apart from an awareness of "the realm of the ultimate" at least in a "non-analytical" manner that does not ask, "Is this how the object actually exists, or does it just appear that way to my mind?"⁷² Guy Martin Newland paints an excellent and concise illustration of this aspect of Tsongkhapa's thought:

> Take the situation of students looking up at a blackboard where the instructor has scratched out the shape of the letter A. In recognizing the letter, the students at least initially perceive the letter as being set up "out there," from its own side. It appears to be objectively established, and they experience themselves as attentive but passive recipients of the message it is sending out. Yet after a moment of reflection on the conventional nature of language, the lack of any "A nature" among the bits of chalk and so on, students come to see they are participating in the establishment of the A. The conventional consciousness that recognizes the shapes that can serve as a basis for imputing the A—and ascribes A rather than B in relation to the shape—is not wrong. It is *not* the basis of all misery; it is a practical and correct conventional mind. What *is* wrong is the habitual and usually unchallenged sense that the A is naturally or objectively *there*, on its own, without its "being posited through the force of awareness."⁷³

Hence, in Tsongkhapa's mind, while conventional "truths"—such as the validity of identifying a letter as an "A"—are falsities in the sense that they lack any natural,

---

69. Lopez, "*Vigrahavyāvartanī* 29," 169.

70. Jinpa, 65.

71. Ibid., 166–7.

72. Cowherds, 60, quoting from Tsongkhapa's *Great Treatise on the Stages of the Path to Enlightenment* (*Byang chub lam rim che ba*).

73. Cowherd, 63. Emphasis original.

independent identity from "their own side," nevertheless pragmatically they can be viewed as "true" or valid in that they are "fully capable of functioning": "It works in words; it works as a grade. It does its job perfectly well even though it has no trace of the objective existence we unconsciously attribute to it."[74] This is what is meant when individuals, such as Thupten Jinpa, ascribe "realism" to Tsongkhapa's epistemology. Worldly experience can be illusory and obstructive on an ultimate or ontological level, while still being informative, influential, and veridical in the sense that they assist individuals in properly responding to and conducting actions within the conventional realm of interdependence. This is the fundamental difference that exists between conventional knowledge and knowledge of the ultimate, one is considered valid by an assessment of its pragmatic value to communicate and function while from the other standpoint only the cognition of emptiness can be considered valid or "genuine knowledge."[75]

Part of the reasoning behind this distinction in Tsongkhapa's thought is based on the generally accepted position within Tibetan philosophy that an object of knowledge and one's perception of that object are mutually dependent. "One does not exist prior to the other, nor does one enjoy a greater ontological status than the other. Objects exist in relation to perceptions, while cognitions exist in relation to their objects. For Tsongkhapa, the idea of a content-free consciousness is conceptually incoherent."[76] At least superficially, Gendun Chopel would completely agree with this assumption that an object of knowledge cannot be understood apart from subjective perception. However, he interprets this supposition as leading to a very divergent conclusion. Whereas Tsongkhapa wants to use this understanding in order to hold that claims to knowledge cannot be separated from the perceptive state of the knower and, subsequently, to conclude that it is possible for one to have valid knowledge from a conventional level of perception while remaining ontologically nominalist from the level of ultimate perception, Gendun Chopel wants to use this similar understanding to contend that, along the lines of Dharmakīrti, "mental and material events interact in a constantly ongoing and fluctuating process" of successive evanescent moments. Accordingly, the idea of valid experiential knowledge (*pramāṇa*) is fundamentally distinct from Western conceptions of knowledge in that it does not refer "to an endurable quality possessed by the knowing person ... but to a mental event that cognizes the object as a momentary knowledge event," which after the immediate event itself can only be reproduced through conceptual recollection (*smṛti, dran pa*).[77]

As a consequence Gendun Chopel contends that apart from a correct ontological awareness of these momentary objects, any conventional conceptuality is entirely obstructive, deceptive (illusory), and unreliable because of its inherent reification. And therefore, it is pragmatically unefficacious in actually ever steering

74. Ibid.
75. Jinpa, 166–7.
76. Ibid., 159.
77. Dreyfus, *Reality*, 287–8. Cf. Lopez, *Science*, 110.

one to a proper ontological awareness. For example, in verses 24 and 26 of the *Adornment* Gendun Chopel uses an illustration of the "miracles" of the Buddha to emphasize this point that the reification of concepts is inherent to conventional and consequently inextricably deceptive:

> But if this mind of ours is a valid consciousness, we conclude that an atom is the smallest material form and we conclude that a world is extremely vast. We conclude that the great does not fit inside the small. (284) Therefore, no matter how great the magical powers and abilities of the Buddha may be, how is he able to destroy principles that are established by valid knowledge? ... To decide that in general an atom and a world differ in size, but then to have to make many exceptions, such as saying that the Buddha's doing so is a special case, is in fact proof that the bag of our valid knowledge is leaking in all directions ... To our conceptions, existence and nonexistence, is and is not, large and small, good and bad, and so on are all simply mutually exclusive ... Thus, one must understand that we, and not the Buddha, are the real magicians.[78]

Because experiential knowledge is virtually defined entirely by our sense organs "conventional reality appears to [unenlightened beings] as though it is truly (intrinsically) existent—as more than merely conventional." And in this sense it is essentially "obscurational, confusing, and veiling."[79]

For Gendun Chopel then, as in the example above, any recognition of validity within conventional conceptions of experience entails a reifying effect that makes any type of nonconceptual existence or anything beyond the conventional purview—such as "the Buddha can make an aeon equal to an instant" or "the Buddha can place a world system inside an atom"—seem impossible, illogical, or even nonexistent.[80] This realization, as Sonam Thakchöe clarifies, causes Gendun Chopel to come to three connected conclusions:

> First, what is ontologically unreal and deceptive must also be epistemically flawed. Since all conventional cognitions are ontologically deceptive and illusory in virtue of being causally conditioned, they must be epistemically flawed. Thus, the so-called conventionally reliable cognition must be rejected unequivocally. Second, mundane cognitions (conventional consciousnesses) all reify their objects under the influence of primal ignorance. Thus, they are all flawed and epistemically unreliable. Third, since no conventional cognitions enable one to perceive ultimate reality directly, they are hence unreliable.[81]

---

78. Chos phel, "Adornment," 53–4, v. 26.
79. Cowherds, 31. Cf. Lopez and chos phel, *Madman*, 133.
80. Lopez and chos phel, *Madman*, 134.
81. Cowherds, 40.

Since for Gendun Chopel all conventional knowledge is "flawed" and consequently "unreliable," then it cannot even live up to the pragmatic standards put forth by Tsongkhapa as the means for determining the validity of conventional knowledge within its own framework. If it cannot guarantee any correspondence to things perceived conventionally, it therefore cannot ensure the ability to produce desired outcomes within that reality. At the same time, however, more questions still remain. If all direct perceptions (and their inseparable conceptual interpretations) are foundationally unstable and thus invalid, then is there any kind of valid experiential knowledge? Moreover how can the Buddha's, or any other enlightened being's, own teachings be considered "truthful" since they are steeped in conventional language, concepts, and assumptions? Can an enlightened being currently existing in *saṃsāra* still convey any knowledge of reality to unenlightened beings? This leads us to a discussion of the next two types of existential phenomena in the experiential world, the slightly and thoroughly hidden objects of knowledge, which can be known primarily through inference.

To this point we have observed how for Prāsaṅgika Mādhyamikas (those who accept and practice the Prāsaṅgika interpretation of the two truths) within the conventional realm of direct perception, both the perceptive and inferential modes of knowledge (*pramāṇas*) function inseparably in a dialectical manner in which one's direct perception of "real individual things" is simultaneously interpreted according to inferential constructs of "universal" categories that then shape one's past and future perceptions of "knowledge events." In this way, as Gendun Chopel at one point reflects, "even the perception of a shape does not exist objectively apart from the power of the mind or of human language."[82] Ontologically speaking, however, both of these modes of knowledge are utterly blemished by the delusion of conventional existence and, therefore, can at best be used to help one practically function within the conventional world (Tsongkhapa)—and for Gendun Chopel not even that.[83] Thus the question remains, is there any possible valid knowledge that can be imputed solely on the basis of inferential knowledge? And if so, does this apply to the means of knowledge derived from the Buddha's, or any other bodhisattva's, teaching?

As we already observed in our discussion of Gendun Chopel's depiction of the Buddha's authority, the precedent set by Dharmakīrti regarding inferential knowledge through teaching (whether written or spoken) is that assertions themselves cannot be self-validating. "At best, they can inform us of the speaker's subjective *intentions* ... [Thus] Valid cognition based on valid testimony understood as direct understanding of the object expressed by a statement is to be rejected." In other words, any inferential knowledge based on another's words must be confirmed independent of the other's testimony itself. Dreyfus provides a helpful example of what Dharmakīrti means by this assertion:

82. Loepz, *Science*, 110.
83. See note 65.

If I say to you "this is my rocking chair," you can infer from my words the nature of my communicative intention. You cannot, however, infer that the object I am referring to is a rocking chair from my words only. To do this, you must first know the chair. Hence, knowledge based on communication is not a sui generis form of knowledge. The only sure information obtained from testimony concerns the speaker's intentions.[84]

Similarly, Dreyfus cites another popular example to further elaborate this point, this time using the idea of foreign countries. According to this illustration, people can learn "a great deal" about foreign countries to which they have never been personally. Is this cognition based on inference from the communication of another person actually valid as "knowledge"? Dreyfus explains that the "answer of the Buddhist epistemologist" is not exactly clear in this regard. In the end, however, Dreyfus determines that "the answer seems to be that these cognitions are not knowledge but mere opinions." Even if one can establish that the speaker providing the information is "generally trustworthy," say in the case of Śākyamuni Buddha or another bodhisattva, this type of inference still cannot be considered "valid knowledge" unless it is verified by the individual on any particular topic.[85] Well then, one could ask, how does this apply to information provided in the teachings of Buddhas and Bodhisattvas that cannot be verified directly by the individual such as the laws of *karma* and *impermanence*? This leads into discussions of slightly hidden and thoroughly hidden phenomena, and Gendun Chopel's extensive discussions of the Mādhyamika having "no thesis."

"Slightly hidden" phenomena are those realities that cannot be directly perceived in ordinary sense experience, but whose existence nonetheless can be verified through one's inference. Thus this label is often applied to realities taught by the Buddha (and others) that one probably would not logically perceive on one's own but nonetheless help make sense of the world around an individual after being told about them. Examples of such phenomena include the teachings of "subtle impermanence, the law of karma, rebirth, and emptiness."[86] Because these slightly hidden phenomena can be at least indirectly verified based on one's perception of and inference from the world around them—much like directly encountered phenomena—these teachings at least superficially fit Dharmakīrti's standard of "knowledge" rather than "mere opinions." However for Gendun Chopel, even if these teachings of the Buddha meet Dharmakīrti's standard of experiential verification, it does mean that these statements of Buddha (or anyone else) can be taken as *literally* true. According to verse 121 of the *Adornment*, as long as others still exist and perceive reality within the three conventional realms of *saṃsāra* (v. 120), even though one might have already directly realized emptiness, "one must involuntarily assert whatever was asserted earlier … [so that] when someone who

---

84. Dreyfus, *Reality*, 294–5.
85. Ibid., 295.
86. Lopez and chos phel, *Madman*, 172.

has no such assertions is asked what is out there, he will be bound to say that it is a mountain, it is a tree, and that is a human." Otherwise, he quips, by not asserting the conventional one could be accused of succumbing to "the danger of falling into nihilism."[87] This then becomes the basis for Gendun Chopel's interpretation of Nāgārjuna's illustrious statement that "the Mādhyamika has no thesis."

Statements referring to Nāgārjuna's oft-cited statement that the Mādhyamika has no thesis can be found littered throughout his corpus;[88] however, probably two of the most cited and significant references for our discussion are the *Vigrahavyāvartanī* 29 and the *Mūlamadhyamakakārikā*. In the former account Nāgārjuna responds to an accusation by an opponent that if Nāgārjuna's assertion that all things lack an intrinsic nature (*svabhāva*; lit. "own-being") is true, then his own statement must also lack one as well (and consequently be self-defeating). Nāgārjuna rebuts this charge by declaring, "If I had some thesis, I would incur that fault; because I have no thesis, I am faultless." Ruegg and Lopez concur that the intention of the wielding of this phrase is to insist that although the Mādhyamika (in this case Nāgārjuna) might have many philosophical theses, it refrains from asserting any "propositional thesis that entails the existence of independent entities."[89] The latter one from the *Mūlamadhyamakakārikā* (XXV.24), on the other hand, is a much more subtle position. In this passage Nāgārjuna proclaims, "The cessation of all objects, the cessation of all elaborations is auspicious. The Buddha did not teach any doctrine anywhere to anyone."[90] Here the passage seems to be indicating something beyond the simple distinction between philosophical theses in general and those asserting "independent existence." Instead, it appears to be claiming that the Buddha (and by implication any other enlightened being) does not literally speak *at all*, but remains in "noble silence." Ruegg and Lopez posit the insinuation of this statement to mean that Mādhyamikas do not make any assertions from their own position, but rather adopt the logic of others in order to deconstruct that logic with their grasp of the reality of the two truths. Therefore, although Mādhyamikas do make assertions based on conventional existence as "merely a compassionate concession to the ignorant world,"[91] "within their own system they have not a single thesis."[92]

On the surface it might seem as though these two prominent understandings of the Mādhyamika not having a thesis would easily correspond in Gendun Chopel's mind with the "slightly hidden" and "thoroughly hidden" phenomena respectively. Following this logic then, the "slightly hidden" phenomena would be those realities that the Buddha spoke of and taught in accordance with the philosophical tenets of specific times and places. Since they were taught in the linguistic framework of

---

87. Chos phel, "Adornment," 80, v. 120–1.
88. Lopez, "*Vigrahavyāvartanī* 29," 163.
89. Ibid.
90. Lopez, Hermeneutics, 48.
91. Lopez, "*Vigrahavyāvartanī* 29," 170.
92. Ibid., 168.

worldly conventions it would seem possible to verify these teachings by whether they function in conformity with and help make sense of conventional existence. Conversely then, "thoroughly hidden" phenomena would be those truths only perceivable by an enlightened being, which thus must remain divorced from the conventional world. Hence when enlightened beings "compassionately concede" to speak in the conventions of the ignorant world they are never actually speaking of the "thoroughly hidden" truths to which they are constantly aware. And to an extent, this interpretation could be more or less helpful in navigating Gendun Chopel's thought. However there is still one significant caveat. Remember Gendun Chopel's thoroughgoing anti-realism causes him to maintain that as soon as conventional language or concepts are applied to one's direct experience of reality, these understandings become utterly deceptive, reifying, and unreliable; consequently they cannot be deemed "valid knowledge." Thus, for him, once one begins logically analyzing one's own statements so as to consider and explain whether the statement "I have no thesis" is itself a thesis, that person has already become completely immersed in the "realm of conventional analysis."[93] So Gendun Chopel rejects the notion that a Mādhyamika could assert valid philosophical theses that simply do not "entail the existence of independent entities."

Once again one must remember that for Gendun Chopel, whether intended by the speaker or not, conventional reality has the effect of appearing to unenlightened beings as though it is intrinsically existent and more than merely conventional, and so these claims obstruct, confuse, and veil the truth of existence in toto. In this regard, they can at best be adjudicated along purely pragmatic grounds with no deeper assessment of the actual correspondence to reality. In other words, for him they are like the instructions of a mother forbidding her child to go outside by the empty threat that either "If you go outside, there is a tiger" or "If you go far away, I'll cut your ears off!" Although neither is based in "reality" per se, the intention of the mother is not to explain the actual reasons why the child must not stray outside the house but rather only to keep the child from going outside.[94] Similarly the logical and philosophical assertions concerning the "slightly hidden" truths of phenomena, even if they seem to be verified by one's own experience, are not "valid" in the sense of actually depicting reality as it is, rather they are just relatively effective in conveying the speaker's intention and consequently producing a desired action. Or as Lopez phrases it, they are at best to him "a lie told for a noble purpose."[95]

In light of his anti-realist epistemological proclivities, it makes sense that Gendun Chopel would want to emphasize "thoroughly hidden" realities as the source of any experiential valid knowledge. Accordingly, for Gendun Chopel the primary referent of the Mādhyamika having no thesis is the idea of the "noble silence" of the Buddha. This imagery of the silence of the Buddha, however, should

---

93. Ibid., 172.
94. Chos phel, "Adornment," 80, v. 120–1.
95. Lopez and chos phel, *Madman*, 176.

not be understood in accordance with the theories of thinkers, such as Vajrapāṇi and others, who understood the Buddha's silence in a *literal* fashion so that they believed "the Buddha was actually silent throughout his life, remaining constantly absorbed in *samādhi*, without speech, without thought, without breath." In Vajrapāṇi's mind then, the Buddha functioned more "like a speaking prism" that, while remaining "perfect, impassive, [and] with no color of its own," when approached by "the faith, the development, the questions, the intentions of sentient beings" simply appeared to speak by refracting those beings' own contextually situated words and ideas in an appropriate way.[96] For Gendun Chopel, the Buddha and other enlightened Mādhyamikas clearly *did* and *do* speak, just never from the perspective of the ultimate—thus never about the "thoroughly hidden" elements of reality themselves.[97] In this way while "compassionately conceding" to speak for the sake of sentient beings, the Buddha in fact remained entirely silent about any "truth" or "valid knowledge" of ultimate reality. Thus this understanding attempts to make sense of the Buddha's statements claiming "Whatever the world says exists, I also say exists." In other words, as soon as language and concepts are used the Mādhyamika is no longer engaging or conveying any part of ultimate reality itself, and subsequently is no longer communicating "valid knowledge."[98] Still, the question remains, if even the words of the Buddha are fundamentally deceptive and come nowhere near actually touching upon the "thoroughly hidden" truths of reality, what then is the purpose of speaking at all? Can someone speak in a thoroughly deceptive way that is completely divorced from reality itself, and yet still do so in a soteriologically efficacious way that might assist in bringing an individual to an ultimate awareness of emptiness? This is where an understanding use of Buddhist "negative dialectics" becomes essential for comprehending Gendun Chopel's experiential epistemology.

Within the Geluk scholastic tradition of Tibetan Buddhism, Dreyfus explains, one cannot understand the role of negative dialectics apart from the prominence of debate as pedagogical tool in the Geluk curricula.[99] In fact, in agreement with the analysis of José Cabezón, Dreyfus maintains that within the Geluk tradition debate has tended to replace exegetical commentaries as the primary source for creatively deciphering possible interpretive meanings of the various scriptural texts.[100] Although the implication of the use of "dialectics" within the Western tradition typically is viewed as "the controversial art of 'seeking and sometimes arriving at the truth by reasoning,'" Dreyfus warns that Geluk dialectics of debate

---

96. Lopez, *Hermeneutics*, 49.

97. Lopez, "*Vigrahavyāvartanī* 29," 170. Cf. Chos phel, "Adornment," 64, v. 77.

98. Lopez, "*Vigrahavyāvartanī* 29," 172-3. Cf. Chos phel, "Adornment," 65, v. 80.

99. For an informative discussion of the role of "Debate as Dialectic" within Geluk scholasticism, see Dreyfus, *Hands*, 200-11.

100. Dreyfus, *Hands*, 193. Cf. José Ignacio Cabezón, *Buddhism and Language: A Study of Indo-Tibetan Scholasticism*, Suny Series, toward a Comparative Philosophy of Religions (Albany: State University of New York Press, 1994), 83-5.

do not completely match up with this definition. Rather he insists that, more in the mode of Aristotelian dialectics, the Geluk dialectics of debate tend to function "as a game" with "no other immediate goal outside itself," yet one that can still indirectly have implications toward "a higher purpose."

In other words, the dialectics of debate aim at teaching a critical (or even "deconstructive") logic rather than uncovering "universal truths" through deductive reasoning so that this critical logic might assist the debater in "reaching [a] greater understanding" through "developing crucial intellectual habits, such as a spirit of inquiry and critical acumen."[101] Hence the purpose of debate is not to lead the participants to greater positive assertion of knowledge, but instead is meant to "lead students to the Madhyamaka insights into the limits of theoretical rationality" by continually challenging and destabilizing the grounds for any epistemological postulate.[102] In doing so, it attempts to break Geluk thinkers of "the dualistic tendency to grasp objects by reifying differences."[103] And in the end, then, its intent is not to enable the debaters, and observers, to better articulate "truth" but rather to make them discover the "uncertainties in what [they] thought to be well-established truths," accordingly exposing the "fragility of human knowledge" and subsequently gesturing toward the essencelessness of all language and assertions by preventing the mind to lock onto any alternative as definitive truth.[104] So for this reason Dreyfus identifies the role of debate as negatively alluding to the truth of emptiness through emphasizing the pervasiveness of "knowledge's deconstructability" and leading students "to realize that whatever is said can be undermined, however self-evident it may at first seem."[105] This, as we will see for Gendun Chopel, corresponds rather fittingly with the role of the Mādhyamika speaking conventionally while remaining silent in the absolute sense regarding the "thoroughly hidden" truths of reality. In this sense, the Mādhyamika speaks in a way so as to "deconstruct" the value of linguistic and conceptual ideas and thus expose the hearer to the limits of language, conventional concepts, and knowledge in order to "bring others to the silence of emptiness."[106]

By understanding the role of the Mādhyamika's speech as the thorough deconstructive negation of knowledge with an end result of arriving at a "non-implicative negation" or "a negation that leaves no room for any affirmation or implication in its aftermath,"[107] Gendun Chopel believes his anti-realist epistemology can possibly assist in guiding individuals to an experience of enlightenment, the direct experience of the "non-affirming negative" of ultimate emptiness. And thus, by utilizing concepts in a fundamentally "self-canceling way"

101. Dreyfus, *Hands*, 200–1.
102. Ibid., 237.
103. Ibid., 240.
104. Ibid., 245.
105. Ibid., 312.
106. Lopez, "*Vigrahavyāvartanī* 29," 177–8.
107. Jinpa, 57.

that unmasks all linguistic and conceptual "knowledge" as "powerless to describe reality" or provide any "accurate vision of reality,"[108] Gendun Chopel considers his epistemology as capable of fulfilling the soteriological function that Buddhism, and specifically Tsongkhapa, demands.[109] It enables the hearer to possibly *intuit* "the real" through a "state of nonconceptuality" brought about by the deconstruction of all concepts and language.[110] So in this way, somewhat similar to Schillebeeckx's "mystical" element of experiential knowledge, Gendun Chopel argues that his anti-realist epistemology can actually serve as the basis for an authoritative experiential knowledge of the truth of reality, albeit in a nonconceptual, inexpressible, and utterly *negative* manner.

III. Knowing Negatively: "Apophatic" Knowledge through the Limits of Language and Thought

A. Schillebeeckx: Knowledge Derived from the "Dark Light" of Experience

So far this chapter has examined the philosophical and religious sources for both thinkers' conceptualization of the authority of experiential knowledge, observing how both individuals view experiences of negation—whether language, concepts, or theoretical postulates about the truth of reality—as paramount for indirectly uncovering the inexpressible, nonconceptual nature of reality. This prioritization of the negative quality of knowledge perpetuates in each system a dialectical process of articulation and negation that unveils an imminent encounter with ultimate reality, which then leads one to restart the cycle. In this section, however, the discussion will now turn to examine how Schillebeeckx's (critically) realist epistemology rooted in the Christian tradition in opposition to Gendun Chopel's anti-realist epistemology formulated through his own interpretation of the Madhyamaka philosophy of the Buddhist tradition serves as the source for both some of the resemblances as well as some of the distinctive variances in the theological and philosophical outcomes of their respective applications of experiential authority. This will then set up in the conclusion of the chapter a final array of comparative observations and a resultant collection of questions to be addressed as a part of the constructive conclusion of this project in the chapter to follow. But first, we must still flesh out how this seemingly common characteristic that I am identifying as "apophaticism" is manifested in, and at the heart of, each thinker's construction of his individual system of religious thought.

In the previous section regarding the experiential component to Schillebeeckx's epistemology, it was observed how Schillebeeckx culled language and concepts

---

108. Dreyfus, *Reality*, 460–2.

109. Jinpa, 62. In this passage Thupten Jinpa quotes Tsongkhapa's *Essence of Eloquence* (*Drang nges legs bshad snying po*) to describe this "soteriological dimension" to Madhyamaka logic.

110. Ibid., 28.

from modern thought, and specifically Critical Theory, in order to address some seemingly perennial questions of religious epistemology. Some of these questions included, for example, whether it is possible for anyone to have actual and reliable knowledge of reality itself (God); if it is possible to experience or express any transhistorical elements of reality from within the confines of historical and locational particularity; and finally if there can be any viably positive awareness or "mystical awareness" of the truth of ultimate reality through the negating "limits" of conceptual failures, pervasive suffering, and interest-driven perceptions—all of which constantly remind humanity of the "radical finitude" (or "absolute limit") to all its truth claims and even very existence. And despite his transition away from the phenomenological orientation of his earlier epistemology to the hermeneutical and historically conscious orientation of his later thought, the previous section already assessed how two constant axial planes nevertheless function as the basis of Schillebeeckx's epistemology throughout what Kennedy describes as his theological and philosophical "mutation" or evolution beginning in the mid-1960s.[111] According to Kennedy, these two "epistemological axes" are first his superintending conviction of the validity of a relational ontology and second the principle that the *locus* of a "divine-human cognitional nexus" is fundamentally *negative*. Both of these axes, moreover, are based on his interpretation of a Thomistic epistemology. However in his earlier thought (prior to his "clean break" with De Petter's phenomenology) he wanted to explain this negative factor within conceptual knowledge *abstractly* through emphasizing the conceptual limits of our own cognitional processes, whereas his later conception of epistemology situates the apophatic authority of experiential knowledge preeminently in the historical experiences of profound and unavoidable suffering.[112] For as he himself would later present it, the challenges posed to claims of religious truth and belief by "the reality of suffering and threatened humanity is, in my view, the central problem for us as we enter the third millennium."[113]

As will be made apparent in this section, Kennedy insists that this new emphasis on experiences of suffering and "radical finitude" undeniably adds "a certain intellectual ferment and sense of urgency" to Schillebeeckx's later theology.[114] For example, as a result of this shift in orientation Schillebeeckx explicitly positions his later theological epistemology as no longer focusing on the plight of Christians seeking simply to justify their faith against the critiques of contemporary philosophy, but instead focusing on all of suffering humanity who are yearning for a basis of hope that can be founded on the nature of existence itself. And for this reason, he refers to "suffering humanity" as evidently the new "chosen people of God."[115] With this in mind then, this section will now briefly attempt to

111. Kennedy, *Deus*, 152–3.
112. Ibid., 145–6.
113. Thompson, ix.
114. Kennedy, *Deus*, 159.
115. Schillebeeckx, *Future of Liberation*, 188.

display how Schillebeeckx reappropriated the notions discussed in the previous section of this chapter (experience, ethics, mysticism) specifically from within the "Christian tradition of experience" in order to provide a theological response to the "existential and sociocultural questions and doubts" concerning the possibility of actual knowledge of truth within contemporary culture.[116] Accordingly, this reappropriation manifests itself in Schillebeeckx's thought through the correlative ideas of negative contrast experiences (experience), orthopraxis (ethics), and the grace of inexpressible hope, or *humanum* (mysticism) as the elements of new experiences that can serve as a source for an authoritative knowledge of reality.

As a realist, Schillebeeckx consistently maintains that claims to belief and knowledge of God must be rooted in, and therefore reconcilable with, "the experienceable world."[117] However for many, the innumerable instances of egregious suffering and apparent "nonsensical" elements of our existence serve to negate one's ability to believe that there is an ordering principle to reality, and subsequently a larger universal meaning or purpose driving human history. In response to this dilemma, Schillebeeckx looks to ideology critique[118] in order to flip this assumption on its head. In other words, Schillebeeckx wants to assert that the potential for human knowledge about ultimate reality (God) is in actuality located precisely in these seemingly nonsensical instances of history. Hence he proclaims, "Never before in history has God's presence in the world been so intimate and so tangibly real as now, in our time, yet we do nothing but proclaim [God's] absence everywhere."[119] This is because, Schillebeeckx contests, these seemingly nonsensical or even dehumanizing instances within historical existence in actuality do not obscure or disprove the existence of God but in fact are privileged moments of awareness through which one's consciousness of God can become acutely poignant. These are the exact instances where reality interrupts our preconceived notions, exposes the radical finitude of ourselves, our language, and all our knowledge and consequently the absolute limit of our awareness by gesturing toward a reality beyond the purview of our interpretative horizon, toward an unseen reality resistant to our conceptions and expectations.[120] And as

---

116. Thompson, xiii.

117. Schillebeeckx, *Church*, 99.

118. What is implied by this expression, "ideology critique," among the critical theorists of the Frankfurt School is the practice primarily employed to unmask those beliefs and postulates claiming to be explanations of reality that widely go unnoticed or seem self-evidently true or desirable within a given cultural context. Schillebeeckx himself defines "ideology" as "a false consciousness or a speculative assertion for which no empirical or historical basis can be provided and which therefore has a broken relationship with reality." (See Schillebeeckx, *Understanding*, 163 n.90.) For an excellent expanded discussion on Schillebeeckx's appropriation of ideology critique, see the previously referenced article, William L. Portier, "Edward Schillebeeckx as Critical Theorist: The Impact on Neo-Marxist Social Thought on His Recent Theology," *The Thomist* 48 (1984), 341–67.

119. Schillebeeckx, *World and Church*, 78.

120. Schillebeeckx, *Church*, 78.

such, he proclaims, "no matter in what circumstances we find ourselves ... there is no situation in which God cannot come near to us and in which we would not be able to find [God]. Those who believe in God can still create meaning even in situations where we really experience meaninglessness."[121]

Schillebeeckx labels these privileged experiences as "negative experiences of contrast" and asserts that their privileged status results from the fact that they serve as possibly the most basic and universal experiences to all humanity.

> I now want to radicalize what I have previously, indeed repeatedly, called important human experiences, namely negative experiences of contrast: they form a basic human experience which as such I regard as being a pre-religious experience and thus a basic experience accessible to all human beings, namely that of a "no" to the world as it is ... This reality is full of contradictions. So the human experience of suffering and evil, of oppression and unhappiness, is the basis and source of a fundamental "no" that men and women say to their actual situation of being-in-this-world. This experience is also more certain, more evident than any verifiable or falsifiable "knowledge" that philosophy and the sciences can offer us.[122]

When these "negative contrast experiences" elicit a response of the "fundamental 'no'" to the common human perceptions of "the world as it is," what they essentially do is cause individuals to recognize that there is no articulation of faith or supposed "knowledge of God" that is not at least "in part historically determined and therefore changeable." The direct result of this new awareness then is the subsequent recognition that there is no understanding or depiction of reality that will "remain valid forever" across all historical and cultural consciousnesses.[123] Thus these moments of disruption then not only assert the existence of a reality that is resistant to complete conceptual encapsulation but also provide "the real seed ground for the new image of God in our new culture" by impelling humans to form *new* theories of ultimate reality in light of the unexpected resistance to their previous conceptions.[124] In this sense these negative contrast experiences function as a new version of "natural theology" for Schillebeeckx, wherein they provide the only plausible occasion to discuss a common human encounter with reality that transcends the boundaries of contextual situatedness and thus take on a revelatory status.[125]

Still Schillebeeckx reminds his readers that not simply every "negative experience" is a "negative *contrast* experience." However all negative experiences have the potential to function as contrast experiences. According to how

---

121. Ibid., 11.
122. Ibid., 5.
123. Schillebeeckx, *God the Future*, 180.
124. Ibid., 181.
125. Schillebeeckx, *Interim Report*, 5; "Erfahrung und Glaube," 76–7.

Schillebeeckx defines the term, negative experiences of contrast are not just direct encounters with the nonsensical and irrational components of reality but are negative encounters that *must produce a positive result*. For Schillebeeckx, this positive result is manifested first and foremost as the prophetic protest against the way things currently are and the subsequent "hope for a better future"—"that things *can* be done differently, *must* improve and *will* get better through our commitment."[126] And yet because this hope is connected to an openness to a still "unknown" future situation in which circumstances and one's vision of reality will be different, Schillebeeckx asserts the content of this hope can never be defined in a positive way since it is essentially "a better, other world, which in fact does not yet exist anywhere."[127] Hence, according to this new "natural theology," Schillebeeckx argues that revelation is not a permanent and static realization of the unchanging structures of existence or nature of God in Godself, but rather a "utopian" hypothesis—an experimental projection that emerges completely out of the context of human history and therefore must be continuously applied, tested, and refined through the practical application of resistance to its antithesis of the way reality currently appears.[128]

By looking at "revelation" in this new fallibilistic way in which the source of a future hope is founded in reality but any articulation of an exact outcome of that hope is not, Schillebeeckx believes he "places 'religious truth' within a horizon that is ever open to shifting and often new cultural environments and ways of thinking."[129] This is because now rather than understanding "religious truth" as the formulation of a singular positive assertion of knowledge that must withstand the development, change, and variances of conceptual constructs for all time, he suggests it can be conceived as "a vague consciousness" or an "unarticulated feeling of value" that reminds individuals that human history is still unfinished and as such a possible universal meaning of reality is yet to come. Hence, the knowledge of "revelation" is not the passive comprehension of an object but the active participation in the creation of the "truth" we hope to know.[130] And therefore, these negative experiences of reality simultaneously criticize the current structures of knowledge and consciousness while also empowering individuals to practically participate in the creation and development of reality through the "actual ethical conduct" of praxis and the production of hope through reflection on the indeterminate and mysterious future of reality.[131]

This essential practical-participatory element to the formation of any understanding of reality is exactly why he rejects a purely speculative hermeneutical approach to the determination of knowledge. As he summarizes this point, "it is

---

126. Schillebeeckx, *God the Future*, 158.
127. Schillebeeckx, *Church*, 6.
128. Schillebeeckx, *God the Future*, 157–60.
129. Thompson, xiii.
130. Schillebeeckx, *Jesus*, 633–5; *Christ*, 650–2; *Understanding*, 92.
131. Schillebeeckx, *Jesus*, 621.

not interpretation which has the *last word*, but orthopraxis."¹³² What he intends by this declaration is not that interpretation is not an integral part of thought and comprehension but rather simply that an idea's ability to correspond with and produce the desired outcomes of humans' lived existence and actual conduct within history is ultimately a theory's final measuring stick. And for this reason, Kennedy charts how Schillebeeckx originally explained "God's knowability" from "primarily in the context of religion" wherein the "*sacramental* experience [is seen] as the apex of human contact with God"; to speaking of "God's accessibility in the context of *ethics*" (1966); to furthering it even more so that "God is accessible *above all* in a praxis of Justice" (1986); to then focusing it once again by propounding "that God is *only* accessible in such a praxis" (1987); and finally concluding "that God is not accessible *apart from* a praxis of justice and love" (1989).¹³³ Moreover, he clarifies, this accessibility through "a praxis of justice and love"—what he often refers to as "the coming kingdom of God"—does not necessarily remain the same from one historical instantiation to the next. Or, in other words, it "does not know the human logic of precise justice." Instead, it is an "alternative form of action" to whatever norms or ideologies are viewed as unquestioned within a particular society and yet practically fail to "make sense" of human existence.¹³⁴ The consequence of this is that "orthopraxis" remains a culturally conditioned construct that is determined situationally and as such means that there are multiple ways to a knowledge of ultimate reality, or "God."¹³⁵

Furthermore, since he understands "orthopraxis" as "alternative forms of action," he believes it plays a central role in the dialectic of critical negativity from which one develops a sense of viable or "orthodox" conceptions of God. After all, for Schillebeeckx the validity of assertions of truth can only be determined in the end by the way in which they correspond to one's experience of reality—meaning one's ability to predict or understand the pragmatic results of activity within the world—and so "valid knowledge" or "right belief" cannot be assessed simply through theological speculation. This is because, according to his reading of linguistic analysis, language primarily functions as one of the most blatant forms of ideology and distortion. Since any tradition of language, or "language game," at least in part determines the meaning of the words that belong to it, any attempt to analyze the validity of a truth claim purely through the abstractions of linguistic-based concepts inherently smuggles in presupposed definitions and a logical circularity that at best can only decipher an internal cogency and not an external applicability or correspondence to the perceived universe.¹³⁶ And so this is where the need for praxis comes back in. By putting theoretical, theological postulates into practical action, believers and theologians are confronted with

---

132. Schillebeeckx, *God the Future*, 186.
133. Kennedy, *Deus*, 220. Emphasis original.
134. Schillebeeckx, *Church*, 117.
135. Ibid., 101.
136. Schillebeeckx, *Understanding*, 69.

"disturbances of communication" that arise as a result of breakdowns between the ways truths are expressed and the ways empirical reality is experienced.[137] Hence theology should be considered not as definitive, or even possible, articulations of the true nature of God, but rather a "critical self-consciousness of Christian praxis in the world and church."[138] Accordingly, the type of knowledge produced by negative contrast experiences is what he labels "practical-cum-critical," or an applied critical evaluation of the incongruities between the way things are described and the way they are experienced and felt.[139]

At the same time, however, it is also equally important to note that although he generally defines orthopraxis as any ethically good action directed toward overcoming any threat to the persistent hope of humanity's survival and potential meaning in history (the *humanum*),[140] Schillebeeckx does not believe that any particular manifestation of praxis is self-authenticating either. Citing the French Revolution as one example, Schillebeeckx discusses how this uprising was "essentially a process of liberation" originating from the promotion of "the freedoms and human rights which we now treasure [as] part of our modern personality structure." Nonetheless, he continues, this "bourgeois liberation" eventually itself became an "oppressive and repressive" force within society that asserted one group's freedom at the expense of many others. In other words, praxis *too* is itself a concept that has proven multivalent in its meaning, has a specific history, and must be applied differently in a diversity of particular contexts.[141] Hence, the simple repetitious application of any one form of praxis would function no differently than asserting outmoded theological language that might distort or obscure the very reality it seeks to purport.

Moreover if a particular action is only mechanically employed with no regard to a critical awareness of exactly *what* outcome it is actually advancing, praxis itself can be used basically to justify an ideological belief as "universally true" through the consistency of its praxis. Simply put, a belief's consistent ability to reproduce specific actions "in no way settles the truth value of the theory which is defended. In that case, for example, the stubborn loyalty with which some people followed the Nazi ideology would prove the truth of Nazism!" Therefore praxis itself cannot be the end goal in the search for ultimate truth, for it is only one side of the dialectical process. Rather the end goal of theoretical formulation and its evaluation through its experiential application in praxis is still the eventual critical unity of theory and praxis. In this way, "liberating action in faith does not call for less but *more* critical-theoretical analysis."[142] As a Christian theologian, Schillebeeckx believes the "orthos" in "ortho-praxis" still needs to be assessed

---

137. Schillebeeckx, *Language of Faith*, 89–90.
138. Schillebeeckx, *Understanding*, 154.
139. Schillebeeckx, *Jesus*, 621; *Understanding*, 86.
140. Schillebeeckx, *Christ*, 659.
141. Schillebeeckx, *Church*, 53.
142. Ibid., 178.

in light of the broader tradition and particularly whether it corresponds to the authoritative reorientation toward one's experience based on the Jesus narrative. This does not mean, however, whether a belief or the action it produces mimics the actual actions of Jesus, but whether it emulates the intentional *thrust* behind his actions—humanity's wholeness through "the conquest of all human, personal and social alienations."[143] By this measure, even if any specific human plan for creating happiness is relativized by its historical and contextual localization,[144] Jesus's narrative can still set the orientation for "the praxis of the kingdom of God"[145] as the tangible and visible outworking of the hope for "a new type of liberating relationship among men and women, within a reconciled society in a peaceful ecological setting."[146] Or as he elaborates on this unification of theory and actual experience elsewhere,

> The correlation between Christian faith (with its own narrative-practical structure and the distinctive cognitive, critical and liberating power given in it) on the one hand and contemporary experiences within a modern society on the other can ultimately be carried through in a productive way only on the basis of a praxis which seeks to realize salvation for all and as a result seeks to allow truth to come into its own as universal truth.[147]

Nevertheless lest one think that Schillebeeckx is implying a system in which humans come to a better knowledge of the universe *solely* on the basis of their own efforts of formulation, experimentation, evaluation, and reformulation, because of his commitment to the first axial plane of his epistemology—the superintending postulation of a relational ontology—Schillebeeckx refuses to depict the formation of knowledge as simply one-directional from the human (creation) side alone. Or to phrase it differently, he rejects any suggestion that the creation of the truth of a better world and existence (salvation) can be achieved "by purely human means."[148] Instead, Schillebeeckx suggests that within negative contrast experiences there is also manifested "the hidden magnets of reality" that assert an implicit awareness in our consciousness of something perceived in our experiences that is still "not completely objectifiable or capable of articulation." In this sense, the authority of new experiences is at least in part related to the positive contribution back from reality itself that is ingrained in all finite experiences and that impels individuals to attempt to inquire further about those elements of their experiential awareness that inevitably fall outside the confines of their linguistic description.[149] Within

---

143. Schillebeeckx, *Christ*, 814.
144. Thompson, 57.
145. Schillebeeckx, *Church*, 176.
146. Schillebeeckx, *For the Sake*, 106.
147. Schillebeeckx, *Church*, 178.
148. Kennedy, *Deus*, 231–2.
149. Schillebeeckx, "Erfahrung und Glaube," 92.

negative contrast experiences, this positive contribution manifests itself as "the meaningless residue of history which theoretical reason cannot grasp" that "remains a power, a cognitive stimulus to practical reason which ... is as a result prompted to liberating action which seeks to remove the meaninglessness from history."[150] Thus these new experiences provide humans with a "cognitive, critical, and productive" hope (*humanum*) that a fuller understanding of the true nature of reality can still be fathomed—albeit never *exhaustively*—through the cognitive reconciliation with and active surmounting of these perceived nonsensical, meaningless, and evil facets of existence.[151]

Once again, therefore, one is reminded that experiential knowledge is thoroughly dialectical in Schillebeeckx's system. However it is not dialectical in the sense of simply being "a philosophical or purely conceptual, dialectical *thought-process*" but instead it is dialectical in its interplay between reflective interpretation and the critical-practical application of actual conduct.[152] One experiences the world, and particularly those elements of suffering and meaninglessness that seem to interrupt one's preconceived conception of human meaning and purpose, and is brought face to face with an unexpected, unforeseen reality that challenges one's comprehension of truth. Consequently, one must reflect *again* in order to attempt to give an account for these discrepancies. This new reflection provides a theoretical *hope* that reality's nonconformity to one's conceptions does not imply a fundamental arbitrariness or meaninglessness to existence but rather that "surprising, unexpected, new ways of perceiving [can be] opened up in and through the resistance presented by reality."[153] As a consequence of this hope that the humanization of existence can prevail over the threat of meaninglessness (*humanum*), the individual is then compelled to practically *re*engage with the world now armed with a new affirmation of the truth (God) that "is to come."[154] However, in the end, the individual will once again only be subsequently "surprised" by how "reality is always more than and different from what we imagine it to be,"[155] thus initiating the dialectical process over again. At the same time, since our theoretical reflections and descriptive language still in many ways *do* seem to correspond with much of our experiences (just not completely) and *do* seem to perceive new elements of reality through each cycle of the process (while never exhausting them), a fundamental hope continues to emerge out of the revelation of how our practical encounters and cognitive reflections do seem to improve the way we perceive reality.[156] For this reason Schillebeeckx exclaims, "Hope is surprised by the constantly unexpected, but never disappointed!"[157]

150. Schillebeeckx, *Church*, 175.
151. Schillebeeckx, "*Erfahrung und Glaube*," 90.
152. Schillebeeckx, *Church*, 77.
153. Schillebeeckx, *Christ*, 35.
154. Schillebeeckx, *God the Future*, 199.
155. Schillebeeckx, *Christ*, 55, 47.
156. Ibid., 35; Schillebeeckx, *Jesus*, 634.
157. Schillebeeckx, *Christ*, 57.

The mystical aspect of experiential knowledge (the *via eminentiae*), then, he proclaims, is not obtained as a simple outcome of a conceptual negation (*via negativa*) but in a practical or experiential one.[158] It is not comprehended directly, but only indirectly in the constant "surprising more" of experienced reality that exposes all our images of God to be human products of interpretation and conjecture. It is the understanding that is derived from the unexpected, indeterminant, and thus inexpressible or "apophatic" nature of reality that ensures our "earlier images of God will constantly be shattered and new possibilities will come to life."[159] Hence, he directly challenges common misrepresentations of "mysticism" when he insists, "Authentic mysticism is never flight from the world but, on the basis of a first disintegrating source-experience, an integrating mercy with all things. It is approach, not flight."[160] It is an awareness that can only arise out of the actual felt tension of the contingent limits and fortuitous potentialities within lived human existence. And yet despite the deeply negative quality to this "knowledge," Schillebeeckx also points out that the "positive power" of this experience of limitless potentiality within one's contingent relationship with reality also functions as a grace that continues to exert a constant pressure on believers and theologians "to name this ultimate reality and not leave it in anonymity"[161] in the hope that doing so might bring about a better world through a more profound understanding of existence and the creation of new realities.[162]

For this reason, Schillebeeckx describes himself as "a theologian who all his life did nothing but seek what God *can* mean for men and women, tentatively and stammeringly."[163] Thus, Schillebeeckx's recognition of the negative element to all descriptions of God as ultimate reality, a recognition of their inherent cultural and linguistic relativity, does not make him want to do away with "God talk" or even metaphysics altogether. In fact, Portier explains that Schillebeeckx actually decries the anti-metaphysical trend in modern thought and suggests in light of modern awarenesses and sensitivities that metaphysics should just be reconceived in a "non-essentialist" manner.[164] He attempts to establish this new "non-essentialist" metaphysic by putting a markedly *eschatological* spin on "God talk" so that metaphysics becomes the end goal of theological inquiry, not the starting point.[165] What this effectively means is that theologians should no longer speak of God in terms of *actus purus*, or "pure actuality" (to borrow an expression

---

158. Schillebeeckx, *Church*, 77.
159. Ibid. Cf. Thompson, x. Here in writing the foreword to Thompson's book he proclaims, "The absolute and grace-filled presence of divine Mystery repeatedly shatters all our images and representations of God."
160. Ibid., 72.
161. Schillebeeckx, *Christ*, 57.
162. Schillebeeckx, *God the Future*, 191; *Christ*, 57.
163. Schillebeeckx, *Church*, xv. Emphasis added.
164. Portier, "Critical Theorist," 362.
165. Schillebeeckx, *God the Future*, 199.

from Aquinas), because such a perspective tends to paint the theological task as naively trying to decipher a static, unchanging truth that transcends all time and space. However people do not actually *experience* the ultimate reality of God in that way. Instead humans experience the truth of God *as a part of* reality, not apart from it. And consequently they encounter the transcendence of God not as the knowledge of a "wholly other" but of that which is constantly "wholly new"—as the surprising unfolding of a yet unknown future. Hence, Schillebeeckx suggests individuals begin to speak of God as the One who is, "was and is to come" (or "the Coming One"); "who is our future, who creates the future of mankind anew"; "eternally young"; "a constant surprise"; "new each moment"; and "the source of pure positivity."[166] In this way, Schillebeeckx believes he has taken the experientially *negative* knowledge of the "absolute limit" of all our language, concepts, and beliefs and translated into a *positive* formulation of the apophatic reality of God as the pure potentiality and positivity of the future.

In summary, then, Schillebeeckx puts forth a theory of experiential knowledge in which knowledge emerges out of a critically conscious, practically oriented, and inevitably surprising encounter with the boundlessly complex and intermingled forces of suffering, hope, and resistance that shape our perception of ultimate reality. His hermeneutic for deciphering, indeed *creating*, meaning, and knowledge within this realm of inseparable complexity is based on a relational model of ontology where God as creator is constantly in direct contact with the contingent existence of the created universe. At the same time, however, though this relationship is reciprocal, it is not *symmetrical*. Because of the relative limits of finitude (i.e., historicity, contextuality, and mortality), humans as a part of contingent creation can only comprehend the transcendent and non-historical elements of ultimate reality *negatively* as the absolute limit of possible knowledge. As a result, the cognitive or epistemological aspect of a mystical or theological faith has at least two sides—a creative and imaginative side where experience is reflectively interpreted through language, concepts, and symbols culled from a variety of diverse sociocultural contexts of human society and history; and another practical or "lived" side where out of the "relative limits" of negative contrast experiences, especially those of suffering and dehumanization, one is faced with the absolute limit of human knowledge—the recognition that our grasp of reality can never conceptually encompass all of reality—that reveals an indirect and unthematic cognitive awareness of the limitless creative potential within reality.

Consequently, however, once the historicity of human knowledge is recognized as an unavoidable reality, Schillebeeckx concludes that the goal of theology can no longer be defined in the terms of a participation in the totality of meaning but rather in the *anticipation* of the unforeseen potential meaning within history. Thus, he becomes more and more uncomfortable with the current "God talk" within

---

166. See the essay "The New Image of God, Secularization and Man's Future on Earth" in Schillebeeckx, *God the Future*, 169–207. Also see Schillebeeckx, *Church*, 4, 101, 122, 129; Schillebeeckx and Strazzari, *Happy*, 81; *Western Culture*, 62.

Christian metaphysics as promoting not an openness to experiencing the ultimate reality of God as future potentiality and "Pure Positivity," but rather as perpetuating "an antiquated image of God," one that envisions God within "a former picture of the world and society, [as] the God of a handful of rich people, to the detriment of those who have to live on the periphery of society."[167] In response to this perceived dilemma, Schillebeeckx argues for the implementation of a new "non-essentialist" metaphysic within theology that places metaphysical language about the ultimate truth of God as the end goal of a purely ontic and eschatological interpretation of God through the hopeful experience of the consistently oncoming and surprising potential of the future. This potential of a purely positive future simultaneously reveals how the world as it is does not match our understanding of the ultimate good that is possible, while also providing the undetermined hope (*humanum*) that reality can be better than it currently appears. This hope (*humanum*) then becomes the impetus for further reflection and articulation of what that purely positive future might be and how it can be achieved, which is then tested and challenged through active praxis in the world. Hence, Schillebeeckx asserts, "Belief in God radicalizes efforts for a better world. Christian belief in what is humanly possible, namely a radically new improvement of the world, automatically drives Christians to quite specific political action."[168]

This constant dialectical interplay between active resistance to an unthematized apophatic awareness of reality through negative contrast experiences of suffering and the consequential positive (cataphatic) articulation of a hope brought about through a mystical reflection on those negative experiences then becomes the new medium through which God is solely known. Thus with his call for a new "non-essentialist" metaphysic, Schillebeeckx believes he can maintain a Thomistic realist epistemology based in the unthematized negative encounter with reality itself through contrast experiences, while also being capable of giving an account for the historical nature of all human conceptions of God as the imperfect and hypothetical articulations of that valid experience. As such, he thinks that theology can avoid the extremes of propagating destructive ideology through unverifiable, transhistorical assertions about ultimate reality while also not succumbing to the "reductionist material analysis" found in thinkers such as Habermas, "which would view religious ideas as human creations with a purely social basis."[169] Accordingly, in the end for Schillebeeckx the task of theologians is not completely to comprehend or name ultimate reality (God) as it is, but literally *to search* for what it *might* be as a part of a better future reality.[170] And so, as we now turn to the next section examining the negative dialectics of Gendun Chopel's epistemology, we will be able to observe how Schillebeeckx's dialectical interplay between linguistic affirmation and unthematized negative experiences of

---

167. Schillebeeckx, *Church*, 11.
168. Schillebeeckx, *Christ*, 781.
169. Portier, 363–4. Cf. Schillebeeckx, *Jesus*, 618–19.
170. Schillebeeckx, *For the Sake*, 85.

reality both strikes a seeming resonance and noticeable dissonance with Gendun Chopel's Madhyamaka epistemology—specifically in Schillebeeckx's attempt to justify positive articulations of the Ultimate. In the end, however, we will be able to see how both seek to establish a "non-essentialist" way of speaking about ultimate reality, and thus might be able to inform, challenge, and assist the other in his own system of experiential negative dialectics.

B. Gendun Chopel: Conviction in the Dharma as Conviction in the "Inconceivable State"[171]

Because of their divergent epistemological commitments—Schillebeeckx's realism and Gendun Chopel's anti-realism—it seems unlikely that these two thinkers would come to any agreement regarding the epistemic authority of personal experience. What is so arresting, however, is the fact that both individuals ground their entire epistemological outlooks essentially in (what I am terming) an "apophatic," or inherently non-affirming and negative, encounter with reality itself. Moreover, in another way apparently similar to Schillebeeckx, Stoddard proclaims that Gendun Chopel's intention behind his Madhyamaka epistemology expressed in the *Adornment* (which he believed he had accomplished) was to "introduce Madhyamaka philosophy in language appropriate to his [modern] age."[172] Still, at the same time, Lopez states that he finds this claim by Stoddard particularly perplexing since, as he aptly notes, "Whether [Gendun Chopel] believed this or not, there appears to be nothing in the work that is marked by such modernity."[173] Its principally "intra-Buddhist" philosophical argumentation notwithstanding, by placing Gendun Chopel's dialectically negative experiential epistemology in comparison with Schillebeeckx's negative dialectic of experiential knowledge, which explicitly seeks to respond to and engage modern philosophy, one might begin to see how Gendun Chopel could have believed as Stoddard professes despite the glaring omission of "modernity" from the text itself. And therefore, it might actually be quite possible to hold that Gendun Chopel's approach is *both* overtly and exclusively sourced from within the Tibetan Buddhist philosophical tradition as Lopez points out (so that determining whether any of the ideas are indeed "unique to him" is difficult if not impossible) and also intended to give an argument for "a transhistorical and transrational vision of enlightenment" that might withstand the scrutiny of the modern systems of science and philosophy.[174]

Thus this section will briefly seek to lay out the experiential grounds for valid knowledge within Gendun Chopel's Madhyamaka epistemology through a use of negative dialectics focused on deconstructing all "knowledge" of the conventional realm. In so doing, we will be able to better understand how by utilizing solely

---

171. Chos phel, "Adornment," 81, v. 128.
172. Stoddard, 275.
173. Lopez, "*Vigrahavyāvartanī* 29," 178.
174. Ibid.

traditional language and logic Gendun Chopel is able to present a philosophical theory of the existence of a "transhistorical and transrational" realm that can implicitly give an answer to the same modernist concerns that Schillebeeckx also explicitly hopes to address. Thus we will be able to observe how by demarcating a philosophical system centered on better perceiving "the boundary between the universe of things that can be stated and the universe which cannot be spoken [of] because it cannot be thought,"[175] Gendun Chopel could hope that, despite the inherent confines of his conventional language and concepts, his epistemology might "reveal the path of vast benefit in the presence of my unseen friends,"[176] possibly even those steeped in modern thought.

It seems that in almost every chapter there has been at least some reference to Gendun Chopel's somewhat jarring and certainly controversial opening poem to the *Adornment* traditionally known as "the expression of worship" (*mchod brjod*). Nonetheless, this chapter will be no different. This is because, as Lopez mentions, Gendun Chopel's intentionally provocative question—"what intelligent person would honor you [Śākyamuni Buddha] as a friend for protection from the great enemy, fearful saṃsāra?"—signals the "dominant mood" of the *Adornment*, one that consistently utilizes traditional philosophical conventions in Buddhism to make a rather unconventional point.[177] Moreover this passage in particular also marks the foundational basis of the argument that will be worked out throughout the rest of the work, namely that the knowledge of all enlightened beings (including the Buddha) is something that cannot be known or established through conventional reasoning of the world.[178] For him, conventional reasoning is fundamentally based in false distinctions of the mind that obstruct the mind's natural state, one which he defines as a "primordial sphere of reality" that is "aimless," "without base, without foundation," "empty," or, in other words, "perfect buddhahood." Thus according to this logic, to experientially perceive means to make distinctions about existence and therefore be actually obstructive to realizing the indistinguishable reality of ultimate emptiness. Hence, he challenges his readers to not "pursue perceptions" and to instead "look directly at the perceiver itself" in order to see one's "own inexpressible face." In doing so, he encourages that one will find that "the path to achieve buddhahood is not far."[179] Likewise, this theme of critically examining and dialectically negating all of one's conventional perceptions and knowledge of reality as a means to lead indirectly to buddhahood is an apparent staple to the entire argument of the piece.

There are many ways in which Gendun Chopel attempts to exhibit this problem of perception instinctively making interpretive distinctions, but probably one of his most poignant illustrations places in tension any possible "valid consciousness"

---

175. Ibid., 179.
176. Lopez and chos phel, *Madman*, 38–9.
177. Lopez and chos phel, *Madman*, 127.
178. Ibid., 126.
179. See the poem by Gendun Chopel in Chos phel and Lopez, *Forest*, 26–9 (esp. 29).

with the professed acts of the Buddha. He contends that even in its most basic recognition, before labeling an item with a universal categorization but instead simply observing an object as a "mere thing," the supposed "valid consciousness" of the mind "perceives" the condition of size so that "we conclude that an atom is the smallest material form and we conclude that a world is extremely vast." Moreover, similarly, "we [logically] conclude that the great does not fit inside the small." However, he points out, the Buddha is repeatedly said in the sutras to perform great feats that invert these seemingly primordial observations of categories, thus destroying "principles that are established by valid knowledge." Gendun Chopel asks how this can be. In an attempt to resolve this tension he cites how many philosophers have to go out of their way to contort our understanding of this "valid knowledge" in order "to make many exceptions, such as saying that the Buddha's doing so is a special case." Such special pleading, however, in Gendun Chopel's mind just serves as unequivocal "proof" that even the most seemingly basic perceptions are indistinguishably mixed with the interpretations of the perceiver, so that "the bag of our valid knowledge is leaking in all directions."[180] For this reason, he later concludes, "In the end, the knower is mixed with the object of knowledge with which it is of one taste," and as such there cannot be a "commonly appearing object of knowledge" between beings with conventional opinions and ones with the valid knowledge of enlightenment even at the most basic perceptive experience.[181]

One of the major causes for this inseparable relationship between direct perception and the interpretation of distinctions according to Gendun Chopel is the reifying power of language that permeates all thoughts of the mind. Accordingly, he bemoans the pervasive assumption within the mainline of Geluk scholastic philosophy (based in the teachings of Tsongkhapa) that reasoned analysis that is still grounded in language can ever lead to an improved or valid conceptual grasp of reality.[182] Consequently, he contends, one can see in the Geluk philosophical tradition a series of newly developed linguistic and conceptual categories—"such as 'validly established,' 'trustworthy,' 'infallible,' 'undeniable,' and so on"—that attempt to push beyond universal distinctions but in fact only produce "nothing other than what merely appears through the changing of orientations of this conventional consciousness."[183] In other words, no matter how many linguistic qualifications one can tack onto a statement, as long as the inherent distinctions of language are involved a perception can never come close to transversing the chasm separating conventional perceptions and the nonconceptual awareness of emptiness—the only truly valid knowledge. Hence, he insists that the furthest a Mādhyamika can go within the confines of conventional consciousness, perception, and language is

---

180. Chos phel, "Adornment," 53–4, v. 24.
181. Ibid., 107, v. 211.
182. Ibid., 57, v. 36. Cf. Lopez and chos phel, *Madman*, 138.
183. Chos phel, "Adornment," 59, v. 47; Cf. 84, v. 136; Lopez and chos phel, *Madman*, 178.

to say "this pot is something that appears to me. However, it *does not exist at all* in the way that it appears."[184]

Nonetheless, Gendun Chopel anticipates that such an assertion of an epistemological anti-realism regarding all conventional experiences and their subsequent claims to knowledge might be met with accusations of "nihilism" by followers of the standard Geluk line of thinking. Thus, he preemptively attempts to counter any of these charges by simplifying his argument according to possibly the most basic formulation of the Madhyamaka view: "Such a thought is the Madhyamaka view of the composite appearance and emptiness, which understands that although things appear, they do not exist in the way that they appear."[185] Therefore, he contends, his anti-realist approach to conventional knowledge cannot be considered "nihilism," because it in fact articulates this standard Madhyamaka view.[186] Furthermore elsewhere he concludes that since conventional language permeates all of our perceptions and understandings, "as long as we remain in this land of saṃsāra, it is true that there is no other method than simply making decisions, having placed confidence in this mind in which one can have no confidence in any of the decisions that it makes."[187] Likewise, Lopez elaborates, in Gendun Chopel's mind this conviction is not a judgment against the character of those avowing the validity of conventional knowledge, it is simply the unavoidable plight of the unenlightened who are trapped in the confines of language and concepts to which there is no alternative for them.[188]

In fact, Gendun Chopel professes that the danger of "falling into nihilism," which is the typical Prāsaṅgika rejoinder to systems that tend to identify the proper object of negation too broadly, is that the real threat of nihilism is found in systems (including those of most Prāsaṅgikas) that do not identify the proper object of negation *broadly enough*. For him, the much larger and more illogical dilemma facing a Madhyamaka understanding of reality is the notion that some parts of the conventional realm can be accepted as "existent" while at the same time "asserting that some [other] parts" are "nonexistent." This is because the categories of "existent" and "nonexistent" are linguistic constructions themselves, and thus deciphering between the "truly existent" and "utterly nonexistent" amounts to nothing more than the reshuffling of a complex language game in which *everything* can eventually be deemed nonexistent. According to Gendun Chopel, however, if one is aware that even this notion of "nonexistence" is subsumed within the realm of conventional language, then any notion of "nonexistence" becomes self-negating so that it too must be viewed "within the nonexistent things which are free from the elaborations of the four extremes." Hence, he maintains that as long as one recognizes that even one's understanding of nonexistence is ultimately

---

184. Ibid., 59, v. 43. Emphasis added.
185. Ibid.
186. Ibid. Cf. Lopez and chos phel, *Madman*, 142.
187. Chos phel, "Adornment," 51, v. 14.
188. Lopez and chos phel, *Madman*, 131.

nonexistent, "there is no possibility of falling into nihilism."[189] As just another invalid form of conventional awareness, any perceived threat presented by "utter nonexistence" to the completely separate ultimate nature of reality in the end has no teeth because "these ideas of the world are incapable of going even a little way toward the other side." Thus, he continues, "regarding these appearances of the world, deep despair about all reasonings, terms, and conceptions appears to be the view of emptiness."[190] In this way, Lopez explains that Gendun Chopel in his discussion of nonexistence's ultimate nonexistence seems to be endorsing "the understanding of nonexistence gained by a 'reasoning consciousness' (*rigs shes*), a meditative awareness that sets out to investigate the final mode of being of an object and discovers in the end that the object cannot be found." To Gendun Chopel, this is a much more profound understanding of nonexistence than can ever be achieved through syllogistic reasoning that aims solely from the outset to refute the existence of something.[191] Therefore, the end goal is not an understanding of the absence of intrinsic existence in a way that allows one to portray it accurately to another, but instead an understanding of it that produces the serenity of a mind untainted by conceptual distinctions altogether.[192]

If Gendun Chopel truly believes in this conviction, however, that language inherently entraps beings into projecting conceptual images and interpretations of reality that cause them to persist in the utterly invalid realm of the conventional,[193] then it would seem justified for one to inquire as to how anyone might achieve the "valid knowledge" resultant of a direct perception of emptiness apart from any concepts or language within his system. In response to this line of inquiry, Gendun Chopel presents two possibilities: the first in the tantric practice of sexual yogas and the second in the Mādhyamika's strategy of making assertions for others; with the latter being discussed extensively in the *Adornment* and the former discussed almost exclusively in Gendun Chopel's previously mentioned Tibetan rendition of the Kāmasūtra, the *Treatise on Passion* (*'dod pa'i bstan bcos*). According to its own proclamation, this is a text that was completed by Gendun Chopel sometime in 1938 during a visit with a "[girl-]friend with the same life-style" in the city of Mathurā, India.[194] What is particularly interesting about this text moreover, Lopez explains, is that it repeatedly exalts the sexual yogas of the *Anuttarayoga tantras* as the supreme means of passing into a state beyond language and thought.[195]

In his well-known English translation of the work, *The Tibetan Arts of Love*, Hopkins concurs with Lopez's assessment proclaiming "the compatibility of sexual pleasure with spiritual insight" as the underlying theme of the entire book. In fact

---

189. Chos phel, "Adornment," 85–6, v. 141. Cf. Lopez and chos phel, *Madman*, 180–1.
190. Chos phel, "Adornment," 106, v. 206.
191. Lopez and chos phel, *Madman*, 180.
192. Chos phel and Lopez, *Forest*, 28–9.
193. Chos phel, "Adornment," 69, v. 93.
194. Hopkins and Chöpel, 166, 275.
195. Lopez, "*Vigrahavyāvartanī* 29," 175.

Hopkins tells how, relying on the guidances of "Indo-Tibetan Tantrism," Gendun Chopel throughout the work frequently references "the spiritual value of sexual pleasure" as being capable of producing a consciousness within the participants that "can reveal the nature of reality with tremendous force" and subsequently with a "dynamic import for the spiritual path."[196] This is because, as Gendun Chopel insists in accord with the tantras, when one experiences the height of an "ecstatic orgasm" the ensnaring nets of conceptual perception dissolve into "the great spacious bliss" of a "clear and nonconceptual" state of mind.[197] This "fundamental innate mind of clear light (*gnyug ma lhan cig skyes pa'i 'od gsal gyi sems*)," Hopkins expounds, "is the most subtle, profound, and powerful level of consciousness" possible, which Gendun Chopel refers to as "the goal of life."[198] Gendun Chopel articulates this level of consciousness produced by sexual ecstasy in a poetic section of the *Treatise*:

> As much as one approaches the nature of a thing,
> So much do the words of scholars become dumb.
> Hence it is said that by nature all subtle phenomena
> Pass beyond proposition, thought, and verbalization.
> Having set the mind in the realm of emptiness endowed with all aspects,
> Who could view this wheel of illusory appearances
> With a mind of asserting is and is not
> That even the hand of Buddha does not prevent!
> The small child of intelligence swoons in the deep sphere of passion.
> The busy mind falls into the hole of a worm.
> By drawing the imaginations of attachment downwards
> Beings should observe the suchness of pleasure.
> Wishing to mix in the ocean of the bliss of the peaceful expanse
> This wave of magician's illusions separated off
> By perceiving the non-dual as dual, subject and object,
> Does one not feel the movement and igniting of the coalesced!
> To what could this reality devoid of projection move?
> Where could this mind devoid of pursuit run?
> Since, having abandoned their nature, they do not stay still,
> Move these two—appearances and mind—in the direction of bliss.
> Even taking a single step is for the sake of seeking bliss.
> Even speaking a single word is for the sake of seeking bliss.
> Virtuous deeds are done for the sake of bliss.
> Non-virtuous deeds also are done for the sake of bliss.
> Eyeless ants run after bliss.
> Legless worms run after bliss.

---

196. Hopkins and Chöpel, 11.
197. Ibid., 96–7, 241.
198. Hopkins and Chöpel, 101, 266–7.

In short, all worldly beings one by one
Are running, faster and slower, in the direction of bliss.
If one really considers the fact that the one billion worlds of this system
Are suddenly swallowed into a gigantic asteroid devoid of perception or feeling,
One understands that the realm of great bliss
Is that in which all appearances dissolve.
Though they have attained the glory and wealth of the three billion worlds,
    they are not satisfied
And therefore come to be renowned for burning ravenous passion.
In fact they seek the sky-kingdom of bliss and emptiness
With the dumb child of a mind knowing nothing.[199]

This somewhat lengthy poem is worth citing at this point for multiple reasons. First, it provides a helpful summary to the entire discussion of this section so far regarding the problem of experience as an authoritative source for knowledge: it speaks of the incapability of language to capture "the nature of a thing"; yet it also acknowledges language's power to compel the "illusory appearances" of what "is and is not" within the mind; and finally, it also explains how the "peaceful expanse" of emptiness (or "bliss") is completely cordoned off by the perceptive illusion of "the non-dual as dual" and "subject and object." Second, it depicts the intensity of sexual orgasm as being a profound moment when an individual can be uniquely raptured in "the suchness of pleasure" so that one's immediate perception can in fact possibly become separated from conceptual and linguistic interpretation. The result is a profound experience of reality where "all appearances dissolve" in a way that allows the individual to encounter "the realm of great bliss" directly. Lastly, and maybe most importantly, in an interlinear note to this poem Gendun Chopel defines the experience of "bliss" produced by sexual ecstasy as the positive counterpoint to the awareness of the "non-affirming negative" of emptiness: "Therefore, here regarding the inexpressible meaning that is the final nature of the stable [environment] and moving [living beings], when one considers it from a negative viewpoint it is empty, and when it dawns from a positive viewpoint, it is bliss."[200] Hence, despite any difference in the orientation of the perceiver and the subsequent experience itself, Gendun Chopel insists that both the experiences of "bliss" and "emptiness" reveal the same inexpressible final nature to reality. And so, it is in the performance of an action (sexual intercourse) that Gendun Chopel believes one can come the closest to *positive* experience of ultimate reality, which everywhere else he only refers to as a "non-affirming negative."

Nevertheless, apart from this specific action that can possibly induce a momentary and fleeting direct positive perception of reality, one is still left

---

199. Ibid., 266–8.
200. Ibid., 268.

wondering how an individual is to speak positively about reality in a way that might reveal the truth of emptiness regardless of the fact that language itself is the prime force preventing unenlightened beings from perceiving it. As alluded to above, for Gendun Chopel the solution to this dilemma is the Mādhyamika's strategic use of making assertions for others.[201] And so, at this point, Gendun Chopel's attention once again returns to focus on the figure of the Buddha, particularly on the tension between the Buddha's extensive teachings and the traditional imagery of the "noble silence" of enlightened beings.[202] However, as Lopez is quick to mention, although Gendun Chopel in the *Adornment* argues powerfully for a fundamental return to the Buddha as the source for experiencing and understanding the nature of reality, as is similarly the case with "so many Buddhist modernists" one finds that the Buddha to which Gendun Chopel wants to return to "is a very different Buddha."[203] This is because even though he still describes the Buddha as the "guide for beings of the three worlds" who leads "worldly beings from the path of worldly conventions to the sphere beyond the world,"[204] the means by which he believes the Buddha achieves this are quite different than the beliefs of many of his fellow Tibetans.

His agreement with Tsongkhapa (and consequently most Prāsaṅgikas) about the Buddha's speech merely being "a compassionate concession to the world"[205] which he himself does not believe in his heart[206] notwithstanding, Gendun Chopel's conception of the intention and technique behind making "assertions for others" is quite distinct from Tsongkhapa and the standard Prāsaṅgika line of thought. Both thinkers agree that even after one has a direct yogic perception of the ultimate state of emptiness, which subsequently constitutes the basis of maintaining "the noble silence" from an ultimate perspective, as long as one still persists in the conventional realm among unenlightened beings when asked by the unenlightened "what is out there, [the enlightened one] will be bound to say that it is a mountain, it is a tree, and that it is a human." Similarly, even if an enlightened being speaks of emptiness—that "nothing exists"—it will still be apprehended by the minds of the unenlightened as a conventional construct.[207] Accordingly, both agree that when the Mādhyamika is compelled to speak and make assertions for the benefit of others, that individual is bound by the nature of language to abide within the conventions of the world as a means to bring others to "the silence of emptiness."[208] However Lopez notices a significant difference between the two thinkers in regard to the implication behind the Mādhyamika's use of worldly

---

201. Lopez, "*Vigrahavyāvartanī* 29," 175.
202. Ibid., 168.
203. Lopez and chos phel, *Madman*, 252.
204. Chos phel and Lopez, *Forest*, 36–7.
205. Lopez, "*Vigrahavyāvartanī* 29," 170. Cf. *Madman*, 152.
206. Chos phel, "Adornment," 78, v. 118.
207. Ibid., 80, v. 121.
208. Lopez, "*Vigrahavyāvartanī* 29," 177–8. Cf. *Madman*, 159.

conventions to guide others to an enlightened awareness of emptiness. First of all, Tsongkhapa holds that only followers of the Prāsaṅgika-Madhyamaka philosophy who are already themselves enlightened ("*ārya Prāsaṅgikas*") have "gained the right" to say that they have no assertion, while unenlightened followers ("*pṛthagjana Prāsaṅgikas*") are "obliged to uphold the reflection-like appearances of dependently arisen phenomena until the point of gaining the direct vision of emptiness in which all appearances are destroyed."[209] On this point, Gendun Chopel makes no such distinction.

Concerning a second and more significant point of contrast, furthermore, Gendun Chopel rejects Tsongkhapa's notion that it is valid for Mādhyamikas (whether enlightened or not) to claim that they "have no assertion" when conversing with the common beings. Instead Gendun Chopel portrays the essence of having "no thesis"—and thus making assertions *for others*—as being the Mādhyamika's willingness to tell "a lie for a noble purpose." In other words, the Mādhyamika "has no assertion but claims he does in order to defeat the opponent."[210] This is where the influence of Gendun Chopel's training in the dialectics of debate begins to surface. Gendun Chopel deems the role of the Mādhyamika in making assertions for others as not being to introduce increasingly subtle ideas about reality so as to lead common beings gradually to more profound levels of ultimate—this would mean that conventional reasoning could (however inadequately) articulate the truth of emptiness, and as we have seen Gendun Chopel fiercely maintains that conventional language and logic cannot come close to touching "the other side." Rather he considers the role of the Buddha and other Mādhyamikas to be one of the deconstructing debate partner that situationally determines the best false assertion to defend as a means to destroy the other's reasoning with reasoning, and consequently expose the inherent limit and fault with all language and distinctions.[211] Hence, the authority of an enlightened being's speech is dialectically negative and fundamentally deconstructive. Its validity does not rest in the statement itself—that assertion is just "a lie told for a noble purpose"—but in its pragmatic ability to deconstruct the reifications of language, thus possibly exposing the hearer to glimpse at the nonconceptual "absence," the "non-affirming negative" of emptiness, that rests beyond the limits of all language and thought. Its purpose is solely to provide the possible experience of "a 'non-implicative negation', namely, a negation that leaves no room for any affirmation or implication in its aftermath" as opposed to guiding others simply to a new "better" affirmation of something else.[212]

---

209. Lopez, "*Vigrahavyāvartanī* 29," 176–7.

210. Ibid. Cf. *Madman*, 158.

211. Chos phel, "Adornment," 61–2, v. 55.

212. Jinpa, 57. Cf. Lopez and chos phel, *Madman*, 192: Lopez describes the direct perception of emptiness Gendun Chopel intends as perceiving "only an absence; emptiness is a nonaffirming negative that implies nothing."

This is why for Gendun Chopel a hardline anti-realist position regarding conventional knowledge is paramount. Because he fears that if one allows for some knowledge and language to be accepted as "valid," even just conventionally, it limits the possibility for enlightened beings to take up a contradictory view toward some positions and assertions. This then would make even the use of language by the enlightened impotent in bringing others to an experience of a "non-implicative negation."[213] Therefore, even affirming any claim about the ultimate as valid—including emptiness itself—fundamentally subverts the possibility for this type of ultimate negation. For this reason, Gendun Chopel emphatically contends: "Even ultimate truths exist conventionally; they do not exist ultimately. An ultimate mode of being is unfounded. Even the ultimate is established in a way which is not ultimate. This means that it is conventionally established."[214] In the end "emptiness" itself does not depict the ultimate nature of reality, it is just a useful deconstructive tool for dismantling *other* conventional conceptions of the ultimate reality, hence the famous Buddhist proclamation of the "emptiness of emptiness."[215] As such, in accordance with Lopez and Thupten Jinpa,[216] it can be said that Gendun Chopel upholds a fundamentally "apophatic" understanding of "valid knowledge" in which one can only recognize "the nature of the ultimate from the negative side, the 'is not' side and the 'does not exist' side," and where there is no method "to encounter the mode of being from the positive side, the 'is' side and the 'exists' side."[217] Accordingly, therefore, toward the conclusion of the *Adornment* he proclaims that within this conventional realm of saṃsāra the "famous 'valid knowledge and reasoning'" of which the majority of common beings (even Geluk Buddhists) are so enamored that they can at best "refer to just a faint comprehending awareness" of the absence beyond all language and thought "that falls between two uncomprehending awarenesses" of the persistent projection of distinctions and linguistic reifications by the ignorant.[218]

Overall then, by observing his position and conclusion in comparison to Schillebeeckx's adaption of apophaticism in light of the negative dialectics of critical theorists (namely Adorno) in modern philosophy, one can begin to see

---

213. Chos phel, "Adornment," 104, v. 202.
214. Ibid., 84, v. 137.
215. Jinpa, 47.
216. See Lopez, "*Vigrahavyāvartanī* 29," 166; *Hermeneutics*, 57; Jinpa, 182. In each of these passages the scholars use the terminology of "apophaticism" (i.e., apophasis, apophatic, etc.) as a way of describing the knowledge resultant of this type of ultimate negation. It should be noted, however, that in the passage by Thupten Jinpa he points out that stopping at this type of extreme deconstructive negation (which Gendun Chopel champions) is in direct opposition to Tsongkhapa's system that maintained the necessity of following such a negation with "a reconstructive approach to relate the apophatic experience back to the reality of the everyday world."
217. Chos phel, "Adornment," 70, v. 94.
218. Ibid., 110, v. 221. Cf. Lopez and chos phel, *Madman*, 210.

how Gendun Chopel might have been able to view the *Adornment* as presenting an epistemological system (according to Stoddard) that is compatible with modernity despite the entirely intra-Buddhist nature to its discussion of the type of "valid knowledge" possible through personal experience.[219] It is certainly studious for Lopez to highlight that the text *never* directly engages, let alone mentions, modernity or modern philosophy. Nevertheless, in many ways one can see how Gendun Chopel's system appears to be at least somewhat analogous to Adorno's neo-Marxist negative dialectic, which seeks only a continuous negation over a "true" unified synthesis to one's understanding of reality (as suggested by Hegel's dialectical method). Moreover, whether he was directly aware of any of these modern philosophical trends or not (most of which he probably was not), one can surely glean how—like Schillebeeckx's critically realist thought—Gendun Chopel's anti-realist system of epistemology also could provide a "middle way" between the extreme poles of a Kantian subjectivism and scientific positivism within modern philosophical thought. Conversely, however, by this time it should also be apparent that it would be a complete misnomer to contend that Schillebeeckx's and Gendun Chopel's epistemologies are identical virtually in any way, whether in starting point, intention, process, or conclusion. Therefore, it is to this process of comparison we must now turn to in the concluding section of this chapter.

IV. Conclusion: Comparative Observations and Questions for Further Reflection

In summation, this chapter considered the question posed by the previous one as to how both Schillebeeckx and Gendun Chopel understood the authoritative knowledge about reality to be deeply "experiential" as well as how each thinker believed this heuristic form of knowledge is manifested in everyday living. We observed how both Schillebeeckx and Gendun Chopel viewed linguistic and conceptual interpretation of experience as inseparable from one's direct empirical perception of reality, and thus how all knowledge of reality gleaned from one's experience in the world is limited by the confines of language and is incapable of capturing or depicting the nature of reality as it is itself. Consequently in its final form then, we noted how both individuals believed any such authoritative knowledge about reality itself is at its foundation deeply "apophatic"—negatively known by a way of recognizing what something "is not"—and essentially beyond all expressions and concepts. In this sense, both thinkers would seemingly agree with Richard Rorty's proclamation that "the world is out there, but descriptions of the world are not."[220] Moreover, we also noticed how both thinkers sought, somewhat analogously, to utilize both forms of negative dialectics as well as language from traditional religious practice concerning the process of negatively

---

219. Stoddard, 275.
220. Rorty, *Contingency, Irony, and Solidarity*, 5.

"unknowing," or deconstructing, one's interpretative perceptions of ultimate reality in order to cultivate a profound immanent encounter with that reality. Yet once again our analysis also conversely displayed how as a result of the almost antithetical differences in their epistemological and religious starting points for engaging the topic of experiential knowledge, each thinker's system appears to possess divergent objectives, methods, and implications for discerning the nature of both knowledge and religious experience. Hence, similarly to the previous two chapters, this concluding section will briefly compare and contrast Schillebeeckx's and Gendun Chopel's thought regarding the nature and authority of experiential knowledge in order to highlight particularly poignant "points of contact"— whether of resonance or of friction—as a means to tease out further questions to be addressed in the subsequent concluding chapter.

Yet, as has been the case with both of the preceding chapters, it seems important to note that at least on the surface there appear to be numerous similarities between both the method and outcomes of each person's epistemological system. For example, both Gendun Chopel and Schillebeeckx acknowledge that within existence an individual's perception of an object of reality as "out there" cannot be separated from an instantaneous linguistic and conceptual interpretation of that object from the subject's side. Thus, for both of them, one's experience of reality is constantly maintained within a dialectical tension between one's encounter with something "out there," which influences and gives shape to any possible interpretation, while at the same time remaining limited by preconceived interpretations of the object engaged. Hence, both necessarily reject any simplistic notion of a clear subject–object distinction in the formation of knowledge. Rather, any "knowledge" or belief derived from an experience of the empirical world contains elements so intermingled within perception and inference that distinguishing what contributions toward knowledge come from the objective or subjective side is nearly impossible. And as such, if Stoddard's research and analysis of Gendun Chopel's Madhyamaka is accepted, then both Gendun Chopel and Schillebeeckx believed their respective epistemological system could present the practitioners of their own religious tradition with a defensible and more consistent alternative response to the emergent epistemologies within the prominent modern philosophical systems (i.e., subjectivism and positivism). Accordingly, because of this concern to provide a functioning alternative for their religious communities, we also observed how both thinkers actively and explicitly tied their philosophical method to well-known spiritual methods already established within their respective religious traditions for the cultivation of an "apophatic" or "negative" awareness of ultimate reality—Schillebeeckx with the *triplex via* and Gendun Chopel with the dialectics of debate. And finally, through this retrieval and reinterpretation of "mystical" elements within their own tradition, both of their philosophies *do* posit the possibility and benefit of "positive," or "cataphatic," elements of experiential knowledge situated principally within a process of human action (Schillebeeckx's as "orthopraxis" and Gendun Chopel's as tantric sexual bliss). Therefore, it would seem to be justified for one to conclude their systems appear to contain elements of analogous resemblances and correspondences that might not have been recognizable upon first glance.

Nevertheless, once again, because of their significantly divergent convictions about the nature and source of knowledge (Schillebeeckx's realism as opposed to Gendun Chopel anti-realism) as well as their understanding of human beings' ontological relation with ultimate reality, one is also confronted by a series of predominant differences in almost every component of their epistemological systems. Gendun Chopel's anti-realism causes him to perceive an entirely asymmetrical relationship between contingent beings and ultimate reality so that there is almost an unbridgeable chasm between the two sides. This results in his fundamental rejection of "valid knowledge" within the conventional world apart from one miraculously reaching the other side and achieving a proper ontological perspective (or "perspectiveless perspective") through the experience of enlightenment. Whereas for Schillebeeckx, on the other hand, with the foundation of his system being a conception of a "relational ontology"—grounded in the Creator/creation distinction—he maintains that the apparent lack of ontological contact between beings and ultimate reality is essentially one-sided, persisting only from the side of the finitude of creation and not from the side of an infinite ultimate reality that directly sustains and inseparably permeates all finite and contingent existence. Thus for Schillebeeckx, even if humans can never directly contact ultimate reality itself, that reality (God) is nonetheless always in contact with humanity through an ontological relationship he describes with the paradoxical expression of "mediated immediacy."

This divergence in the foundational orientations of their systems instigates noticeable differences in their methodological approaches for, and the subsequent outcomes of, determining the nature and validity of experiential knowledge as well. Yet again Gendun Chopel's anti-realism and complete rejection of any valid conventional knowledge compels him to view the intention of epistemological inquiry not as the discovery of a defensible "valid knowledge" that can be positively articulated in language, but instead the constant and utter negation of all language and concepts so as to produce the experience of a "non-implicative negative" and hence possibly an awareness of the absolute *absence* (or "non-affirming negative") that is ultimate reality. Consequently, one could say that Gendun Chopel's use of the negating dialectics of the Tibetan debating courtyard might actually be more analogous to Adorno's system of "negative dialectics," which intends to produce nothing beyond further negation than Schillebeeckx's thought. Conversely, Schillebeeckx's conviction that all "true knowledge" rests in its indirect, or "mediated immediate," contact with reality itself (even if the nature of this relationship can never be fully known) causes him persistently to reemphasize the importance of making positive assertions about reality despite the fact that no linguistic and conceptual affirmation can ever capture ultimate reality as it is in itself. Rather even if humans' awareness of ultimate reality can only be manifested negatively, still the proclamation of positive, or "cataphatic," affirmations about "truth" being made and exposed as inadequate is the only way to maintain this fundamentally negative consciousness of ultimate reality

(God). Thus Schillebeeckx's negative dialectic must maintain the hope of a clearer or better articulation of the truth of reality in order to fuel further action and reflection. And in this way it is recognizably distinct from both Gendun Chopel's and Adorno's dialectical processes of negation.

And finally by broadening the methodological scope of the comparison between these two distinct thinkers we can begin to see yet again how even though in this instance both thinkers consciously utilize and incorporate common elements from their religious traditions, nevertheless how they do so in relation to their traditions is quite different and therefore produce different reactions among the intellectuals, institutions, and common practitioners of their respective traditions. As our discussion regarding the "debate" between Stoddard and Lopez in the previous section highlighted, Gendun Chopel might have intended on producing a Madhyamaka epistemology that could withstand the scrutiny of modern philosophy in the *Adornment* but, if he did so, this intention was carried out in a thoroughly intra-Buddhist manner that only utilized traditional terminology and debates with no direct reference to modernity itself. And as such, it is quite reasonable to assume that this saturation in Buddhist thought might have helped contribute to the eventual wider acceptance of his thought among many contemporary Tibetan Buddhists. In Schillebeeckx's thought, on the other hand, although explicitly including elements from the long theological tradition of apophaticism and mysticism within the history of Christian thought, its reference to and incorporation of alien, especially "secularist" or "atheistic," Western philosophical ideas once again seem to cause his theological system to be received somewhat polemically within the Christian community. The result being one where many Catholic academics and intellectuals laud his theology for its innovative reinterpretation of the tradition as well as its distinctly "progressive" political orientation, while others remain rather critical and suspicious of it venturing too far beyond the bounds of orthodox interpretation—never mind the fact that the sheer breadth and scope of its philosophical references and sources are so large that the nuances of his ideas probably remain inaccessible to the theologically untrained believer. Yet it is still important to note that both thinkers' emphases on and utilization of negative dialectics within their philosophies at least initially placed them in clear tension with many of the mainstream assumptions of their scholastic contemporaries. Hence this begs the final question of this comparison as to whether a system of religious philosophy that is rooted in a conviction of a negative or "apophatic" experience of reality as being the primary authoritative source for all other religious faith and knowledge can still be religiously efficacious in evoking a spirituality of committed belief and action among everyday believers. Or alternatively, are either or both of these systems (whether individually or dialogically) simply fated to elicit among receptive practitioners an unrelenting cynicism toward their traditions at best, and a faithless skepticism at worst? And so, it is to this concern of how one might defend the former rather than the latter of these two possible outcomes (as well as the other concluding questions raised in the previous two chapters) that we will now briefly attempt to discuss in the dialogically constructive assessment within the final chapter of this work.

Conclusion

POSSIBLE MADHYAMAKA IMPLICATIONS FOR CATHOLIC THEOLOGY

I. Introduction: Where Do We Go from Here?

Each of the last three chapters has closely examined the writings and thought of both Edward Schillebeeckx and Gendun Chopel around the constructed comparative topics of "perspectivalism," "hermeneutics," and "apophaticism" with the hope of creating possible points of comparative contact between these two religious thinkers despite any perceivably wide discrepancies in the nature of their religious vocabularies, traditions, and convictions. However, since the use of these conceptual topics was intended to elicit interpretations and comparisons of each thinker's ideas through a third conceptual vocabulary rather than just attest to a simple similitude between the various components of their thought, each of these comparative "case-study" chapters did not end with the assertion of a series of unified conclusions regarding the topic explored but instead finished by raising more questions that were prompted as a result of the comparison's exposed differences with regard to the specific topic. As promised throughout this project, therefore, this chapter will now seek to return to these open-ended questions left at the conclusion of the previous three chapters in order to imagine how both Schillebeeckx and Gendun Chopel might have responded to each other's thought as well as these broader questions in light of their encounter with the other person's system.

Still the overall goal of this brief imaginative dialogue between the two thinkers will not be to give any definitive answers to these larger questions—making such an argument to surely constitute another project (if not many) in and of itself—but rather only to suggest possible avenues and trajectories for addressing these questions in the future. Nonetheless, while not purposing any definitive judgments to these larger questions themselves, this chapter will still aim to expand the purview of this comparison beyond the sole assessment of the two thinkers regarding the particularities of their theories of religious knowledge and authority purely on the conceptual level to also addressing how the interaction of their particular thoughts might assist believers in speculatively approaching these broader issues on the level of judgment. Accordingly, as discussed in the methodology of the first chapter, after attempting to suspend (as much as possible) my own theological commitment to the Roman Catholic tradition, it is in this chapter that I will specifically seek to return to my own religious community and tradition so as to show how the undergoing of this project has provided me with new perspectives and new tools for engaging the daunting questions of religious authority, knowledge, and belief for Catholics in the contemporary world. Hence the theological tone and orientation of this chapter will generally center around what I believe Christian theology might learn from the Madhyamaka Buddhist traditions (and more specifically Gendun Chopel's version of Madhyamaka), and conversely will not attempt to critique or to tell Buddhists what they should learn or appropriate from the Christian theological tradition. In the end, therefore, this chapter will briefly return to assess how this comparative project might assist contemporary Catholics in responding to the larger question of maintaining religious belief amidst the current postmodern tendencies toward notions of intellectual anti-representationalism and relativism regarding the question of truth in the contemporary world. And so the conclusion of this chapter and this overall project, then, aspires to show how both thinkers might be better able to impact and contribute to forming new, broader trajectories for thought and spiritual practice for religious believers in the contemporary postmodern world.

II. Perspectivalism: Fallible Humans, Fallible Knowledge, and the Necessity of a Fallible (and Critical) Community

The third chapter's discussion concerning the elements of both Schillebeeckx's and Gendun Chopel's thought that can be, at least in some ways, labeled as "perspectivalist" concluded by asking the primary question of whether one can hold a position of epistemological perspectivalism in regard to religious truth in a way that nonetheless does not cause the individual to logically slide into forms of a radically relativistic individualism and/or communal isolation. In other words, the main issue surrounding both thinkers' notions of the perspectival limits of knowledge—namely, how the cognitive processes of the individual limit the perception and interpretation of one's own phenomenological experiences—is a question of incommensurability. Or, how radically do their notions of the perspectival nature of knowledge limit the ability of individuals (or even groups) to actually share "knowledge" beyond the confines of one's own mind and interpretation? Moreover, this more acute question about the scope of the perspectival limits of an individual's ability to accurately interpret the totality of one's phenomenological experiences in the world led to a more specified theological question concerning the ability and authority of religious traditions in the formation of knowledge. Hence, the chapter concluded without answering the larger theological question of whether, according to Schillebeeckx and Gendun Chopel, it is possible for a community comprised of individuals' personally fallible conceptions of knowledge to be an actual conduit of an infallible reality of ultimate truth. As was displayed within the interpretative readings of, and comparisons between, the two thinkers within the body of that chapter, it is clear that the differences to each thinker's response to these questions rest in the fundamental disagreement of whether it is possible for there to be imperfect knowledge that is still based on an apprehension of reality as it really is—that is, the difference between assuming an epistemological *realism* (Schillebeeckx) or *anti-realism* (Gendun Chopel) to individuals' truth claims.

As the body of that chapter noted, despite a gradual metamorphosis in his emphasis about the way individuals' understandings and presumed "knowledge" of reality is simultaneously shaped and limited by the natural confines of their cognitive processes of interpretation, Schillebeeckx throughout his life consistently maintained that these individually shaped interpretations at least *could* be—albeit always incompletely and thus fallibly—in touch with and partially based on an encounter with reality in itself. And for this reason most scholars aptly choose to label Schillebeeckx a *critical* realist,[1] that is, someone promoting an epistemology that bases the ability to adjudicate between propositions of truth at least in part on those claims' correspondence to a reality "out there" while nevertheless remaining cognizant of the fact that no notions of truth ever fully correspond to that reality in its totality. Early in his career, based on his training and collaboration with philosophical theologian De Petter, Schillebeeckx sought to strike this balance between correspondence and the perspectival interpretation of the individual through what he and De Petter termed "phenomenological Thomism," and more specifically a notion of "implicit intuition." According to this system, in every phenomenological encounter with reality the individual has an implicit and intuitive prehension of the entirety of all reality. However, based on the natural limits of individuals' cognitive processes of interpretation, this implicit intuition of reality can never be fully known in an individual's explicit conceptual consciousness and thus all conceptual knowledge is always limited and fallible in a way that consistently leaves any propositional or conceptual articulation of truth open to further refinement and development in understanding.

In his later theology, Schillebeeckx maintains the general aspects of his perspectivalism—again situating the permeating fallibility of knowledge within the cognitive limits of an individual's conceptual interpretation—but would alter his emphasis regarding the primary cause for this limitation. After his self-described "clean break" with De Petter and increased interest in hermeneutics and Critical Theories in the latter half of the 1960s, Schillebeeckx began to focus on the inescapable realities of the hermeneutics of history and the (even self-deceptive) forces of personal and institutional self-interest that influence and confine an individual's interpretation of reality. Nonetheless, his commitment to a relational ontology (which is the backbone to both the early and later manifestations of his epistemology) caused him to insist that an individual's claims to truth indeed

---

1. Though this is the interpretation of an overwhelming number of Schillebeeckx scholars, it is still certainly not an unanimous interpretation of his thought. For one example of an interpretation of Schillebeeckx's epistemology as being fundamentally based in "non-realism," see Corneliu C. Simut, *Critical Essays on Edward Schillebeeckx's Theology: From Theological Radicalism to Philosophical Non-Realism* (Eugene, OR: Wipf & Stock, 2010), esp. 220–46.

still *can* be grounded in an actual experience of reality itself, even if it is only experienced indirectly and negatively through reality's resistance to human efforts and conceptual circumscription. And therefore, in the end, Schillebeeckx consistently maintains throughout his career that knowledge is always limited and fallible due to individuals' limited capacities of linguistic and conceptual interpretation while at the same time equally attesting to the conviction that these incomplete and fallible understandings can be grounded in, and thus assessed by, a correspondence to an encounter with a perceptible reality outside of one's self.

Conversely, Gendun Chopel's own Madhyamaka system of epistemology—based on a particular non-realist rendering of Dharmakīrti's epistemology—rejects any notion of epistemic half-measures, ones where linguistic and conceptual interpretations of reality or "truth claims" can be fundamentally fallible and flawed but still be based on an actual valid perception of reality. For him, the epistemological validity of cognition cannot be separated from the ontological premises according to which an object is apprehended. This assumption, in conjunction with his Madhyamaka belief in the ontological primacy of "emptiness," the non-affirming negative or absence in reality of all conceptuality, causes him to view all linguistic and conceptual renderings of reality—and hence, any articulation about reality—as fundamentally divorced from the ultimate truth of emptiness. So for this reason, Gendun Chopel contends that it is impossible for anyone to know something "in part"; either one knows the valid nonconceptual and non-dual reality of emptiness in its entirety or not. And so accordingly, he argues that all individuals can be divided into two distinct categories or "realms": first the conventional one of "common beings" where there can be no valid knowledge of reality because all awareness is mired in the delusion of conceptuality, language, and distinction; and another ultimate one of "enlightened beings" in which individuals are persistently aware of the nonconceptual and non-dual nature of reality in its entirety. The significance of this last point cannot be overstated. This is because since Gendun Chopel does not reject the possibility of *any* valid knowledge but rather just insists there can be no valid knowledge according to the conventional terms of worldly existence (*saṃsāra*), he believes he avoids the classic Buddhist fear of falling into a form of nihilistic relativism. Rather, he contends that what he upholds is simply a conventional non-realism that divorces all language and conceptions from reality itself. As a consequence of this position, then, he repeatedly rejects any assertion that grants authority to the Buddhist tradition's teachings, ideas, or images in and of themselves.

There can be little doubt that Schillebeeckx would seriously challenge numerous points of Gendun Chopel's non-realist position, particularly with regard to its implications on traditional authority. Schillebeeckx's commitment to the Christian faith, which is rooted in the belief in a creator God (and hence for him an ontological relation between contingent creatures and ultimate reality), would make him quite suspect of any epistemological theory that would suggest a complete break between an infinite creator and a finite creation. In fact, for him, without there being some kind of analogous relation between the truth of reality and the finite, fallible depictions of it through the experiential language, images, and concepts of the created order, there would be no possibility for a revelation of ultimate truth that could transverse the chasm between the finite and infinite. As a consequence of this, in Schillebeeckx's eyes such a non-realist position would severely limit, if not render *impossible*, any soteriological hope for individuals based on a knowledge and acceptance of a revelatory understanding of the nature of all reality, and subsequently one's own condition in relation to the perfection of that reality. Hence, functionally speaking, Schillebeeckx would probably be compelled to pose a question to Gendun Chopel as to whether his distinction between "common beings" and "enlightened" ones actually solves the problem of a nihilistic relativism. Although such a distinction might allow Gendun Chopel to attest that his philosophy is not "relativistic" in the sense that he does affirm a universal truth for all reality, still his equal persistence that the validity or reality of this truth is completely separate from all conventional language and conceptions—and as such it is seemingly unobtainable by the unenlightened minds of "common beings"—implies an equivocal relativism to the experiences of the vast majority of past, present, and future beings with little (if *any*) hope of them ever being able to break out of this perpetually delusional state. In other words, Schillebeeckx would probably wonder whether, and if so *how*, any individuals could actually come to a state of enlightenment without any experience (either direct or indirect) of the ultimate reality of emptiness itself. Gendun Chopel might be able to use the negative dialectics of Tibetan debate as an illustration of the potential for an understanding and awareness that can be gleaned from the process of negating all language and concepts, but if there is truly no possible positive cognition or outcome from the process of negation how does this actually induce an experience of enlightenment and not just produce the same continual refining of conventional falsities for which he so doggedly chides his fellow Gelukpas?

Moreover, as shown by his own efforts to balance rather than completely undercut any institutional and traditional authority in his theology through the dialectical exchange of the community's role as both a "teaching church" (*ecclesia docens*) and also a "learning church" (*ecclesia discens*), it is reasonable to believe that Schillebeeckx would be very troubled by the brash individualism promoted by much of Gendun Chopel's rhetoric and philosophy. In fact, for the most part it seems that Gendun Chopel's philosophy exclusively emphasizes only the root problem of "delusion" (skt. *muha*; tb. *gti mug*) much to the neglect of the other two poisons (*triviṣa*; *dug gsum*) of greed (*rāga*; *'dod chags*) and hatred (*dveṣa*; *zhe sdang*) in his theory of Buddhist epistemology. Although traditionally Buddhists *have* seen delusion as the primary problem for beings both epistemologically as well as soteriologically, Gendun Chopel at times takes this prioritization to such an extreme that he virtually ignores the roles that the other two poisons play in the epistemological dilemma. Especially later in the development of his thought following the influence of hermeneutical and Critical Theories, Schillebeeckx would challenge Gendun Chopel's perception of the overwhelmingly passive state of delusion as the primary, if not sole, epistemological obstruction. If the determination of truth in Gendun Chopel's mind is purely based on the individual's own decision of what one accepts as "knowledge" or "truth" (particularly concerning any conventional claims), then what is there to possibly restrain the individual's own self-delusion driven by the forces of self-interest, fear, and power? In other words, Schillebeeckx would certainly have to inquire as to how Gendun Chopel might reconcile the more "active" causes of suffering by the other two poisons within his epistemology. Once suffering is no longer seen simply—or even primarily—as the passive outcome of an atmospheric-like state of delusion but as also something actively being imposed on one's self and others as a result of these two other related forces, what effect would it have on Gendun Chopel's seemingly intransigent individualism?

Undoubtedly, on the other hand, Gendun Chopel would have some significant issues of his own with Schillebeeckx's epistemological system as well. In many ways not so different from his criticisms of the critically realist interpretations of Tsongkhapa's epistemology that are prevalent within Prāsaṅgika Madhyamaka, Gendun Chopel would certainly challenge whether Schillebeeckx's "critical realism" actually maintains a consistent "middle way" between reification (or in Schillebeeckx's terms "idolatry"[2]) and relativism. Gendun Chopel would have a profound skepticism toward whether any form of "critical realism" is actually capable of taking the radical state of contingency that permeates the conventional world seriously. For remember, much in accord with his challenges to other Prāsaṅgika Madhyamaka interpretations, Gendun Chopel does not see the real threat of nihilism as resting in the potential of one to define the scope of valid truth too narrowly, but rather in the tendency to define it too *broadly*. According to Gendun Chopel's system, a much greater issue arises when one (such as Schillebeeckx) attempts to maintain that some part of conceptuality and language is in touch with reality as it exists in itself while other parts of these elements of the conventional world are utterly nonexistent in reality, even if one can never precisely situate which elements correspond to reality and how.

As discussed in the previous chapter, this is because for him the categories of "existent" and "nonexistent" (or "corresponding" and "not corresponding") are linguistic constructions themselves, so that deciphering between the "truly existent" and "utterly nonexistent" amounts to nothing more than a complex rearranging of language that makes it possible for *everything* to be eventually deemed "nonexistent." Conversely, for Gendun Chopel, if one is aware that even the very notions of "nonexistence" and "non-correspondence" are linguistic concepts and therefore contingent constructs themselves, then these notions become self-negating to the extent that they seek to invalidate the possibility of the "utter

---

2. Edward Schillebeeckx, "Prologue: Human God-Talk and God's Silence," in *The Praxis of the Reign of God: An Introduction to the Theology of Edward Schillebeeckx*, ed. Mary Catherine Hilkert and Robert J. Schreiter (New York: Fordham University Press, 2002), xiv. Here Schillebeeckx explicitly gives his concise definition of "idolatry" as "offering to creature the worship that is only accorded to the divine mystery. Idolatry is a worship of an object upon which the glory of God has come down, or a thing upon which human beings project their own unsatiated desire and glory."

nonexistence" of all concepts or meaning in reality, *nihilism*, by actually affirming the linguistic categories on which that concept is based as corresponding with an aspect of reality beyond language. So once again, for him as long as one recognizes that even one's understanding of nonexistence is ultimately nonexistent, "there is no possibility of falling into nihilism."[3] Thus the only real threat of nihilism would be the partial recognition of language and concepts as being correspondent to existence while rejecting others as not, because that way of thinking assumes that language and concepts can reflect actual aspects of reality. However, Gendun Chopel observes that—especially within modern philosophy—an awareness of the historical contingency of all language and ideas seems to be ever expanding in reach so that increasingly truth claims or "knowledge" about the nature of reality that were once perceived to be transhistorical or transrational are being exposed as more and more historically constructed and culturally conditioned. Accordingly, in Gendun Chopel's mind, the threat of a nihilistic worldview is not the result of accepting all language and concepts as utterly contingent and fallible, but in fact is more the result of the constant disintegration of individuals' beliefs as their linguistic propositions and abstract concepts are continually further revealed to be undeniable reifications of their own vocabularies, thoughts, and images, each with its own history.

Furthermore, as it relates to the question of traditional and institutional authority, Gendun Chopel would probably perceive a creeping authoritarianism, or at best majority rule, within Schillebeeckx's realist interpretation of epistemology. Although Schillebeeckx attempts to balance his realist conviction with his understanding of traditional authority through an actively critical dialectic between religious institutions and the beliefs of the individuals that comprise them (the "teaching church" and "learning church" dialectic), Gendun Chopel would seem to argue that Schillebeeckx undervalues the power of language and group dynamics in the shaping of one's perception. Hence, as we observed in the third chapter, one is brought back to Gendun Chopel's discussion of Āryadeva's *Four Hundred Verses* (*Catuḥśataka*) and Candrakīrti's response to its question: "Therefore, why is it incorrect to say that the whole world is insane?" Candrakīrti's response is the story about the king whose kingdom is rendered insane by drinking tainted rainwater. Even though the king (due to a prophetic warning against drinking the water) does not partake in the water and consequently is "the only one whose mind remained normal," after some time, since no one else can understand his way of thinking, his subjects collectively begin to label *him* as insane. And so, in the end, the king eventually has to drink the water and cause himself to go insane in order to be able to effectively communicate with his subjects and live in the world by "[agreeing] with everyone else."[4]

This story can serve as a metaphor of Gendun Chopel's problems with Schillebeeckx's understanding of traditional authority in two ways. First it shows

---

3. Chos phel, "Adornment," 85–6, v. 141. Cf. Lopez, *Madman*, 180–1.
4. Chos phel, "Adornment," 49, v. 7–8.

the all-encompassing and inescapable power of language to shape individuals' perceptions and interpretations of reality. Notice that in Gendun Chopel's paraphrase of the story, the king's main problem was not that he was experiencing any part of reality distinct from his subjects, but rather that he was no longer capable of speaking in, or "playing," their language game ("all the people did not agree with the way of thinking and the way of speaking of the king"). As a result of this disparity in language games, the members of the new and "delusional" tradition of language (the royal subjects) end up deeming the earlier and "untainted" tradition of the king irrational and incoherent. Similarly for Gendun Chopel, as he goes on to explain in the verse immediately following this story, religious traditions are much like the delusional language game of the king's subjects in that those who have drunken the waters of their vocabularies are then incapable of seeing coherence, rationality, or even sanity in any perception that does not fit within their own system of language and symbol sets. That is why he follows his parable by providing a "moral to the story" that is worth repeating when he explains:

> Thus, due to the single great insanity from our having continually drunk the crazing waters of ignorance from time immemorial, there is no confidence whatsoever in our decisions concerning what exists and does not exist, what is and is not. Even though a hundred, a thousand, ten thousand, or a hundred thousand of such insane people agree, it in no way becomes more credible.[5]

And therefore even with Schillebeeckx's argument for the balance of traditional authority in the church through his "teaching-learning" dialectic between the traditional institution and "critical communities," Gendun Chopel would still view these two groups as belonging to and agreeing upon the same general language game in which neither can ever fully know if, and how much, their perceptions and communications actually correspond to the reality they encounter "out there," or rather if they are trapped in a completely delusional way of thinking and speaking that has no basis in reality whatsoever. At best, then, Schillebeeckx's perspectivalism as manifested through his insistence on the necessary dialectic between traditional authority and "critical communities" of individuals can simply function to effectively regulate its own language game and not assess its ultimate truth or validity. But then, in this sense, it is still simply a case of the blind leading the blind.

Second, furthermore, this illustration also challenges Schillebeeckx's view of traditional authority according to the power of group dynamics. This is because, following Gendun Chopel's rendition of the parable, the king in the story *knows* that the language of his subjects is delusional and does not correspond to reality. However once the majority begins to deem *him* insane and incoherent, he is eventually overcome by the pressure to be accepted by, and seen as credible within, the rest of the group so that he embraces a state of self-delusion by willingly

---

5. Ibid., 49, v. 8.

partaking of the tainted waters himself. Hence, the first issue that this point of the story raises is Gendun Chopel's conviction that criticism from truly outside of a language game will always be ineffective in speaking to and changing the inner structure of that vocabulary because it will not fit with the categories of language through which the "delusional" tradition of language understands the world. Therefore, there can be no true check on traditional thinking and authority besides maybe tinkering with the periphery of thought from within. But more than that, even if someone from within the tradition was by chance capable of breaking out of the delusional state individually, that person would immediately be considered illogical, heretical, or insane according to the inner logic of that system of meaning and consequently probably ostracized from the community. Thus even if one was capable of truly critiquing the community from within, more than likely they would be either easily disregarded as outside the scope of "truth" and reliability or pressured to suppress such understandings and practice a form of active self-deceit in order to conform to and remain within the standard of the traditional community. And so, Gendun Chopel would likely perceive a creeping authoritarianism in Schillebeeckx's (or any other) system that wants to give a special possession of truth to any tradition or community—even if regulated—because the historical and social dynamics inherent in such traditions make any acceptance of its authority be based on its ability to efficaciously communicate and utilize language to influence one's interpretations of reality, and not on its ability to objectively present the world as it is in itself.

So, then, one is left wondering what might be learned about the role of traditional authority in contemporary theology from comparing these thinkers in terms of their use of "perspectivalism." If both Schillebeeckx and Gendun Chopel would view the other as potentially teetering on the edge of "nihilism" or "relativism" for seemingly antithetical reasons (either for defining the object of negation too broadly or too narrowly), then is there any way that these two voices might collectively help guide a theological understanding of the authority of tradition moving forward? The answer to these questions I believe actually rests less in their theories of "perspectivalism" and more in the common concerns that they seem to be addressing with those ideas. Both thinkers are suspicious of the ability of concepts and language to efficiently and accurately help individuals interpret their own experiences of reality, not to mention any *transhistorical* aspects of that reality. Thus both of them have elements that can resemble an epistemological perspectivalism—the limitation of knowledge resulting from the interpretative constraints of using abstract concepts (or "universals") in describing particular encounters with reality—in order to express their own belief that language and concepts cannot completely depict the realities they wish to convey as they are in themselves. In terms of traditional or communal authority, therefore, both Schillebeeckx and Gendun Chopel are seeking to answer the question of what is the purpose of communal teachings, doctrines, and beliefs if one acknowledges that ultimate truth is beyond all concepts and words. Or put somewhat differently, how can a community of individuals with personally fallible conceptions of knowledge be a conduit of the infallible reality of ultimate truth that is beyond all language, concepts, and history?

It is in Gendun Chopel's persistent awareness and conscious unmasking of the radical contingency (or "conventionality") of all thought and language where his epistemology truly seems to contribute something significant to a theological reimagining of traditional authority within contemporary society. His generally deconstructive mindset toward all instantiations of language and concepts as being completely historically laden and socially contingent in nature not only seems to resonate with the suspicions of contemporary anti-representationalist philosophers and theologians but also sufficiently preserves, indeed *emphasizes*, the common notion between Schillebeeckx and himself (and possibly even Christian and Buddhist traditions more broadly) that human language and concepts can never completely reflect or circumscribe the authentic nature of ultimate truth behind all reality. As such, this philosophical orientation specifically raises a necessary conscious suspicion in Gendun Chopel toward both the idolatrous reification of language and imagery as well as the power of institutions and groups to use such processes of reification to manipulate, oppress, and intimidate others in order to fulfill their own self-interests. Accordingly, this orientation demands a necessary critical inquiry when approaching claims to knowledge or truth that are based solely on the testimony and authority of others. Moreover, it reminds practitioners that their traditional vocabularies, images, and practices are not the *source* of truth and knowledge but rather at best an indirect *means* to experiencing, and thus gaining knowledge of, reality for one's self. So, in the end, Gendun Chopel's version of Madhyamaka philosophy beneficially reminds religious believers and theologians of the constant potential for theological reification and idolatry lurking in all conceptual expression of ultimate truth, and as such it relentlessly calls for a greater sense of humility in all articulations and convictions regarding that ultimate truth.

For the most part, Schillebeeckx would probably agree with (and to an extent admire) Gendun Chopel's convictions in this area. At the same time, however, he would certainly feel quite uneasy with the deep-seated individualism implied by Gendun Chopel's rhetoric and logic. Schillebeeckx would view both the authoritative voice of religious communities and their traditions alongside the experience, interpretation, and judgment of individual practitioners as vitally important for regulating the tendency of both institutions and individuals toward the active will to power and self-interest in all promotion of "knowledge." Thus he would not reject Gendun Chopel's suspicion toward traditional language, teachings, and concepts as potentially powerful reifications of human desires and will, but would rather insist that such a suspicion be equally applied to both sides of the relationship between traditions and their individual followers. Hence, this is where Schillebeeckx's dialectical approach to traditional authority that emphasizes the roles of traditions as both "teaching" communities and "learning" communities becomes quite useful. For Schillebeeckx, the rightful suspicion toward traditional images and doctrines should never be separated from the communal suspicion concerning the motivations behind the critical and deconstructive inquiries of individual believers. It is in this sense that Schillebeeckx's model of traditional authority genuinely seeks to forge a middle way between the potential for a traditional authoritarianism and a debilitatingly isolationist individualism. By emphasizing the need for the critique of both communal as well as individual conventional constructions of belief based on interpretations of reality, Schillebeeckx's approach seems to find a way to highlight the shared concern between the two thinkers that all interpretations and articulations (read "conventions") of the ultimate nature of reality always fall short of capturing that reality in itself, whether communal or individual. And as such it promotes a notion that I believe both thinkers would appreciate and accept, a conviction that any valid knowledge and awareness of ultimate truth comes not from any religious ideas themselves but in the experience of the continually negating back-and-forth process between individual and communal constructions and criticisms of conventional beliefs, meanings, and practices.

And so, out of this comparison between Gendun Chopel and Schillebeeckx concerning the perspectival nature of knowledge and the authority of religious tradition, one avenue of theological inquiry that I believe should be further pursued in the future is what I am terming a "critical conventionalism." One could utilize more recent theological positions such as William Dean's theory of "sacred conventions" in order to discuss the historical- and cultural-conditionedness of all theological statements and doctrines alongside the need for traditional critique and correction in the individual and communal quests for ultimate truth. Dean's theory utilizes Thomas Haskell's seminal article, "The Curious Persistence of Rights Talk in the Age of Interpretation,"[6] in order to propose a concept of "sacred conventions" as an effective theological "middle way" between realism and non-realism, or objectivism and subjectivism, in understanding the correspondence between religious symbols, beliefs, doctrines, and the reality "out there" they claim to be depicting. According to Dean's appropriation of Haskell's theory, all religious doctrines, beliefs, and symbols are social conventions, or "public constructions," that are "always formed by an objective public past interacting with a current subjective creativity" in a way that "is not reducible to either of those causes or to their combined effects."[7] More specifically then, for Dean the sources of a religion's normative claims are what he terms "sacred conventions," which he defines as the images, metaphors, and ideals that are derived and constructed out of the materials of history and yet nonetheless eventually take on "a life of their own" and "can turn back on society and in ways that were not originally intended."[8] Hence,

---

6. Thomas L. Haskell, "The Curious Persistence of Rights Talk in the 'Age of Interpretation,'" *Journal of American History* 74, no. 3 (December 1987): 984–1012.

7. William D. Dean, *The Religious Critic in American Culture* (Albany: State University of New York Press, 1994), 107, 136.

8. Dean, *Religious Critic*, 134. To be clear, Dean's actual position regarding "sacred conventions" (at least in this passage and his earlier works) would probably be much more analogous to Gendun Chopel's understanding of religious conventions in that both Dean and Gendun Chopel would question any connection between sacred conventions and a

by acting independently and unpredictably, these socially constructed ideas take on an ontological status that neither corresponds completely to an objective reality "out there" (such as a divine supernatural person) nor to a mere subjective reality (such as the projection of a wish) but is instead a third kind of "ontological reality" that is not reducible to either side of the objective–subjective binary.[9]

Moving forward, I believe that Dean's theological use of the idea of "sacred conventions" might be helpful in developing a theological position that can mediate between Schillebeeckx's critical realism and Gendun Chopel's non-realism regarding linguistic and conceptual depictions of reality and ultimate truth (particularly as pertaining to the authority of religious traditions) in his attempt to balance the notions of the active, subjective, and creative construction of all linguistic propositions and concepts with the passive, objective, and receptive influences of a reality "out there" in the shaping of all religious beliefs. Dean articulates how sacred conventions encompass both sides of this dichotomy when he elaborates,

> The sacred, I am proposing is a living and evolving convention about what is ultimately important. Although it is continually reinterpreted, the sacred is not just passive to the influence of a people's interpretations of what is ultimately important. It is also *active*, influencing a people's estimate of what is important.[10]

Accordingly, Dean's theory of sacred conventions acknowledges the constructed and conventional aspect to all religious beliefs and concepts while also preserving the notion that these conventions are not just pure subjective projections that are completely detached from experiences of an objective reality by individuals. Dean does this by contending that the reality of religious experiences, and the subsequent ultimate commitments they produce, are not determined solely by the interpretation of the one experiencing it alone, nor by an objective thing being experienced alone, but materializes out of the relation of an unpredictable chain interaction between the two so that they are realities which are "partly determined by observer choices and the traditions those choices create."[11] Moreover, since Dean views these conventions as (at least in part) social constructions that nonetheless have *real implications* for both the religious traditions that cherish them and the societies that envelop those traditions more generally, Dean's

transhistorical, transcultural aspect of reality. However, as I hope to show in the following paragraph, I do not believe that this assumption is inherently indicative of the use of sacred conventions more broadly conceived. In fact, in more recent years Dean has written a number of texts that have openly begun to tie his understanding of sacred conventions to realities of ultimate "mystery" and "transcendence" in a way that he believes might be *sui generis* to religious language.

9. Dean, *Religious Critic*, 134–6.
10. Ibid., 133.
11. Ibid., 118.

theory of sacred conventions appears to inherently require the sort of dialectical balance between theoretical construction and critical regulation by both religious communities (traditions) and the individual voices that comprise them as was discussed above in our constructive synthesis of Schillebeeckx's and Gendun Chopel's unique positions. In other words, by utilizing a variation of Dean's notion of sacred conventions in a theological epistemology of religious authority, one can potentially maintain a theological recognition of the radical contingency of all linguistically based ideas (and as such the thinkers' mutual recognition that concepts and descriptions can never capture the reality itself) while also demanding for the continuous regulation of the development of these conventions by both the historical traditions and the individual practitioners that claim them. Moving forward, then, out of the comparative dialogue between Schillebeeckx and Gendun Chopel—with the use of William Dean's theory of conventions and others like it—one can see the possibility for a Christian theology that can relate and respond to non-realist (or anti-representationalist) theories of epistemology on the social and conceptual level, while preserving a differing judgment as to whether those conventions actually correspond to a greater reality "out there."

III. Hermeneutics: Jesus as the First among Many Local Theologians

As a direct result of their shared suspicion toward the ability of language and concepts to accurately and effectively capture the reality they are meant to describe, both Schillebeeckx and Gendun Chopel are led to reinterpret their own understanding of the teaching authority of the founders of their respective religious traditions. Chapter 4 discussed how both thinkers (each in his own way) creatively reimagined the authority of their traditions' historical founders to be located less in those teachers' actual words and teachings, and more in their ability to reorient the mindset, or "perspective," of their followers toward a fundamental openness to the ever-potential inbreaking of new meanings that can emerge out of one's own crisis-ridden experiences of history. For Schillebeeckx, then, this new emphasis in understanding Jesus's authority caused him to resituate the locus of that authority in Jesus of Nazareth's ability to serve as an exemplar for contemporary individuals on how they can construct a sense of purpose and meaning in their lives by pursuing right actions ("orthopraxis") that in turn help instill a sense of hope in others who are suffering.[12] Whereas for Gendun Chopel, on the other hand, his own renegotiation of traditional Buddhist hermeneutics caused him to identify the Buddha's teaching authority in his teachings' ability to shape a fundamentally deconstructive orientation to the perspective of his followers that can eventually lead them to their own experience of the silent wisdom of Buddhahood in the face of the non-affirming negative, or absolute "absence," that is the ultimate nature of all reality. In this way, therefore, by the end of the chapter one was able to see how

---

12. Schillebeeckx, *Christ*, 809. Cf. Schillebeeckx, *Interim Report*, 29.

both thinkers' suspicions toward the correspondence between linguistic concepts and reality as it is in itself guided both Schillebeeckx and Gendun Chopel to place the authority of their traditions' historical founders similarly more in those figures' methodological approaches for orienting others toward the awareness of an ineffable reality that is exposed through the constant collapse of prior meanings, and thus the potential meaninglessness, of history rather than in the perceived meaning of any one of their teachings itself.

Despite this methodological similarity in their understanding of the authority of these figures, however, the chapter also fleshed out some notable differences in their theories of teaching authority and the hermeneutics of deciphering past meanings. The most significant difference was how each thinker depicted the ontological nature that was to be attributed to the founder of each thinker's respective tradition, along with the effect that those figures' nature had on their standing as an authoritative voice for others. For example, while never denying the honorific theological titles that were later ascribed to Jesus as being "the Christ" or "the Son of God" by the Christian tradition, Schillebeeckx viewed any requirement that such titles be presupposed by an individual in order for the person to understand the authority of Jesus's message as a potential hindrance to contemporary, more historically conscious individuals. Rather, for Schillebeeckx, Jesus's epistemological authority regarding the nature of reality and truth could only effectively come from the discovery of the efficacious appropriation of his message of hope in the face of suffering that emerges out of the narratival retelling of Jesus's life story in new historical contexts. Hence, for him it is completely valid for one to determine and believe that Jesus was divine (that he truly was the "Son of God"), but that is a belief (and title) that can only be ascribed to the figure of Jesus following one's own discovery of the authoritative nature of his message.

Conversely, Gendun Chopel takes the exact opposite tact in discussing the nature of Śākyamuni Buddha. Chapter 4 showed how throughout his writings, Gendun Chopel not only refuses to shy away from presupposing and invoking the honorific titles of the Buddha in his discussion of the Buddha's teachings but also regularly cites them as source of a meditative experience and awareness of the ultimate nature of reality the Buddha sought to expose. Nevertheless, relying on his own interpretation of the "four seals" for understanding the authentic teachings of the Buddha within the tradition, Gendun Chopel would still hold that the words of the teachings themselves are not what can be taken as literally authoritative—for all language and concepts are just the pedagogic use of "expedient means"—but instead it is the experience they produce in the mind of individual hearer (the "spirit" of the teaching) that makes them authoritative. Thus in reality even the honorific titles attributed to the Buddha are only just another form of linguistic and conceptual "expedient means" for producing this type of authentic experience and awareness. Therefore, for Gendun Chopel there is no inherent danger or obstruction associated with the use of such titles because, if they assist in orienting the individual hearer's mind toward an authentic experience of emptiness, such titles eventually and necessarily will be negated anyways. And so, whereas Schillebeeckx sees the use of honorific titles attributed to his founder as a possible hindrance to understanding the true authoritative reality behind his teachings, Gendun Chopel views the use of honorific titles not as hindrance at all but just another potential tool for expediently bringing others to the authoritative experience of ultimate truth that the Buddha intended.

Nonetheless, regardless of the difference in approaching and describing the nature of the founders of their tradition, the methodological similarity of situating those figures' teaching authority not in their words but in those teachings' efficaciousness in producing desired outcomes caused Chapter 4 to conclude with a series of unanswered questions. The first was whether (and if so, *how*) both thinkers' reinterpretation and new formulations of traditional terms and ideas about the teaching authority of their traditions' spiritual founders might impact the efficaciousness of those figures to speak to their own religious communities either positively or negatively. Similarly it raised the question of whether the reimagining of the nature and role of such prominent figures as Jesus of Nazareth or Śākyamuni Buddha can actually *hinder* the soteriological potential of these figures within those very communities that have traditionally recognized them as authoritative. In other words does Schillebeeckx's refusal to presuppose Christianity's traditional honorific titles to Jesus as (at least in part) the source of his epistemological authority, in fact, potentially make Jesus's teachings less effective in producing the orientation and pursuit toward the "orthopraxis" of working on the behalf of the oppressed and suffering—the ushering in of the "Kingdom of God"—that Schillebeeckx believes Jesus intended for his followers with his life and message? Or in the case of Gendun Chopel, might his willingness to negate the teachings of the Buddha that are commonly considered by other Buddhists to be the "definitive" (*nītārtha*) meanings of Śākyamuni's teachings actually cause some Buddhists to lose faith in the capacity of the Buddha's teachings at all, and so potentially *prevent* them from expediently realizing the ultimate negation that Gendun Chopel believes the Buddha intended with his words and actions? In other words, is Gendun Chopel's own approach toward understanding the Buddha's authority really a use of "skillful means" with regard to Buddhists or does it actually obstruct them from realizing what he believes to be the end goal of the Buddha's teachings? Lastly, then, these questions produce another further one as to whether such figures as Jesus of Nazareth and Śākyamuni Buddha indeed *require* an authority fundamentally distinct and superior to any other individual within their respective tradition's understanding of history. Or put somewhat more pointedly, do these figures need to be seen as the *exclusive* authority on knowledge in order to remain soteriologically meaningful and effective within their religious traditions?

Because of the general similarity in their methodological resituation of the different uses of language pertaining to their spiritual founders as displayed in Chapter 4, however, it is somewhat easy to imagine how both Schillebeeckx and Gendun Chopel might respond to the questions above in similar ways. Regarding the first question about the impact of new formulations of traditional images and ideas on the figures' authoritative voice among their followers, I believe Schillebeeckx would find a lot of resonance with Gendun Chopel's imagery of the Buddha's teachings being like "strings on bow" that need to be continually adjusted and retightened in every new moment and context in order for them to remain perpetually effective.[13] Thus both would certainly recognize the potential impact, both positively and negatively, that "resetting" these formulations might have within their own religious traditions, and yet at the same time both would also argue that this type of reformulation is fundamentally necessary if there is any hope of these figures' messages to remain relevant in new future contexts. Both would have to argue that the greater possible risk of negatively affecting these figures' voices within their communities would be not to make *any* adjustments *at all* based on the modern context the traditions find themselves in, and as such insisting on using outmoded and unrecognizable terminology from the past that can no longer make sense in the current historical and cultural contexts.

So consequently, this comparison between Gendun Chopel and Schillebeeckx around the presumed nature and role of the figures of Jesus of Nazareth and Śākyamuni Buddha as sources of truth within their traditions presents some interesting trajectories of inquiry to be explored by Catholic theologians in order to answer the other remaining questions above. In response to the question of the implications on the soteriological potency of both figures' messages within their communities, similarly to the rejoinder in the previous paragraph, I believe that both thinkers are fairly explicit about their opinions that the soteriological efficaciousness of these figures is *already* being negatively affected by the traditions' inability to speak to contemporary individuals with their at times outmoded and unintelligible vocabularies, meanings, and symbols from the past. And therefore, by placing Schillebeeckx's hermeneutic for contextually reinterpreting and appropriating past understandings of Jesus's message in comparative dialogue with Gendun Chopel's hermeneutic for deciphering the "very hidden" meaning behind all of the Buddha's teachings apart from the expedient means of contextual language and imagery, both thinkers collectively might challenge Catholic theologians to reconsider what it would mean and look like for Christians to reinterpret Jesus's soteriological message solely in terms of its pragmatic ability to assist current believers in finding hope amidst the contemporary instantiations of needless suffering, oppression, and meaninglessness apart from any presupposed notions of Jesus's divinity or superior ontological relation to ultimate reality. Furthermore, Gendun Chopel's own theory concerning the "very hidden" meaning of all truth both could reinforce and also add depth to Schillebeeckx's call for Catholic theologians to begin to actively and intentionally reimagine the traditional concept of "revelation" in terms of the "surprising" potential for traditional beliefs and symbols to take on new more understandable meanings in the contemporary context, rather than depicting it as the "unveiling" of static and unchanging "truths" that are buried in the layers of the historical past.[14]

---

13. Dge 'dun Chos 'phel, Jinpa, and Lopez, *Grains*, 407.
14. Schillebeeckx, *Jesus*, 622; *Christ*, 35, 47, 55; *Church*, 77. Cf. Thompson, x.

Moreover, and more significantly, Gendun Chopel's unique attempt to both maintain the traditional language and imagery of Śākyamuni Buddha while radically reconsidering the authoritative nature of his teachings I believe also pushes Schillebeeckx's challenge to other Catholic theologians to think of the New Testament as a collection of "local theologies"—which "have no greater value than the theologies of our own period"[15]—to its even further logical conclusion: that is, what would it look like in Catholic theology to consider Jesus's authority as being the first among many "local theologians"? Is the soteriological potency of Jesus's message necessarily tied to an assumption of his divinity? Schillebeeckx would surely respond to such an inquiry with a resounding "No!" Without denying Jesus's divinity, Schillebeeckx strongly believed that it was the efficacy of Jesus's life and message as a historical person that should guide individuals to a deeper understanding of his nature and relation to ultimate reality, not the other way around.[16] For Schillebeeckx, Jesus did not come teaching doctrines and theology, but instead encouraged the more practically oriented mindset of social and political resistance to all forms of oppression and suffering. And so, in light of this dialogue with Gendun Chopel, one could certainly see Schillebeeckx pressing other contemporary Catholic theologians on thinking of ways that Jesus can still be considered an authoritative source of truth to both individuals that recognize him as divine and those who do not alike.

Indeed, some Catholic theologians currently have already begun to give examples of what this type of authority might look like when fleshed out more fully in a specific cultural and philosophical context. One example of a theologian contemplating what such a new trajectory for understanding Jesus's authority might look like is the Indian Jesuit Michael Amaladoss in his 2006 book *The Asian Jesus*. In the portion of this work that addresses the image of Jesus as a contextual "teacher," and more specifically the possible "universal resonance" of his teachings as authoritative, Amaladoss notes:

> The teaching of Jesus does not give us information about heavenly realities. He does not speak about God's inner being or life. He does not describe life in heaven. He does not set up a ritual organization focused on the sacred. When he finally leaves a sign for his disciples to remember him by, it is the common gesture of sharing a meal in community, eating and drinking together in his memory. He tells us how to live and how to relate to one another and to God. He talks in the context of life in this world. He uses ordinary examples with which everyone is familiar: the lilies in the field, the sower going out to sow, the growing corn, the trees and the birds of the air that come to rest on them, the sea and those whose living depends on it, the suffering and the marginalized poor, unjust rulers, the loving and forgiving parent.[17]

---

15. Schillebeeckx, *God Is New*, 59.

16. Peter Hebblethwaite, *The New Inquisition?: The Case of Edward Schillebeeckx and Hans Küng*, 1st U.S. ed. (San Francisco: Harper & Row, 1980), 13.

17. Michael Amaladoss, *The Asian Jesus* (Maryknoll, NY: Orbis Books, 2006), 33.

Similarly, moving forward then, one can see how both Gendun Chopel's and Schillebeeckx's discussions about separating their spiritual founders' teaching authority from the later notions of their superior (and even exclusive) ontological status might help expound on ways that the soteriological messages of their teachings might still be deemed as true even by those who either cannot or choose not to recognize them as having any elevated ontological status within humanity. And therefore, through this comparative dialogue between Gendun Chopel and Schillebeeckx—even more when in conjunction with Christologies such as Michael Amaladoss's image of the contextual teacher—Catholic theologians might be able to see the possibility of future theologies and Christologies that can effectively argue for the authority of Jesus's teachings through their pragmatic efficaciousness to produce liberative actions among those who hear them, whether those hearers accept the epistemological judgment of Jesus as the divine Son of God or not.

IV. Apophaticism: Toward a Christian Metaphysic of Emptiness?

Finally, stemming from Chapter 4's comparison of how Gendun Chopel and Schillebeeckx situated the teaching authority of their spiritual founders in those figures' ability to produce a specific type of experiential knowledge, Chapter 5 then turned to focus on the question of what exactly each thinker meant by claiming that valid "knowledge" is fundamentally experiential rather than cognitive. Accordingly, what the analysis of the chapter uncovered was how Schillebeeckx and Gendun Chopel both seem to be in agreement as to the *nature* of that "experiential knowledge" of reality, although the means by which each thinker conceived individuals as gaining an awareness or "knowledge" of that reality differed. Namely, both thinkers claim this knowledge to be an awareness of the ineffable nature of reality that only comes from the experiential discovery of what reality is *not* through the failure of all language and concepts to encapsulate the many facets of reality's unpredictable and dynamic complexity. Hence, in conjunction with the argument of Chapter 2, this chapter claimed that both thinkers could rightly be said to hold an "apophatic" (though Gendun Chopel never used that phrase), or fundamentally *negative*, theory of valid knowledge. Once again, however, despite this general parallel in description, there still remained some significant differences in that similarity regarding the purpose and manifestation of this experientially negative form of knowledge.

Based primarily on the influence of the critical theorists Theodor Adorno, Jürgen Habermas, and Ernst Bloch, Chapter 5 exhibited how Schillebeeckx developed a theory of valid experiential knowledge emergent out of the dialectical interplay between the affirmation of belief through critical activity in the world and the negating theoretical evaluation of the effects of those actions. Borrowing from Bloch's theory of the *humanum*, Schillebeeckx argues that within the many experiences of severe suffering, oppression, and destruction that render all human theories of purpose, meaning, and order within historical existence seemingly nonsensical and invalid—what Schillebeeckx terms "negative contrast experiences"—there nonetheless remains an implicit and indeterminate hope of a better existence within, and understanding of, reality that never can be expressed in a positive fullness.[18] Hence for Schillebeeckx, it is in fact those very moments of failure, suffering, and injustice, which most acutely expose the fallibility and inaccuracy of all our theories about the nature of reality and how to improve humanity's existence within it, that possess "the hidden magnets of reality" that compel us to persistently pick up the pieces of our broken theories of supposed "truth" and "knowledge" and to craft new theories based on our now widened interpretative horizon of experience. Moreover, one must do this while remaining ever aware that those theories will only meet the same fate of eventually being shattered by reality's resistance to all human concepts and language as well.

Thus, although Schillebeeckx cites Adorno's "negative dialectics" as a foundational source of his own theory regarding the possibility of an apophatic knowledge of ultimate reality, Chapter 5's analysis of his theory showed how he significantly deviated from Adorno's theory by using the dialectics of negation in order to reassert the need for continually constructing new positive formulations of "knowledge" based on one's experiences of reality's utter resistance to human circumscription and control. Schillebeeckx's theory of the apophatic nature of valid knowledge, therefore, can be said to be primarily "experiential" in the sense that it is a knowledge derived from the experiences of testing one's theories through the application of appropriate actions in the world ("praxis") and observing their incessant incapacity for ever depicting the nature of reality in its full potentiality. Furthermore, it can be said to be "negative" in that it is grounded on one's negating experience of the reality as it really is as opposed to one's depictions and theories of it. And, finally, it can be considered dialectical because it situates the experience of true knowledge as indirectly emergent within the back-and-forth process of making and negating one's own affirmations about reality.

Gendun Chopel also derived his theory about the negative nature of any valid experiential knowledge from a recognition of what reality is not and how the ultimate nature of reality consistently eludes all descriptions of language and concepts. However, where on the one hand Schillebeeckx explicitly bases his process on a combination of Adorno's philosophical theory of negative dialectics and the religious mystical practice of the Christian tradition's *triplex via*, on the other Gendun Chopel establishes his theory of knowledge through negation within the rhetorical style and practice of the Gelukpa dialectics of debate. Hence, Gendun Chopel's theory of "apophatic knowledge" is distinct from Schillebeeckx's in at least two significant ways: first in his prioritization of the use of language and concepts in order to negate the validity of all linguistically based truth claims, and second in his thoroughgoing commitment to the process of negation to the exclusion of making any positive assertions about reality that one believes somehow might actually reflect the true nature of reality (even if only partly). Whereas Schillebeeckx's process of negation clearly prioritizes

---

18. Schillebeeckx, *Jesus*, 622.

the embodiment of ideas through practical actions of resistance (praxis), Gendun Chopel focuses his process of negation on one's active participation in the deconstruction of conceptual language through the dialectical rhetoric of debate. For Gendun Chopel, it is only through using language and logic "to make assertions for others" that one can effectively expose the utter limits of conceptual rationality and thereby guide others to their own experience of the "non-affirming negative" of true emptiness that is the nature of all reality. Moreover, since "valid knowledge" is fundamentally nonconceptual in nature, Gendun Chopel emphasizes that this process of negative dialectics through "making assertions for others" means that language must always be seen simply as a tool, or "expedient means," for dismantling other uses of language, and therefore should never be believed to be an accurate description of reality. And so ironically, it can be said that in some ways Gendun Chopel's theory of knowledge through negative dialectics might actually appear more akin to Adorno's theory than even Schillebeeckx's in that Gendun Chopel's system stresses that it is unnecessary, and indeed *unbeneficial*, for a dialectic of negation to produce positive affirmations about a "truth" or "knowledge" of reality. Still these two methodological differences notwithstanding, in this section I will briefly argue that the broader analogous vein that these two systems of thought share might serve as the basis for a new (or probably more appropriately "*renewed*") trajectory in contemporary Catholic theology that situates the focus of its project on negating the asserted "meanings" or "truths" behind traditional doctrines, images, and spiritual practices with the intention of possibly guiding other believers to a profound experience of the *via eminentiae* and, in turn, a strengthened conviction in the judgment of whether there is an ultimate source and purpose to all reality despite one's negation of the validity of all conceptual beliefs about ultimate reality.

And yet, the concluding question of Chapter 5 still remains as to whether a system of religious philosophy that is rooted in a conviction of a negative or "apophatic" experience of reality as being the primary authoritative source for all other religious faith and knowledge can be religiously efficacious in evoking a spirituality of committed belief and action among everyday believers. Indeed some would certainly argue that by negating the correspondence between humans' conceptual language and reality itself, those various symbols would lose the power to evoke faith and incite the type of action and anticipation that Schillebeeckx's theology wishes to promote. This is where I believe Gendun Chopel's point of view can really contribute to the comparison. Since, unlike Schillebeeckx, Gendun Chopel not only does not emphasize the idea that his process of negation should bring about some form of positive affirmation but in fact actively *discourages* it, he accordingly highlights the ultimate negation itself (the awareness of emptiness) as the pinnacle and the most profound moment of an individual's awareness of reality itself. Thus, through a comparative dialogue with Gendun Chopel's system and mindset toward grounding all valid experiential knowledge of ultimate reality through the negation of all propositions, images, and ideas, Schillebeeckx's own system of epistemology might be able to expand its vocabulary and interpretative horizon in order to make a more nuanced and practical theory of an affective Catholic spirituality based on the negation of all theological language and knowledge.

As already discussed in the previous chapter and briefly alluded to again in this section, Schillebeeckx's main reason for insisting on the need for an explicitly positive affirmation about the nature of reality as a result of the dialectical process of negation is that he wants to prioritize the need for a direct responsive action to emerge out of the negative experience of resistance in reality to humanity's circumscription and attempts to control it. However if one analogously applies Gendun Chopel's theory concerning the use of language to deconstruct and destabilize the meaning of all language to Schillebeeckx's theory of the necessary praxis in response to the experience of the absolute negation, then one might be able to see how praxis could still be necessary and directly inspired out of a negative experience and knowledge of reality while not having to insist on it being a positive affirmation about that reality. In other words, just as Gendun Chopel insists upon the use of language and concepts in order to precisely deconstruct the logic behind all linguistic and conceptual knowledge, Schillebeeckx's system could also say that one must use responsive action to resist, expose, and destabilize the reification of the structures of oppression, injustice, and suffering within society. And in this way, Gendun Chopel's theory of the need for a dialectics of negation all the way down as the only means to an experiential awareness of the non-affirming negative or complete "absence" that is ultimate reality can present Schillebeeckx with a system of spirituality in which an experience and knowledge of ultimate reality can be based on the necessary negative dialectics of praxis, while also allowing Schillebeeckx to be more consistent in his resistance to the reification of all images, theories, and traditions of truth (including his own) as being somehow more reflective of reality itself.

This technique of viewing the purpose of theology as being primarily, if not exclusively, a systematic process of negation through thought and action then could set up a type of theology and spirituality that might more readily speak to the current postmodern apprehensions toward essentialist claims about the nature of reality. In a way very resonant with the *triplex via* and the various iterations of negative theology throughout the Christian tradition, this dialectical spirituality of the conventional God could use the non-realist notions of Gendun Chopel's Madhyamaka epistemology to situate the purpose of all theological reflection in the absolute negation of one's beliefs and images about ultimate reality. Hence, as a result of this form of theology that could possibly search for "God" in terms of Gendun Chopel's "non-affirming negative" or ultimate "absence," one could see the evocative spiritual power of theological deconstruction and negation that Wesley Wildman speaks of when he describes the potential "mystical awareness" within a modern theology of "the profound abyss":

> But when we draw close to this dark place, in the midst of the blazing sunshine of the social construction of reality, we find a shady spot under the leafy boughs of an institutionally impossible tree, floating above an impossibly profound

abyss. In that strange place, people gather who see ultimacy most clearly for what it is. They can build nothing and sustain nothing, at least not under the tree. But they can be with one another, speechless and joking, watching and listening. Here there is no liberalism or conservatism, no institutions and no cultural expressions, for it is the place of rest from all such exertions. But it is also a peculiarly demanding resting place because of its impossibly natural rules. There is no dissembling there, no deflection or distraction, and desperation is never defused; rather everything is allowed to be what it will be, in the presence of the few who gather there.

This shady refuge can never be institutionalized. It needs no defense because people can always find it in the cracks of ordinary and extraordinary institutional achievements. It is the underside habitation of spiritual beings in every religious and cultural tradition that has ever existed. It is a fecund place, spilling over with the wisdom of not taking ourselves so seriously. It unobtrusively nurtures the bright topsides of constructive institutional ventures. The traditions of ideas and poetry that describe this place are another way to find it, and those traditions would perish were it not for the dominant top-side religions that bear forward everything with them, including the deep underside traditions that are almost indistinguishable from one another across religions and cultures. To speak of this shady place is to utter the last word before plunging into the abyss of infinite darkness into which all human ventures plunge, into which all human beings plunge, in due course.[19]

This theological process in which a metaphysical awareness of ultimate reality as the "abyss," "non-affirming negative," "ultimate absence," or even "emptiness" behind all reality that Christians identify with the title of "God" might supply a way for theologians to pick up Schillebeeckx's thought and heed his call for the development of a "non-essentialist metaphysic" in which knowledge of God is not established as the starting point of theological reflection but as the always elusive endpoint in the future. This type of theology, therefore, would necessarily be connected to, and emergent out of, the spiritual experience of the absolute reality beyond all language and concepts. Accordingly, theological reflection would be a primarily dialectical process that seeks to expose the contingency, fallibility, and relativity of all beliefs and theological truth claims through the historicization of thought and subversive social action until one is confronted with the reality of the complete absence of concepts and meanings in ultimate reality. However, as Wildman mentions above, this experience of the comforting darkness of reality will always be found to be impossible to sustain. Thus one is compelled to interpret and explain this negative experience, and as such will fuel the construction of new concepts and conventions in order to more accurately formulate this experience of

---

19. Wesley J. Wildman, "The Ambiguous Heritage and Perpetual Promise of Liberal Theology," *American Journal of Theology & Philosophy* 32, no. 1 (January 2011): 61.

reality, thereby reigniting the need for the theological negation of these ideas and starting the process of deconstruction all over again.

Still if some theologians are too uncomfortable with depicting God in the purely negative terms of the absence or negation of all theological meaning, then Schillebeeckx's language of portraying God from the humanly ontic perspective of the dynamic, indeterminate, and therefore ineffable potential of the always oncoming future might help translate this "non-essentialist metaphysic" of emptiness into more explicitly Christian affirmations. According to this way of thinking, since what one intends by "God" is the dynamic and indeterminate process of history, then all conceptions of God and all theological meanings of history can be relativized and exposed as contextually provisional while not subverting the judgment that there is a reality behind and driving all history and meaning. One example of a Catholic theologian already pursuing a similar trajectory of thought in this area is John Haught's discussion of God as "The Power of the Future" in his book *God after Darwin*. While he admittedly borrows much of his terminology and concepts from Alfred North Whitehead and process thought, Haught argues that by envisioning God as the relativizing force of the "Absolute Future" theologians might be able to set forth a metaphysics that can withstand the judgment of absolute relativism presupposed in many people's reading of evolutionary theory. Certainly echoing some of Schillebeeckx's own sentiments, Haught aptly summarizes this position at one point when he writes,

> A metaphysics of the future is already implicit in a certain kind of religious experience. Paul Tillich describes it as a sense of being grasped by the "coming order": "The *coming* order is always coming, shaking *this* order, fighting with it, conquering it and conquered by it. The coming order is always at hand. But one can never say: 'It is here! It is there!' One can never grasp it. *But one can be grasped by it*" … In the experience of faith it is the "future" that comes to meet us, takes hold of us, and makes us new. We may call this future, at least in what Rahner calls its "absolute" depth, by the name "God." In biblical circles the very heart of authentic faith consists of the total orientation of consciousness toward the coming of God, the ultimately real. Beyond all of our provisional or relative futures there lies an "Absolute Future" … Accordingly, by a "metaphysics of the future" I mean quite simply the philosophical expression of the intuition—admittedly religious in origin—that all things receive their being from out of an inexhaustibly resourceful "future" that we may call "God." This same intuition also entails the notion that the cosmic past and present are in some sense given their own status by the always arriving but also always unavailable future … Only a brief reflection suffices to convince us that the past is gone and remains irretrievable, and the present vanishes before we can ever grasp hold of it. The "future," on the other hand, is always arriving faithfully at the green edge of each moment, bringing with it the possibility of new being.[20]

---

20. John F. Haught, *God after Darwin: A Theology of Evolution*, 2nd ed. (Boulder, CO: Westview Press, 2008), 97–8. Cf. Paul Tillich, *The Shaking of the Foundations*

This passage clearly displays how Schillebeeckx's language of "God as future," or the persistent "surprising more" behind all our ideas, might be further developed from the intuitive sense he consistently refers to in his writings using various titles for God. Furthermore, it also shows how thinking of metaphysics in terms of the potential of the "future" can have a relativizing effect on Christian conceptions of the nature of "God," or "ultimate reality," in a similar fashion to the negative theological dialectics possible through a comparison and dialogue between Schillebeeckx and Gendun Chopel. Moving forward, then, whether through the use of purely negative language of "absence" and "emptiness" or the positive translation of those terms into the relativizing force of the dynamic and indeterminate nature of the future, either way this comparison between Schillebeeckx and Gendun Chopel regarding the negative ground of all religious knowledge and experience can certainly make new contributions to contemporary discourses in metaphysics that seek to acknowledge the relativism of all conceptual knowledge while not demanding an ultimate judgment of total relativism to all reality.

V. Conclusion: A Constructed Dialogue with Real Consequences for Thought and Practice

So in conclusion, this chapter returned to the lingering questions posed by the previous three chapters so as to reconsider the potential broader implications of this comparison between Gendun Chopel's and Edward Schillebeeckx's religious epistemology on more recent trajectories in contemporary theology. It utilized both thinkers' deep suspicions toward all conceptual expressions of belief and traditional institutions in order to present a possible understanding of traditional authority that at the same time both requires the theoretical regulation and social critique from its followers and also acknowledges the necessary role of traditions to also check the limited and self-interested perspectives of individual believers and local communities. Furthermore, it cited Dean's theory of "sacred conventions" as another future avenue to explore as to how contemporary theologians might

---

(New York: Charles Scribner's Sons, 1996), 27 (emphasis added). In this passage Haught also references the writings of Hans Küng and Jürgen Moltmann to highlight the major influence of Ernst Bloch's philosophy on contemporary theology. This point is particularly fitting and significant for our discussion of Haught's resonance with Schillebeeckx's "non-essentialist metaphysics" because of the previous two chapters' discussions of Bloch's similar influence on Schillebeeckx's own thought. This clearly helps explain the intuitive resemblance between Haught's and Schillebeeckx's metaphysical theories, and further links them on an analogous trajectory of theological thought and method. Moreover, for Küng's brief summary of Bloch's broad influence on contemporary theology, see Hans Küng, *Eternal Life?: Life after Death as a Medical, Philosophical, and Theological Problem* (Garden City, NY: Doubleday, 1984), 213–14.

be able to take Gendun Chopel's radical understanding of the contingency of all thought and language seriously while not demanding an ultimate judgment of an individualist relativism to human existence. Next, it focused on assessing how both Schillebeeckx and Gendun Chopel interpreted the teaching authority of the historical founders of their traditions in light of both thinkers' suspicion of language and concepts to display how these figures can still be viewed as authoritative among their respective followers apart from an assumption of their ontological priority. In conjunction with their two theories on this matter, this section concluded by referring to Amaladoss's imagery of Jesus's teaching authority being that of a contextually located teacher to show how Gendun Chopel might help frame Schillebeeckx's Christology in terms of Jesus as the first among many "local theologians." And finally, it observed the similarities and differences in each thinker's understanding of the negative or "apophatic" nature of all valid experiential knowledge, and also each of their own demands for the use of negative dialectics to bring about that valid negative experience of ultimate reality. Then, similarly to the previous two sections, this section concluded by briefly alluding to the thought of two more recent contemporary theologians—Wildman and Haught—as a means to depict how a theologian might use the comparison of Gendun Chopel's and Schillebeeckx's theories of the ineffable nature of ultimate reality in articulating the transcendent nature of God in both more apophatic (Wildman's "abyss") and more constructive or cataphatic (Haught's "Absolute Future") terms.

Moreover in addition to that primary purpose of this final discussion, this chapter also consistently used all three of these topical comparisons to allude back to the original question of this project as presented in its introduction: whether the apparent dichotomy between the commitment of religious belief and an acceptance of anti-representationalist theories of truth truly demands a choice between a trusting realism of faith or the judgment of an absolute nihilistic relativism. In accordance with the analyses and interpretations of the prior four chapters, this final analysis attempted to gesture toward not just one but actually *three* possible alternatives, or "middle ways," on the spectrum between those two epistemological extremes. First, it discussed Schillebeeckx's critically realist epistemology as one method of acknowledging the role of the social construction in all truth claims (and the subsequent level of relativity implied by that), while nevertheless still logically claiming an ability to adjudicate between the validity of conventions based on their at least partial (even if indirect) grounding in an experience of reality. Second, it presented Gendun Chopel's non-realist religious epistemology as another viable alternative to the false realist–relativist dichotomy. This is because, although Gendun Chopel takes a stance more akin to contemporary anti-representationalist epistemologies on the ontic (or "conventional") level of everyday life and experience, he still nonetheless was able to continually maintain a belief in an ultimate truth to all reality, as well as the potential for that truth to be known by individuals, on a separate ontological level. Lastly, then, all three of the preceding sections above also attempted to finish by negotiating and employing elements from both thinkers' systems—alongside other contemporary theological voices—in order to highlight possible future avenues for theological reflection that might still maintain a recognition of the valid authority of religious traditions, the spiritual founders of those traditions, and the personal experiences of their individual followers, regardless of one's judgment as to whether "truth" is something purely made, purely found, or something in between. Hence through this long process of comparison, this project sought to show how Ratzinger's dichotomous fear of the adverse impact that the supposed "dictatorship of relativism" in contemporary culture might have on religious belief was clearly overstated. More than just that, however, it hoped to outline how Schillebeeckx and Gendun Chopel both individually and collectively might be able to more effectively present a true "middle way" of religious epistemology and spiritual vitality: one that might assist contemporary believers in negotiating the tensions between wisdom and ignorance, certainty and doubt, faith and skepticism, that seem to permeate so much of the contemporary postmodern culture. And in doing so, it set forth three different paths for a contemporary theology that might willingly call into question everything one knows because of, rather than in spite of, one's religious convictions.[21]

---

21. Lopez, *Madman*, xi. The last few sentences were a clear play on Lopez's description of Gendun Chopel's Madhyamaka epistemology as presenting "his own middle way, one between wisdom and ignorance, certainty and doubt, faith and skepticism—a middle way that calls everything we know into question because, rather than in spite of, the enlightenment of the Buddha."

BIBLIOGRAPHY

Abe, Masao. "Kenotic God and Dynamic Sunyata." In *The Emptying God: A Buddhist-Jewish-Christian Conversation*, edited by John B. Cobb and Christopher Ives, 3–65. Maryknoll, NY: Orbis Books, 1990.
Amaladoss, Michael. *The Asian Jesus*. Maryknoll, NY: Orbis Books, 2006.
Bauckham, Richard, "Jürgen Moltmann," *The Modern Theologians*, I, 293–310 (294).
Bergoglio, Jorge Mario, and Abraham Skorka. *On Heaven and Earth: Pope Francis on Faith, Family, and the Church in the Twenty-First Century*, edited by Random House Large Print. New York: Random House, 2013.
Borgman, Erik. *Edward Schillebeeckx: A Theologian in His History*. Translated by John Bowden. Vol. I: *A Catholic Theology of Culture* (1914–65). New York: Continuum, 2003.
Bowden, John Stephen. *Edward Schillebeeckx: Portrait of a Theologian*. London: SCM Press, 1983.
Braudel, Fernand. *On History*. Translated by Sarah Matthews. Chicago: University of Chicago Press, 1982.
Buescher, John B. *Echoes from an Empty Sky: The Origins of the Buddhist Doctrine of the Two Truths*. Ithaca, NY: Snow Lion, 2005.
Bultmann, Rudolf. *The New Testament and Mythology and Other Basic Writings*. Translated by Schubert M. Ogden. Philadelphia: Fortress Press, 1984.
Cabezón, José Ignacio. *Buddhism and Language: A Study of Indo-Tibetan Scholasticism*. Albany: State University of New York Press, 1994.
Chenu, Marie-Dominique. *Toward Understanding Saint Thomas*. Chicago: H. Regnery, 1964.
Chöphel, Dge 'dun, and Donald S. Lopez. *In the Forest of Faded Wisdom: 104 Poems by Gendun Chopel, a Bilingual Edition*. Chicago: University of Chicago Press, 2009.
Chöphel, Dge 'dun, Thupten Jinpa, and Donald S. Lopez, *Grains of Gold: Tales of a Cosmopolitan Traveler*. Chicago: University of Chicago Press, 2014.
Clooney, Francis X. *Comparative Theology: Deep Learning across Religious Borders*. Malden, MA: Wiley-Blackwell, 2010.
The Cowherds. *Moonshadows: Conventional Truth in Buddhist Philosophy*. New York: Oxford University Press, 2011.
Davaney, Sheila Greeve. *Pragmatic Historicism: A Theology for the Twenty-First Century*. Albany: State University of New York Press, 2000.
De Petter, D. M. "Impliciete Intuitie." *Tijdschrift voor Philosophie* 1, no. 1 (1939): 84–105.
Dean, William D. *The Religious Critic in American Culture*. Albany: State University of New York Press, 1994.
"Declaration on the Relation of the Church to Non-Christian Religions." In *Vatican Council II: The Conciliar and Post Conciliar Documents*, edited by Austin Flannery, 738–42. New York: Costello, 1988.
Decosimo, David. "Comparison and the Ubiquity of Resemblance." *Journal of the American Academy of Religion* 78, no. 1 (2010): 226–58.

Dilthey, Wilhelm, Rudolf A. Makkreel, and Frithjof Rodi. *Hermeneutics and the Study of History*. Princeton, NJ: Princeton University Press, 1996.

Dreyfus, Georges B. J. *Recognizing Reality: Dharmakīrti's Philosophy and Its Tibetan Interpretations*. Albany: State University of New York Press, 1997.

Dreyfus, Georges B. J. *The Sound of Two Hands Clapping: The Education of a Tibetan Buddhist Monk*. Berkeley: University of California Press, 2003.

Eck, Diana L. *A New Religious America: How a "Christian Country" Has Now Become the World's Most Religiously Diverse Nation*, 1st ed. San Francisco: HarperSanFrancisco, 2001.

Eckel, Malcolm David. *To See the Buddha: A Philosopher's Quest for the Meaning of Emptiness*, 1st ed. San Francisco: HarperSanFrancisco, 1992.

Ellis, Marc H., and Otto Maduro. *Expanding the View: Gustavo Gutiérrez and the Future of Liberation Theology*. Maryknoll, NY: Orbis Books, 1990.

Fatula, M. A. "Dogmatic Pluralism and the Noetic Dimension of Unity of Faith." *The Thomist* 48 (1984): 409–32.

Geertz, Clifford. *The Interpretation of Cultures: Selected Essays*. London: Hutchinson, 1975.

Gyatso, Janet. "Moments of Tibetan Modernity: Methods and Assumptions." In *Mapping the Modern Tibet: Proceedings of the Eleventh Seminar of the International Association for Tibetan Studies*, edited by Gary Tuttle, 1–44. Andiast, Switzerland: The International Institute for Tibetan and Buddhist Studies, 2011.

Haight S. J., Roger. *Ecclesial Existence*. 3 vols. Christian Community in History, vol. 3. New York: Continuum, 2008.

Harrison, Paul. "Commemoration and Identification in *Buddhānusmṛti*." In *In the Mirror of Memory: Reflections on Mindfulness and Rememberance in Indian and Tibetan Buddhism*, edited by Janet Gyatso, 215–31. New York: State University of New York Press, 1992.

Harrison, Paul. "Mediums and Messages: Reflections on the Production of Mahāyāna Sūtras." *Eastern Buddhist* 35, no. 2 (2003): 115–51.

Haskell, Thomas L. "The Curious Persistence of Rights Talk in the 'Age of Interpretation.'" *Journal of American History* 74, no. 3 (December 1987): 984–1012.

Haught, John F. *God after Darwin: A Theology of Evolution*, 2nd ed. Boulder, CO: Westview Press, 2008.

Hebblethwaite, Peter. *The New Inquisition?: The Case of Edward Schillebeeckx and Hans Küng*. 1st U.S. ed. San Francisco: Harper & Row, 1980.

Hilkert, Mary Catherine. "Hermeneutics of History in the Theology of Edward Schillebeeckx." *The Thomist* 51 (1987): 97–145.

Hopkins, Jeffrey, and Gendün Chöpel. *Tibetan Arts of Love: Sex, Orgasm & Spiritual Healing*. Translated by Jeffrey Hopkins and Dorje Yudon Yuthok. Ithaca, NY: Snow Lion, 1992.

Huber, Toni. *The Holy Land Reborn: Pilgrimage & the Tibetan Reinvention of Buddhist India*. Chicago: University of Chicago Press, 2008.

Jensen, Jeppe Sinding. *The Study of Religion in a New Key: Theoretical and Philosophical Soundings in the Comparative and General Study of Religion*. Aarhus: Aarhus University Press, 2003.

Jinpa, Thupten. *Self, Reality and Reason in Tibetan Philosophy: Tsongkhapa's Quest for the Middle Way*. New York: RoutledgeCurzon, 2002.

Keenan, John P., Sydney Copp, Lansing Davis, and Buster G. Smith. *Grounding Our Faith in a Pluralist World: With a Little Help from Nāgārjuna*. Eugene, OR: Wipf & Stock, 2009.

Kennedy, Philip. "Continuity Underlying Discontinuity: Schillebeeckx's Philosophical Background." *New Black Friars* 70 (1989): 264–77.
Kennedy, Philip. *Deus Humanissimus: The Knowability of God in the Theology of Edward Schillebeeckx*, Ökumenische Beihefte Zur Freiburger Zeitschrift Für Philosophie Und Theologie 22. Fribourg, Switzerland: University of Chicago Press, 1993.
Kennedy, Philip. *Schillebeeckx*, Outstanding Christian Thinkers. Collegeville, MN: Liturgical Press, 1993.
Knitter, Paul F. *Introducing Theologies of Religions*. Maryknoll, NY: Orbis Books, 2002.
Knitter, Paul F. *One Earth, Many Religions: Multifaith Dialogue and Global Responsibility*. Maryknoll, NY: Orbis Books, 1995.
Kuhn, Thomas S. *The Structure of Scientific Revolutions*, 3rd ed. Chicago: University of Chicago Press, 1996.
Küng, Hans. *Eternal Life?: Life after Death as a Medical, Philosophical, and Theological Problem*. Garden City, NY: Doubleday, 1984.
Lane, Dermot A. *Foundations for a Social Theology: Praxis, Process and Salvation*, 9–18. Dublin: Paulist, 1981.
Lefebure, Leo D. *The Buddha and the Christ: Explorations in Buddhist and Christian Dialogue*. Maryknoll, NY: Orbis Books, 1993.
Lefebure, Leo D. *True and Holy: Christian Scripture and Other Religions*. Maryknoll, NY: Orbis Books, 2014.
Lindbeck, George A. *The Nature of Doctrine: Religion and Theology in a Postliberal Age*, 1st ed. Philadelphia: Westminster Press, 1984.
Lonergan, Bernard J. F. *Verbum: Word and Idea in Aquinas*, 22 vols., Collected Works of Bernard Lonergan, vol. 2. Toronto: Published by University of Toronto Press for Lonergan Research Institute of Regis College, 1980. Reprint, 2005.
Lopez, Donald S. *Buddhist Hermeneutics*. Honolulu: University of Hawaii Press, 1988.
Lopez, Donald S. *Buddhism & Science: A Guide for the Perplexed*. Chicago: University of Chicago Press, 2008.
Lopez Jr., Donald S. "Dge 'Dun Chos 'Phel's Position on Vigrahavyāvartanī 29." In *Buddhist Forum*, edited by Tadeusz Skorupski and Ulrich Pagel, vol. 3, 161–85. London: School of Oriental and African Studies, 1994.
Lopez, Donald S. *Gendun Chopel: Tibet's First Modern Artist*. 1st ed. Chicago: Trace Foundation's Latse Library Serindia Publications, 2013.
Lopez, Donald S., and Dge dun chos phel. *The Madman's Middle Way: Reflections on Reality of the Tibetan Monk Gendun Chopel*. Chicago: University of Chicago Press, 2006.
Lyotard, Jean François. *The Postmodern Condition: A Report on Knowledge*. Minneapolis: University of Minnesota Press, 1984.
Mengele, Irmgard. *Dge-'dun-Chos-'phel: A Biography of the 20th Century Tibetan Scholar*. Dharamsala, HP: Library of Tibetan Works and Archives, 1999.
Mettepenningen, Jürgen. *Nouvelle Théologie – New Theology: Inheritor of Modernism, Precursor of Vatican II*. New York: T&T Clark, 2010.
Miller, James. "Review of *Overcoming Our Evil: Human Nature and Spiritual Exercises in Xunzi and Augustine*, by Aaron Stalnaker." *Theological Studies Review* 69, no. 1 (2008): 200–1.
Neville, Robert C. *The Human Condition*. Albany: State University of New York Press, 2001.
Neville, Robert C. *Religious Truth*. Albany: State University of New York Press, 2001.
Neville, Robert C. *Ultimate Realities*. Albany: State University of New York Press, 2001.

Nicholson, Hugh. "The New Comparative Theology and the Problem of Theological Hegemonism." In *The New Comparative Theology: Interreligious Insights from the Next Generation*, edited by Francis X. Clooney, xix, 208. New York: T&T Clark, 2010.

O'Donovan S. J., Leo. "Salvation as the Center of Theology." *Interpretation* 36 (1982): 192–6.

Palmer, Richard E. *Hermeneutics: Interpretation Theory in Schleiermacher, Dilthey, Heidegger, and Gadamer*. Evanston, IL: Northwestern University Press, 1969.

Paul VI, Pope, "*Ecclesiam Suam*," http://www.vatican.va/holy_father/paul_vi/encyclicals/documents/hf_p-vi_enc_06081964_ecclesiam_en.html (2014).

Perdue, Daniel, and Byams-pa-rgya-mtsho Phur-bu-lcog. *Debate in Tibetan Buddhism*. Ithaca, NY: Snow Lion, 1992.

Portier, William L. "Schillebeeckx's Dialogue with Critical Theory." *The Ecumenist* 21 (1983): 20–7.

Portier, William L. "Edward Schillebeeckx as Critical Theorist: The Impact of Neo-Marxist Social Thought on His Recent Theology." *The Thomist* 48 (1984): 341–67.

Ratzinger, Joseph. "Pro Eligendo Romano Pontifice," http://www.vatican.va/gpII/documents/homily-pro-eligendo-pontifice_20050418_en.html (2014).

Rego, Aloysius. *Suffering and Salvation: The Salvific Meaning of Suffering in the Later Theology of Edward Schillebeeckx*. Dudely, MA: Eerdmans, 2006.

Rorty, Richard. *Contingency, Irony, and Solidarity*. New York: Cambridge University Press, 1989.

Ruegg, D. Seyfort. "A Tibetan's Odyssey: A Review Article." *Journal of the Royal Asiatic Society of Great Britain and Ireland* 121, no. 2 (1989): 304–11.

Schillebeeckx, Edward. *Christ, the Sacrament of the Encounter with God*. New York: Sheed and Ward, 1963.

Schillebeeckx, Edward. "Exegesis, Dogmatics, and the Development of Dogma." In *Dogmatic vs. Biblical Theology*, edited by H. Vorgrimler, 115–45. Baltimore: Helicon, 1964.

Schillebeeckx, Edward. *Revelation and Theology*. Translated by N. D. Smith. Vol. I: His Theological Soundings. New York: Sheed and Ward, 1967.

Schillebeeckx, Edward. *The Eucharist*. New York: Sheed and Ward, 1968.

Schillebeeckx, Edward. *God the Future of Man*. New York: Sheed and Ward, 1968.

Schillebeeckx, Edward. *Revelation and Theology*. Translated by N. D. Smith. His Theological Soundings, Vol. 2. New York: Sheed and Ward, 1968.

Schillebeeckx, Edward. *God and Man*, His Theological Soundings, Vol. 3. New York: Sheed and Ward, 1969.

Schillebeeckx, Edward. *World and Church*. New York: Sheed and Ward, 1971.

Schillebeeckx, Edward. *The Mission of the Church*. New York: Seabury Press, 1973.

Schillebeeckx, Edward. *The Understanding of Faith: Interpretation and Criticism*. New York: Seabury Press, 1974.

Schillebeeckx, Edward. "Critique Du Monde Sur L'obéissance Chrétienne Et Réponse Chrétienne." *Concilium* 159 (1980): 25–41.

Schillebeeckx, Edward. "Erfahrung Und Glaube." In *Christlicher Glaube in Moderner Gesellschaft*, 25, 72–116. Friedburg: Herder, 1982.

Schillebeeckx, Edward. *Interim Report on the Books Jesus & Christ*. Translated by John Bowden. New York: Crossroad, 1982.

Schillebeeckx, Edward. *God among Us: The Gospel Proclaimed*. New York: Crossroad, 1983.

Schillebeeckx, Edward. *Theologisch Geloofsverstaan Anno 1983*, 3–24. Baarn: Nelissen, 1983.

Schillebeeckx, Edward. *Ministry: Leadership in the Community of Jesus Christ*. Translated by John Bowden. New York: Crossroad, 1984.
Schillebeeckx, Edward. *The Church with a Human Face: A New and Expanded Theology of Ministry*. New York: Crossroad, 1985.
Schillebeeckx, Edward. *Jesus in Our Western Culture: Mysticism, Ethics, and Politics*. 1st British ed. London: SCM, 1987.
Schillebeeckx, Edward. *Church: The Human Story of God*. New York: Crossroad, 1990.
Schillebeeckx, Edward. *For the Sake of the Gospel*. New York: Crossroad, 1990.
Schillebeeckx, Edward. *Christ: The Experience of Jesus as Lord*. Translated by John Bowden. New York: Crossroad, 1993.
Schillebeeckx, Edward. *Jesus: An Experiment in Christology*. Translated by Hubert Hopkins. New York: Crossroad, 1995.
Schillebeeckx, Edward. *The Language of Faith: Essays on Jesus, Theology, and the Church*, Concilium Series. Maryknoll, NY: Orbis Books, 1995.
Schillebeeckx, Edward. "Prologue: Human God-Talk and God's Silence." In *The Praxis of the Reign of God: An Introduction to the Theology of Edward Schillebeeckx*, edited by Mary Catherine Hilkert and Robert J. Schreiter, ix–xviii. New York: Fordham University Press, 2002.
Schillebeeckx, Edward, Huub Oosterhuis, and Piet Hoogeveen. *God Is New Each Moment*. New York: Continuum, 2004.
Schillebeeckx, Edward, T. M. Schoof, and Catholic Church. Congregatio pro Doctrina Fidei. *The Schillebeeckx Case: Official Exchange of Letters and Documents in the Investigation of Fr. Edward Schillebeeckx, O.P. By the Sacred Congregation for the Doctrine of the Faith, 1976-1980*. New York: Paulist Press, 1984.
Schillebeeckx, Edward, and Robert J. Schreiter. *The Schillebeeckx Reader*. New York: Crossroad, 1984.
Schillebeeckx, Edward, and Francesco Strazzari. *I Am a Happy Theologian: Conversations with Francesco Strazzari*. New York: Crossroad, 1994.
Schleiermacher, Friedrich. *Hermeneutics and Criticism and Other Writings*. New York: Cambridge University Press, 1998.
Schwöbel, Christoph. "Wolfhart Pannenberg." In *The Modern Theologians*, edited by David F. Ford, I, 257–92, 2 vols. Oxford: Blackwell, 1989.
Simut, Corneliu C. *Critical Essays on Edward Schillebeeckx's Theology: From Theological Radicalism to Philosophical Non-Realism*. Eugene, OR: Wipf & Stock, 2010.
Smid, Robert W. *Methodologies of Comparative Philosophy: The Pragmatist and Process Traditions*. Albany: State University of New York Press, 2009.
Smith, Jonathan Z. "Religion, Religions, Religious." In *Critical Terms for Religious Studies*, edited by Mark C. Taylor, 269–84. Chicago: University of Chicago Press, 1998.
Stalnaker, Aaron. *Overcoming Our Evil: Human Nature and Spiritual Exercises in Xunzi and Augustine*. Washington, DC: Georgetown University Press, 2006.
Stoddard, Heather. *Le Mendiant De L'amdo*, Recherches Sur La Haute Asie. Paris: Société d'ethnographie, 1985.
Thompson, Daniel Speed. *The Language of Dissent: Edward Schillebeeckx on the Crisis of Authority in the Catholic Church*. Notre Dame, IN: University of Notre Dame Press, 2003.
Tillemans, Tom J. F. *Scripture, Logic, Language: Essays on Dharmakirti and His Tibetan Successors*. Boston, MA: Wisdom, 1999.
Tillich, Paul. *The Shaking of the Foundations*. New York: Charles Scribner's Sons, 1996.

Truett Anderson, Walt. "Introduction: What's Going on Here?" In *The Truth about the Truth: De-Confusing and Re-Constructing the Postmodern World*, edited by Walt Truett Anderson, x, 260. New York: Putnam, 1995.

Van Erp, Stephan. "Implicit Faith: Philosophical Theology after Schillebeeckx." In *Edward Schillebeeckx and Contemporary Theology*, edited by Lieven Boeve, Frederiek Depoortere and Stephan Van Erp, 209–23. New York: T&T Clark International, 2010.

Westerhoff, Jan. *The Dispeller of Disputes: Nāgārjuna's Vigrahavyāvartanī*. New York: Oxford University Press, 2010.

Wildman, Wesley J. "The Ambiguous Heritage and Perpetual Promise of Liberal Theology." *American Journal of Theology & Philosophy* 32, no. 1 (January 2011): 43–61.

Williams, Paul. *Buddhism: Critical Concepts in Religious Studies*. 8 vols. Critical Concepts in Religious Studies. New York: Routledge, 2005.

Wittgenstein, Ludwig, G. E. M. Anscombe, P. M. S. Hacker, and Joachim Schulte. *Philosophische Untersuchungen = Philosophical Investigations*. Rev. 4th ed. Malden, MA: Wiley-Blackwell, 2009.

Wuthnow, Robert. *America and the Challenges of Religious Diversity*. Princeton, NJ: Princeton University Press, 2005.

INDEX

Note: The letter "n" following page number refers to footnote.

Abe, Masao, 25 n.8
absolute Being concept, 41
absolute limit, 59 n.179
Adornment, 36–7, 37 n.71, 38 n.75,
  39 n.82, 40 n.85, 48, 49–50, 51
  nn.142–4, 52 n.146, 53 n.151, 59–60,
  60 nn.181, 183, 61 nn.189, 190, 62
  nn.195, 196, 198, 63 n.203, 75, 79, 80
  nn.70, 74, 81, 82 n.79, 83 nn.84, 86,
  88, 84 n.90, 85 n.96, 97, 97 n.164, 98
  n.170, 99–100, 99 nn.174, 177, 100
  n.180, 103 nn.189, 190, 192, 193, 133,
  133 n.94, 150, 157, 157 n.197, 177,
  182 n.78, 184, 185 n.87, 186 n.94,
  201 n.171, 203 n.180, 203 n.183, 204
  n.187, 205, 208, 208 n.206, 209 n.211,
  210 nn.213, 217, 211
*Adornment to Nagarjuna's Thought,
  The*, 26
Adorno, Theodor, 64 n.207, 168
Amaladoss, Jesuit Michael, 231, 231 n.17
analogia fidei (analogy of faith), 93
anamnesis (remembrance), 92
Anderson, Walter Truett, 3, 3 n.6
Anno, 93 n.137, 94 n.147
Anscombe, G. E. M., 16 n.44
anti-realism, 80 n.76
anti-realist epistemology, 177–89
anti-realist ontology, 78–81
apophatic knowledge, Chopel's, 201–11
  anti-realist position, 210
  conviction in dharma, 201–11
  Prāsaṅgika-Madhyamaka
    philosophy, 208–9
apophatic knowledge, Schillebeeckx's,
  189–201
  Dark Light of experience, 189–201
  limits of language and thought, 189–211
  negative contrast experiences, 192
  non-essentialist manner, 198
  orthodox conceptions of God, 194
  radical finitude, 190
apophatic knowledge of ultimate reality,
  163–214 (*see also under* experiential
  knowledge)
apophaticism, 164–89, 232–8 (*see also
  under* experiential knowledge)
apophaticism, Chopel's, 59–64
  dualistic distinctions, 60
  Madhyamaka and, 61–2
  perspectivalism, 60
  subsequent attainment, 63
  supramundane qualities, 62
  tantric practices, 63
apophaticism, Schillebeeckx's, 53–9
  actual "divine Mystery", 58
  critical consciousness of faith, 58
  engagement with Critical Theory, 55
  epistemology after "Death of God", 53–4
  ethical praxis, 58
  humanum of history, 56
  sense of "truth", 58–9
  theoretical/hermeneutical
    approaches, 57
Aquinas, Thomas, 74, 113
Āryadeva, 52, 76 n.55, 101, 221
Asian Jesus, The, 231, 231 n.17
assertion for others, Madhyamaka
  principle, 51
assessment, 129 nn.78, 790, 133 nn.93, 95,
  135 n.105, 136 n.108, 137 n.113
Augustine of Hippo, 12

Barth, Karl, 123
Bergoglio, Mario Jorge, 10, 11 nn.20, 21
Blavatsky, Helena Petrovna, 155

Bloch, Ernst, 56, 123
Bodhisattvabhūmi, 129 n.78, 137
Borgman, Erik, 54 n.155, 70 nn.12, 14, 71
   nn.19, 21, 23, 73 n.37, 74 nn.45, 47,
   94 n.150
Bowden, John Stephen, 54 n.155
Braudel, Fernand, 44, 44 n.108, 120
bridge concepts, 12–20, 12 n.29, 23–67
   interreligious and cross-cultural
     comparison, 12–20
   its materials and, 23–67
Broido, Michael M., 136 n.111
buddhānusmṛti, 131
Buddhist Hermeneutics, 49 n.136,
   125–138, 127 n.71, 128 n.74, 134
   n.98, 136 n.111
Buddhist hermeneutics, New Old World
   of, 125–38
   Bodhisattvabhūmi's conclusion, 129
     n.78, 137
   Madhyamaka epistemology, 127
Buddhology, Chopel's, 149–59
   anti-realist philosophical
     conviction, 153
   expression of worship, 151
   trusting the inexpressible, 149
Buescher, John B., 127–8, 127 n.72,
   128 n.76

Candrakīrti (Madhyamaka philosopher),
   84 n.93, 135
Catholic theology, 5, 215–40
   fallible humans, 216–27
   fallible knowledge, 216–27
   Madhyamaka implications for, 215–40
   necessity of a fallible (and critical)
     community, 216–27
   phenomenological Thomism, 217
Catuḥpratisaraṇasutra (Sūtra of the Four
   Refuges), 127, 133
Chandrakīrti, 179
Chenu, Marie-Dominic, 41–3
Chopel, Gendun, 5, 14, 20–1, 24 n.8, 26–7,
   35–7, 37 n.67, 51 n.141, 52, 60 n.182,
   59–64, 76 n.55, 85 n.95, 96–104,
   107 n.200, 154 n.178, 206 nn.196,
   198, 210
Christ: The Experience of Jesus as Lord,
   93 nn.140, 142, 95 n.154, 112, 112
   n.1, 117 n.25, 122 nn.52, 142 n.128,
   147 n.145, 166 nn.6, 9, 167 nn.15,
   16, 168 n.21, 169 n.29, 170 n.31, 174
   n.49, 175 n.53, 176 n.55, 193 n.130,
   195 n.140, 196 n.143, 197 nn.153,
   155, 157, 198 nn.161, 162, 200 n.168,
   227 n.12
*Christ, the Sacrament of the Encounter
   with God*, 29 n. 24, 87
Christology, Schillebeeckx's, 139–48
   experience, teaching, and
     action, 139–48
   hypostatic union, 141
   Kingdom of God, 148
   Revelation-in-Reality, Jesus's story
     as, 139–48
   Thomistic hermeneutical principle, 139
Church: The Human Story of God, 55,
   55 n.162, 72 nn.28, 30, 31, 34, 90
   nn.120, 122, 91 nn.126, 128, 94
   n.149, 95 n.157, 118 n.31, 122 nn.50,
   124 n.64, 125 n.68, 142 n.130, 144
   nn.133, 137, 147 n.150, 165 n.3, 167
   n.18, 168 n.22, 169 n.27, 170 n.33,
   171 n.37, 174 n.51, 176 n.56, 191
   nn.117, 120, 193 n.126, 194 n.134,
   195 n.141, 196 nn.145, 147, 197
   nn.150, 152, 198 nn.158, 163, 199
   n.166, 200 n.167
Clooney, Francis X., 6–7, 6 n.3, 7 n.6,
   10 n.18
collective community intelligence in
   knowledge formation, 67–110
Commentary on Valid Knowledge,
   Dharmakīrti's, 77
common beings, 218–19
communal knowledge, perspectivalism
   applied to, 85–104
community of individuals, 67–8
Comparative Religious Ethics (CRE), 12
comparative theology, religious diversity,
   and the question of ultimate
   truth, 5–22
comprehensiveness of knowledge of God,
   71 n.21
Congar, Yves, 41
Continuity, 56 nn.165, 178
conviction in dharma, 201–11
creation perspective, 72–3

credibile prout intelligibile (credible as intelligible), 88
critical negativity, 168
Critical Theory, 28, 58 nn.173, 176, 112 n.3, 164, 164 n.1

Davaney, Sheila Greeve, 2, 2 n.3
De Petter, D. M., 30 n.33, 31, 31 nn.35, 39, 42, 32, 33 nn.50, 52, 34 n.55, 68–75, 68 n.2, 114
Dean, William D., 225 nn.7, 8, 226 n.9
"Death of God" theology, 53–4
Decosimo, David, 23–4, 23 nn.2, 3, 24 n.6
deep-seated individualism, 224
determinate negation, 64 n.207
Deus, 113 n.7, 115 n.18, 116 n.20, 118 n.29, 121 nn.46, 48, 124 n.62, 125 n.66, 139 n.118, 141 n.124, 142 n.125, 164 n.1, 165 n.5, 166 nn.8, 13, 14, 169 n.26, 170 nn.30, 33, 172 nn.42, 43, 173 n.48, 174 n.50, 190 nn.111, 114, 194 n.133, 196 n.148
Dge ' dun Chos ' phel, 75 n.50, 107 n.199, 127 n.73, 128 n.77, 149 nn.157, 158, 150 n.160, *151 n.165*, 152 nn.168, 170, 153 n.172, 173, 174, 175, 154 n.181, 158 n.199, 230 n.13
Dharmakīrti (Indian Madhyamaka commentator), 39, 75–85, 178
dialectical thought process, 197
Dilthey, Wilhelm, 126 n.70
doctrine of emptiness (*śūnyatā*), 136
doctrine of no-self (*anātman*), 136
Dreyfus, Georges B. J., 76 n.53, 77–81, 77 n.57, 78 nn.60–2, 79 n.64, 80 nn.71–3, 75, 76, 81 nn.77, 78, 99 n.176, 103, 103 n.194, 135 n.104, 138 nn.115–16, 154 n.180, 178 nn.59, 63, 64, 65, 179 n.66, 181 n.77, 184 n.84, 187–188, 187 n.100, 188 n.101, 189 n.108

ecclesia discens (learning church), 86, 92, 94, 219
ecclesia docens (teaching church), 86, 92, 94, 219
Ecclesiam Suam encyclical, 8–9, 8 n.12
Echoes from an Empty Sky: The Origins of the Buddhist Doctrine of the Two Truths, 127, 127 n.72

Eck, Diana L., 6, 6 n.1, 7 n.5
Eckel, Malcolm David, 25 n.8, 129, 130 n.80
Eckhart, Meister, 175
effective history concept, 46
emptiness (*śūnyatā*) concept, 84, 179
enlightened beings, 218
Entrance to the Boddhisattva Deeds (Bodhicaryavatara), The, 85
epistemological anti-realism, Dharmakīrti's, 75–85
Essence of Eloquence That Distinguishes between the Provisional and Definitive Meanings of the Scriptures, The, 51, 189 n.109
ethical praxis, 171–2
Eucharist, The, 28 n.21, 75 n.48
experiential knowledge and apophaticism, Chopel's, 164–89
  anti-realist epistemology, 177–89
  dialectics use, 187
experiential knowledge and apophaticism, Schillebeeckx's, 164–89
  absolute limit of reality (God), 173
  actual conduct of praxis, 173
  as authoritative and ultimately negative in nature, 163
  ethical praxis, 171–2
  in modern world, ethical, mystical, and experience in, 164–76
  nonantithetical conception of reality, 169
  phenomenon and noumenon, comparison, 166, 173
  positivism, 165
  principle of nonidentity, 169
  relational ontology, 167
  religious–secular divide, 171
  theological foundations of, 164–89
  Thomistic phenomenology, 164
  triplex via, 175
  via affirmativa (way of affirmation), 175
  via eminentiae (way of eminence), 175
  via negativa (way of negation), 175
expression of worship (*mchod brjod*), 202

Four Hundred Verses (Catuḥśataka), 101, 202, 221
fulfillment (salvation), 119

Gadamer, Hans-Georg, 54, 114
Geertz, Clifford, 7, 7 n.11
Geluk curriculum, 76 n.52
God after Darwin: A Theology of Evolution, 237, 237 n.20
God and creation relationship, 72
God and Man, 70, 70 n.11
God the Future of Man, 53, 89 n.117, 92 n.136, 113 n.6, 115 nn.17, 19, 116 n.24, 119 n.37, 120 n.43, 122 nn.49, 51, 53, 123 n.56, 124 n.61, 125 n.67, 144 n.134, 145 n.139, 148 n.155, 192 n.123, 193 n.128, 194 n.132, 197 n.154, 198 nn.162, 165, 199 n.166
Grains of Gold: Tales of a Cosmopolitan Traveler, 75 n.50, 127 n.73, 128 n.77, 149 n.158, 150 n.160, 151 n.165, 152 n.170, 153 nn.173, 175, 154 n.181, 158 n.199, 230 n.13
Great Treatise on the Stages of the Path of Enlightenment, The, 82, 180 n.72
Gylepo, Lhodrak Namkha, 153

Habermas, Jürgen, 54, 123
Hacker, P. M. S., 16 n.44
Harrison, Paul, 131, 131 nn.84, 88, 89
Haskell, Thomas L., 225 n.6
Haught, John F, 237 n.20
Hebblethwaite, Peter, 231 n.16
Heidegger, Martin, 114
Hermeneutical orientation, Chopel's, 47–53
　Buddhist modernism concept, 47
　contextual limitations of Buddha teachings, 51
　historical manifestation as source, 47–53
　nihilistic relativism, 49
　Schillebeeckx's and, 53
　unenlightened mind, limit of, 47–53
hermeneutics, Chopel's, 125–138 (*see also under* Buddhist hermeneutics)
hermeneutics, Schillebeeckx's, 112–25
　epistemological crucible, 112
　four philosophical themes, 113
　fulfillment (salvation), 119
　hermeneutical circularity, 121
　meaninglessness, threat, 117
　ressourcement movement, 115
　theological and theoretical sources, 112–38
　theological knowledge, 112–25
　ultimate reality, 118
　ultimate truth (revelation), 119
Hermeneutics and the Study of History, 126, 126 n.70
Hermeneutics of interpretation, Schillebeeckx's, 41–7
　absolute Being concept, 41
　effective history concept, 46
　historicity concept, 44
　"Revelation-in-Reality" to "Revelation-in-History", 41–7
Hilkert, Mary Catherine, 26 n.15, 28, 28 n.19, 29 n. 22, 30 n.31, 32, 32 nn.45, 4735 n.59, 42, 42 nn.94, 96, 44 n.104, 45 nn.112, 114, 116, 53–5, 53 n.153, 54 n.157, 55 n.161, 114, 114 n.10, 123, 123 nn.55, 60
historical founders for contemporary believers, 111–61 (*see also under* hermeneutics)
　deciphering knowledge, 111
　religious knowledge, conveying, 111–61
　universal truths within teachings, 139–59
historicity concept, 44
History of Buddhism, 153
Hoogeveen, 121 n.45
Hopkins, Jeffrey, 48 n.125, 50 nn.137, 139, 51 n.145, 60 n.182, 154 n.178, 206 nn.196, 198
Huber, Toni, 76 n.55
humanum concept, 91–3
hypostatic union in Christ, 141

illimitable pluralism, 90–1
Illumination of [Candrakīrti's] Thought (dBu ma dgongs pa rab gsal), 82
individual intelligence in knowledge formation, 67–110
interreligious and cross-cultural comparison, Aaron Stalnaker's, 12–20
　clusters of related ideas, 19
　conceptual *diversity*, 14–15
　conceptual *relativism*, 14–15
　language games theory, 16

new comparativism, 16
semiotic method, 14
vocabularies of social life, 14
"intra-Buddhist" philosophical argumentation, 201
"Irony of Atheism" argument, 59 n.179

Jensen, Jeppe Sinding, 15–16, 15 n.41, 19
Jesus: An Experiment in Christology, 44 n.106, 57, 57 n.170, 55 nn.163, 164, 68 n.2, 72 n.34, 112, 112 n.1, 114 n.14, 117 n.26, 118 n.34, 119 n.40, 139 n.120, 144 n.136, 146 n.141, 147 nn.148, 149, 148 n.151, 168 n.23, 176 n.54, 193 nn.130, 131, 195 n.139, 197 n.156, 200 n.169, 230 n.14
Jesus as first theologian, 227–32
Jesus in Our Western Culture: Mysticism, Ethics, and Politics, 57 n.172, 92 nn.130, 132, 116 nn.21, 23, 141 n.123, 142 n.126, 143 n.132, 145 n.140, 172 n.42
Jinpa, Thupten, 75 n.50, 76 n.55, 81, 82 n.80, 82 n.80, 84 nn.93, 94, 103 n.194, 127 n.73, 128 n.77, 149 n.158, 150 n.160, 151 n.165, 152 n.170, 153 nn.173, 175, 154 n.181, 158 n.199, 179 n.67, 180 n.70, 181, 188 n.107, 189 nn.108, 109 n.109, 209 n.212, 210, 210 n.215, 210 n.216, 230 n.13

Kennedy, Philip, 26 n.15, 27, 27 n.17, 30 n.28, 30 n.32, 32 n.43, 32 n.46, 44 n.105, 56 n.165, 59 n.178, 69, 73, 74, 69 nn.3, 5, 9, 70 nn.13, 16, 71 n.20, 73 nn.36, 39, 74 nn.41, 46, 91 n.124, 113 n.7, 116 n.20, 118 n.29, 121 n.46, 124 n.62, 125 n.66, 139 n.118, 141 nn.122, 124, 142 n.125, 164 n.1, 165 n.5, 166 nn.13, 14, 169 n.26, 170 nn.30, 33, 172 nn.42, 43, 173 n.47, 174 n.50, 190 nn.111, 114, 194 n.133
Knitter, Paul F., 2, 2 n.5, 3 n.7
knowledge formation, 67–110, 183
individual and collective community, 67–110
perspectivalism, in community of individuals, 67–8
perspectivalism, philosophical, 68–85

Kuhn, Thomas, 120, 120 n.42

Lamotte, Étienne, 128 nn.74, 75, 129 n.78, 132, 132 n.90, 133 nn.93, 95, 134 n.100, 135 n.105, 136 n.108, 137 n.113
Lane, Dermot A., 124 n.62
language games theory, 16, 18
Language of Dissent: Edward Schillebeeckx on the Crisis of Authority in the Catholic Church, The, 26
Laṅkāvatārasūtra, 62, 132, 136
Lefebure, Leo, 16 n.46
Lindbeck, George, 16, 16 n.47
Livingston, James C., 16 n.46
local theologians, 227–32
Lopez, Donald S., 26, 26 nn.10, 11, 35 n.62, 37 n.70, 38 n.77, 39, 39 nn.78, 79, 80, 81, 40 n.87, 47 nn.123, 124, 48 n.125, 48 nn.125, 128, 129, 49 nn.132, 134, 135, 50 n.138, 51 nn.140–2, 51 nn.140–1, 143, 52 n.150, 59 n.180, 61 nn.186, 187, 62 nn.194, 197, 63 n.202, 75 n.50, 77 n.59, 79 nn.66, 67, 83 n.85, 84 nn.89, 92, 96 nn.161, 163, 97, 97 n.165, 98 n.171, 99 n.173, 100 n.179, 102 nn.187, 188, 103, 103 n.192, 104 n.196, 107 n.199, 126, 127 nn.71, 73, 128 n.77, 134 nn.98, 99, 135, 135 nn.101, 107, 136 n.110, 137 n.112, 138 n.117, 149 nn.157–9, 150 n.160, 151 n.165, 152 nn.166, 168, 170, 153 nn.172–5, 154 n.181, 156 n.194, 157 n.196, 158 nn.199, 178 nn.59, 61, 180 n.69, 181 n.77, 182 nn.79, 80, 183 n.82, 184 n.86, 185 nn.88, 90, 91, 186 n.95, 187 nn.96, 97, 188 n.102, 201 n.173, 202 nn.176, 177, 179, 203 n.182, 204 nn.186, 188, 208 nn.201, 203, 208, 209 n.209, 209 n.212, 210 n.218, 230 n.13, 240 n.21
Luther, Martin, 123
Lyotard, Jean-François, 2, 2 n.4

Madhyamaka epistemology/philosophy, 39, 51, 61–2, 96, 127
assertions for others, 51
Bhāvaviveka's conception, 129–30

implications for Catholic
theology, 215–40
Prāsaṅgika tradition of, 51
to Buddhapālita and Candrakīrti,
76 n.55
Madhyamaka theory, Chopel's, 75
emptiness of emptiness, 84
individualistic interpretation, 75–6
Nāgārjuna's, 76, 76 n.55
Madhyamakāvatāra, 135, 136 n.110
Majjhima Nikāya (Collection of Middle-Length Discourses of Buddha), 132, 132 n.92
Makkreel, Rudolf A., 126 n.70
Mapping the Modern Tibet: Proceedings of the Eleventh Seminar of the International Association for Tibetan Studies, 49 n.131
meditative equipoise, 83
Mengele, Irmgard, 47 n.122, 96 nn.162, 175
metamorphosis, 69
Methodologies of Comparative Philosophy: The Pragmatist and Process Traditions, 13
Metz, Johann Baptist, 124, 124 n.62
Miller, James, 12, 12 n.29
modernism, 8–9
dialogue need of, Pope Paul VI on, 8–9
as Naturalism, 8 n.13
Moltmann, Jürgen, 124
Mūlamadhyamaka-kārikā (Fundamental Verses of the Middle Way), 135, 185

Nāgārjuna, 62, 76 n.55, 97, 103
nature and grace, 74
negative contrast experiences, 233
negative dialectics, 64 n.207
Neville, Robert Cummings, 12–13, 25 n.8
Nietzsche, Friedrich, 29 n. 26
nihilism, 204, 221, 223
nonantithetical conception of reality, 169
non-Christian traditions, religious truth question in, 9
Buddhism, 10
Hinduism, 10
nonexistence notion, 204

"nonidentical" source of knowledge, 64 n.207
"nonrealism", 217 n.1
Nostra Aetate (In Our Age), 9–10
noumenon, 166, 173

O'Donovan, Leo, 112, 113 n.4
objective "truth" problem, 1–4
Oosterhuis, 121 n.45
Overcoming Our Evil project, 12, 23–4

Pannenberg, 124
Perdue, Daniel, 178 n.62
personal experience in apophatic knowledge of ultimate reality, 163–214 (*see also under* experiential knowledge)
perspectivalism, 67–85, 114 n.11, 216–27
communal knowledge, 85–104
in community of individuals, 67–8
philosophical, 68–85
perspectivalism, Chopel's, 35–41, 75–85
afflictive obstructions, 38
anti-realist ontology, 78–81
Dharmakīrti's epistemology, 78–81
Dharmakīrtian anti-realism and, 99–100
enlightened perspective, 36
individualistic interpretation of Madhyamaka, 76
individualized theory of knowledge, 75–6
Prasaṅgika-Madhyamaka philosophy, 78
transforming reality in radical ways, 38
Two Truths philosophy, 77–9, 83
ultimate truth, 83
unenlightened beings, 96–104
unenlightened mind, 35–41
valid cognition, 75–85
perspectivalism, Schillebeeckx's, 28–41, 29 n. 26, 68–75
applied to communal knowledge, 85–96
church in the individual's theological knowledge, 33
collective truth, 85–6
conviction, 71
De Petter's philosophical, 68–75
God and creation relationship, 72–3

God's salvation
  (revelation-in-reality), 74
Implicit Intuition, 31
individually fallible knowledge, 85–6
"perspectivalist" epistemology, 29
phenomenological Thomism, 68–75
revelation-in-reality, 29, 33
revelation-in-word, 33
ultimate truth, 28
Phenomenological Thomism, 25 n.9, 27, 68–75
phenomenon, 166, 173
pluralism notion, 7
Pope Paul VI, 8–9, 8 n.12
Portier, William L., 29 n. 23, 58, 54 n.160, 58 nn.173, 176, 96 n.158, 200 n.169
Pramāṇavārttika, 178
Prāsaṅgika-Madhyamaka philosophy, 51, 78, 183, 209
primordial sacrament, 88 n.110
principle of nonidentity, 169
problem of 'universal' history, 114 n.13

radical contingency (conventionality), 224
radical finitude (absolute limit), 190
Ratzinger, Cardinal Joseph, 1–3, 1 n.1
real composition, 2
"realism", 80 n.76
real synthesis, 2
reasoning consciousness (*rigs shes*), 205
Recognizing Reality: Dharmakīrti's Philosophy and Its Tibetan Interpretations, 78, 78 n.61
Rego, Aloysius, 55 n.164
relativism, 2, 4, 9
religious diversity, 5–22
  church's awareness of, 8–9
  for religious epistemology, 5–12
  ultimate truth and, question of, 5–22
religious epistemology, 5–12
religious–secular divide, 171
Ricoeur, Paul, 114
Rodi, Frithjof, 126 n.70
Rorty, Richard, 3, 211 n.220
Ruegg, David Seyfort, 75, 75 n.49, 98 n.172, 99 n.173

sacred conventions concept, 225
Śākyamuni Buddha, 98, 127

salvific knowledge of God, 89
Samādhirājasūtra, 136
Saṃdhinirmocana, 136
Schillebeeckx Reader, The, 30, 30 n.29, 69
Schillebeeckx, Edward, 14, 27–28, 28 n.19, 29 nn. 24, 25, 30 nn.29, 33, 32 n.44, 33 nn.49, 53, 34, 34 nn.54, 56, 57, 35 n.60, 43 nn.99, 100, 101, 44 nn.106, 109, 45 n.113, 46 nn.118, 119, 120, 121, 54 nn.156, 160, 55 n.162, 56 nn.166-7, 57 nn.170-2, 58 n.177, 59 nn.178, 179, 64 n.207, 68 nn.1-2, 68 n.2, 69 nn.3, 5, 7, 8, 9, 70, 70 nn.11, 13, 16, 71 nn.20, 24, 72 n.25, 27, 28, 30, 31, 33, 34, 72 n.32, 73 nn.35-6, 38-9, 74, 74 nn.41, 42, 43, 44, 75 nn.48, 86 nn.99, 100, 101, 102, 103, 104, 87 nn.105, 106, 88 nn.108, 109, 110, 112, 89 nn.116-17, 90 nn.120, 121, 122, 123, 91 nn.124, 125, 126, 127, 128, 129, 92 nn.130, 131, 132, 134, 136, 93 nn.137, 138, 140, 142, 143, 94 nn.144, 145, 146, 147, 148, 149, 95 nn.152, 153, 154, 156, 157, 96 n.159, 107 n.200, 113 n.6, 114 n.14, 115 nn.16, 17, 19, 116 nn.21, 22, 23, 24, 117 nn.25, 26, 28, 118 n.31, 32, 33, 34, 35, 36, 120 n.43, 121 nn.44, 45, 47, 122 nn.49, 50, 51, 52, 53, 54, 123 n.56, 124 nn.61, 63, 64, 125 nn.65, 66, 67, 68, 139 n.120, 141 nn.122, 123, 142 nn.126, 128, 130, 143 nn.131, 132, 145 n.138, 144 nn.133, 134, 136, 137, 146 nn.141, 143, 147 nn.145, 146, 148, 149, 150, 148 nn.151, 152, 155, 165 nn.3, 4, 166 nn.6, 7, 9, 167 nn.15, 16, 18, 168 nn.21, 22, 23, 25, 169 nn.27, 28, 29, 170 n.31, 171 nn.34, 37, 38, 172 nn.42, 45, 173 nn.46, 47, 174 n.49, 51, 175 n.53, 176 nn.54, 55, 56, 190 n.115, 191 nn.117, 119, 120, 192 nn.123, 125, 193 nn.126, 128, 129, 130, 131, 194 nn.132, 134, 136, 195 nn.137, 138, 139, 140, 141, 196 nn.143, 145, 146, 147, 149, 197 nn.150, 151, 152, 153, 154, 155, 156, 157, 198 nn.158, 161, 162, 163, 165,

200 nn.167, 168, 170, 220 n.2, 227 n.12, 230 n.14
Schreiter, Robert, 30, 30 n.29, 69, 69 n.7
Schulte, Joachim, 16 n.44
To See the Buddha: A Philosopher's Quest for the Meaning of Emptiness (Malcolm David Eckel), 129, 130 n.80
sensus fidelium (communal unity of faith), 94
sensus plenior (fuller meaning), 86
sequela Jesu (following of Jesus), 92
Simut, Corneliu C., 217 n.1
Skorka, Rabbi Abraham, 5, 10, 11 nn.20, 21
Slightly hidden phenomena, 184
Smid, Robert W., 13
Smith, Jonathan Z., 14, 14 n.34
Sobre el cielo y la tierra (On Heaven and Earth), 5, 10–12
Sound of Two Hands Clapping: The Education of a Tibetan Buddhist Monk, The (Georges B. J. Dreyfus), 76 n.53, 77, 77n.57, 103 n.194, 135 n.104, 138 n.115, 154 n.180, 179 n.66, 187 n.100, 188 n.101
Stalnaker, Aaron, 12–20, 12 nn.28, 29, 13 n.31, 14 n.35, 17 nn.50, 51, 18 n.51, 23, 23 n.1
Stoddard, 99 n.173, 201 n.172, 211 n.219
Strazzari, 68 n.1, 72 n.27, 199 n.166
Structure of Scientific Revolutions, The, 120, 120 n.42
Study of Religion in a New Key: Theoretical and Philosophical Soundings in the Comparative and General Study of Religion, The, 15, 15 n.41
Sūtrālaṃkāra, 133–4, 134 n.97

Thakchöe, Sonam, 182
Thérèse of Lisieux, 175
Thompson, Daniel Speed, 26–7, 26 n.14, 27 n.16, 27 n.17, 28 n.19, 29, 30 n.27, 31 n.41, 42 n.97, 43 nn.99, 102, 45 nn.111, 115, 54, 54 n.158, 57 n.169, 58 nn.174, 175, 69, 69 n.4, 71 n.18, 72, 72 n.29, 85 nn.97, 98, 87 n.107, 89 n.118, 94 n.149, 95 n.155, 112 n.2, 113 n.5, 114 n.9, 115 n.15, 167 n.19, 190 n.113, 191 n.116, 193 n.129, 196 n.144
threat of relativism for religious practitioners in the modern world, 1–4
Tibetan Arts of Love, The, 154, 205
Tillich, Paul, 237 n.20
triplex via, 175, 212, 233, 235
true cognition (*pramāṇa*), 180
Tsongkhapa (1357–1419), 36, 76–84, 84 n.93, 179–80, 180 n.72
Two Truths philosophy, 24 n.8, 77–9, 83, 178

ultimate reality, apophatic knowledge of, 163–214 (*see also under* experiential knowledge)
ultimate truth (*paramārthasatya*), 25 n.8, 119
unenlightened beings, 96–104
universal truths within particular teachings, 139–59
    Chopel's, 149–59 (*see also under* Buddhology)
    potential of, 139–59
    problems of, 139–59
    Schillebeeckx's, 139–48 (*see also under* Christology)
universals, 80 n.76

valid knowledge, 84 n.93
Van Erp, Stephan, 26 n.15, 31 nn.34, 38, 42 nn.93, 98
Verses on the Essence of the Middle Way, The, 130
via affirmativa (way of affirmation), 175
via eminentiae (way of eminence), 175
via negativa (way of negation), 175

Wellmer, Albrecht, 164 n.1
Wildman, Wesley J., 236 n.19
Williams, Paul, 131 n.85
Wittgenstein, Ludwig, 16, 16 n.44
Wuthnow, Robert, 6–7, 6 n.4, 7 n.8

Xunzi (Confucian philosopher), 12

zero-sum game, 4

www.ingramcontent.com/pod-product-compliance
Lightning Source LLC
Chambersburg PA
CBHW072138290426
44111CB00012B/1914